IKE'S
MYSTERY
MAN

IKE'S MYSTERY MAN

The Secret Lives of
ROBERT CUTLER

PETER SHINKLE

STEERFORTH PRESS
HANOVER, NEW HAMPSHIRE

For information about permission to reproduce selections from this book, write to:
Steerforth Press L.L.C., 45 Lyme Road, Suite 208,
Hanover, New Hampshire 03755

Book design by Peter Holm, Sterling Hill Productions

Cataloging-in-Publication Data is available from the Library of Congress

ISBN 978–1–58642-243-1 (Cloth)

First Edition 2018

Printed in the U.S.A.

1 3 5 7 9 10 8 6 4 2

To my parents

JUDITH CUTLER SHINKLE & JACKSON JOHNSON SHINKLE

who taught me the importance of finding the truth

CONTENTS

PREFACE

A Republican and a devout Christian, Robert Cutler was a retired army general and bank president who helped Dwight Eisenhower win the presidential election of 1952. A lifelong bachelor, Cutler, whom everyone knew as Bobby, became a close friend of Ike's — and someone the president trusted deeply. Shortly after the election, Ike appointed Bobby his top assistant for national security affairs. Two months into the new Eisenhower administration, in March 1953, Bobby proposed a reform of the National Security Council (NSC) that would create the position of special assistant for national security affairs, later referred to simply as national security advisor. Ike swiftly implemented Bobby's reform and named him the first person to hold the position, and Bobby managed the NSC in the following years to help the president make decisions on a broad array of Cold War national security issues, from nuclear weapons strategy to how best to undermine Soviet Communism. Bobby knew many of the nation's high-level Cold War secrets, worked long hours, kept a low profile, and refused to speak to the press. He was soon dubbed the Mystery Man of the White House.

Yet something in addition to policy and national security may have heightened Bobby's insistence on secrecy. After taking office in 1953, Bobby hired a Russian-speaking naval intelligence officer, Tilghman B. "Skip" Koons, to work on the NSC staff. Though he was twice Skip's age, Bobby developed passionate feelings for the young NSC staffer, an emotional obsession that lasted for years, as Bobby's private diary reveals.

The fact that Bobby fell in love with a young male employee of the NSC may not be shocking today. What *is* striking is that Bobby's passion for Skip blossomed in the superheated crucible of the White House national security apparatus amid the Cold War, McCarthyism, and the purge of homosexuals — the so-called Lavender Scare — that gripped the federal government in the 1950s. Bobby didn't let questions about his sexuality stop him from accompanying Ike on his 1952 campaign train, meeting with Joe McCarthy, and being friendly with Director of the Federal Bureau of Investigation J. Edgar Hoover — even after Hoover investigated him for homosexuality.

Bobby played the role of the straight bachelor out of necessity, and he played it very well. In early 1953, for instance, he steered the drafting of Ike's notorious Executive Order 10450, which banned gays from employment by the federal government. Yet behind the mask of the highly skilled national security specialist, in a secret life amid all the secrets he kept, Bobby was a man who struggled profoundly to find, recognize, and accept his sexual and romantic orientation.

Bobby was an unusual figure in American political life, a Republican who easily crossed party lines and worked closely with Democrats, almost unthinkable in today's intensely polarized political climate. In 1944, he carried out President Roosevelt's policy to enable all soldiers overseas to vote, clashing with segregationists in Congress who saw the move as a bid to gain access to the ballot box for black southerners. In fact, Bobby crossed all sorts of lines. He advocated for J. Robert Oppenheimer after the controversial nuclear physicist raised concerns about the dangers of the nuclear arms race. Yet when Oppenheimer fell under investigation for his Communist ties, Ike asked Bobby to help engineer Oppenheimer's ouster. Bobby did so, but still embraced Oppenheimer's cause and later advanced a plan to sharply reduce the US nuclear weapons buildup.

The razor's edge on which Bobby walked is illustrated by his relationship with Hoover. The FBI director needed Bobby's help because Bobby was his primary conduit to Eisenhower, and Bobby needed Hoover's help with national security matters. Both men, aging bachelors with a fondness for male company, were trailed by suspicions of homosexuality. When Hoover himself investigated Bobby's ties to other White House homosexuals in 1957, Bobby must have felt intense pressure.

The story of Bobby Cutler's hidden life came to my attention in the summer of 2006, when my aunt, Patricia Cutler Warner, told me a family secret about Bobby, who was her uncle. She said "Uncle Bobby," who had died in 1974, was gay. Sitting beside me, my mother, Judith Cutler Shinkle, quietly confirmed her sister's account. I was stunned. Having grown up in Missouri, far from my East Coast cousins, I had neither met my great-uncle nor heard his story. I interviewed family members who knew Bobby, many of whom supported Aunt Pat's account. Harry

Lodge — son of one of Bobby's closest friends, Senator Henry Cabot Lodge Jr. — told me Bobby let family and friends believe he was gay. "He didn't bother to hide it when he wasn't at work," he said. Bobby's autobiography, *No Time for Rest*, mentions Skip Koons and some other young male friends, but it says nothing explicit about his or their sexual orientation. The vast amount of scholarship on Eisenhower and his presidency is silent on the subject. I dug through thousands of pages of formerly secret documents at the Eisenhower Library, but none raised a question about Bobby's sexual preferences. He was, indeed, a mystery man.

Then an Eisenhower Presidential Library archivist introduced me to Stephen Benedict, who had known Bobby personally and had given the library thousands of pages of documents related to him. Benedict had come to know Bobby well when they both worked on the Eisenhower campaign train in 1952. They subsequently became colleagues on the White House staff and remained good friends through all the years of the Eisenhower administration and beyond. When Steve and I first met in the summer of 2008, he revealed an astonishing story: He said that he himself was gay, that Skip Koons had been his lover, and that he had introduced Bobby to Skip, setting the stage for their story to unfold. Steve, who had been executor of Skip's estate after his death in 2005, provided me with thousands of pages of documents and photographs. The crown jewel of these documents was Bobby's six-volume diary, in which he pours out his feelings for Skip.

Bobby was noted for his desire to remain behind the scenes, which is one reason why he disappeared from public view so thoroughly after the Eisenhower years. Because of the way he ran the NSC, Bobby had a much lower profile than many who held the national security advisor's post in the decades after he did — people like McGeorge Bundy, Henry Kissinger, John Poindexter, Colin Powell, and Condoleezza Rice. Indeed, many histories of the Eisenhower era make very limited mention of Bobby. And yet it appears his role was greater than previously thought. Eisenhower's has been called the Hidden-Hand Presidency in good part because of his unseen use of the NSC to steer his administration, set national security policy, and control his advisers.[1] Thus, because of his critical role in the NSC, Bobby perhaps may be considered the unseen arm of the hidden hand. Indeed, when Bobby announced his first resignation in 1955, Ike compared his departure to "losing my right arm."

Bobby served the nation's strategic defense and national security interests brilliantly while living in private agony as a closeted homosexual, deprived of the affections for which he longed. After his love for Skip disrupted his emotional equilibrium, he broke free of his strictures and enjoyed the companionship of a number of young gay men later in life. As his great-nephew, I can only hope he ultimately found happiness. It might be said that by revealing Bobby's passion for Skip, I am "outing" my great uncle, betraying his privacy. After studying Bobby's life and letters for more than a decade, I am confident that his love for Skip was so great that if he were alive today — with our era's liberated view of homosexuality — he would want this story told.

Peter Shinkle

St. Louis, August 2018

1

BOSTONIAN REPUBLICANS

In 1635, John Cutler, a native of Norfolk, England, sailed to the New World with his wife and children and settled in the village of Hingham, Massachusetts. By the early 1800s, his Cutler descendants had moved to Exeter, Maine.[1] The fierce independence of Mainers, who embraced Puritanism and thrived on such rugged industries as timber harvesting and shipbuilding, was distilled in the Cutlers. From the Civil War on, they were Republicans and unionists. One of John Cutler's descendants, Lysander Cutler, a general in the Union army, fought at Gettysburg and resigned his command in 1865 at the age of fifty-eight only after he was severely injured by a shell fragment that struck him in the face.

One of Lysander Cutler's great-nephews, George Cutler, owned and operated lumber mills in Maine.[2] He and his wife, Mary, had resided in Bangor for much of their lives. In 1889, George and Mary moved to the prosperous Boston suburb of Brookline, where their five sons grew up in a Republican household and with friends who came from powerful families with names like Cabot, Lowell, and Lodge. While they shared the political party of the Boston Brahmin families, the Cutlers were not part of the Brahmin aristocracy.

George raised his boys to be outdoorsmen, taking them on annual trips to fish for salmon on the Bonaventure River in Quebec and on trips to New Brunswick in the dead of winter for curling on a frozen lake. As a young man, George had been athletic, playing sports at Phillips Exeter Academy. Like his father before him, George went to Harvard, where he played baseball, graduating in 1879. His three older sons — John, Elliott, and Roger — were athletes, too, excelling in sports at the Volkmann School in Boston. George, the fourth of the boys, was less athletic and was given the brutal nickname "Fat." Born into this world of competition on June 12, 1895, the youngest Cutler boy, Bobby, came to view George as a "buffer state" who would shield him from the tough older boys. George and Bobby gravitated toward the arts. Mary Cutler brought up all her sons — but particularly the younger ones — to embrace literature, history, and music. She took them to Shakespeare's plays at the Castle Square Theatre in Boston, first taking care for their proper understanding: On the day before the matinee, she often gathered with the boys and read parts of the play they were to see.

Mary read aloud to her children; by the time Bobby was seventeen, she had read all of Charles Dickens. The books that filled the house included Jack London's *White Fang* and Arthur Conan Doyle's Sherlock Holmes stories. "Little wonder I became an omnivorous reader," Bobby observed, "always with a book in hand."[3] Bobby also took to writing as a boy, producing his own small "newspaper," which he dubbed *Cutler's Weekly*, featuring the latest opera news and items such as his own retelling of the life of Alexander Hamilton. He delved into politics, too, embracing President Teddy Roosevelt's brand of Republicanism and adopting the president's *bully* as a phrase of his own.[4]

Mary wanted her boys to appreciate opera, and Bobby came to love it. He haunted the second balcony of the Boston Opera House, exhausting his allowance on cheap seats and standing-room-only tickets. He saw Caruso a dozen times. Bobby noted, "There was always make-believe lurking in me. I didn't see myself as I was, but as I imagined myself to be." And when it came to performances, Bobby often played the role of a woman. In 1911, the year he turned sixteen, he took the role of a married woman in a school play, wearing one of his mother's gowns. When the audience burst into applause, he acknowledged it by singing a portion of his favorite aria in Italian from *La Traviata*. He recalled that "in the dazzle of the footlights" he was Emma Calvé "in black velvet and diamonds and trailing a long Russian sable stole," as she had appeared to him the previous Saturday afternoon on the stage of Symphony Hall, "her seductive mezzo-soprano sweeping the audience up and to her."[5]

After the famed Russian ballerina Anna Pavlova came to Boston, Bobby took to dressing up in a negligee and white slippers of his mother's, a veil upon his head. He recalled in his memoir: "In our darkened parlor after supper, to incidental Tchaikovsky on the Victrola, I would present an imitation of the Incomparable Anna dancing *La Mort du Cygne*." His performance featured "tiptoe runs across the room, followed by undulating gestures as I folded into death upon the floor."[6]

The Cutler boys were raised to express their affection openly, kissing each other on the cheek routinely, a common practice in Europe. "It would never have occurred to us, any more at sixty years than at sixteen," he reflected, "not to greet a brother with a handclasp and a kiss. Here was a way to show our parents, long after death, outgoing gratitude for their gift to us of a 'family life.'"[7]

The family suffered a cruel blow when Mary contracted cancer, which tormented her for years. The two younger boys, George and Bobby, would read aloud to her in bed, as she had read to them. Mary Cutler had her second operation for cancer in the summer of 1912, and that fall Bobby entered Harvard.

The younger Cutler boys faced great expectations at Harvard engendered by the achievements of their older brothers. The eldest, John, was quarterback and captain of the undefeated Harvard football team of 1908 and rowed crew with his brother Elliott. John roomed at Harvard with Teddy Roosevelt Jr. and stayed at the White House for the wedding of his sister Alice Roosevelt. The middle Cutler brother, Roger, captained Harvard's crew team.

When John became engaged to the daughter of a prominent New York political family, the society pages of local newspapers mythologized the couple. "Football Goal Won Bride for Harvard Star," said the headline of one article. "A romance of the gridiron involving one of Harvard's greatest athletes and an heiress, the daughter of one of the richest men in the United States, was revealed today through the announcement of the engagement of Miss Emily Rosalind Fish, daughter of Hamilton Fish of Washington and New York, and John W. Cutler, a member of the famous Cutler family of Harvard athletes." Emily Fish, who went by the name Rosalind, had visited her brother, Hamilton Fish III, the captain of the Harvard team that year, at practice, where she made the acquaintance of John Cutler. As the society pages account had it, Rosalind Fish accepted John Cutler's proposal of marriage on the condition that Harvard defeat Yale in their annual game. Harvard won, and the couple wed two years later in October 1910; four private railcars carried guests from Grand Central Station to Garrison, New York, for the event.

Rosalind was the granddaughter of Hamilton Fish, whose father had named him after a close friend, Alexander Hamilton.[8] Hamilton Fish served as New York's governor from 1849 to 1850, then as US senator from

New York. A Republican supporter of Abraham Lincoln, Fish later served as secretary of state under President Ulysses S. Grant. His son, Hamilton Fish II, Rosalind's father, was a lawyer and real estate investor in New York who also served as a US congressman. Rosalind's first cousin, also called Hamilton Fish, was among the volunteers who died while fighting with Teddy Roosevelt's Rough Riders in Cuba in 1898. Rosalind's brother, Hamilton Fish III, the All-American football captain, would go on to prominence as a Republican US congressman.

When Bobby arrived for his freshman year at Harvard in 1912, a newspaper sports section carried a story headlined, "Another Cutler Comes to Harvard." "Young Cutler is the fifth of a famous rowing family. He has been rowing in the Volkmann second boat and shapes up well." Bobby was welcomed at Harvard's Newell Boathouse "like an heir apparent," but it soon became obvious that he was not on par with his older brothers. "It was like a sudden death in the family, cruel, not to be mentioned: a Cutler who just *couldn't* row," he admitted wryly in his autobiography.

Bobby followed all four of his brothers into the Porcellian Club, which dated to 1791 and was among the elite Harvard student societies. Its members included Justice Oliver Wendell Holmes and President Theodore Roosevelt. The club derived its name from the tale of an eighteenth-century student who brought a pig into a classroom to squeal in order to upset a much-disliked professor. The Cutler brothers amassed a collection of small pig ornaments and figurines, which they kept on shelves just inside the front door of their house in Brookline. Later in life, whenever Bobby met other members of "the PC," they had an instantaneous bond of common experience.

In his freshman year, Bobby met an older man, Owen Wister, who would become a mentor, someone he greatly admired and with whom he would forge an extremely close bond. Wister wrote *The Virginian*, published in 1902 and widely considered the first great cowboy novel. Wister was thirty-four years older than Bobby, and yet the two discovered they had many common interests, including profound loves of literature, drama, and music. Wister, also a PC member, insisted on being called Uncle Dan, and Bobby gladly agreed. "Easy and agreeable with younger men, his meticulous, matchless courtesy disarmed shyness and drew comradeship," Bobby wrote.[9]

The son of a wealthy Philadelphia financier and his wife, Wister was schooled in music as a child. At Harvard, he befriended Teddy Roosevelt; both were members of the PC and would remain close friends for life. Wister was a gifted pianist and performed in university theater groups. After graduating in 1882, he traveled to Europe and played one of his compositions for Franz Liszt, whom Wister met while visiting the home of Richard Wagner. A sensitive aesthete who had reached the heights of Europe's cultural elite, Wister suddenly found himself ordered back to a more banal reality when his father summoned him to a job in finance in Philadelphia. He acquiesced and worked in Philadelphia until his health "broke down," as he vaguely described it. Seeking a recovery, he traveled to a Wyoming ranch in 1885.

In Wyoming, Wister discovered his deep admiration for the manly directness and unadorned machismo of cowboys, who often had strained or distant relationships with women. In *The Virginian* and other writings, his cowboy characters often recite their troubles with women and marriage, an avowal that typically opens the door to greater intimacy among the men. Indeed, *The Virginian* is often noted for its homoerotic aspects, which emerge on the book's very first page, when the narrator, an East Coast dandy who has come west for the first time, sees "a slim young giant, more beautiful than pictures." The dandy, recounting the experience in a first-person narrative, admires this cowboy's body, which has "the undulations of a tiger, smooth and easy, as if all his muscles flowed beneath his skin." This "ungrammatical son of the soil," as the dandy describes him, is the Virginian. The conversation immediately turns to the failures of cowboys to find women to marry them, and the dandy says of the Virginian, "Had I been the bride, I would have taken the giant, dust and all." The narrator goes on to tell an enraptured tale of the Virginian's physical beauty, his feats of courage and strength, and his righteous struggles with rustlers and other ne'er-do-wells. Ultimately the Virginian is married to a schoolmarm who barely plays any role in the novel, romantic or otherwise. Instead, accounts of swimming naked together with the narrator and other adventures in the open Wyoming spaces provide the romance.

Wister was a close friend of Justice Oliver Wendell Holmes, a Republican from an abolitionist family who had been wounded while fighting for the North in the Civil War. He also was close to Henry Adams, an author and scholar descended from two presidents, and Henry Cabot Lodge, a

US senator and ally of Teddy Roosevelt's known for supporting America's intervention in Cuba.[10] All three — Holmes, Adams, and Lodge — were Harvard graduates. Holmes and Lodge were Porcellian members like Wister. When Bobby met Wister at Harvard, the freshman student must have felt as if a god had stepped down from Olympus to befriend him. While a student, Bobby wrote a novel, and Wister recommended that the Macmillan Company, which had published Wister's works, publish Bobby's first novel, *Louisburg Square*. Wister acted as a "kindly midwife to my literary accouchements," Bobby wrote.

Bobby also had at least one close relationship with a fellow student, Oliver Ames, what he called "my first great friendship with a fellow my own age."[11] Ames, too, was a Porcellian member. "Although we were of an age, he used to call me — because I was a class ahead — 'Old Boy' or 'Funny Old Boy'; linking his arm in mine as we walked along. There was no touch of tarnish in Ollie anywhere — in body, or spirit or courage."

Though Bobby failed to follow the family tradition of athletic prowess, he made up for it by excelling academically. He was elected to Phi Beta Kappa, the academic honor society, was chosen class poet, and graduated cum laude.[12] He also wrote for the Hasty Pudding Theatricals, a student group known for putting on humorous plays in which male students often dressed as girls and women, an activity that stemmed from the lack of female students on campus but also conveniently coincided with Bobby's delight in cross-dressing.

As a lover of literature, Bobby was likely well acquainted with the homosexual and homophilic inclinations of some of Harvard's leading literary figures, including Frederick Loring, whose novel *Two College Friends*, published in 1871, featured two Harvard students who loved each other dearly and fought for the Union cause. In 1882, Oscar Wilde gave a speech at Harvard that was attended by a large number of students. Wilde's poems at the time revealed a strong aesthetic appreciation for men, though years would pass before he was convicted in England of "gross indecency" for his sexual relationship with a young man in 1895.

Harvard's gay literary history includes an incident in which the poet of the senior class, E. E. Cummings, gave a speech at commencement in 1915 reading a poem by Amy Lowell, known for her romance with actress Ada Dwyer Russell, in which she laments her lover's absence.[13] The lesbian themes in Lowell's poetry were considered scandalous, and one lady was later overheard denouncing the poem as "lascivious." Cummings made this oration while Lowell's brother, Harvard president A. Lawrence Lowell, notoriously conservative and likely displeased with any allusions to his sister's lesbianic poetry, was sitting just a few paces away.[14] By this time, Amy Lowell had earned a reputation for crossing gender boundaries — including her habit of smoking cigars. She helped found a theater company that put on many avant-garde dramas, including a 1907 production of Oscar Wilde's *An Ideal Husband*, a bold statement not long after Wilde, pilloried as a homosexual, had died in exile in Paris.

As Bobby entered his senior year, Mary Cutler's cancer worsened, and she summoned Bobby to her bedside to tell him how short her time would be. She took from her finger the wedding ring of her mother, Mary Elliott Carr, and put it in Bobby's hand. After his mother died in 1916, Bobby had the initials MEC-MWC-RC inscribed inside the ring, and had it made large enough to slip over the little finger of his right hand, where he wore it until the end of his life.[15]

As Harvard's commencement ceremony approached in June 1916, Bobby was selected for an unusual trio of honors. First, a hymn he composed was selected as the Baccalaureate Hymn for the class of 1916 and was sung in the university chapel; Bobby's verses urged love of God as the only true way to find a path to success in life. Then, as class poet, he read before the student body his poem gently chastising fellow students for wasting their time and failing to study, and praising the university for enabling students to grow wise and build friendships that would last a lifetime. Finally, a committee of professors chaired by a dean selected Bobby to give a speech at commencement. The committee made sure President Lowell would be spared the embarrassment of Cummings's performance the year before as Bobby was to give a speech that was an exhortation to military preparedness. On commencement day, with painter John Singer Sargent on the stage to receive an honorary degree, before a stadium filled with thousands, Bobby spoke in praise of the "Harvard Regiment" that had gone off to prepare for military service, and he called for universal military training to ensure a strong national defense. "This nation should teach all her sons to defend her, should teach all her sons that the duty of each to serve under arms is as much the part of liberty and manhood as the duty to vote." These three expressions — a hymn on devotion to

God, a poetic ode to hard work, and a speech in support of national defense — traced the arc that Bobby's public philosophy would follow for the rest of his life.

Yet if Bobby's public performances were infused with duty, religiosity, and military service, privately Bobby had a soaring romantic spirit that sought expression through literature and crossed the lines of socially acceptable tastes. In early 1917, he published an essay praising Amy Lowell in *The Nation* magazine for her imagist poetic style. "She has done the world imperishable service; she has cleaned out our old wine bottles and left them pure, sweet and welcoming for new wine," Bobby wrote.[16] His praise of Lowell skirted the issues raised by her sexuality. Soon Bobby's own literary creation would explore what it means to search for love with a member of the opposite sex — but be unable to find happiness.

Bobby's novel *Louisburg Square*, completed while he was a senior at Harvard, was published on April 3, 1917. The novel tells the story of imaginary characters from a very real, prominent Boston family, the Copleys. The fictive Singleton Copley lives out his life a bachelor, spending time with other prominent Boston men in a place called the Sarcophagus Club. The club's name was undoubtedly a gentle jibe at the Somerset Club, the elite gentlemen's club of Beacon Hill housed in a stately mansion looking out over Boston Common. The Somerset Club's exterior wall bears a memorial to John Singleton Copley, a famed portraitist of the colonial era. In *Louisburg Square*, shortly before his death the aging bachelor Singleton Copley warns his illegitimate son Eric not to let his life go unfulfilled by love. "Don't make your life like mine . . . ruined," he tells Eric. "Loneliness. At night — by day," he explains. "Love some one, boy; keep that some one." This advice would later have strong echoes in Bobby's life; it was almost as though Bobby were penning a note to himself to read decades later, encouraging himself to resist the fate of the lonely unwed life that he foresaw. Ironically, Bobby eventually became a Somerset Club member and lived life as a bachelor for four decades with his own apartment in the club's adjacent "annex" at 41 Beacon Street, one of the few men to have that privilege.

After graduation, Bobby worked as an English instructor at Harvard but soon joined the army. In May 1917, he began basic training in the Plattsburgh Barracks in upstate New York beside Lake Champlain. "Dear Bro Wister," Bobby wrote his mentor, using the Porcellian term

Brother for members, after Wister had inquired about Bobby's work on a new book. "Just now my novel languishes. Learning how to serve one's country and learning how to write a book do not combine successfully. However the lay off of a month will probably have a salutary effect."

By August 1917, Bobby was promoted to a second lieutenant in the infantry. With Americans dying on the battlefield, his feelings about the war veered from one extreme to the other. He told Wister at one moment that he wanted to "test my hand against a German hand"; the next that "I am 'the baby of a girl,' and don't want war, will have none of it, and cry inwardly against the hazarding of such beautiful young lives."[17] In June 1918, Bobby was ordered to board a ship to join the American Expeditionary Force in France. He wrote Wister: "America is new, filled with snap and vigor — you know the West yourself, and there are thousands of Westerners here, 'mad,' as they say, 'to polish off the Germans and get back.' There is something typically breathless in the feeling. 'Come on, boys! Let's hurry like Hell, and we can get back before the World Series!' All the same, it is not braggadocio: I have seen finer American soldiers here than I had dreamed could be."

Bobby, now with the rank of first lieutenant, was stationed in Bordeaux, then moved to central France. The terrible cost of the war, which left millions dead, touched Bobby directly. Bobby's close friend Oliver Ames fell victim to a German sniper's bullet near the River Ourcq northeast of Paris in July 1918. He also lost another close friend, Walker Beale. Days after the armistice was signed in November 1918 ending the war, Bobby visited the devastation of Verdun, seeing the land scarred and blackened by countless shells and gunfire, pocked with holes dug in mud by soldiers desperate for protection. He wrote his father, lamenting his friend Beale, killed just a month earlier:

> Who could look at such ground without tears! I kept wondering which of these holes Walker had huddled in those noble days and nights before he died . . . His death has stung my heart like a scorpion. I cannot see how he must be killed and others so less worthy live. Perhaps his grave is on one of those raw, bare hillsides; perhaps he bled to death at a roadside I have passed, gushing his blood into the grassy soil and grey thick mud.

With the war over, Bobby became a military police officer with the Third Army first in Bitburg, then Coblenz. The grim mayhem of war lingered, yet he managed to find a few lighthearted pleasures, such as joining other Porcellian Club members for a round of drinks. "Such songs, such a lifting of glasses to laughing lips, such humor — all appreciated," he wrote Wister. After Teddy Roosevelt died in January 1919, Bobby wrote Wister to express his sadness over the loss. "He was in a thousand ways my ideal; the rallying flag for my political and moral faith. We have so long been accustomed to his strenuous activities, his frank, fearless opinions, his daily appearance before our eyes in the journals — and now our most vigorous and valuable light is extinguished."

In May 1919, Bobby was awarded the Victory Medal Service Ribbon for his duty in Europe, and the next month he returned by ship to the United States. In August, he was honorably discharged at Camp Dix, New Jersey. Upon his return to Boston, his father encouraged him to enroll in Harvard Law School. Bobby opposed the idea of more years in school, but quickly changed his mind when Wister told him that the mental discipline of law school had helped his own writing more than anything else in his life.[18] The next morning, Bobby applied to Harvard Law, and he was admitted. He soon discovered he loved the law, and his excellent grades helped him become a *Harvard Law Review* editor.

2

BACHELOR

In the summer of 1921, Bobby went on a tour of Europe with Uncle Dan Wister and some young male friends from Boston. They crossed the Atlantic by steamship, arriving in London in July, and found themselves caught up in a whirl of parties hosted by American high society ladies, including Alice Astor and Grace Vanderbilt. Yet Wister had a special treat in store for Bobby. He took his young protégé alone to dine at the home of E. F. Benson, an English novelist whose works are lightly homoerotic and who is now considered by some scholars highly likely to have been gay. A friend of Oscar Wilde, Benson was associated with the Uranians, a group who praised love between men and whose members included Wilde, his young lover Lord Alfred Douglas, and others engaged in homosexual affairs. Benson and another friend of Wilde's, Reggie Turner, attended the premier of Wilde's play *Lady Windermere's Fan* in 1892, each wearing a green carnation, noted in that day as a symbol of homosexuality.[1] Benson had played a minor role in the scandal that led to Wilde's 1895 conviction on a charge of gross indecency.[2]

Benson's father was the Archbishop of Canterbury, and for years Benson lived in the archbishop's historic palace, attended state dinners, and associated with nobility. Owing perhaps to his social position, and perhaps to his close experience with Wilde's destruction, Benson did not overtly espouse Uranian views in his published writings. Yet he was a lifelong bachelor who favored the company of handsome young men and shared a villa on the Italian island of Capri with an openly gay man who had previously been writer Somerset Maugham's lover.[3] In Benson's 1920 novel, *Queen Lucia*, the protagonist, Lucia, has a close male friend, Georgie, a forty-five-year-old bachelor who is described as "womanish," dresses in florid clothes, loves the arts, and does needlework. Georgie has a "handsome young chauffeur" named Dicky, who drives him on vacations to the seashore. And approximately once a month, Georgie stays home and refuses to go out with his circle of friends, saying he is "busy indoors," a mysterious occupation that no one questions. "His business indoors, in fact, was a perfect secret, from having been public property for so long," the narrator says.[4] In the character of Georgie, Benson suggested homosexuality itself had become the perfect secret — well accepted in England. Despite the series of hints, the novel never reveals Georgie's secrets or sexual orientation.

The year after *Queen Lucia* came out, Wister, the master behind the coyly homoerotic *Virginian*, brought Bobby to Benson's home. Bobby described the scene in a letter to his father: "After a most interesting dinner talk we drove to Benson's lovely house on Brompton Square and Uncle Dan played the piano and sang, and he and Benson talked literature — Wells, Henry James, George Eliot, the Freudian analysis — and Benson showed us his notebook with all kinds of funny letters and pictures that he has cut out and preserved."[5] The next night, Benson invited Wister and Bobby to his house again, and they stayed up well past midnight. Bobby described Benson as "light, quick, and amusing."

Uncle Dan then accompanied Bobby to Paris, where again they held a Porcellian Club dinner with some of Bobby's young friends. Uncle Dan and Bobby then traveled alone to Amiens, visiting the town's spectacular thirteenth-century Gothic cathedral, which overlooks the River Somme, and to the World War I grave of Bobby's beloved friend Ollie Ames. They also toured a vineyard. Back in Paris, "Uncle Dan and I dined quietly together and went to *Les Huguenots* at the Grand Opera. It was splendidly sung and I thought it very grand," Bobby wrote his father.[6] He described his travels with Wister as "our Odyssey — as diverting and engrossing a week as I have ever spent."

It is natural to wonder whether the relationship between Uncle Dan and Bobby had become what Wilde called in his trial "the love that dare not speak its name," a romantic relationship between an older man and a younger. Wilde testified in defense of such relationships by pointing to the affection that David bore for Jonathan in the biblical book of Samuel II. The practice of an older man having a sexual relationship with a young man — illegal in London at the time — was well known among the ancient Greeks and a millennium later in Renaissance Florence.[7] Had Bobby become the youthful muse to Uncle Dan Wister, the wise, worldly, and elder author? There is no question that Uncle Dan and Bobby had developed a profound bond of affection — and Bobby gave a hint about the passion of their relationship late in his life — yet there is no evidence that it ever became sexual.

After graduating from Harvard Law School in 1922, Bobby went to work for the prominent Boston law firm Herrick, Smith, Donald & Farley. He helped represent the firm itself after it was sued in a massive fraud case, *Willett v. Herrick*, which resulted from the collapse of a business. The case, which included a trial that lasted 185 days over thirteen months, dragged on for years and ultimately landed in the US Supreme Court.

Socially, Bobby continued to enjoy the company of Wister, who had been among those who in 1884 founded Boston's Tavern Club. In 1922, with Wister's help, Bobby joined the club. The Tavern was a place where intellectuals, artists, businessmen, and politicians gathered to enjoy conversation, dining, or entertainment. Its members included many prominent Boston figures — painter John Singer Sargent, jurist Oliver Wendell Holmes, Senator Henry Cabot Lodge, and novelist Henry James. The Tavern's brick clubhouse on Boylston Place, a stone's throw from Boston Common, featured a sitting room with wood paneling and a fireplace, and a library lined with bookshelves containing volumes by members of the club and others, and with paintings by club members on the walls. Members ate in a dining room on the second floor.

The club truly came to life when its members performed their own plays for their own private enjoyment.[8] The plays — presented in a theater on the clubhouse's third floor — often were satires that called for male members to play female roles in women's clothing. Plays at the Tavern were fit to order for Bobby, who continued to delight in dressing as a woman. Shortly after joining the club, he played the lead role in *Doll Tearsheet*, based on the story of a prostitute by the same name in Shakespeare's *Henry IV, Part 2*.

In 1923, with Prohibition just a few years old, Wister wrote a classically inspired operetta called *Watch Your Thirst*, in which Ganymede is a bootlegger who sells his illicit hooch to the wealthy men of Athens even though alcohol has been banned by the gods on Mount Olympus. The operetta is about hunger for prohibited pleasures — and not just alcohol. In Greek and Roman mythology, Ganymede is a beautiful boy who symbolizes the ancient practice of pederasty. A myth tells the tale of the king of the gods, Jupiter, swooping to earth in the form of an eagle and capturing Ganymede to take him back to Mount Olympus so the boy can serve at his pleasure, inflaming the jealousy of Jupiter's queen, Juno. In Wister's retelling, Ganymede is now an adult man wooing a beautiful Greek maiden, Zoë Moo, who encourages him to collect money from his bootlegging so they can build a beautiful house. In Wister's production of his operetta, he asked Bobby to play Zoë Moo, requiring Bobby — in full drag — to attract Ganymede's attention and receive embraces and kisses from him. When Wister placed Bobby in the role of Zoë Moo, it may have revealed a hint about Wister's relationship with Bobby. Bobby later wrote in his autobiography, perhaps with a wink, that "Wister's operetta was as tuneful and gay as Offenbach."[9] While it can be risky to read too much into word choice, it should be noted that by this time the word *gay* was already being used to mean "homosexual." Bobby would use the word again, as will be seen, to describe Wister himself in a memorial tribute following his death.

Wister's play with homosexuality and gender roles in *Watch Your Thirst* extended beyond the characters of Ganymede and Zoë Moo. The classically educated Wister included a traditional figure of Greek drama, the choregos, who blames Prohibition on "crazy societies of male women and female men and all of the neuter gender . . ." The goddess Minerva mentions a woman from Lesbos, known as the home of the lesbian poet Sappho. The play also offers a vision of sexual liberation, as Zoë Moo questions the institution of marriage and proclaims, "We are advanced thinkers. We believe in free love." Wister's publisher, Macmillan, quietly issued a thousand copies of the operetta, which Wister signed and dedicated to the Tavern Club.[10] Books with open homosexual or lesbian themes were very seldom published in this era in the United States, and a larger printing of Wister's daring operetta might have encountered opposition.

That same year, Bobby completed his second novel, *The Speckled Bird*. The title refers to the biblical prophet Jeremiah, who sees his homeland under attack and says, "Mine heritage is unto me as a speckled bird, the birds round about are against her." The novel tells the story of a young woman, Abigail Vane, whose prominent New England family is in decline. Abigail's father, Harry Vane, dies in battle while serving in Cuba with President Roosevelt's Rough Riders. When she is older, Abigail goes with her uncle, John Vane, to the White House to attend the wedding of

President Roosevelt's daughter. In Bobby's literary world, the Vane family is tinged with the history of the Cutlers and Fishes.

Like Bobby's first novel, *The Speckled Bird* is a tale of unrequited love. Philip Chester, son of a New York financier, falls in love with Abigail but, under pressure from his mother, marries another woman from a prominent family. After Philip is blinded in World War I, Abigail, serving as a nurse, cares for him in a hospital in Cannes. Philip recovers and tells Abigail he loves her and wants her to go with him to live on the shore of Lake Lugano. When she objects that he is already married, he responds: "Did you come to Cannes merely to save my life and then to fling it down? Are you so cruel? . . . I have only loved and wanted you." Abigail, however, rejects him, and the book closes with her walking down a dark path alone. The novel presents, ultimately, bleak prospects that men and women will ever find true love in a marriage.

The depiction of failed relationships between men and women in *The Speckled Bird* presents a starkly clear reflection of Bobby's own life. His letters reveal profound affections for men, and an early photo shows him warmly embracing an unidentified male friend. There are no similar experiences with women. Instead, Bobby spent much of his social life in the all-male environs of the Somerset and Tavern Clubs, where quite a few members were bachelors.

In 1923, Bobby wrote his own play for the Tavern, *Beyond the Behind*, a title at once humorously anatomical and curiously metaphysical. The play tells the story of Mrs. Margaret Harding, described as "forty but still very beautiful," who had a child out of wedlock many years prior in an affair with a British cabinet minister, Sir John Elphinspoon.[11] Now the illegitimate child, John Harding, has an affair with Sir John's wife, Lady Cicely Elphinspoon. By having an affair with Lady Cicely, Harding unknowingly cuckolds his own father, giving the play a decidedly oedipal theme. Sigmund Freud's theory of the Oedipus complex, with its explanation of the origins of homosexuality, was gaining recognition at this time, and thus the play was Bobby's humorous rumination on Freud's theory. The cast was a typical blend of Taverners. Bobby played Mrs. Margaret Harding, in a dress. Boston philanthropist George Peabody Gardner Jr. played Sir John Elphinspoon. The painter Ives Gammell played their illegitimate son, John Harding. Poet Archibald MacLeish played Lady Cicely. As icing atop all the gender capering, Tavern Club president James Huntington played a French maid, as Bobby's script put it, in "very short skirts and silk stockings."

Bobby soon became extremely close to one of his younger friends, Chandler Bigelow, a Tavern Club member. Bobby was attending law school when he first met Chan, as Bobby called him, then still a Harvard undergraduate and a member of the Porcellian Club. Bobby described the friendship in his autobiography in warm terms: "When Father traveled overseas, I would visit at Chan's home on the North Shore and he would stay with me in Brookline. We came to share much of our enjoyment together . . ."[12] Bobby wrote that their "great friendship" had endured "in comfort and joy, thanks to my friend's loving-kindness, faith, and good principle." Chan introduced Bobby to the Episcopalian faith, to which he converted from the Unitarianism in which he was raised. Bobby and Chan took a monthlong tour of Europe in 1930, touring ruins at Pompeii and Paestum in Italy, and visiting Florence, Siena, Paris, and London.

Bobby cast Chan and another good friend, Henry Cabot Lodge Jr., grandson of Senator Lodge, in his next production at the Tavern, *England Expects Every Man to Do His Duty*, presented in the club's 1931 Christmas production. The play tells the story of an English princess, Louise, who disguises herself as a Buckingham Palace chambermaid so she can go freely among the public.[13] Once she is outside the palace, a bobby — or policeman — Officer Bangle, becomes smitten with her. Bobby cast himself as Officer Bangle and Theodore Spencer, a poet and Harvard English professor, as Princess Louise. Spencer was a confidant of W. H. Auden, the gay English poet, who sent his manuscripts to Spencer for review.[14] In the closing scene, Officer Bangle — Bobby — embraces Louise — Spencer — as the curtain falls.

Such gender play was not unusual — after all, many Taverners had emerged from all-male Harvard, where Hasty Pudding and other drama societies routinely required male actors to play women's roles. Many members of the Tavern were either artists or writers themselves, or patrons of the arts, and so might be tolerant of homosexuality. Yet there is no indication that the Tavern ever approved of homosexuality — like many institutions in those days, it was simply silent on the subject.

Some club members even had a record of opposing homosexuality. One of these was A. Lawrence Lowell, who had served as Harvard's president since 1909. Lowell reportedly once demanded that an elderly professor, exposed as a homosexual, resign immediately. When the professor asked what Lowell would have done, had he been in the professor's position, Lowell replied, "I would get a gun and destroy myself."[15]

Lowell also quietly cracked down on gay students at Harvard. In 1920, after a student committed suicide, allegations emerged that he was among a large group of homosexuals on campus. Lowell convened a secret disciplinary panel that questioned about thirty students.[16] Some of the students and an assistant professor confessed to homosexual activities, and one described parties where the male students danced together, dressed in women's clothes, and there was "kissing." The panel secretly expelled eight students and terminated the assistant professor. A second student committed suicide after learning he had been expelled. (The whole affair remained unknown until Harvard's student newspaper revealed it in 2002.) Yet just a few years after Lowell completed this secret homosexual purge, Bobby fluttered across the Tavern Club stage dressed as a series of female leads — the prostitute Doll Tearsheet, Zoë Moo, and Mrs. Margaret Harding.

Bobby also indulged his flair for cross-dressing occasionally in social settings. In 1933, he went on a cruise in the Caribbean with Chan Bigelow and their friend Lodge, Lodge's wife, Emily, and her sister Jean Sears. A picture of the group shows a costume party in which Chan, dour and in bland attire, is sitting at Bobby's side.[17] Bobby is wearing a florid woman's dress, with a white flower in his hair and holding a parasol.

As the years passed, Bobby seemed to move closer to that solitary bachelor lifestyle that he lamented in *Louisburg Square*, with its depiction of the Sarcophagus Club. In 1934, at the age of thirty-nine, he took up residence in what was called the Somerset Club's annex, a small apartment building attached to the club at 41 Beacon Street. This made his regular haunts remarkably close at hand — the Tavern and his church, St. Paul's Episcopal Cathedral, were just a quick walk away across the common. One of his neighbors was Tavern member F. O. Matthiessen, a prominent Harvard English professor and the author of an important book on American nineteenth-century literature. Matthiessen had fallen in love with a much younger painter, Russell Cheney. The pair lived quietly in Louisburg Square, just a few blocks from Bobby's residence at the Somerset.[18]

Bobby's Tavern Club member file holds a two-page document, festooned with a red heart at the top of the first page, followed by the words, TO MY VALENTINE, from a person identified only as "XXXX."[19] The second page presents a poem titled "To my Valentine — Robert Cutler, Esq." The poem praises the breadth of Bobby's intellect and humor, including his "anecdotes of sex," and implores Bobby to

> *Abandon art's delusive charms,*
> *My proffered charms embrace*
> *And let this shy Philistine help*
> *To elevate the Race.*

Was this an expression of true romantic attraction, somehow fallen into club management's hands? A prank? A sarcastic or abusive taunt? A harmless and playful jest from some humorous Valentine's Day party that involved gender play? The answer is unknown.

Bobby did apparently once seek a romantic relationship with a woman. This was Ellen "Nell" Sears, who was in an unhappy marriage with a Bostonian named David Sears when she traveled in February 1928 with Bobby, his brothers John and Elliott, and a group of other friends to Nassau, in the Bahamas. "I had already become deeply involved with Bobby Cutler. He was the one who persuaded me to leave David," Nell wrote in a memoir.[20] An album from the trip has a photo of Bobby lying adoringly beside Nell on the beach and another of him holding her hand as she steps over a low wall.[21] After Nell divorced Sears, she married Charles C. Cabot, another friend of Bobby's. She later wrote about Bobby: "He was a brilliant man, and a very emotional one! I'm afraid I made him a very unhappy one!"[22]

Bobby later suggested he was responsible for the relationship's failure. "When I did essay a great love in my thirties, I failed; my failure being more worthy than my love. But this matter is still between God and me," he wrote in his autobiography. Bobby gave an ambiguous explanation for his bachelorhood, saying, "Usually, after initial steps with someone my own age, I would draw back. An unreadiness to plunge? A retreating deep into work and the comradeship of cherished friends rather than sail ahead into the uncharted seas?"[23]

It was not a lack of passion that led him to bachelorhood. To the contrary, Bobby overflowed with emotion. "From childhood, my disposition has been extremely affectionate," Bobby wrote. "There was in me a restless need to love and to find a return of that love. I sought one or more persons to devote myself and share with, in a continuing flow of intercommunication."[24] Withholding names, he continued:

> I am highly susceptible. There was no halfway about my emotional response to a person: at a first meeting, there was either warm acceptance or cold turning away . . . When I was strongly drawn to a person, it was as if all my spirit gathered together in one overriding sweep. My intense nature would drive me into a high pitch of joy or, as quickly, into a pit of gloom at some fancied slight. These swift alterations would baffle those for whom I cared and splinter my own reserves.

After Nell, there is no sign that any woman inspired such emotionalism, and he spent his time with male friends like Chan. It was a blow to Bobby when Wister died in 1938. The Tavern has a long-standing tradition of memorializing deceased members by having a friend write a tribute to the departed. Bobby gave Wister's tribute, lionizing both Wister's willingness to befriend young men and his seemingly endless curiosity about life. "And in this consuming interest, which enjoyed everything it did to the top of the bent, he was akin with the liveliest and gayest of men of all ages," Bobby said.

Bobby found what may have been his greatest calling when he entered the political realm, helping Cabot Lodge seek election to the US Senate in 1936. The elder Lodge's son, the poet George Cabot Lodge, died young in 1909, and his son had a very close relationship with his grandfather. Cabot Lodge graduated cum laude from Harvard in 1924 and was elected as a Republican to the Massachusetts House of Representatives in 1932.[25] Owing to his close relationship with his grandfather, he was called Henry Cabot Lodge Jr. A liberal Republican, he took positions friendly to labor groups and the working class, which helped him win election even in the Great Depression.

When a US Senate seat became open in 1936, Cabot Lodge threw his hat in the ring, and Bobby became his campaign finance chairman.[26] Lodge's opponent was James Michael Curley, the governor of

Massachusetts and a controversial Democrat who ran a powerful political machine in Boston. Curley, who as a child emigrated from Ireland to Boston's Roxbury section, had been embroiled in a series of scandals and had twice been convicted and imprisoned while holding office.[27] An imposing figure with deep roots in Boston's Irish community, Curley had won election as Massachusetts governor despite his repeated run-ins with the criminal justice system. As the Senate election drew closer, Bobby wrote Lodge that the contest between the two men made Lodge look "like young St. George in shining armor anxious to stick a spear into the entrails of the dragon . . ."[28]

Bobby used his slightly bawdy humor to defuse tension and lighten the mood during what was expected to be a tough political contest. After Lodge won the Republican primary, Bobby wrote, "Dear Cabot, What a vote! What a vote! What a vote!" He added, "The doorman at the Parker House just told me that you were going to take Curley 'like Grant took Richmond.' But even if you only take him like Caesar took Cleopatra, you will always be the delight of your affectionate Bobby."[29]

On Election Day in November 1936, Bobby stayed up through the night with Lodge and Emily, Chan, and another friend, former Harvard football star Mal Greenough — and they celebrated when Lodge defeated Curley.[30] This campaign forged a friendship — and a political alliance — between Bobby and Lodge that would last for the rest of their lives. While it was founded on a shared political philosophy, the two men had similar educations and many common acquaintances in the worlds of politics, business, and law. For a 1939 event in support of Lodge, Bobby invited a group of twenty businessmen and friends, including Chan, to a dinner at the Somerset Club. Lodge sent Bobby a thank-you letter days later: "It is seldom that an opportunity for constructive achievement goes hand in hand with an evening of conviviality and friendship, but this was true on Monday night. The memory of it will always be with me and the greater satisfaction is that you were willing on my account to make such an effort and provide such a splendid evening for everyone concerned."[31]

Bobby took part in many civic activities, making himself well known in town. He raised money for the Community Fund, which supported charities in Boston, and eventually served as the fund's chairman. He soon got to know Boston's Democratic mayor, Maurice Tobin. Tobin's parents had emigrated from Ireland and, like Curley, he had grown up in Roxbury. Tobin had once been a close ally of Curley's but broke ranks with him and then defeated him in the 1937 mayoral election in Boston. Bobby became friends with Tobin and even went on vacations with him and his wife, Helen. Devout Catholics, the Tobins once went to Bobby's Episcopalian house of worship, St. Paul's Cathedral, to hear Bobby preach a sermon in support of the Community Fund.[32]

In 1940, Tobin asked Bobby for help in a reelection campaign for the mayor's office that again pitted him against Curley. Seeking to bolster his image as a candidate for good government, Tobin asked Bobby to become Boston corporation counsel — the city's chief lawyer. The move also was calculated to help Tobin win the support of Republican voters. Bobby accepted Tobin's offer and was sworn in on October 30, 1940.

This new position for Bobby — amid a tough Democratic race — drew attention to one of the Cutler brothers' outings. Even as their careers led them far afield, the five Cutler brothers, known for their fierce loyalty to one another, continued to hold regular reunions. At such events, the brothers often lined up for photographs in their birth order, with John, the eldest, on the left, and Bobby, the youngest, on the right. Bobby's appointment as Boston's corporation counsel sparked public interest in the brothers' reunion in October 1940, which took place not far from John and Rosalind Cutler's home in Garrison, New York. *The Boston Globe* sent a reporter to hike through the mountains to the cabin where the brothers were staying. "Famous Cutler Brothers Relax in Mountains," the headline said. The article reported:

> Waldo, N.Y., Oct. 26 — Every Fall and Spring, five of the most successful brothers in Boston gather in a rude log cabin on a small mount here in the foothills of the Catskills, where they can look back over the course they have traveled through life thus far, appreciate it, relax, and do a bit of hunting and hiking.
>
> They are the Cutler brothers, celebrated in medicine, law, finance, business and adventure.
>
> The appointment of Robert Cutler, the "baby" of the five, to be corporation counsel of the city of Boston, came on the eve of one of these reunions, and he was here today dressed in slacks, heavy walking shoes, a brown coat,

although he remained a Beau Brummell of the outdoors
by sporting a bow tie.

The article went on to note that Roger Cutler, who "stroked the
Harvard crew to victory in 1911" and six years later sank a German subma-
rine from an airplane, could not attend because the secretary of the navy
had commissioned him a day previous as a lieutenant commander and he
was back in the service. George Cutler, the president of a trust company
in Baltimore, also was not present, as he was required in Florida for business. Attending the reunion along with Bobby that day were John Cutler,
now a partner at the finance company Smith Barney in New York, and
his brother Elliott, who had gained international fame for a pioneering
heart surgery and also was president of the Harvard Alumni Association.
The *Globe* reporter wrote that he wanted to talk to the brothers awhile,
but Elliott said the group had to make the nine-mile hike back to John's
house in Garrison.[33] The reporter tartly ended his story: "Note to the
boss: The next time you want these guys interviewed, send the Foreign
Legion." While entertaining, the story also was brilliant political show-
manship: No one could miss the point that Tobin was now backed by a
Republican with elite Harvard credentials.

As Boston corporation counsel, Bobby plunged into a world of legal
wrangling over public parks, land for Boston's new airport, tax rates and
appeals, bills in the state legislature, placement of birth control books
in a public library, and a proposal by Mayor Tobin to build an elevated
highway through the city's downtown. Yet it was Tobin's reelection battle
against Curley in the 1941 mayoral race that landed Bobby in the middle
of Boston's rough-and-tumble Democratic politics.

During a previous term as mayor of Boston, Curley was accused of
violating the public trust in a city license fraud scheme, and he had been
ordered in court to repay the city more than forty-two thousand dollars.
After taking office as corporation counsel under Tobin, Bobby launched
an investigation into how Curley failed to repay the money while he
managed to live in a magnificent house and drive a fine car. Bobby filed
suit to obtain payment and won an order forcing Curley to repay five
hundred dollars per month.[34] Bobby wrote statements attacking Curley
for Tobin's supporters to use in radio ads. He also drafted a letter supporting Tobin, to be signed by Bobby and other Republicans, for distribution

in a ward where Republican voters would respond favorably. In the end, Tobin won reelection, defeating Curley by a vote of 125,786 to 116,430. Curley launched a suit alleging voter fraud and improper campaigning by Tobin, but Bobby successfully defended the mayor and Tobin took office for another term.

Bobby's prominent role in this Boston political race — as a Republican who crossed party lines to work for a Democrat — won him recognition. With the outbreak of the Second World War, and President Franklin Roosevelt looking for Republicans who would back the war effort, Bobby's ability to bridge the political divide in Boston soon led to a summons to Washington, where he would be called upon to perform another political balancing act — this time on a national stage.

3

WARTIME

Prior to American entry into the war, President Franklin Delano Roosevelt called for strong US support of England, but isolationists in Congress accused him of pushing the nation into the European war. In July 1940, in an effort to broaden support for his pro-British views, Roosevelt asked Henry L. Stimson, who had served as secretary of state under Republican president Herbert Hoover, to lead the nation's military as his secretary of war. Stimson in turn asked Harvey H. Bundy, who had been Stimson's assistant secretary of state, to return to Washington as his special assistant. Bundy, a Harvard graduate and prominent Massachusetts Republican, was a friend of Bobby Cutler, whom he had gotten to know while practicing law in Boston.

In June 1942, seven months after the Japanese attack on Pearl Harbor, Bobby got a phone call from a friend urging him to come to Washington to serve in the War Department. The friend offered Bobby the rank of colonel and the position of assistant deputy director of the Army Specialist Corps. The unit had recently been established to bring people with special qualifications — scientists, technicians, and professional managers — into the US war effort. Bobby accepted. It is unclear who exactly made this offer, but it seems certain that Bobby's appointment came from Bundy or owed much to him.[1]

Stimson was notoriously taciturn and given to occasional bursts of anger. However, he knew Bobby's older brother Elliott, who was later to become the army's chief medical officer in the European theater. Bobby later wrote that when Bundy introduced Bobby to Stimson as Elliott's younger brother, his reaction was "like a brief sunshaft in the wintry sky of Vermont . . . In a moment, as he turned to Bundy, the cloud of urgent work waiting to be done closed down again upon him."[2]

Stimson had expressed strong support for the Army Specialist Corps and had appointed Dwight Davis, a St. Louisan who had served as governor general of the Philippines under Hoover, to run it. With a thousand employees, it occupied a former munitions building in Washington.[3] Yet Bobby soon perceived the agency to be inept, mired in bureaucracy and in conflict with the army's existing officer-recruitment operations. As for Davis, Bobby said he was "an amiable, lovable man, soon adrift in red tape and internecine jealousies." After four months of operation, the corps had commissioned just one officer.[4] After about six weeks of watching the Army Specialist Corps operate, Bobby wrote a memo calling for its abolition and combining its functions with another agency. Stimson approved the transition, and Bobby moved to run the new agency, the Officer Procurement Service (OPS). In less than a year, the OPS commissioned approximately thirty thousand officers.[5]

After the OPS had shown success in its mission, Stimson asked Bobby in October 1943 to serve in the Office of the Secretary of War in the Pentagon and to manage voting by US soldiers during the presidential election of 1944. With approximately ten million soldiers deployed away from their homes, voting by soldiers carried the potential to determine the outcome of the election. President Roosevelt and northern Democrats wanted soldiers — all soldiers — to vote in the election, but southern Democrats saw this as a threat to the state laws that kept black voters disenfranchised, and northern Republicans viewed it as a ploy to drum up votes for Roosevelt.

Roosevelt had won his third consecutive term in 1940, prior to US entry into World War II. He had won his first two elections — in 1932 and 1936 — by significant margins, with the Great Depression of the '30s driving support for his programs to assist the poor and regulate the risky practices of Wall Street. By the early 1940s, he was still widely admired for his handling of the nation's economy and his leadership in the fight against fascism in Europe and Japan. Roosevelt also had built an alliance with black leaders that would remake the face of American politics by convincing black voters to leave the Republican Party and support the Democratic Party. Seeking to respond to demands for racial justice by A. Philip Randolph and other black leaders, Roosevelt in 1941 issued an executive order prohibiting racially discriminatory employment practices by federal government agencies and defense industries. His order created the Fair Employment Practices Committee (FEPC), empowered to enforce this prohibition. In 1942, the FEPC held public hearings and issued rulings requiring employers to hire black workers under certain circumstances. In 1943, President Roosevelt issued an executive order requiring all federal contracts to include a clause prohibiting discrimination on the basis of race, creed, or color. Issues of interest to black citizens also drew support from First Lady Eleanor Roosevelt. She urged passage of a law against lynching, a barbaric crime that at that time claimed as many as one hundred black lives per year, primarily in the South. And after singer Marian Anderson was denied permission to sing at a private concert hall in Washington, the First Lady led an effort to have her perform on the steps of the Lincoln Memorial. Together, the Roosevelts had won supporters among black citizens, and that promised strong support from black voters in the next presidential election.

As 1944 approached, it became clear that the soldier vote could play a major role in the outcome of the election, in which President Roosevelt would seek an unprecedented fourth term in office. George Gallup, who issued poll findings and other assessments that were sometimes less than scientific, issued a statement in June 1943 that "all current evidence" suggested that soldiers largely favored the Democratic Party. "Hence, the larger the soldier vote the better off the Democrats will be," he wrote.[6]

Roosevelt and his Democratic allies wanted all soldiers to have a right to vote in the 1944 presidential election. Two Democratic senators, Scott Lucas of Illinois and Theodore Green of Rhode Island, introduced a bill that would provide a simple blank ballot that would enable soldiers to write in the name of the candidate, or a political party, they supported for president and a US House and Senate candidate from their state in the general election. Lucas argued that soldiers were fighting for democracy and deserved an opportunity to cast a vote. Some states did not permit absentee voting, and others had onerous absentee voting rules that would require multiple mailings for each soldier, which would burden the military transportation system, Lucas argued. Significantly, the bill would enable soldiers to bypass the poll taxes that eight southern states had established. As a burden on poor voters, poll taxes were commonly perceived as a way to reduce the number of blacks who voted.

Southern Democrats, who had earlier used the states' rights rallying cry to defeat anti-poll-tax and anti-lynching legislation, quickly raised the same objections to the Lucas-Green soldier voting proposal. Led by Representative John Rankin, a staunchly segregationist Democrat from Mississippi, opponents charged that the Lucas-Green proposal violated the Constitution's clause that gave the states the power to set "times, places and manner" of holding elections. Rankin said he agreed soldiers should vote, but they should use the existing absentee voting procedures available under state laws.

Stimson appointed Bobby the secretary of war's coordinator for soldier voting, making him the top-ranking officer in charge of soldier voting matters. Bobby quickly assembled information on US soldier voting in wartime, including the presidential election of 1864 during the Civil War.[7] Testifying before a congressional committee, Bobby explained the hurdles soldiers would face in trying to vote under state absentee voting laws: Each soldier would require as many as five mailings — first requesting an application for a ballot, then receiving the application, sending in the application, receiving the ballot, and sending in the completed ballot. As an example of how long this sequence of mailings might take, five mailings to or from Springfield, Illinois, and the European theater of the war would require sixty-one days, he said.[8] Bobby also noted that the armed forces were already struggling with a shortage in transport planes. Further complicating the matter, the states had a patchwork of laws regarding absentee voting. Some states permitted no absentee voting at all, or only by people physically located in the state. It was clear that many state laws made it impossible for soldiers — using multiple mailings from stations thousands of miles overseas — to cast absentee ballots. In some states, an absentee ballot could be requested only a few days before an election. In eleven states, no more than twenty days could pass between receipt of an absentee's application and the absentee's executed ballot being received back in the state offices to be counted. "I thought it a cruel hoax to carry a ballot to a soldier overseas which could not be returned in time to be counted," Bobby later wrote.[9]

"With all deference to Colonel Cutler," the segregationist Rankin said on the House floor, "he is a Boston lawyer and a graduate of Harvard, and probably has a different slant on holding elections from that of our people down in the fork of the creek."[10] Rankin urged passage of bills by southern Democrats that would merely recommend — rather than require — states to make changes to absentee voting procedures.

In December 1943, after the Lucas-Green bill passed from committee to the Senate floor, three southern Democratic senators sponsored a substitute bill that would merely recommend how states might amend absentee voting laws to make them more amenable to soldier voting. One of these senators, John McClellan of Arkansas, insisted he wanted soldiers to vote, but said, "I appeal to those who believe in the fundamentals of states' rights, of state sovereignty, of the states controlling their own election machinery, and of the states being able to say who is eligible to vote."[11]

Proponents of the Lucas-Green bill stepped forward to combat the southerners' arguments. Senator Lucas denied that his bill disregarded the Constitution: "I yield to no man in my reverence for states' rights." He warned McClellan's bill would have a devastating impact: "Those who vote for the pending amendment will have to assume the responsibility of denying practically every man overseas an opportunity to vote. As I pointed out a few days ago, from the statement given by Colonel Cutler of the Army, under the amendment, not a single boy from the state of Illinois who is now serving beyond the limits of the continental United States, could vote in 1944. Does the Senate want to deny them that privilege?"[12]

In the end, the alliance of segregationist southern Democrats with northern Republicans proved too powerful. On December 3, 1943, the Lucas-Green measure went down in defeat as the substitute bill passed in the Senate by a vote of 42–37.[13] A total of twenty-four Democrats joined eighteen Republicans to secure victory for the states' rights bill.

The bill's passage set off a firestorm of controversy. A group of twenty-five House Democrats released a letter calling the bill a "slap in the face" to soldiers. Senator Joseph Guffey, a Pennsylvania Democrat, charged that southern Democrats had entered "an unholy alliance" with northern Republicans to defeat the Lucas-Green bill.[14] Senator Josiah Bailey, a North Carolina Democrat, countered that if liberal Democrats pushed Roosevelt's bill, the southern Democrats might break free and form their own party, a step that would doom Democratic hopes for reelecting Roosevelt. Speaking on the floor of the Senate, Bailey warned that without southern Democrats, "there would never again be a man elected President of the United States on the Democratic ticket."

Once McClellan's bill arrived in the House for consideration, Rankin quickly embraced it as the alternative to a soldier ballot bill proposed by a liberal Texas Democrat, Eugene Worley. Rankin went to the House floor repeatedly to denounce supporters of Worley's bill as black radicals or Communists, lacing his comments with anti-Semitic remarks.

After Walter Winchell, the influential columnist, voiced support in the left-leaning newspaper *PM* for the Worley bill, Rankin gave a speech on the House floor attacking Winchell as "the little kike." Rankin went on to call the editorial staff of *PM* "that bunch of communistic kikes."[15] As an example of hate-filled anti-Semitic speech in Congress, Rankin's performance has few rivals.

Another opponent of the national soldier ballot bill was Representative Hamilton Fish, a conservative Republican from New York who was among the most vocal critics of Roosevelt's New Deal. Fish's sister, Rosalind, was Bobby's sister-in-law. Fish made it clear that his brand of Republicanism had shifted toward states' rights. "We are opposed to further regimentation and bureaucratic domination by the defunct New Deal for political purposes or any other, and the destruction of the few remaining rights of the states and their sovereignty," he said on the House floor on January 10, 1944.[16]

President Roosevelt went on the offensive, delivering a message to Congress that denounced McClellan's bill as a "meaningless measure" that did nothing other than make a recommendation to states. "I consider such proposed legislation a fraud on the soldiers and sailors and marines now training and fighting for us and for our sacred rights. It is a fraud upon the American people," the president said.[17]

Republicans countered that the Lucas-Green bill itself was a fraud because it promised soldiers a federal ballot, but states could ultimately reject that ballot or challenge it in court. Senator Robert Taft, the powerful Ohio Republican, also charged that the federal ballot bill would enable officers to compel soldiers to vote in a certain way. Lucas rejected the notion that US military officers would do such a thing, saying Taft's comment was "the most ridiculous and asinine and absurd statement any senator has ever made since I have been in the Senate."[18] Taft also charged that Stimson was "partisan" and "working for a fourth term of President Roosevelt."[19] Secretary of War Stimson, a Republican, had served in that same post under Taft's father, President William Howard Taft, also a Republican. When Bobby and Harvey Bundy reported Taft's accusation to Stimson, he responded with disdain, "Why, the young puppy . . . I loved his father."

Southern Democrats, meanwhile, made it clear that this voting rights issue rankled them deeply — and had its roots in generations of racial and regional bitterness dating back to the post–Civil War Reconstruction era, when Union soldiers occupied southern states and supervised elections, including some that black candidates won. After Reconstruction collapsed, white hegemony over the black population, enforced by brute force, terror, and Jim Crow laws, gripped the South. Rankin warned that the war ballot bill "invades the rights of the states, the very thing the white people . . . have protested against ever since the close of the Civil War."[20]

On February 3, 1944, the House voted, with a few southern Democrats refusing to join the states' rights group. Yet in the final vote, the states' rights coalition held together and McClellan's bill passed by a vote of 328–69.

Because there were differences between the bills passed in the House and Senate, the measures had to be reconciled by a conference committee with members from both bodies. Remarkably, the final compromise that emerged from the conference committee created a federal War Ballot Commission to administer voting by soldiers using a federal ballot. But the bill permitted soldiers to use the federal ballot only if certain conditions were met, including a requirement that the soldier's home state had to approve use of the federal ballot. The bill also gave the forty-eight states until July 15 to inform the federal government whether they intended to accept the federal ballot. After the bill won final approval from the House, President Roosevelt said, "The Bill is, in my judgment, wholly inadequate to assure to servicemen and women, as far as is practically feasible, the same opportunity they would have to vote if they were at home."[21] Yet after the drawn-out battle in Congress, it was clear no better alternative would pass, and Roosevelt let the bill become law.

Within days, the War Ballot Commission was established and Bobby was appointed its executive director, with staff and offices in a War Department building in Washington.[22] Yet the disputes over soldier voting were far from over. The next month, a top assistant to President Roosevelt, Sam Rosenman, raised concerns that the army's voting process was being run completely by Republicans. Bundy told Bobby that Rosenman questioned Stimson, provoking an irate response. "Are you suggesting to me, sir, that I am rigging something here?" Stimson fired at Rosenman. "Cutler was corporation counsel to a Democratic Mayor of Boston. I don't give a damn to what party he belongs. How dare you address such an innuendo to me?"[23] Bobby spent three hours in Rosenman's White House office on a Saturday morning, outlining his plans and the protections to be put in place for secure voting by servicemen. Ultimately, Bobby defused the issue by quietly agreeing to place a Democrat on his staff.

Senator Taft, concerned that Stimson and his officers were trying to aid Roosevelt in winning reelection, had inserted a lengthy section in the soldier voting law that banned the army from distributing "political argument" of any kind intended to affect the result of the elections. Taft's provision also gave the War Ballot Commission authority to judge whether materials violated the ban and made it a crime to violate the ban. Bobby, as the commission's executive director, prepared a directive spelling out the ban. When the army refused to distribute fourteen books, including one by influential historian Charles Beard, the public erupted with letters accusing the army of banning books and censoring information for soldiers. Bobby appeared in a public forum with Taft and stated simply that the directive merely complied with requirements of the law Taft supported. A *New York Times* editorial said, "The Army ought not to be required to police the minds of the young men who are doing the fighting for us."[24] Soon thereafter, Taft met with Bobby in Senator Green's office and agreed on a compromise easing the restrictions on reading material. The Senate and House swiftly passed the amendment, and President Roosevelt signed it into law on August 21.

Ultimately, only twenty of the forty-eight states agreed to accept the federal ballot for soldiers, and while the War Ballot Commission sent 3.3 million executed absentee ballots to the secretaries of state for counting in the election, most were state absentee ballots; only 9 percent were federal ballots.[25] In the November 1944 election, President Roosevelt was reelected to his fourth term in a landslide.

For Bobby's work in defusing the political firestorm over soldier voting, Stimson awarded him the Distinguished Service Medal before a crowd in the Pentagon in September 1945. Stimson praised Bobby a few years later in his book *On Active Service in Peace and War*, written with Harvey Bundy's son, McGeorge Bundy. "Both in the War Ballot Commission and in the Army, soldier voting was so smoothly and fairly handled that Stimson felt a deep personal debt to Cutler. No job entrusted to his supervision during the entire war had held more explosive possibilities, and none was accomplished with less friction."[26]

Bobby became embroiled in another politically explosive matter in late 1944, when the Republican-dominated House Military Affairs Committee accused forty-two officers and enlisted men in the army of being Communists or Communist sympathizers. Working with Stimson's assistant John McCloy, Bobby went to the House committee and looked into the files on the soldiers, and he began to whittle down the list of possible Communists. Bobby reported that "five men were under surveillance because of suspected sexual perversion," then a derisive but official term for homosexuality.[27] Another soldier was dead. Another had married a Japanese girl. A number of the soldiers were of foreign birth and had gotten involved with subversive or Communist issues as young men. Bobby worked his way through the files and whittled the list down to "a hard core of some dozen cases." One of these was Joseph Lash, an army trainee with a long record of Socialist and Communist involvement. Eleanor Roosevelt had taken an interest in Lash, and he had visited the president and Mrs. Roosevelt's home in Hyde Park, New York.[28] A committee investigator "clung to this young trainee like a limpet to a rock," Bobby noted. But after President Roosevelt died in April 1945, and Mrs. Roosevelt moved out of the White House, Bobby convinced the investigator to drop the matter by promising him that the army would assign Lash to a minor post in the Deep South, where he could do no harm. Bobby and the investigator shook hands on the matter. Ultimately, when the committee held a hearing in the summer of 1945, Bobby called Major General William Donovan, director of the Office of Strategic Services, as a witness to testify about the valuable contributions of foreign-born intelligence agents. The committee investigation quietly faded away.

Another of America's revered wartime leaders with whom Bobby worked was General George C. Marshall, the army chief of staff throughout the war. In May 1945, a congressional committee that was considering possible changes in military recruitment asked Marshall to testify. Marshall, aware of Bobby's assistance to Stimson and McCloy on the matter of universal military training, asked Bobby to prepare a "checklist" of ideas on the subject. When Bobby presented a two-page document to Marshall on the morning of his testimony, the general reviewed it carefully and said simply, "Thank you, Cutler."[29]

Working behind the scenes to resolve two potentially explosive issues — the furor raised by Democratic segregationists and Republicans over the soldier vote in 1944 and charges by Republicans in Congress that Communists and homosexuals had infiltrated the army — Bobby had become recognized as an effective fixer, a man with a sharp legal mind who knew how to solve a problem by working the levers of power in Washington, and striking a compromise when necessary, to get something done. He could work with Democrats and Republicans, in Congress or in executive agencies. After Bobby left the War Department in late 1945, General Marshall recommended him for the Legion of Merit and also promotion to the rank of brigadier general, both of which President Truman approved. Undersecretary of War Robert Patterson later sent Bobby a letter recalling Marshall's fondness for him.[30] Patterson's note captured the respect that Bobby's political and writing skills had earned him, as well as his striking personality: "I think of you so often, and I think of General Marshall's reference to you as a rose among cabbages."

The feeling of admiration was mutual. Bobby's interactions with Marshall left him with lifelong reverence for the general's acute focus on the issues before him and careful manner of speech. "George Marshall," Bobby wrote in his memoir, "was the most august person that I ever saw or came to know."[31]

4

FROM OLD COLONY TO PSYCHOLOGICAL WARFARE

As the war ended, Bobby was in a unique position in Boston politics. He was a prominent Republican and close friend of Henry Cabot Lodge Jr., whom he had helped win election to the US Senate in 1936 and 1942. He also had forged strong ties with Democrats both in Boston city government and in the Roosevelt and Truman administrations, and he had relationships with important figures in the War Department. He moved back to Boston and resumed his residence at the Somerset Club, the staid institution on Beacon Hill that overlooked the gently rolling landscape of Boston Common and was just a few minutes' walk from the State House. In February 1946, Old Colony Trust, a division of the First National Bank of Boston and the nation's largest trust company outside New York, named Bobby its president.

Bobby's new position at Old Colony put him in regular business dealings with many of Boston's wealthy elite, including T. Jefferson Coolidge III, a direct descendant of President Thomas Jefferson and scion of the wealthy Coolidge family.[1] Coolidge, whose father had been among the founders of Old Colony in 1890, was chairman of United Fruit Company, the banana conglomerate based in Boston. Coolidge, like Bobby, was a member of the Somerset and Tavern Clubs and was both a social friend and a significant business associate. For five decades, Old Colony had provided financial services to United Fruit as the company grew to be one of the nation's largest agricultural concerns thanks to its banana plantations, railroad lines, and shipping businesses in Latin America. United Fruit had a unique business relationship with both Old Colony and First National. At the bank, this arrangement was called the interlock. Since 1907, United Fruit had placed a member on the board of directors of First National Bank, and the bank held a seat on United Fruit's board.[2] When Bobby arrived in his new post, the interlock had a powerful lineup: Coolidge, United Fruit's chairman, was a First National Bank board member, while Channing H. Cox, a longtime First National

Bank executive who was Massachusetts's former Republican governor, sat on United Fruit's board.

Bobby's hard-driving work ethic guided his management of Old Colony. He "brought to the trust company a kind of energy and leadership it had never seen before," an authorized history of the bank says.[3] As president, Bobby worked closely with Coolidge, chairman of the bank's trust committee. He was "affectionately known as Bobby to everyone who ever met him," yet his ferocious drive to get things done inspired a certain degree of dread. Comparing Bobby and Coolidge, the history said: "Those two strong men, so disparate in personality and style, worked well together, but Bobby was so forceful and energetic that no one wanted to be in his way." Trust company employees called Bobby's office "hurricane corner."[4]

While the bank became the center of his work life, Bobby continued to engage in politics, particularly supporting the political aspirations of his close friend Henry Cabot Lodge Jr. Lodge had given up his Senate seat to serve in the army in 1944, and with the war over he decided to win back his old seat in an election set for 1946. As the election approached, Bobby organized a rally in support of Lodge and other Republicans. Lodge wrote Bobby in early October thanking him for his support and noting that the large rally, to be held the Sunday before the election, could have a major impact on the outcome. Lodge also outlined some ideas for drawing a bigger crowd to the event, including hiring Frank Sinatra to perform.[5] Lodge said the suggestions "are for you to consider and for you to decide, as I have complete confidence in your judgment on this as on all other matters." Sinatra did not sing, but Massachusetts voters nonetheless handed Lodge a major victory on Election Day: He defeated Democratic incumbent David Walsh by a margin of 968,840 to 644,043.[6] It was a resounding victory that signaled Republicans had returned to power in New England.

After Lodge took his place in the Senate in January 1947, Bobby continued in his role as political adviser and confidant to his old friend. Bobby criticized the Truman administration for failing to respond to the threat of Communist expansion with a coordinated national security strategy, and he shared his views with Lodge, who was among the internationalist Republicans who sought a strong US role in defense of Europe, as opposed to the isolationist wing of the Republican Party led by Senator Robert Taft of Ohio. "Dear Cabot," Bobby wrote in a March 1947 letter. "It was very nice having lunch with you and Emmy and the boys yesterday. Quite like old times. Our debate on foreign policy cultivated both heat and light, a rare enough happening. If our present steps in Greece and Turkey are to be part of a consistent foreign policy of aggressive strength, well and good; but I feel otherwise if we are just to be little Peters running about to put our fingers in the dike whenever it leaks."[7]

As a bachelor with no children of his own, Bobby extended his close bond with his brothers to relationships with his nieces and nephews. When his brother John's daughter, Judith, was engaged to marry St. Louisan Jackson J. Shinkle in June 1947, Bobby wrote her a congratulatory letter. "Growing old alone is, I find, a disenchanting thing. That is, if you are a naturally affectionate person. So long I've been embracing the marble statue of WORK and DUTY and CHARITY; but my Galatea never comes to life. So I think you are a smart girl to find someone you love to share things with. Affly, Uncle Bobby."[8] Bobby was referring to the Greek myth of Galatea, in which a sculptor falls in love with one of his creations. As told in Ovid's *Metamorphoses*, the sculptor, Pygmalion of Cyprus, witnesses the lewd behavior of prostitutes and concludes he is "not interested in women," and so creates a sculpture of a beautiful ideal woman to admire. When he kisses his sculpture, it comes to life — and he falls in love with her.[9] In his letter, Bobby was not just congratulating his niece — he was explaining why he remained a bachelor.

Judith Cutler Shinkle said she was convinced Bobby was gay from the time she was a young woman. Her sister, Patricia Cutler Warner, agreed and noted that she had discussed the subject with her mother, Rosalind Fish Cutler, Bobby's sister-in-law. "Mother's theory was that he worked so hard that he sublimated his sexuality under all of his work," Patricia Warner said.

Bobby always remained professional in work settings but was very different in social settings, said Harry Lodge, son of Cabot Lodge and Emily, who was born in 1930 and knew Bobby well. "He would dress in fairly outlandish things, with a dahlia in his buttonhole, and drink lots of martinis and tell very funny stories. He was generally the life of the party." He recalled an instance of Bobby's slightly ribald humor when Bobby was at the Lodge family home in Washington and was standing near a reproduction of a Gauguin painting showing two bare-breasted Polynesian women. "What a lovely painting of Emily and Jean," Bobby quipped, referring to

Mrs. Lodge and her sister, provoking an outburst of laughter. As for being gay, Harry Lodge said, "He didn't mind you inferring that he probably was."[10] He said he personally was so sure that Bobby was gay that he came to look upon him as "an advance man for the gay movement." Bobby's orientation seemed confirmed when he became very close to a man who was a bodybuilder, Lodge said. "He brought him over to cocktails. We would walk on the beach . . . Bobby was absolutely captivated by him."

The man was William H. Sullivan, who apparently worked at a health club that Bobby frequented in Boston. "I met Bill in August/46 in an elevator going up to the Health Club and was, like a lightning flash, attracted by his physical beauty — only later coming to know his good qualities of mind and spirit that have tied us together," Bobby recorded in his diary.[11] Sullivan, about twenty-six years younger than Bobby, had been in the military. Later, after Bobby bought a country house in 1949 near the town of Harvard west of Boston, he invited Sullivan, who by then had a wife named Ruth, to live in the home. The Sullivans made it their home and raised their six children there. Bobby named the house "Fair Harvard," which also is the name of Harvard University's anthem. When Bobby was at the house, the children would visit him in his rooms on the third floor, recalled the Sullivan's daughter, Maura Sullivan Dudley.[12] She said Bobby had a large globe in his room, liked to take cold baths, and loved working outdoors and splitting wood with her father. Bobby was "very caring" and asked the children to call him "Uncle Bobby."

In 1951, the Sullivans had a boy whom they named after Bobby, Robert Cutler Sullivan. "My father was a big relief for Bobby," Robert Cutler Sullivan recalled decades later. "They would talk and talk and talk." He said that his father was "teaching squash and tennis" at the club where Bobby first met him.[13] "Both my father and Bobby were well read and liked poetry and this probably started their friendship."

Not long after Judith Cutler's engagement in the summer of 1947, sad news struck the family. Elliott, fifty-nine, the second eldest of the five Cutler brothers, lay dying of cancer at the family home on Heath Street in Brookline. During World War I, he had led a Harvard medical team in France.[14] He went on to perform pioneering surgeries on the heart and the thyroid gland. In 1923, at a Cleveland hospital, he performed the first known surgical procedure on a heart valve. During World War II, he served as chief of surgery in the European theater of operations, at one point traveling to Russia to study Soviet medical care.[15] A colonel, Elliott directed care for soldiers on D-Day and throughout the invasion of Normandy. At General Eisenhower's recommendation in April 1945, he was promoted to general. At the time of his death, he was a professor of surgery at Harvard and surgeon in chief at Peter Bent Brigham Hospital in Boston. He also had served as president of the Harvard Alumni Association and as a member of the Harvard Board of Overseers. Bobby later recalled his beloved older brother's dying days at the family home on Heath Street. "On spring and summer days before his death, Elliott lay on a chaise longue beyond the giant maple tree, surrounded by dogs, cats, two pet Nubian goats, and an ever-changing stream of old and young Cutlers." It was a testimony to family unity, Bobby wrote.[16] Elliott died on August 16, 1947.

In the postwar years, attitudes toward homosexuality began to shift. Until this time, it was often ignored in social settings and prosecuted — usually with little public attention — in the courts; it was not commonly discussed in the news media or literary or scholarly publications. The English writer Radclyffe Hall's lesbian-themed novel, *The Well of Loneliness*, was banned upon publication in 1928 in England. The turmoil of World War II, uprooting legions of young men and women from their homes and casting them together in the fatalistic enterprise of war, had created vast potential for sexual encounters.

The year 1948 saw publication of two groundbreaking works on the subject of homosexuality. The first of these was Gore Vidal's novel *The City and the Pillar*, the first major American novel to depict a homosexual protagonist, Jim Willard, as an average American. Growing up in Virginia, Jim is a high school athlete who plays tennis and is well liked. After he has a sexual encounter with another boy, Bob Ford, the purity of that relationship becomes an ideal that Jim clings to as he moves through life and has many other gay relationships. At the core of the novel is the idea that Jim is a good person driven to desperate actions by the clash between his sexual orientation and societal prohibitions. The book also unveiled the world of anonymous homosexual encounters, gay men passing as heterosexuals in Hollywood, bisexuality, and gay men marrying women for convention's sake. It revealed that most gay men preferred the term *gay* to the clinical-sounding *homosexual*, and it defined the term *queen*.[17] An earlier gay-themed novel, John Horne Burns's 1947 work *The*

Gallery, had broken barriers and won critical acclaim for its description of gay American soldiers in Naples, Italy, though it cast them as players in a hellish scene of moral degradation in a distant land upended by fascism and war. In Tennessee Williams's 1947 play *A Streetcar Named Desire*, Blanche DuBois breaks down after acknowledging her young husband had a secret sexual relationship with an older man. Blanche says she was disgusted by her husband, who committed suicide. In contrast, Vidal's novel gave gay people a vibrant reality in America, a moral compass, and a significant — if turbulent — place in American society. *The City and the Pillar* unsettled many Americans, and *The New York Times* at first refused to carry ads for it, yet after its publication in January 1948 the novel quickly rose to the top of the bestseller lists.

The second major work published in 1948 was the groundbreaking scientific study *Sexual Behavior in the Human Male*, led by Alfred Kinsey. Kinsey and his team found that homosexuality was astonishingly prevalent: The report estimated that 37 percent of males have at least one homosexual experience in their lives. It also estimated that 10 percent of men are exclusively homosexual for three years of their lives. The study said homosexuality is not a "yes or no" trait and that many men have some degree of homosexual experience before ultimately living primarily as heterosexuals. "Males do not represent two discrete populations, heterosexual and homosexual," the study said. "The living world is a continuum in each and every one of its aspects."[18] Kinsey's report, too, soared to the top of the bestseller lists.

By recognizing that homosexuality was a significant part of American life, Vidal and Kinsey helped launch a revolution in public perceptions. While the two groundbreaking works offered hope that gays could look forward to a day when their conduct would be accepted socially and perhaps even respected under law, homosexuality in fact remained illegal in most states, was considered a disorder by the American Psychiatric Association, and was widely viewed as a moral failing. By raising homosexuality in the public consciousness, the Kinsey and Vidal books may ironically have contributed to a period of heightened discrimination. Americans who feared and loathed homosexuality went on the offensive, forcing many gays to take extra measures to conceal their sexual orientation.

Meanwhile, globally, Communism continued to spread, causing deep concerns among Americans. In China, the Communists continued to advance against the Nationalist forces of Generalissimo Chiang Kai-shek, despite military support that the United States provided to the latter. In February 1948, the Communist Party of Czechoslovakia seized control of the country, outlawing other political parties and clamping controls on the economy and citizens. Alongside Communist takeovers in East Germany, Hungary, and Poland, the coup in Czechoslovakia gave the Soviets control over most of Eastern Europe and intensified concerns in the United States and around the world that Communist aggression was a grave threat.

In March 1948, Bobby was at home in his Somerset Club apartment recovering from an illness when the telephone rang. Secretary of Defense James Forrestal was calling on behalf of General George Marshall, whom Truman had appointed his secretary of state. Marshall, Forrestal said, wanted Bobby's help winning approval from the Senate of a hotly disputed military budget bill for 1949 and needed Bobby to come to Washington to "stage-manage" appearances by top military leaders before the Senate Armed Forces Committee. Marshall wanted Bobby to help Forrestal resolve a dispute over the budget among branches of the military. "I was hooked. The use of Marshall's name had done it, just as Jim guessed it would," Bobby wrote later.[19] Bobby quickly took a three-week leave of absence from Old Colony to go to Washington.

On March 14, 1948, Bobby met with Forrestal at his Georgetown home and discussed the dispute over drinks, something he would do repeatedly in the coming weeks.[20] The National Security Act of 1947 was at the core of the dispute, as it had not provided the secretary of defense with sufficient power to compel each of the military services — army, navy, and air force — to accept a unified policy and budget. The act was a major piece of Cold War legislation. It created the Department of the Air Force and the Central Intelligence Agency and established a new organization called the National Security Council to improve the president's ability to coordinate national security policy. However, the new post of defense secretary — which Forrestal occupied — did not have the authority to command the secretaries of each of the military services. Forrestal could only persuade them, and this was the crux of the problem.

The first air force secretary, Stuart Symington, was now demanding the largest share of a proposed military spending increase to build a strategic bomber force capable of dropping nuclear bombs on the Soviet Union. Forrestal was unable to convince Symington that the air force should get a smaller share of the budget increase. Forrestal and Marshall sought Bobby's help in resolving the matter. Bobby was given an office in the Pentagon one floor above Forrestal's office.[21]

The air force wanted to achieve nuclear supremacy over the Soviet Union, which at this time still had not detonated a nuclear bomb. It hoped to develop a strike force, the Strategic Air Command, with a fleet of B-36 bombers capable of delivering nuclear weapons to Soviet territory from the United States. The navy, meanwhile, wanted to develop a nuclear strike force based on aircraft carriers.[22] Forrestal sought to maintain a balance among the army, navy, and air force that placed less emphasis on air strike capabilities.

With support from Marshall and Forrestal, Bobby began working toward the goal of winning Senate approval of a three-billion dollar increase in military spending for a "balanced force" among the service branches. First, Bobby undertook an orchestrated series of meetings with military budget officials and representatives of the army, navy, and air force. He also drafted a thirteen-page opening statement for Forrestal to make before the Senate Armed Forces committee on March 25, warning of the need for a strong defense to protect the country from Communism.

Forrestal wanted to make it clear to the Senate committee that if the air force expansion urged by Symington was to be balanced by proportionate increases for the army and navy, the entire program would cost an additional eighteen billion dollars, far in excess of the three billion in spending that the Truman administration had proposed. Bobby began collecting additional data from each of the services for a draft response that would address questions the senators might ask.[23] The army and navy cooperated with Bobby's efforts to craft the new report, but in a meeting in Bobby's office the air force representatives said Forrestal should send no reply to the senators. That response "fell like a bomb," and Bobby erupted, telling the representatives, "I must expect to receive Mr. Symington's written comments or corrections on last night's draft not later than tomorrow noon." Half an hour later, Symington contacted Bobby via the intercom, nicknamed the squawk box, and denounced Bobby's draft as slanted and inaccurate, and soon the two men were shouting at each other. According to Bobby, Symington "called me an offensive name," and Bobby cut off the squawk box in the middle of a statement by Symington.

Bobby walked into Symington's office a short while later to confront the air force secretary in person. "Stuart," Bobby said. "You can't talk to me like that. I came down here as a volunteer, at the request of Jim and General Marshall, to help them."[24] Bobby extended his hand and Symington shook it, setting in place a working truce. But the damage was done, as Symington had revealed his intentions. The next day, as Bobby and Forrestal ate breakfast at Forrestal's home, Bobby told him about the conflict and said that he suspected Symington was quietly "making hay" in Congress in an attempt to win the funding the air force sought. Angered, Forrestal asked Bobby whether he should go to the White House and tell President Truman "either Symington or I must go." Bobby replied that he did not know enough to answer that question — "I only know that I trust you." At that point, Forrestal leaned back and said, "No, of course you can't know enough. It was a silly question, Bobby. It's *my* fight. I have to fight it alone. You know that I can't *make* Stu obey me. My job is to persuade him that I am right and he is wrong. I have to *convince* him to come over to my view, because it's the right way."[25] Forrestal paused, then said in a distant tone: "If I can't persuade him to my way of thinking, then I'll have failed. After all, I shall have come out a failure." To Bobby, the thought of the highly accomplished Forrestal being described as a failure seemed preposterous, yet the defense secretary's doubts were deep-seated.

General Eisenhower, a national hero for his leadership of Allied forces in Europe, who had recently served as army chief of staff, was the last witness Bobby needed to prepare to testify to the Senate Armed Services Committee. Bobby met with Eisenhower in his Pentagon office on April 2, 1948, the day before Eisenhower was to address the committee. With the final testimony completed, Bobby's mission for Marshall and Forrestal was done and he returned to Boston and his duties at Old Colony. Forrestal sent him a picture of himself inscribed WITH DEEP APPRECIATION.

The budget dispute soon boiled over, however, when Congress approved the air force budget that Symington sought, procuring the bombers for the Strategic Air Command and sowing further discord in the military. Forrestal supporters accused Symington of insubordination, a charge Symington denied. The dispute led to an amendment of the National Security Act in 1949 that gave the secretary of defense authority over the service branches and their budgets and created the position of chairman of the Joint Chiefs of Staff to build unanimity among the three service branches.[26] A year after Bobby finished his work for Forrestal and Marshall, President Truman asked Forrestal to resign, ending his highly praised record of military service. After Forrestal went to Bethesda Naval Hospital in Maryland for treatment of depression, he was found dead on May 22, 1949, having plummeted from the hospital's thirteenth story, an apparent suicide.[27] To Bobby and many others, his death was a devastating loss.

After returning to Boston, Bobby soon entered a political fray as the Republican Party was preparing for its national convention in Philadelphia in June 1948. Cabot Lodge had gained increasing recognition for his role in the internationalist wing of the Republican Party, which included his support of the Truman administration's Marshall Plan for European recovery. Now Lodge was selected as chairman of the party's Resolutions Committee, which would write the party platform. He called on Bobby to be his chief of staff, and so Bobby traveled to Philadelphia for the arduous work of hashing out the platform. "I got up at half past seven and worked till half-past 12 at night," Bobby said.[28] The platform called for standard Republican principles such as reducing taxes, balancing the federal budget, and blocking expansion of Communism. Yet the committee bore the strong imprint of these two progressive Republicans who resisted the conservative Republican endorsement of states' rights and instead sought to restore the party as the inheritors of the legacies of Abraham Lincoln and Theodore Roosevelt. The committee's activities included a meeting with NAACP executive secretary Walter White.[29] Ultimately, the platform called for a ban on lynching as well as passage of an equal employment opportunity law, a ban on the poll tax, and desegregation of the armed forces. It also called for passage of a constitutional amendment guaranteeing women equal rights, and said the party favored "equal pay for equal work regardless of sex." Lodge also got Senator Arthur Vandenberg, leader of the Republican internationalists, to write the foreign policy plank of the platform, which included support for the United Nations, for a new nation of Israel, and for collective security agreements in Europe and elsewhere. Under Lodge's and Bobby's management, the final platform was a high-water mark for progressive Republicanism in the twentieth century.

At the convention, one of the contenders for the presidential nomination was Harold Stassen, a Republican who had been elected governor of Minnesota at the age of thirty-one, resigned that post in 1943 to join the navy, and later helped write the United Nations Charter. Yet it was another progressive Republican, New York governor Thomas Dewey, who ultimately vanquished both Stassen and the conservative Taft to become the presidential nominee. However, President Truman preempted the Republicans on civil rights by signing an executive order on July 26, 1948, desegregating the US military. This reaffirmed the Democratic Party as an ally of black citizens, though it also caused southern segregationists like Senator Strom Thurmond, Democrat of South Carolina, to split off into a states' rights party known as the Dixiecrats. When Congress came back into session, the Republicans failed to pass significant civil rights legislation. President Truman capitalized on that to attack the Republicans as unable to stand by their own progressive platform, which the president labeled "hypocritical." On Election Day, in what was widely expected to be a close contest, Truman decisively defeated Dewey.

Conflict with Communism worldwide, meanwhile, was reaching a crescendo. In June 1948, the Soviets had blocked the Allies from traveling to Berlin, the city inside Soviet-controlled East Germany. Truman had responded by using an airlift to get food and supplies to Berlin, successfully preserving West Berlin as an outpost of democracy inside the Communist bloc. In September 1949, the Soviet Union detonated its first nuclear bomb and announced it was building its own nuclear arsenal. The next month, Chairman Mao announced that his Chinese Communist Red Army had defeated the Nationalists and established the People's Republic of China. In June 1950, Communist North Korea, backed by Soviet and Chinese Communists, invaded South Korea, a US ally, and the United States sent forces under United Nations auspices to defend the south.

The spread of Communism internationally heightened concerns of a domestic threat inside the United States. Senior Treasury Department official Harry Dexter White testified in August 1948 before the House Un-American Activities Committee that he was not a Communist, though evidence mounted that he had secretly funneled information to Soviet officials. He died of a heart attack days after testifying. That same month, former *Time* magazine editor Whittaker Chambers testified he had been a Communist spy for decades and identified former senior State Department official Alger Hiss as a member of an underground Communist group. Hiss denied the allegation in his own testimony, though he acknowledged having met Chambers and was eventually convicted of perjury. President Truman's Justice Department launched criminal prosecutions against eleven leaders of the Communist Party of the United States in 1949, winning convictions on charges of advocating the violent overthrow of the US government.

Concerns over Communist infiltration of the government reached near-hysteria after Senator Joseph McCarthy, a Wisconsin Republican, spoke to a Republican women's group in Wheeling, West Virginia, on February 9, 1950. He asserted that the State Department was under Communist influence, denounced Truman's secretary of state, Dean Acheson, as a "pompous diplomat in striped pants," and claimed he had a list of 205 Communists working in the department.[30] This thundering accusation was later recognized as the opening salvo of McCarthyism. In the following weeks, McCarthy continued his charges but backed away from the number of 205 State Department employees, eventually cutting the tally to 81. The State Department responded to the allegations by denying it harbored Communists and insisting that McCarthy identify any alleged Communists publicly so that the remaining employees of the department could continue their work free from the taint of McCarthy's accusations. The department acknowledged that, as part of its regular security work, it had dismissed 202 people for security reasons. Under testimony on February 28, Acheson acknowledged that those dismissed were considered security risks. Then Undersecretary of State John Peurifoy stated that of 91 people dismissed recently, "most of these were homosexuals."[31]

Almost immediately, with Peurifoy's utterance, McCarthy's Red Scare had sparked a separate yet closely related hunt for homosexuals in government. McCarthy stoked the flames, announcing in March that a homosexual dismissed as a security risk by the State Department, whom he did not name, had been hired by the Central Intelligence Agency. McCarthy continued to raise additional questions about both gays and Communists in hearings and public statements. Thus, homosexuality and Communism became inextricably intertwined as evils threatening the American way of life. In the coming weeks and months, McCarthy and other members of Congress demanded more information from the Truman administration about dismissed homosexuals and debated the effectiveness of Truman's security program, while newspapers across the country carried stories about gays in the State Department, prompting citizens to write letters expressing outrage. Conservative columnist Westbrook Pegler warned that homosexuals are inclined to be Communists. "The obvious fact is, of course, that Communists, having no morals, have no objection to practices which are to normal people depraved and in most Western countries are crimes. This offers an important social inducement to queeries," Pegler sneered.[32]

The Republican-dominated Senate quickly authorized an investigation into homosexuals in federal agencies, and the hunt for gay Americans — the Lavender Scare — entered a new phase. Senator Clyde Hoey, a North Carolina Democrat who was chairman of the Committee on Expenditures in Executive Departments, led the investigation. The committee's chief counsel, former FBI agent Francis Flanagan, soon learned that the navy had a list of eight thousand sex deviants, the army had a list of five thousand, and the State Department and Washington police each had lists of three thousand.[33] Under President Truman's instructions, however, the White House refused to release the actual names or related files to the committee, and the administration sought to downplay homosexuality and portray it as a medical issue facing federal workers.

When Hoey's hearings began behind closed doors in July 1950, Director of the Central Intelligence Agency Roscoe Hillenkoetter testified that homosexuals posed a threat to national security because they could be blackmailed if an enemy learned of their sexual practices. To prove his argument, Hillenkoetter outlined the case of Colonel Alfred Redl, head of Austrian intelligence prior to World War I. Russian intelligence officers learned of Redl's sexual preferences, supplied him with an attractive "newsboy," and then burst in on him "in an act of perversion" in a hotel room, Hillenkoetter said.[34] Threatening to expose Redl, the Russians then blackmailed him into providing them hundreds of secret documents, including war mobilization plans, the CIA director claimed. It was a "classic case" that showed "what can be done to a country's security by a homosexual strategically placed." However, while Redl was indeed a gay double agent, he had accepted large cash payments from the Russians, and greed played a significant role in his betrayal. The suggestion that the Russians supplied him with a newsboy has been discounted as a fabrication.[35] What's more, Hillenkoetter turning to a decades-old case in a foreign country underscored the lack of evidence to support the claim that homosexuality posed a significant risk of blackmail. Despite this lack of evidence, the Hoey committee's final report, issued in December 1950, declared: "It is an accepted fact among intelligence agencies that espionage organizations the world over consider sex perverts who are in possession of or have access to confidential material to be prime targets where pressure can be exerted."[36]

The report, titled "Employment of Homosexuals and Other Sex Perverts in Government," said the military had investigated 4,380 "sex perversion cases" from January 1, 1950, through October 31, 1950. The report also warned that homosexuals, once employed in a federal government office, will try to get other homosexuals hired or convince others into their "perverted practices." It proclaimed: "One homosexual can pollute a Government office."

One Hoey committee witness cited in the report was FBI assistant director D. Milton Ladd, who testified that Russian intelligence agents were under orders to investigate the private lives of federal employees to find "a weakness upon which they might capitalize."[37] Following the issuance of the Hoey report, FBI director J. Edgar Hoover dramatically expanded what he called the FBI's Sex Deviates Program. On June 20, 1951, Hoover launched the enhanced program by distributing a memo under the heading: "Re: SEX DEVIATES IN GOVERNMENT SERVICE."[38] Three months later, Hoover issued another memo saying that if an allegation that a federal employee is a sex deviate surfaces during an investigation of the employee's loyalty, "this allegation should be completely and fully developed and the facts reported. This procedure must be placed in effect immediately and followed closely."[39] Hoover's orders quickly gave the FBI a major role in investigating suspected homosexuals.

Hoover himself had been the subject for decades of rumors that he was gay. A lifelong bachelor, he had an extremely close relationship with Clyde Tolson, the FBI associate director and second highest ranking official in the agency. The two men worked together, ate together on a daily basis, and took regular vacations together. Hoover took hundreds of pictures of Tolson, even some while his friend was sleeping.[40] While celebrating New Year's Eve 1936, Hoover and Tolson held hands as they rode in an FBI limousine, according to Luisa Stuart, a woman in the limousine with them.[41] Ultimately, the outcome of the debate over whether Hoover was gay depends on a close review of large amounts of circumstantial evidence, which this book will not attempt. And even if Hoover himself was gay, that would not change the impact that his fervid hunt for homosexuals had on the lives of countless Americans.

As McCarthy and other Republicans attacked the Truman administration as rife with Communists and homosexuals, President Truman responded in July 1951 by ordering a little-known government organization, the Interdepartmental Committee on Internal Security (ICIS), to explore whether federal employment rules should be tightened to protect national security.[42] ICIS chairman Raymond Whearty, a senior Justice Department official who had handled prosecutions of Alger Hiss and Soviet spy Judith Coplon, soon drafted new security rules for federal employees that would have a major impact on gays.

At this time, Bobby was in Boston, far removed from Washington's war on homosexuality, but he remained in contact with Eisenhower, who in 1948 had left the military to become president of Columbia University. In 1950, Eisenhower announced he was creating the American Assembly, an organization intended to be a nonpartisan venue for business, professional, and government leaders to discuss important issues. In late 1950, Bobby planned a dinner in honor of Ike and to raise funds for the American Assembly. The event, which Bobby hosted at the Tavern Club on November 22, was attended by many of Boston's business and political leaders, including United Fruit chairman Coolidge, board members of Old Colony Trust and First National Bank of Boston, and friends of Bobby's like Cabot Lodge, Harvey Bundy, and Sinclair Weeks, a member of the Republican National Committee.

"Dear Bobby," Ike wrote a week later. "I met so many interesting individuals and was so intrigued by everything I saw and heard that the day was one for me to remember with real satisfaction. Of course, the fact that everyone that I met seemed to take such a specific and objective interest in the American Assembly was most gratifying." Eisenhower also mentioned fondness for Bobby's late brother Elliott.[43] "Not only did I hold him high in my affection, admiration and respect but I have always felt that his cool courage in the final days of his life provided an example that I should like to be able — under similar circumstances — to emulate." Bobby wrote back to say that Boston was still "rocking" from Ike's visit to the city and to note also that Elliott's son, Elliott Cutler Jr., had been fighting in Korea since July. "Heaven watch over you, too,

Sir, whether here or — for a short time — in Europe." Bobby's closing comment was a reference to the fact that around this time President Truman asked Eisenhower to return to military service as the first supreme Allied commander of the newly formed North Atlantic Treaty Organization (NATO), a role that would require him to relocate to Paris.

In early 1951, Eisenhower urged Bobby to take a position in the State Department's Office of International Security Affairs, which was supporting the effort to rearm European nations against Soviet aggression. Ike wrote, "I merely sought to insure that you knew of my conviction that the job was deserving of the talents and caliber of a man such as yourself." But Bobby declined the position, pointing to his responsibilities to Old Colony as well as organizations like the Harvard Board of Overseers and a new group he recently helped launch, the Committee on the Present Danger.

Harvard president James Conant, former army undersecretary Tracy Voorhees, and Vannevar Bush, a prominent engineer who had advised President Roosevelt on technology during World War II and guided the Manhattan Project in its early phase, had announced the creation of the Committee on the Present Danger in December 1950. Identifying the "present danger" as Soviet expansionism, the committee urged rearming Europe with conventional weapons, as opposed to the isolationism that Senator Taft and other Republicans advocated. In addition to Bobby, other founding members included Robert Patterson, President Truman's former secretary of war; and John McCloy, former assistant to Secretary of War Henry Stimson.[44] Conant, Bush, and another member of the Committee on the Present Danger, nuclear physicist J. Robert Oppenheimer — all of whom played leading roles in the development of the atom bomb — also had become increasingly concerned about the rapid growth of the US nuclear strike capability. As members of the Atomic Energy Commission's General Advisory Committee, Conant and Oppenheimer objected — within the top-secret confines of the committee — to the proposed development of a weapon that would be far more powerful, the hydrogen bomb.[45] Thus, at least some members of the Committee on the Present Danger were concerned not only about Soviet expansionism and American isolationism but also the threat of the nuclear arms race.

Responding to the Soviet threat, President Truman had initially embraced the policy of "containment," which senior diplomat George

Kennan had proposed in his famous "Long Telegram" written from the US embassy in Moscow in 1946. Yet as Truman's Republican critics denounced him as weak on Communism, he pushed for a more aggressive response to the Soviets. In the spring of 1950, after the Korean War erupted, a State Department team led by Paul Nitze drafted a policy calling for sharply increased military expenditures and a harder line against Soviet expansionism. Kennan and another diplomat, Charles Bohlen, argued that the proposed policy was not financially feasible, was too aggressive, and could provoke further Soviet aggressions. But Secretary of State Dean Acheson urged its adoption, and Truman agreed. The National Security Council adopted Nitze's policy as NSC-68.

Bobby began to take an increasing interest in national security affairs. At some point in 1951, he began advising the CIA as a consultant.[46] Bobby's role as an outsider involved in national security increased again when Truman moved to improve coordination of covert and overt operations to confront Communism. In April 1951, the president issued a directive creating the Psychological Strategy Board (PSB) to coordinate "psychological operations" by various government agencies. The board, which reported to the NSC, was aimed at countering the Soviet government's powerful propaganda machine.[47] The new CIA director, retired general Walter Bedell "Beetle" Smith, served as the PSB's first chairman. Truman named Gordon Gray, the former secretary of the army, as the PSB's first executive director. Gray, an acquaintance of Bobby's, asked Bobby to serve as his deputy director. In August 1951, Bobby once again took unpaid leave from Old Colony, this time to help Gray run the PSB.

The PSB began working on US psychological warfare activities around the world, including Radio Free Europe's anti-Communist broadcasts. It also developed a plan to exploit a possible collapse in the peace talks over the war in Korea.[48] From the start, however, the PSB was hobbled by ambiguity in Truman's directive about its authority as well as disputes among federal agencies over the extent of the PSB's powers. The State Department, in particular, sought to defend its own role in crafting psychological warfare actions and so sought to minimize the PSB's responsibilities. At one point in a debate on the issue, the State Department's Nitze told Gray imperiously, "Look, you just forget about policy, that's not your business; we'll make the policy and then you can put it on your damn radio."[49]

As the dispute over the PSB's powers boiled, Gray asked Bobby to prepare a report on a "strategic concept" for psychological operations in waging the Cold War.[50] To prepare the report, Bobby concluded that the PSB needed more information on what the agencies were already doing to undermine Soviet power. On Bobby's recommendation, the PSB ordered State and CIA to turn over the information. The PSB's demand for information said it needed to know about all projects intended "to mount psychological war designed to detach each of the satellites from Moscow" and "psychological war designed to eliminate the threat from the Kremlin."[51]

State and CIA both refused to comply with Bobby's demand for information. Bobby may have been used to having his orders from the president's office at Old Colony quickly executed, but the demand from the fledgling PSB was quickly dismissed. Charles Marshall of the State Department's Policy Planning Staff sent a memo to Nitze accusing the PSB of trying to make itself into the "general staff" for Cold War operations.[52] Faced with this refusal, the PSB was in a state of near-paralysis. After a series of meetings, Nitze proudly reported to his boss, Dean Acheson, that the "PSB capitulated on all fronts . . ."[53]

From this internecine and bureaucratic conflict, Bobby concluded that the PSB's mission was flawed from its conception and was not serving the nation well. "As time wore on, none of us could grasp the concept of a 'psychological strategy' that ran along beside the great elements of foreign and military policy like an independent fifth wheel. The Board's role appeared more and more unreal," Bobby wrote in his autobiography.[54] Bobby's role as Gray's special assistant ended abruptly and somewhat obscurely, and he returned to Boston to resume his role as Old Colony's president. His experience with the PSB, however, left him convinced that the president needed an independent, powerful, and integrated mechanism for setting national security policy. This insight guided the advice Bobby would provide in the coming months to Eisenhower, who was soon to become the Republican presidential nominee.

5

WITH IKE TO VICTORY

Dwight D. Eisenhower's popularity was supreme in America at the war's end. In June 1945, an estimated thirty thousand spectators attended a parade in Ike's honor in his hometown, Abilene, Kansas, which had a population of just six thousand.[1] The following month, Kansans launched a foundation to build a shrine to their war hero that would include the Eisenhower family home, a tiny gingerbreaded Victorian house. David and Ida Eisenhower had raised their six sons in its twelve hundred square feet of floor space. David worked in a creamery while Ida remained home, and the family lived a simple life. Ike was an American ideal — a man of modest origin who had made his way in life through perseverance and served the nation spectacularly through one of its darkest chapters. As his fame soared after the war, Ike persistently rejected suggestions that he enter politics. When a New Hampshire newspaper publisher urged him to run for president as a Republican in 1948, Eisenhower declined to do so in a letter stating that "the necessary and wise subordination of the military to civil power will be best sustained . . . when lifelong professional soldiers, in the absence of some obvious and overriding reasons, abstain from seeking high political office."[2] In the spring of 1948, Ike left the army to become president of Columbia University. Months later, when Walter Winchell asked listeners of his radio program to send Eisenhower letters urging him to run for president that year, some twenty thousand letters and telegrams swamped Eisenhower's office at the university within a week.[3]

Eisenhower's tenure as president of Columbia bolstered his reputation as a man with compassion for those less fortunate than himself or not in the mainstream of American society. In May 1948, he gave a speech calling for greater attention to mental health, noting that in 1944 he had struggled to find enough soldiers to fill the ranks, while as many as two million men had been rejected from military duty due to mental illness or disorders. "The man power of the United States is not inexhaustible. It is one of our most treasured assets that we must do our utmost to maintain."[4] Eisenhower urged his listeners to think of people suffering from mental illness as one of them.[5] Eisenhower worked with a Columbia professor of economics, Eli Ginzberg, to create the Conservation of Human Resources Project, which would study problems undermining the preparedness of American soldiers and workers.[6]

In 1950, President Truman asked Eisenhower to return to military service and take the role of the first supreme Allied commander of the newly formed North Atlantic Treaty Organization (NATO). Ike accepted the assignment and moved with his wife, Mamie, to Paris, where members of both major parties continued to urge him to take up their banner. Bobby Cutler's friend Cabot Lodge spearheaded the Republican effort, serving as chairman of a national group, Eisenhower for President. Lodge flew to Paris to urge Ike to run. Meeting in the general's office on September 4, 1951, Lodge laid out a slate of reasons why Ike should become the Republican nominee, including the preservation of the two-party system in the United States. The Democrats had won the past five elections, from 1932 through 1948, and another Democratic victory could end the two-party system, Lodge warned. He also decried a trend of "paternalism" in the federal government's relationship with citizens and constant deficit spending. He reviewed the potential candidates and concluded that Ike was "the only one who can be elected to the Presidency by the Republicans."[7] Ike had known Lodge since the war, when Lodge had stepped down from his Senate seat to join the army, and his argument carried weight. "Cabot, an associate and friend of mine from wartime days, presented his plea with the ardor of a crusader," Ike later wrote.[8] He promised Lodge that he would consider the matter, abandoning his long-standing practice of bluntly refusing to enter politics.

Senator Robert Taft, the powerful Ohio Republican and son of former president William H. Taft, had already thrown his hat in the ring. Taft had consolidated his support among Republicans nationwide with his attacks on the Truman administration, which he blamed for the loss of China to the Communists and for the Korean War. However, Taft also had opposed Truman's efforts to recommit US forces to Europe to prevent the spread of Communism. This had led to charges that Taft was a "neo-isolationist." Eisenhower, who in his role as NATO leader advocated for a strong US military presence in Europe, quickly became a leading candidate for internationalist Republicans opposed to Taft.

Yet Ike was still serving in Europe and had still not declared himself a member of any party. Cabot Lodge set out to change that. In November 1951, Lodge met in New York with Ike's good friend retired general Lucius Clay and Republican New York governor Thomas Dewey, who had lost the 1948 presidential race to Truman. The men agreed that Lodge would act as Ike's campaign manager. The next month, he appeared in New York on a television news program, NBC's *Meet the Press*, and vowed that Ike would announce his candidacy soon. "Those who think he is a Democrat are wrong," Lodge insisted slyly.[9] A month later, on January 6, 1952, Lodge placed Eisenhower's name on the ballot as a Republican candidate for president in the New Hampshire primary elections to take place in March. Still, from Allied headquarters near Paris, Eisenhower refused to make any public statement confirming he was a candidate.

Ike's strategy was ingenious: He positioned himself as a military man who refused to sink into the mire of politics, but this posture also made him an elusive target for opponents. Meanwhile, Ike's very capable supporters, led by Lodge and New Hampshire governor Sherman Adams, defended him vigorously and made the case for Ike to the American public. An organization called Citizens for Eisenhower, created by two young businessmen, quickly opened branches across the country. Supporters had filled Madison Square Garden on a Friday night in December 1951, with singer Ethel Merman performing, movie stars Humphrey Bogart and Lauren Bacall appearing in support of the general, and the crowd chanting "We like Ike."

As the New Hampshire primary approached, Ike held his ground and refused to comment publicly, leaving the nation unsure whether he was actually running. Adams, a progressive Republican ally of Lodge and Bobby who had attacked Taft's foreign policy positions, defended Ike against complaints that his views were unknown. On March 11, New Hampshire voters cast their ballots in the Republican primary, giving Ike a stunning victory over Taft, 51 to 39 percent, with several other candidates trailing far behind. When reporters asked Ike the following day at an airport outside Paris to comment, he said, "I was deeply moved. Any ordinary American would be if other Americans felt that way about him."[10] Yet he was still a soldier on duty, and he refused to comment on whether he would return to the United States and run.

A week later, more than one hundred thousand voters cast write-in ballots for Ike in the Republican primary in Minnesota. Minnesota governor Harold Stassen received more votes, but Ike's vote total was five times Taft's, and the write-in campaign by Eisenhower supporters confirmed that there was a national groundswell among Republicans for Ike unlike anything seen in decades. Still, Ike held his silence in Paris. One of the Republicans who soon met with him was John Foster Dulles, a former US senator from New York who called for liberating "captive nations" living under Communist rule in Eastern Europe. The two men began a dialogue about foreign policy, and Ike later reported, "my interest was excited by his theories."[11]

Bobby, still Old Colony Trust's president, began working for the Massachusetts Ike Committee. Days after the Minnesota primary, Bobby squared off with former congressman Hamilton Fish (the brother-in-law of Bobby's older brother John) and other Republicans — radio commentator Tex McCrary and political operative Kenneth Bradley — in a debate at Harvard Law School. Bobby cast doubt on the ability of Ike's opponents to lead the nation at a time of serious international threats. "We need one thing and we need it quick: a captain, a sure, capable, moral hand at the helm; a leader who can attract the free world to his banner." Fish said Taft was "better qualified mentally, morally, spiritually, and from a standpoint of experience to be president" than any other candidate.[12]

In a letter he wrote to Ike days later, Bobby described the debate. "I put so much brio in it — for I believe every word — that Bradley and Fish the rest of the evening complained of my 'emotional' delivery. A genuine expression of feeling seemed to bother them as much as it seemed to please the audience."[13] Bobby suggested Ike need not rush back to the United States to enter the political fray:

> If we can do New Hampshire and Minnesota and last night without you physically here, my "five cents worth" is for you not to hurry home. Obviously, there should be a time for that in June. But many people on the street agree with me that all this speculation in the press about your coming home, and when, is not helping and may hurt. The enormous belief the American people have in your integrity and sincerity is the greatest asset for victory. Nothing must be permitted to derogate from it.

Bobby also told Ike of his fund-raising efforts, noting that the Massachusetts Ike Committee had raised $53,000 to date. "I have personally collected over $14,000 here from some seventy people. Takes time, but it's good, clean fun. More to come." He closed with a personal note:

> I know Cabot worries about delegates, and that's just right for him to do. But, to an ignoramus like me, it looks as if the Voice of the American people is going to make itself heard at last and that voice is beyond any doubt for you. These days are more exciting than the Circus to a kid. Reminds me of Wordsworth's "Bliss was it then to be alive . . ." God bless you and keep you safe, and please don't answer this note which is intended as a minor diversion . . . Bobby.

Working closely with Lodge, Bobby continued marshaling votes for Ike in Massachusetts, and their efforts paid off. In the Massachusetts primary, on April 29, Ike swept to victory, capturing 70 percent of the Republican vote, well above Taft's 30 percent. Amazingly, Ike also got strong support in the Democratic primary: He got 16,007 write-in votes, or 30.5 percent of the total, second behind Senator Estes Kefauver of Tennessee, with 56 percent.

On June 1, after resigning as supreme commander of NATO forces, Ike returned to the United States and went promptly to Abilene, where three days later he announced his candidacy, denouncing the futility of isolationism, calling for a vigorous defense against Communism, and opposing excessive taxes. He set up his campaign headquarters in Denver, his wife Mamie's hometown and a city strategically located near the western states where he needed to win Republican support.

After the initial burst of support for Ike in the Northeast, the momentum had shifted in Taft's favor, as primaries in other regions showed strong support for the Ohioan. Taft won primaries in his own state and in Nebraska, Illinois, West Virginia, and South Dakota. In several states, bitter intra-party disputes broke out over selection of delegates to attend the national convention and determine the presidential nominee. In Texas, supporters like Dillon Anderson claimed that Ike had won numerous delegate elections, but pro-Taft Republicans controlling local party machinery managed to hold repeat elections under favorable terms and packed the state delegation with Taft supporters. Taft supporters, meanwhile, charged that Democrats improperly voted for Eisenhower in the Republican primary. Similar disputes erupted in Louisiana, Georgia, and other states.

Ike and Lodge attacked the activities of the Taft supporters and took their protest to the Republican Party's Credentials Committee, which would meet in Chicago prior to the start of the convention. Bobby's friend Sinclair Weeks, a Republican national committeeman from Massachusetts, asked Bobby to join the fight over delegates in the Credentials Committee. Bobby traveled to Chicago and for four days battled for Eisenhower in the trenches of committee meeting rooms. Yet the committee balked at seating any disputed delegates, forcing the Eisenhower team to take the issue to the full convention floor.[14]

As the convention opened, Taft held a significant advantage. With 604 votes needed to win, Taft had already lined up 530, of which 72 were contested by Eisenhower. Eisenhower had lined up only 427, of which 21 were contested by Taft. If Taft retained all of the delegates Eisenhower was challenging, Taft would have a very strong lead.

Bobby moved quickly to launch a salvo at the Taft forces: He drafted a political broadsheet, measuring two feet by one foot, to be distributed on the convention floor on its first day. Using his bare-knuckles Boston political savvy, along with his literary skills, Bobby worked to "state objectively the sordid facts in clear, hard-punch prose." With Republicans of every stripe denouncing the Democrats for corruption, Bobby's strategy was simple: Tar the Taft forces with corruption. While Anderson found funds to pay for the printing, Bobby went to the printer's shop and "spent four early morning hours coaxing, urging, proofreading, and correcting."[15] The final broadsheet said in large boldface type:

THE EYES OF TEXAS
NOT ONLY THE EYES OF TEXAS, BUT THE
EYES OF EVERY AMERICAN, ARE ON THE
REPUBLICAN NATIONAL COMMITTEE TODAY.
THE REPUBLICAN PARTY WILL WIN IN
NOVEMBER ONLY IF IT COMES TO THE
VOTERS WITH CLEAN HANDS.

"A copy of the broadsheet was on every seat in the convention hall at the opening session. It was a ten-strike," Bobby recounted later.[16] The broadsheets were distributed just as Cabot Lodge delivered a speech on the convention's first day in support of a rule that would resolve the delegate dispute in Ike's favor. Lodge's rule, which he dubbed the "Fair Play Amendment," was adopted by the convention in a vote of 658–548. The rule mandated that no contested delegate could vote on any candidate or the seating of contested delegates. This meant that Taft's large number of contested delegates could not vote to support one another's seating, and that they could not vote for Taft unless the entire convention voted to seat them. It was a blow to Taft that gave Eisenhower's campaign significant momentum.

Two days later, the convention voted to seat all the Eisenhower delegates from Texas and another contested state, Georgia. Ike, meanwhile, had chosen as his running mate Senator Richard Nixon, a young Republican from California who had made a name for himself by hunting for Communists in the federal government. On July 11, after the first nominating ballot, Ike led with 595 votes — 9 votes shy of the total needed to win — to Taft's 500. Then, in a dramatic turn, Minnesota's delegation announced it would switch its 19 votes from its favorite son, Governor Harold Stassen, to Eisenhower, giving Ike the nomination victory with 614 votes. Learning the news, Ike fought through throngs to cross the street to Taft's hotel, where he told Taft he hoped "we can work together."[17]

In the days that followed, Eisenhower, Lodge, Adams, and other Republican leaders worked assiduously to establish a plan for the presidential campaign. Ike already had operations set up in the Commodore Hotel in New York, which would be the center of campaign operations.

Even before the convention was over, Bobby had begun trying to tackle the biggest problem Republicans perennially faced in Massachusetts — winning converts among the state's large bloc of Democratic voters. Bobby was in a unique position to reach out to Democrats because of his years of work for Boston's Democratic mayor Maurice Tobin, his support for other Democrats, and his work in Roosevelt's War Department. Bobby drew on these friendships and connections to build support among Democrats for Eisenhower, Lodge, and Christian Herter, a friend of Bobby's running for governor of Massachusetts. On July 8, freshly back from the Republican convention in Chicago, Bobby met with Boston's archbishop, Richard J. Cushing.[18] Cushing agreed to meet with Herter and to keep the archdiocese's newspaper out of the political contest. "He spoke warmly of Ike as being the strongest candidate and expressed admiration for his leadership," Bobby said in a memo to Herter.

As the Republicans ramped up their campaign to retake the White House, they intensified efforts to taint Ike's Democratic opponent, Senator Adlai Stevenson of Illinois, by associating him with alleged Communists and homosexuality. On August 4, Senator Everett Dirksen of Illinois, chairman of the Republican senatorial campaign committee, smeared Stevenson for his connections to former colleagues in the State Department, where he had worked. Dirksen growled: "Just how well does he think his associates look — Alger Hiss, Dean Acheson . . . and the lavender lads of the State Department?"[19] Lavender had become associated with gays, and the sneering sobriquet "lavender lads" would soon appear in scandal magazines like *Confidential*. Years later, the phrase Lavender Scare would come to refer to the tactics that McCarthy, Dirksen, and others used to smear opponents with a supposed threat from homosexuals in government.

After the Republican convention, Lodge urged Ike to go campaigning on a train, making whistle-stops at towns along the way so he could address crowds. It quickly turned into a strenuous program for Eisenhower, with long hours and lots of pressures, said Cabot Lodge's son Harry, who also was active in Ike's campaign. "Ike was getting less and less happy with life," Harry Lodge said. It was at that point that Cabot Lodge recommended Bobby join Ike on the train to bolster the candidate's spirits. "Pa thought, 'My God, I'm going to get Bobby Cutler to come on the train and help him have a great time.'" Cabot Lodge asked Bobby to come to his home in Beverly, and there he asked Bobby to join Ike's campaign train, called the Eisenhower Special.

Adams made arrangements for Bobby to come to New York on September 12 and stay at the Commodore Hotel and discuss joining the campaign train. "Needless to say, General Ike was quite hopped up about the prospects of your coming aboard, and is looking forward to seeing you on the 12th," Adams wrote Bobby. "I am looking forward with some personal anticipation to having you around where you can help keep me out of trouble."[20]

Bobby went to New York and met with Ike at the Commodore. He later recalled Ike's words: "Bobby, this is what I hope you can do for me. I need someone on the train during the next month, whom I can turn to and talk with. Nobody has time to talk to the Candidate! . . . It would be a great favor to me if you could arrange your affairs to do it."[21] Bobby quickly agreed to Ike's request, although he first needed to get Old Colony's directors to grant him leave from running the trust company. Days later, Bobby was in his own cabin aboard the Eisenhower Special as it left New York.[22]

Bobby immediately began working with Ike's economic adviser, Gabriel Hauge, and Hauge's assistant, Stephen Benedict, to draft and edit speeches for Ike. Hauge was a former Harvard economics professor who advised Dewey in the 1948 campaign and then was an assistant editor at *Business Week* magazine. Typically, the men began with draft speeches that were prepared in New York by a team led by C. D. Jackson, a former *Fortune* magazine publisher, and then wired to teletype machines on the train.

Jackson had been an assistant to the president of *Time* magazine and a key ally of media titan Henry Luce, owner and publisher of *Time*, in the 1930s. During World War II, Jackson joined the army and served as deputy chief of the Psychological Warfare Branch in 1943 in Algiers while Eisenhower was supreme commander of the Allied forces there. When Eisenhower moved to England to prepare for the invasion of Normandy in 1944, he took Jackson with him to continue his psychological warfare role and take charge of efforts to convince Europeans trampled by the Nazi war machine to rise up and support the D-Day invasion.[23] After the war, Jackson rejoined the Luce empire, eventually becoming publisher of *Fortune*. After joining the Eisenhower campaign in 1952, Jackson oversaw a stable of writers at the campaign headquarters preparing speeches for the candidate to give at whistle-stops and venues in towns.

Once the speeches from Jackson's team arrived on the train, Bobby, Hauge, and Benedict refined and edited them, with Ike actively reviewing drafts and making revisions. Bobby deployed the language of politics he had learned through two decades of Boston political battles, wrangling in Congress, and Republican Party conventions. "There was a running controversy between C. D. and us," Bobby later explained.[24] "When he read the Candidate's final version, he would declare that a masterpiece had been ruined. But 'campaign speech English' is not intended as a masterpiece; it is a peculiar species, suited for delivery amid a shouting stampede of noise, erupting in applause thirty-five times during a thirty-five minute speech. Hauge had the facility to turn great concepts into nimble language. The meat remained. But in a form digestible by five, ten, twenty, fifty thousand listeners."

Hauge's assistant, Benedict, said the draft speeches from New York occasionally caused Ike to say angrily, "Do they really think I would say this, say things this way?" Benedict added: "As it turned out, most of those drafts that came through were close to worthless . . . Some of them we'd just throw away entirely."[25] Benedict's notes from the campaign trip recorded the team's energetic speechwriting process on the train. He noted on September 21: "Late sessions with GSH [Hauge] & Bobby Cutler on War & Peace speech. Cutler fantastic!"[26]

Benedict was a twenty-five-year-old graduate of St. John's College, Annapolis, who had been active in the world federalist movement. In 1949 and 1950, he had studied music in England and Italy, exploring it as a possible career. He grew up in Westchester County, New York, the son of a Wall Street businessman. Ike's internationalist view of the world appealed to Benedict, while Taft's isolationism struck him as disastrous.

Ike himself dove into the speechwriting process, marking up drafts and discussing them with his team. "Speeches had to be written and rewritten in racing trains and planes, in densely populated hotel rooms, while standing in halls, and even, at times, riding in automobiles," he later recalled. "The work was made all the harder because I have never been able to accept a draft of a suggested talk from anyone else and deliver it intact as my own. Because drafts could be corrected only at odd moments, I never was able to get one completed to my satisfaction without repeated revisions."[27]

The train schedule called for long hours, and the staff was in close quarters with Ike, even when the campaign team left the train to spend the night in hotels in larger cities. Years later, Bobby described how close the living quarters were in his autobiography: "I remember bringing some papers into Ike's hotel room one night in mid-October, while he was rubbing himself down after a shower. He looked lean and fit, pink from the hot water, and vigorous despite the schedule. He must have seen me cast longing eyes toward the bath. He called out with a grin: 'Go ahead, Bobby, take a shower. There's plenty of time.'"[28]

Bobby was usually up at 6:15 AM and back to bed at midnight, as the demanding schedule included one or more campaign stops every day. Ike made whistle-stop speeches from the back of the train or traveled from the train to a local venue. To relax, when the crowds and press had gone away, the campaign team occasionally resorted to hijinks. One night, a skit was arranged in which Bobby, press secretary Jim Hagerty, Republican New York congressman Len Hall, and campaign aide Bern Shanley put on makeup, placed mops on their heads as "female hairdos," and danced "en quartette" as a female revue line.[29] Someone played an accordion, and the four men sang a revised version of Henry Wadsworth Longfellow's poem "The Children's Hour":

> *Between the dark and the daylight*
> *When the night is beginning to lower*
> *Comes a spurt in the day's operation*
> *Which is known as the Eisenhower.*

The lines were almost certainly written by Bobby, who shared Longfellow's Boston roots and Harvard association.

The Eisenhower Special, powered by two locomotives, had two baggage cars and twenty-four Pullman cars. Bobby spent most of his days in the last five. Ike and Mamie had compartments in the rear car, including a study where Ike worked and met with his staff. The rear car also housed a galley and cook, and Ike's longtime orderly, Sergeant John Moaney. Mamie's mother, Elivera Doud, and General Howard Snyder, Ike's physician and friend, also traveled with Ike and Mamie. The next Pullman forward included compartments for Bobby, Sherman Adams, Republican women's leader Katherine Howard, and others. The third car forward served as a room for local delegations to come aboard the train and meet with the presidential candidate. The fourth car forward was the press headquarters, including clacking teletype machines serving the seventy press representatives traveling with the train. The fifth and sixth cars forward housed the campaign staff and the press corps, as well as secretaries who typed constantly even as the train rolled swaying through the night.[30] The seventh car forward was the dining car, with limited seating and slow service, so that Bobby often had to skip lunch and try to pick up a snack from Ike's cook. Twice a week, however, Ike invited

Bobby and Gabriel Hauge — both of whom worked with the candidate on a daily basis in the rear car's parlor — to dinner with the family in the small dining room.[31]

There were efforts to bring some sense of a normal life to the train. One Sunday, an Episcopalian rector came aboard in Montana, recalled Katherine Howard. The rector put on his vestments and read a simple Episcopal service for Ike and Mamie, Sherman and Rachel Adams, Bobby, Howard, and some others. The Adamses and Bobby were devout Episcopalians, and, according to Howard, the three of them "always found a place to go to church."[32] Yet bringing godliness aboard was not the only way to make life on the train seem normal. There was the occasional cocktail hour with Ike and Mamie, too. Howard said, "Sometimes Bobby Cutler and I would come back with them, and Sherm, and we'd sit with them while in their car, and maybe the General would have a scotch and soda, and Mamie [would] have a weak Canadian Club with water at the end of the day."

On September 19, Bobby was with Ike when the news broke that vice presidential nominee Richard Nixon had received sixteen thousand dollars from a fund set up by some supporters. As some critics called for Nixon to be replaced on the presidential ticket, reporters on the campaign train pressed Ike for a comment. Ike had been huddled with Bobby and others preparing for a speech in Kansas City that night. He asked Bobby for notepaper, then wrote Nixon a letter urging him to reveal all the facts of the fund to the public and expressing confidence that Nixon had violated no ethical standards.[33] As Nixon's fate hung in the air, Bobby recommended that Ike ask a former Supreme Court justice to serve as an impartial "umpire" of the matter — and then went so far as to discover that the justice was in fact available to serve. As the tense day unfolded, Nixon sent back to the train a statement denying any impropriety and promising to reveal all the facts on the fund. Bobby then drafted a speech supporting Nixon, including the line: "Knowing Dick Nixon as I do, I believe that when the facts are known to all of us, they will show that Dick Nixon would not compromise with what is right."[34] Ike delivered those supportive words — and also read the statement from Nixon — in his speech before eleven thousand people at Municipal Auditorium in Kansas City that night.[35] Two days later, Nixon gave a live, televised speech arguing that the fund was necessary to avoid having taxpayers pay for campaign activities, though he said he intended to keep a dog named Checkers he had bought for his children with money from the fund. After the "Checkers" speech, Ike met Nixon in West Virginia and expressed renewed support for him, the controversy died down, and the campaign went forward.

In the tumult and stress of these days, Bobby appeared to have earned Ike's admiration and confidence. A few days after the storm of controversy broke over Nixon's fund, Hauge told Benedict that Bobby "might well have become the Louis Howe or Harry Hopkins of the Eisenhower administration," a reference to two close confidants of President Franklin Roosevelt.[36] "Works beautifully with Ike. Ike rages, Bobby just proceeds quietly with the business at hand." While Bobby had the manners one might expect from a trust company president, he also evidently didn't hold back on tough language, Benedict noted. ". . . [Hauge] said Cutler uses the language of the 'lowest sailor' with some amazement!"

Dulles, meanwhile, had continued giving speeches beating the drum of anti-Communism. After one of Foster's press conferences, Ike admonished him for failing to qualify his reference to liberation of captive nations "by all peaceful means."[37] Ike also sought to moderate Dulles's aggressive anti-Communist message through a speech Bobby drafted for him to give in San Francisco on October 8.[38] "Our aim in 'cold war' is not conquest of territory or subjugation by force," Ike said. "Our aim is more subtle, more pervasive, more complete. We are trying to get the world, by peaceful means, to believe the truth. That truth is that Americans want a world at peace, a world in which all peoples shall have opportunity for maximum individual development."[39] Ike's speech called for an effective psychological warfare effort, echoing Bobby's frustrations the year before with the Truman administration's Psychological Strategy Board. "The present administration has never yet been able to grasp the full import of a psychological effort put forth on a national scale . . . In past years, we have lacked leadership to develop such a strategy. The administration in power has failed to bring into line its criss-crossing and overlapping and jealous departments and bureaus and agencies. It has failed to follow up on the policies of the National Security Council." Then, turning to his own plans, Ike said: "We must choose a man of exceptional qualifications to handle the national psychological effort. He should have the full confidence of and direct access to the Chief Executive. I have suggested in other talks that this function may best be worked out through a revitalized and reconstructed National Security Council." With these remarks, Ike turned the NSC into a presidential campaign issue for the first time.

Eisenhower faced a particular challenge in the polarizing, explosive, and politically powerful Senator Joseph McCarthy of Wisconsin. McCarthy had weakened Ike's Democratic opponent, Adlai Stevenson, through attacking him and other Democrats as weak on Communism. Yet McCarthy also had attacked General George Marshall, who was a hero for his role as army chief of staff during the war. McCarthy charged that Marshall, in his postwar role as President Truman's special envoy to China, had betrayed China to the Communists. In June 1951, McCarthy went to the floor of the Senate and denounced Marshall for making "common cause with Stalin" and conspiring with Secretary of State Dean Acheson to facilitate the Communist takeover of China.[40] In 1952, McCarthy published the venomous speech as a book with the mild-mannered title *The Story of General George Marshall*. In their broad outlines, the Republican senator's attacks on Democrats tended to support Ike's campaign, but they also posed the risk that an association with McCarthy would alienate some voters.

Ike was aware of that political risk, and he also was upset by McCarthy's attack on Marshall, whom Ike considered a brilliant wartime leader. Ike wrote in his 1948 book *Crusade in Europe* that Marshall had the "vision and determination" to prepare the US military for war well before the Japanese attack on Pearl Harbor.[41] Marshall had promoted Ike to be a military planner in the Pentagon's Operations Division, and in 1942 he named Ike commander of all US forces in Europe. While on a campaign stop in Denver in August 1952, Ike defended Marshall in a news conference, saying, "I have no patience with anyone who can find in his record of service for this country anything to criticize."[42] Ike himself had faulted the Truman administration for losing China to the Communists, but he did not charge Marshall and Acheson with conspiring to bring about the Communist victory.

As the campaign moved into the fall of 1952, Bobby helped Ike explore how to use McCarthy carefully to win votes in Massachusetts, an issue that Bobby raised with Cabot Lodge because it could affect the senator's race against John F. Kennedy. "Catholic sentiment seems to feel that McCarthy would be a help by speaking in Mass. If he is to speak, his visit should certainly be spaced widely from Ike's," Bobby wrote Lodge on September 17.[43] "Ike says that a decision to have him in Masstts at all would rest of course entirely with you." Bobby's letter indicated Ike was contemplating how to use McCarthy to his advantage — and the risks of doing so. In the end, McCarthy did not appear in Massachusetts during the campaign, but Ike's efforts to use the senator in his campaign soon caused turmoil.

Ike, the brilliant strategist who knew how to forge an alliance in order to achieve victory, had often made peace with difficult personalities — ranging from British field marshal Bernard Montgomery to US general George Patton — to achieve a broader goal. In August 1945, Ike traveled to Moscow to meet with Marshal Georgy Zhukov and Joseph Stalin, even discussing management of occupied Berlin with Stalin while they viewed a parade from atop Lenin's Tomb in Red Square.[44] Thus, it was not out of character when Ike found common ground with McCarthy, bringing the senator to campaign while McCarthy gained the status of being on the Republican nominee's campaign train.

It soon became apparent that Ike, pushed by Republican leaders arguing that party unity increased the chances of victory, had decided to compromise with McCarthy. After initially opposing the idea of campaigning in Wisconsin, Ike agreed to a series of campaign train stops and speeches through the state in early October.[45] Plans also were made for the caustic red-hunting senator to stay on the campaign train overnight, making McCarthy a political ally and boosting his status. On September 29, Senator Frank Carlson, the Kansas Republican who had joined the campaign train, came to see Hauge about the strategy for campaigning with McCarthy. Carlson said McCarthy "will do anything we say! Will appear or not appear as requested," Benedict wrote in notes at the time.[46] Hauge replied that whatever decision was made regarding McCarthy's role, the effect of McCarthy's actions on the Eastern seaboard should be the "predominant consideration."

However, before the rapprochement between Ike and McCarthy could unfold, there was one stumbling block. Speechwriter Emmet Hughes, working from Ike's campaign headquarters on the sixth floor of the Commodore in New York, had drafted a speech for Ike to give in Milwaukee on the night of October 3.[47] It was chiefly an attack on Democrats for dismissing concerns about Communism, yet it also included a defense of General Marshall, which Hughes later said Ike had specifically requested. The speech had already undergone several redrafts by the time the train pulled into Peoria, Illinois, on October 1 for a campaign speech Ike was to give at Bradley University that night.

McCarthy and two of his Republican allies, Wisconsin governor Walter Kohler and Republican national committeeman Henry Ringling, flew to Peoria in a private plane that afternoon. They went to the hotel where Eisenhower was preparing for his speech, and McCarthy went alone to Eisenhower's hotel suite, emerging about thirty minutes later.[48] After the meeting, McCarthy told the media only that he had a "very, very pleasant conversation" with Ike.[49] Then Kohler went to Ike's suite. "Bobby Cutler and the General and I ate dinner at one of the small card tables that had been set up," Kohler later recalled. McCarthy was not invited to the dinner, Kohler said. When Kohler got back to the room where McCarthy was waiting, McCarthy told him he had not spoken with Ike about the contents of Ike's speech when the two met earlier. After dinner, Ike went to the Bradley campus to give his speech, mentioning neither McCarthy nor Marshall.

Later that night, Kohler and McCarthy joined the Eisenhower team on board the campaign train before it departed toward its first stop the next day in northern Wisconsin. It is unclear where on the tightly organized train McCarthy's compartment was located. The next morning, October 3, before the first stop, McCarthy entered Ike's car and a very direct discussion began. "I'm going to say that I disagree with you," Sherman Adams recalled Ike telling McCarthy. "If you say that, you'll get booed," McCarthy replied.[50] Eisenhower shrugged and said, "I've been booed before, and being booed doesn't bother me."

At the first stop, in Green Bay, Ike told the crowd that he shared McCarthy's goals, but not his methods. "I want to make one thing very clear. The purposes that he [McCarthy] and I have of ridding this Government of incompetents, the dishonest and above all the subversive and disloyal are one and the same. Our differences, therefore, have nothing to do with the end result that we are seeking. The differences apply to method," he said.[51] There were no boos heard, Adams noted.[52] Without naming McCarthy, Ike also called for the election of every Republican candidate in Wisconsin, a slate that would include, of course, McCarthy.

The next stop was Appleton, Wisconsin, McCarthy's hometown. Here, McCarthy went out on the rear platform of the train and introduced

Eisenhower before a crowd of some seven thousand people, saying he would "make an outstanding president."[53] Kohler then stood between the two men as Ike delivered his speech. An Associated Press photo that ran in newspapers nationwide the next day showed Ike and McCarthy with big smiles, Kohler standing between them. In his comments, Ike made no mention of Marshall and again called for the election of every Republican candidate in Wisconsin.

After the train left Appleton, Kohler asked Adams if he could review the speech Ike planned to give that night in Milwaukee, expected to be his most important public address in the state. In the text of the speech, Kohler found the paragraph defending Marshall, and he told Adams the paragraph should be removed. Kohler, noting that Wisconsin's twelve electoral votes had gone to Truman in 1948, voiced concern that the rebuff to McCarthy could undermine Eisenhower in a state where McCarthy had wide support.[54] Adams agreed with Kohler's objection and brought Kohler to Ike to raise the issue. "I had only begun when Eisenhower interrupted me impatiently and asked me if I was about to suggest that the reference to Marshall should be deleted," Adams recalled.[55] "'That's what I'm going to recommend,' I said. 'Take it out,' Eisenhower snapped."

At some point — it's unclear when — Bobby worked on the draft speech and inserted language that would soften, rather than delete, the defense of Marshall. This sixth draft includes a phrase — in writing recognized by Benedict as Bobby's — inserted in the Marshall defense: "I am not here in defense of any [judgment] he may have made . . ."[56] Hauge recalled that he and Bobby were working on speeches in the back car when Adams approached them and said, "The paragraph's going out." Hauge said he made a "very strong objection," but Adams said the matter had been decided.[57] "Then the General came back, and I could tell what a terrible thing he'd been through," Hauge recalled. "He was purple way down to the roots of his neck. He was glowering. I had to ask him, for final confirmation, if that paragraph was going out. He said, 'Yes.' He said it in a way that discouraged me from even arguing about it." Hauge later said he had fought alone to keep the Marshall paragraph in the speech, while Bobby had been "silent" when the issue erupted.[58] Adams later described Bobby and C. D. Jackson as "the two strong enemies of McCarthy on our team."[59] But at this point, apparently recognizing that the candidate had made his final decision, Bobby had stayed silent. The

Marshall defense was scratched out of the draft in pencil, and Ike put his initial *D* on it, indicating it was the final version.

Late that day, October 3, the train arrived in Milwaukee, and Ike went to a hotel suite to prepare for that night's speech. Bobby met McCarthy and led him into a hotel suite for a second private meeting with Ike, then remained outside while the two met.[60] "The whole episode was like a bad dream that comes unbidden in the depth of night," Bobby wrote later in his autobiography. "The political amateurs on the train, like me, thought Ike's original intent to praise General Marshall in McCarthy's lair was the right course. We thought whatever Ike said in Wisconsin would not affect his victory."

In his speech that night, Ike made no mention of Marshall. Instead, he attacked the Democratic Party for tolerating Communist penetration of the government and "treason itself." He also again noted that he shared McCarthy's goal of ridding the government of subversives and said he disagreed only with McCarthy's "methods." By deleting his praise of Marshall, Ike upheld the entente between the two men — at least for the time being.

The New York Times, citing unnamed sources, reported the next day that McCarthy himself had told Ike during the meeting in Peoria that Ike's defense of Marshall "probably could be better made before another audience." The newspaper also said that in his Milwaukee speech Ike yielded to McCarthy's request that the Marshall defense be removed.[61] Two days after Ike's speech in Milwaukee, on October 5, McCarthy began campaigning vigorously for Eisenhower, announcing that he was so confident of Eisenhower's willingness to hunt out Communists that he could end his "one-man" crusade against Communists if the Republican ticket won the election. Inexplicably, McCarthy also falsely denied he had ever called Marshall a traitor or accused him of helping lose China to the Communists. His comments portended a bonus for the nation: Electing Eisenhower held the promise of ending the tension created by McCarthy's constant barrage of reckless charges.[62]

Democrats immediately pounced on the Eisenhower–McCarthy dealings, arguing that Eisenhower had made a pact with the devil — he gave up his defense of Marshall in order to win McCarthy's support. On October 7, President Truman denounced Eisenhower for befriending McCarthy and Senator William Jenner of Indiana, who also had accused Marshall of betraying the country. Truman called Marshall "the finest example of a patriotic American." As for the two right-wing senators, Truman said of Eisenhower: "One he has embraced publicly. The other he has humbly thanked for riding on his campaign train. Never a word of criticism — or even of distaste. And why — because he thinks these two unprincipled men will bring him votes in November."[63] Ike's Democratic opponent, Adlai Stevenson, quickly attacked Eisenhower in a speech in Milwaukee for failing to stand up to McCarthy. "I'm worrying about his backbone," he said.

While the Democrats ferociously sought to turn Ike's political compromise with McCarthy against him, Bobby and Lodge began developing a plan to ensure that Ike's McCarthy strategy succeeded in Massachusetts — or at least would not damage Lodge's chances at winning reelection. Bobby wrote his friend from the train asking for a memo on points Ike should make during his speech planned for Boston two weeks later.[64] On October 10, Lodge wrote Bobby asking Ike to pronounce "some good ringing paragraphs about Communism." Lodge added: "Stevenson's attack on McCarthy has not helped him in Massachusetts." In another letter to Bobby a few days later, Lodge drafted specific comments for Ike to make: "Communism is a military threat and a dangerous one; it is a political conspiracy and a diabolical one . . ." Lodge also warned that Ike's reconciliation with the conservative Taft had created a "bad impression" and called for Ike to counter that conservative tinge by voicing support for social welfare programs as a means of fighting poverty. Lodge suggested a specific line: "That means enactment of a social program which meets the needs of the people so completely that Communism can never get a foothold."

On October 21, the Eisenhower campaign train pulled into Boston, and Bobby and Herter rode with Ike in an open convertible through Harvard Square, where a throng of an estimated twenty thousand Harvard students and other supporters surrounded the motorcade. As the crowd pressed in, police officers jumped up on the car for their own safety while souvenir hunters snatched chrome parts and other accessories from the car.[65] The rowdy support underscored that Ike's brand of progressive Republicanism had caught the imagination of young people. Later, Ike spoke at Boston Common, delivering a firm anti-Communist message to an estimated hundred thousand people. "There exists a definite and self-proclaimed threat to the individual lives, the individual freedom, of each one of us here on this ancient common ground. This terrible danger is godless Communism," he intoned. Tracking Lodge's recommendations nearly verbatim, Ike said Communism can exploit poverty in America, and "that means we must have a social program which meets the needs of our people so completely that through this door Communism can never gain access in America." He also praised Lodge as "the first man since the Civil War to resign from the Senate to fight for his country," adding, "Today, he is a valiant fighter for his country against Communism."[66]

Ultimately, Lodge made a separate peace with McCarthy. He announced in a speech that he supported "election of all Republican nominees, including Senator McCarthy of Wisconsin." McCarthy, meanwhile, continued supporting Ike. In a televised speech delivered in Chicago on October 27, a week before Election Day, McCarthy accused Stevenson of sympathizing with and supporting Communists, outlining Stevenson's ties to Alger Hiss in the 1940s.

Four days later, Ike gave a speech in Chicago, playing his role in the political theater of good cop/bad cop. If McCarthy was the bad cop bullying and slinging accusations wildly, then Ike was the good cop who conducted an honest investigation. Ike drew a clear distinction between himself and McCarthy without mentioning the senator by name:

> There are those who believe that any means are justified by the end of rooting out Communism. There are those who believe that the preservation of democracy and the preservation of the soul of freedom in this country can and must be accomplished with decency and fairness and due process of law. I belong to this second school. But at the same time, I say to you that no differences in theory can excuse any failure to see that Communist contamination inside our government is stamped out.

On November 1, the Democratic National Committee issued a rebuttal that faulted McCarthy for eight "glaring falsehoods and distortions." It was too late. The damage was done. Even if the public felt that McCarthy's charges were dubious, the allegations themselves raised the prospect that McCarthy would drag Stevenson — and the nation — through years of highly charged accusations.

On Monday, November 3, for a last night of campaigning before Election Day, Eisenhower traveled to Boston, so he and Nixon could give final speeches in the fifteen-thousand-seat Boston Garden arena. Bobby appeared on the platform with Christian Herter, Katherine Howard, Senator Leverett Saltonstall, and Cabot Lodge, who introduced Ike. The candidate's speech sounded notes of liberalism and moderation, as he called for unity and expressed hope for a nation free from "the faintest strains of prejudice or bigotry." Ike and Mamie returned to New York that night, with Bobby and numerous other aides, to vote the next day and watch the election returns at the Commodore Hotel campaign headquarters.

Ike defeated Stevenson soundly, winning 55 percent of the popular vote and carrying all but nine states. The election was a victory for Eisenhower's strategy of forging an alliance with McCarthy while separating himself from the abuses of McCarthyism. The election also represented a victory for Lodge's drive to make Eisenhower into a Republican president. Ike won Massachusetts, and Herter was elected governor, but Kennedy defeated Lodge in the race for the Senate.

An exhausted Bobby wrote Ike on November 5:

> Before going to bed I have to send one message to you . . . It has been a great privilege to be with you these last seven weeks. It has taught me a great deal. Your warmth, your knowledge, your Christian principle, your generous kindness are beyond what I have known before in man. Comparing my own meager gifts with all you offer really cuts a fellow down to his proper size. I really feel chagrined that I could not bring more with me to be of use to you. But I do have the satisfaction that the only thing I have wanted for my country, — your victory, — has happened and happened with the biggest possible bang.

Bobby noted that Lodge had conceded to Kennedy at 7:20 AM, and said:

> I took the liberty of telling him that you asked several times last night about how things were going with him, and that your last word to me as you went home this

morning from the Commodore was that *you* could use Cabot if Massachusetts couldn't. It gave him quite a lift. I really think he is so pleased over your victory and what it means to the country that it has taken the bitterness right out of his own defeat. I know that his manifold talents can be of great assistance to you. Please give my best love to Mamie. Your affectionate friend — Bobby.

Relaxing in Augusta, Georgia, after the long and hard-fought campaign, Eisenhower wrote in reply thanking Bobby for his work. "Dear Bobby, Of course I know you are quite a wit but I will not, even in the service of humor, have you belittle your efforts as you did in your note to me of November fifth. At the very least you kept me from going completely batty — possibly at times you were doubtful of your success even in this regard," the president-elect wrote.[67] "With my undying thanks for all you did, and particularly for all that you put up with in the form of fairly continuous irascibility, As ever," he closed the note.

Bobby and Ike came from two different worlds; one a dairyman's son from Kansas, the other a Harvard-educated lawyer from Boston. But their lives coincided in the military, and they shared views on what is important in life: service to their country, democracy, respect for honorable men, intelligent leadership, and hard work. Through Bobby's hard work on the campaign train, it also became clear that he placed Ike's interests ahead of his own, preferred to remain behind the scenes, and was self-deprecating almost to a fault. As their relationship evolved in that brief but intense period, Ike had come to consider Bobby a true friend, someone he could rely upon and place great trust in. Years later, after his terms as president were over, Ike wrote in his memoir that Bobby "was one whose company I always enjoyed and who became a very close friend."[68]

6

TRANSITION

In early December 1952, President-Elect Eisenhower arrived in South Korea for a three-day tour of the war zone. In an October campaign speech, he had vowed to resolve the Korean War, and as part of that effort pledged: "I shall go to Korea." Fulfilling that pledge, he met with US generals, visited wounded American soldiers, greeted Korean troops, flew over the battle lines, and saw Chinese fortifications in the hills behind the North Korean lines. His nominee to be defense secretary, Charles Wilson, joined him on the trip. When truce talks had begun in July 1951, American casualties — killed, wounded, and missing — stood at seventy-five thousand, but since then the death toll had continued to mount as negotiations dragged on. "We cannot tolerate the continuation of the Korean conflict," Eisenhower told his advisers en route home.[1] "The United States will have to break this deadlock."

Returning to New York, Ike continued to use offices at the Commodore Hotel as he prepared to address the Korean War and a host of other national security issues, from threats of Communist takeovers in other countries to nuclear weapons production and McCarthy's drumbeat of claims that Communists had infiltrated the US government.

On December 19, Bobby spent two hours with the president-elect. After the Christmas holiday, it became clear that Eisenhower had made up his mind to appoint Bobby to a position managing the NSC. Bobby wrote the president-elect a letter on December 27: "Dear Ike, I know that you consider the Executive of the National Security Council as one of the most critically important posts in the effective functioning of the National Government. I feel my talents unworthy of this position, in which you have asked me to serve in your Administration. However, since you wish me to try to do this job, I accept and will do the best in me for you and the country."[2]

Two days later, Ike's campaign headquarters at the Commodore issued a news release naming Bobby an "Administrative Assistant to the President" in a position that would let Cutler undertake his plans to reform the NSC and Psychological Strategy Board. "Mr. Cutler's special responsibilities will relate to the National Security Council and to coordinating the work of the various departments and agencies with the Council's function." Bobby had drafted the news release himself. It described his career in detail, including his role as president of Old Colony Trust and his two novels, and it mentioned he was a bachelor.

Shortly after New Year's Day, Bobby went to Washington and selected his office in the Executive Office Building, an imposing structure in the French Second Empire style immediately west of the White House. He also met with key existing staff members at the NSC and PSB, asking them to remain in their posts until the new president decided what changes he wanted. He also told Ike in a memo that President Truman had written a letter to Ike proposing an executive order on security clearances, adding that he (Bobby) would review it January 19 — the day before the inauguration — once he had his own security clearance. The NSC staff members showed Bobby three volumes holding "compilations of Top Secret NSC and related papers" as well as documents from the Atomic Energy Commission. "Upon clearance, a first duty of mine will be to familiarize myself with this mass of material for you," Bobby wrote.

Bobby took an apartment in a boardinghouse for prominent bachelors a couple of blocks from the White House, at 1718 H Street Northwest. The house was just a few minutes' walk from the White House — and half a block away from Lafayette Square. Founded by young military aides to President Theodore Roosevelt, the house became known simply as The Family, with a tradition of each bachelor receiving a silver cup upon his marriage.[3] The Family's members included young men from elite backgrounds, many of whom went on to distinguished careers in the Foreign Service. A modest brick house, The Family had hosted guests such as Charles Lindbergh and Franklin and Eleanor Roosevelt. Henry Cabot Lodge Jr. had resided at The Family in earlier decades, and so had Joseph Alsop, a widely published newspaper columnist and friend of Bobby's who was a Harvard graduate and member of the Porcellian Club.

Two striking Washington landmarks flanked The Family. Immediately to its east, on the corner of H Street and 17th Street, was the historic

Metropolitan Club. Founded for Union soldiers in 1863, the club's roster of members was a virtual Who's Who of Washington politics. On the west side of The Family, at 1720 H Street, was Washington's best-known gay bar, the Lafayette Chicken Hut, a colorful place where a piano player usually greeted regulars as they came in.[4] Bobby joined the Metropolitan Club. With an imposing Italian Renaissance structure and ornate interior, it was a comfortable environment for him, akin to his beloved Somerset Club in Boston. There is no record of Bobby visiting the bar known simply as the Chicken Hut, though he likely heard the strains of its piano from his window.

Eisenhower's administration continued to take shape as he named prominent Republican foreign policy expert and international lawyer John Foster Dulles to be secretary of state. Dulles had a family history of remarkable political power. His maternal grandfather, John W. Foster, was secretary of state under Republican president Benjamin Harrison. His uncle, Robert Lansing, was secretary of state under Democrat Woodrow Wilson.[5] His brother, Allen Dulles, five years Foster's junior, was at that time deputy director of the CIA. The two brothers were among those who founded the Council on Foreign Relations in 1921 in New York City. The council and its widely respected publication, *Foreign Affairs*, were considered proponents of internationalism, the concept that America must remain committed financially and politically to maintaining an international order and trade system that made it possible for all economies to grow. Critics maintained that internationalists merely sought to enhance profits of businesses that thrived on international trade.

John Foster Dulles, known simply as Foster, graduated from Princeton in 1908, attended George Washington University Law School, and in 1911 went to work at Sullivan & Cromwell, a powerful New York law firm that often represented corporations seeking assistance from the US and foreign governments. Foster represented the United Fruit Company in its dealings with General Federico Tinoco Granados, who seized control of Costa Rica in 1917.[6] Tinoco's family was deeply in debt to United Fruit, and United Fruit had promoted the coup that placed him in power.

In 1926, at age thirty-eight, Foster Dulles became Sullivan & Cromwell's managing partner, a position he would hold for the next twenty-five years. His rise to the position came two years after he helped plan the Dawes Act, a US law that restructured Germany's reparation obligations from World War I and created immense financial opportunities for American banks.[7] Within a year, he arranged for five banks to lend Germany one hundred million dollars, according to the authoritative dual biography, *The Brothers: John Foster Dulles, Allen Dulles, and Their Secret World War*, by Stephen Kinzer. In the seven years that followed, Foster and his partners brokered another nine hundred million in loans to Germany, or the equivalent of more than a trillion dollars today. In the 1930s, Foster Dulles helped IG Farben, the German firm that was one of the world's largest chemical makers, enter a cartel with American and Belgian companies.[8]

Despite Hitler's rise to power, Foster supported relations with Nazi Germany. He believed Nazism to be a bulwark against Communism, and his defense of it subjected him to public ridicule. Syndicated newspaper columnist Drew Pearson listed Sullivan & Cromwell's German clients who had contributed money to the Nazis and helped them rise to power.[9] Foster's support for working with the Nazis was also the cause of one of the few known disputes between him and his brother, Allen. After an early career in government intelligence, Allen had followed Foster to Sullivan & Cromwell, where the two worked closely for more than a decade, but this did not stop Allen from upbraiding his older brother. "How can you call yourself a Christian and ignore what is happening in Germany?" Allen demanded. "It is terrible."[10] Ultimately, in 1935, Foster agreed to close Sullivan & Cromwell's Berlin office, though he continued to travel to Germany as late as 1939 and attacked President Roosevelt and Prime Minister Winston Churchill as "warmongers."

By the end of World War II, Foster's reputation had recovered to the extent that when a US delegation prepared to attend a conference in San Francisco to frame an agreement to create the United Nations, Republican leaders asked that he be included as a Republican representative. President Truman agreed. Soon, Foster began making speeches and publishing articles that increasingly sounded alarms over the threat that Soviet Communism posed to the United States.

Ike had a detailed vision for using organizational structure to unite the energies of capable men holding strong opinions into a team striving to achieve a single policy or objective. Ike's commitment to organizational structure stemmed from his experiences as a soldier. In *Crusade in Europe*, he described the urgency of his work on the "vital task of operational planning" early in the war, when the massive Japanese and German war machines threatened to defeat America.[11] In the Pentagon's Operations Division, he developed a profound respect for the coordinated work of a staff of officers committed to thrashing out the most effective solutions to the challenges of training, equipping, and mobilizing hundreds of thousands of soldiers into a fighting force. And when he led planning for the Allied invasion of Normandy, Ike said a primary concern was "determination of the most desirable composition of the headquarters staff." He noted: "The scheme which we found most effective, where it was possible for all commanders to meet almost instantly, was to consider the naval, air and ground chiefs as occupying two roles. In the first role each was part of my staff and he and his assistants worked with us in the development of plans; in the second role each was the responsible commander for executing his part of the whole operation." Ike soon adopted this dual-role approach in organizing his administration.

The president-elect summoned Foster Dulles, Charlie Wilson, and other cabinet members, along with Bobby and other top-level appointees, to New York to meet behind closed doors at the Commodore on January 12, 1953, to discuss organization of the incoming administration. At the start of the meeting, the mood was light as Ike reviewed plans for the inauguration and discussed the expected attire, suggesting that the men wear dark homburgs. He said there was no reason for old traditions such as "tri-cornered hats and knee britches." Bobby piped up, mentioning Oveta C. Hobby, nominated as administrator of the Federal Security Agency and attending as the only woman in Ike's cabinet. "If Mrs. Hobby comes in knee britches I want to be in the front row," he joked before the full room.[12]

The meeting became serious when Ike turned the floor over to Bobby to discuss the functioning of the NSC and his and the president's plans to improve it. Bobby assured his colleagues that in his role as Ike's administrative assistant he would be a person who "has a passion for anonymity and makes no speeches except when ordered by the Cabinet or the President." He hinted at the failings of the NSC under Truman and noted that in his campaign speech in San Francisco, Ike had called for a "revitalized and reconstructed" NSC.[13] Bobby went on to say that he had left his position at a "fiduciary institution" to take the post managing the NSC. "We will have a wonderful Cabinet and a wonderful President, but if we don't formulate our national policy effectively and in a rounded, unified, coherent sort of way and have the world understand what we are trying to do, we won't have done the job that we have got to do for the president."

After Bobby finished, Ike made it clear that the NSC was to be the center of his government. "This is a subject in which I am vitally and deeply interested," the president said. He explained that he expected agency heads to perform two distinct roles — contributing to the development of national policy in the NSC, and directing their individual agencies. He also underscored the value he placed on Bobby's role, saying, "Because Mr. Cutler has just gotten up and given you this dissertation it gives me the opportunity to say in front of all of you that there are certain positions that I have filled on the theory that those positions are equally important with any Cabinet position that we have . . . It is an executive committee, and that is the reason why I have asked a man to leave such an important position as — I can't say that word, Bobby. I can't say fiduciary." Here, Ike played the rustic and teased Bobby over his language. "But in any event I felt justified in asking him to be the executive secretary of that body. I hope to call in the best civilian brains to sit with that group." Finally, he told his cabinet members, if Bobby requests a meeting, "get him in quick because it is bound to be important." The importance Ike placed on Bobby's involvement was underscored by the fact that from that day forward Bobby attended not only the NSC meetings that were his domain but also Cabinet meetings.

All Eisenhower White House appointees were subjected to a routine FBI background check, with a report delivered to the president-elect's chief of staff, Sherman Adams. This process soon caused trouble for Arthur Vandenberg Jr., a top campaign assistant whom Eisenhower had named to be his personal secretary in the White House. Vandenberg was the son of Senator Arthur Vandenberg, the Michigan Republican who had died in 1951. While the president-elect was in Korea, Vandenberg Jr. had made key announcements, such as the naming of prominent Republican Nelson Rockefeller to head a committee that would examine government efficiency.

In early December, the FBI had learned that a man linked to Vandenberg had been arrested on a "morals charge" in Lafayette Square and "bounced out of the Navy."[14] Located across the street from the White

House, Lafayette Square was a known cruising place for gays, and while the arrest of the man had escaped public notice, it set off alarms in the Republican Party. Milt Hill, an associate of Republican Party chairman Arthur Summerfield and a friend of Assistant Director of the FBI Louis Nichols, informed Nichols of the arrest.[15] Nichols then sent a memo to Associate Director of the FBI Clyde Tolson saying, somewhat mysteriously, that the arrested man, identified as "George Clayton Irwin or Irvin," was "sponsored by Arthur Vandenberg, Jr.," without elaborating. If Senator Joseph McCarthy learned of the Lafayette Square arrest, he might pursue an investigation of Vandenberg. Such a scandal in the new administration's opening days would have been highly damaging.

Vandenberg disappeared from public view, and the media at first reported he was vacationing in Florida. On December 30, Hoover met privately with Eisenhower at his headquarters in New York, where they reviewed some of Ike's staffing considerations. After Hoover expressed lukewarm opinions about some candidates for the CIA director's position, the conversation turned to Vandenberg. Hoover made it clear that the FBI was proceeding delicately and with respect for the president's appointee. Hoover memorialized the exchange in a memo revealing a new detail about the arrested man — that he lived with Vandenberg:

> I told the General that Vandenberg had asked that we not interview the young man at present living with Vandenberg until he, Vandenberg, came out of the hospital, to which he had gone for physical check over the last week end. The General told me that should Mr. Vandenberg decide that he did not desire to continue in the position to which he had been appointed as Secretary to the President, that I could inform Vandenberg that no report would be submitted as it would then be a moot question.[16]

Ike was proposing a solution in which Vandenberg would relinquish his appointment and, as a result, the FBI would drop its investigation.

Vandenberg, however, was reluctant to surrender the opportunity to work in the White House and maintained the illness story. On January 4, he called Eisenhower's secretary, Ann Whitman, and dictated a letter for Sherman Adams. "Time allotted for rest is not long enough to resolve health problems. In view of urgency of situation in the office, I see no alternative except to suggest that you revise future plans without including me, and consequently that your previous offer of a position to me is withdrawn."[17] But he also told Whitman: "I hope and pray they will continue to wait." As of January 5, according to Hoover, Vandenberg had not decided whether he wanted the background investigation completed. Three days later, Hoover sent Adams a letter stating that the investigation of Vandenberg was done and "there is attached a summary of these inquiries." However, the purportedly attached summary is missing from the archive file.[18]

Vandenberg retreated to the Everglades Hotel in Miami, where he let it be known he was receiving medical care. On January 13, Vandenberg delivered to the president-elect a formal letter stepping down, offering a cover story that suggested illness was the cause. "In my eagerness to fill the post which you offered me, I have made every effort to overcome an adverse condition of health. But I cannot longer delay in yielding to the fact that I will not be able to assume the duties of Secretary to the President on January 20th. Therefore I have no alternative except to request that you grant me an extended leave of absence from your staff." Eisenhower wrote in pen at the bottom of the letter a comment that bolstered the illness storyline and suggested Ike had just learned of it: "I am distressed to learn of Arthur Vandenberg's illness. I sincerely hope he will have an early return to robust health. In this office he will be greatly missed." Vandenberg's letter, along with the president's expression of regret — which vouched for the illness story — was released to the press. To imbue the story with verisimilitude, Press Secretary Jim Hagerty offered the detail that Vandenberg was suffering from a "blood condition."[19]

Three days later, as he and Mamie were preparing for the inauguration, Ike wrote Vandenberg a letter thanking him and expressing concern about him. "When Mamie and I go off to Washington this weekend, one of our great regrets will be that you are unable to be with us," he wrote. "I realize that you have been in this thing from the very beginning and that you have given tremendously of your energies during that period. On that account I feel in some respects guilty. All of us are looking forward to your early return to vitality and health."[20] This letter, which would remain secret for decades, suggests that while Ike sought to oust Vandenberg once his connection with an alleged homosexual threatened to become a political catastrophe, Eisenhower nonetheless reached out personally to express sorrow over the situation.

Ike's sympathy for Vandenberg is consistent with his little-known record of forbearance with respect to homosexuality. When he was commander of Allied forces in Europe at the end of World War II, Eisenhower received reports of lesbians in the Women's Army Corps (WAC). The general called WAC sergeant Johnnie Phelps into his office and asked her to investigate and produce a list of their names so he could take action against them.[21] "Yes, Sir," Phelps told Eisenhower, but she warned it would be a lot of work since by her estimate 95 percent of the nine hundred women in the WAC battalion were lesbians. Phelps also pointed out that the WAC battalion was highly decorated and had extremely low rates of venereal disease infection and pregnancy. Then she dropped a bombshell: "I'll make the list . . . but you've got to know that when you get the list back, my name's going to be first." Eisenhower's secretary then interjected, "Sergeant Phelps will have to be second on the list. I'm going to type it. My name will be first." Eisenhower shook his head and said, "Forget that order. Forget about it."

One person who urged tolerance of homosexuals in the military was Eisenhower's longtime personal physician and friend, Dr. Howard Snyder. A Wyoming native and veteran army doctor, Snyder became personal physician to General Eisenhower in 1945, at the age of sixty-five, and remained Eisenhower's personal physician after the war. When Eisenhower was president of Columbia University, he asked Snyder to serve as an adviser to the Conservation of Human Resources Project, the research group headed by economics professor Eli Ginzberg. In World War II, Eisenhower had struggled with a lack of manpower during the Battle of the Bulge and in the North African Campaign. By the end of the war, the US military had adopted a policy of giving dishonorable discharges to homosexuals along with other soldiers who demonstrated undesirable behavior.[22] When Ike was at Columbia, he urged Ginzberg to undertake research to uncover why so many prospective soldiers were rejected for duty, hoping that manpower could be managed more productively in the future.[23]

In December 1951, Ginzberg asked Snyder about the treatment of gays in the military. In his response, Snyder conveyed his belief that many homosexuals were wrongly dismissed from service and that he found very few cases of homosexuals being "'active' seducers" in the military.[24] Snyder warned Ginzberg that it would be a mistake to let popular attitudes toward gays determine the military's policy on homosexuality. "It is my opinion that a broad-gauged policy, representative of the Personnel Department of the Army, should not be governed by the mores of our society regarding this problem. As is true in the Negro problem, we may have to point the way," he wrote, referring to the fact that President Truman ordered desegregation of the military at a time when many Americans opposed desegregation. "I feel that the saving in manpower which would result from intelligent consideration of these problems in the Services and in society would pay for itself many times."

Snyder illustrated the tragic human cost of intolerance toward gays by describing a horrific case he'd witnessed decades earlier at a US Army base in the Philippines, where soldiers in an artillery battery discovered that one of their comrades was gay. They set up a "stool pigeon" so they could catch the soldier "red handed," then rushed into the tent with pick handles and "blasted this fellow's head to a pulp," Snyder wrote. When Snyder saw the soldier, he was dying in a hospital bed from the blows to his skull.

What Ike may have thought of Ginzberg's inquiry into homosexuality in the military and Snyder's reply remains unknown, though it seems likely that he had some knowledge of the views of a man who served as his personal physician for many years and whom he invited to join the 1952 campaign train. After Eisenhower was elected president, Ginzberg also frequently visited the White House, often playing cards with the president and his friends.[25]

As the transition period continued, the FBI prepared a lengthy report on Bobby that summarized interviews with dozens of his friends and acquaintances, including Chief of Staff Sherman Adams, Henry Cabot Lodge Jr., George Marshall, Old Colony Trust director G. Peabody Gardner, Harold Vanderbilt, and even Somerset Club manager Henry Brown. The report gave Bobby a glowing review. It cited Adams's own comment that Bobby "is a stand-out citizen and a churchman in whose character and loyalty he has the highest faith, adding that Mr. Cutler is a brilliant man whom he unhesitatingly recommends for a high post in the Federal Government."[26] The report also quoted Sinclair Weeks, whom Ike designated secretary of commerce, as telling the FBI: "He has known Cutler for 35 years and considers him to be a superlative person possessing a fine character and enviable reputation." The report made no mention of any homosexuality allegations. In conclusion, the FBI said it found that Bobby was "loyal, of good character and reputation, associates with persons of the same type, and is well qualified for a position of trust with the United States Government."

Other Eisenhower appointees included Henry Cabot Lodge Jr. as ambassador to the United Nations and Gabriel Hauge as an administrative assistant to the president. Hauge brought with him to the White House his assistant from the campaign, Steve Benedict, who had become friends with Bobby on the campaign train.

Born May 8, 1927, Benedict grew up in Scarborough in Westchester County, a prosperous bedroom community north of New York City. His father, Harry E. Benedict, was a Wall Street businessman and close associate of Frank A. Vanderlip, president of National City Bank. John C. Farrar, founding partner of the publishing firm Farrar, Straus and Giroux, was a family friend and neighbor. Farrar's son John was a good friend of Steve, and Farrar often gave the young Benedict armfuls of newly published books to take home and read. Steve was a talented classical piano student and active in the world federalist movement, which advocated creation of a world government. At the age of sixteen, he entered St. John's College in Annapolis, Maryland, whose curriculum was built around the "great books" of Western civilization. As a freshman, Steve became editor of the *Student Federalist*, a national publication about world federalism. He also began working closely with Dr. Stringfellow Barr, president of St. John's and a dedicated world federalist.

After graduating from St. John's in 1947, Steve worked in Chicago as an editor for a world federalist publication, then returned to New York to work as a research assistant to Barr, who had become president of the Foundation for World Government. In 1948, Steve had his first homosexual affair with another world federalism activist.[27] He traveled to Paris to prepare for world federalist conferences in June 1949 but soon decided to move to London to be with another young man he had met and to continue his study of piano. In 1950, while traveling through Cannes, he met Tilghman B. "Skip" Koons, a former US Navy intelligence officer studying for his PhD in Russian history at the Sorbonne. Steve and

Skip became lovers and lived together in Paris and Nice before Benedict returned to the United States and became involved in the Eisenhower campaign in 1952. After joining the White House staff, Steve suggested to Bobby that he consider hiring Skip for an open NSC staff position and wrote to Skip urging him to apply.

7

THE GAY SPY

Born February 25, 1926, in New York City and raised in Plainfield, New Jersey, Tilghman B. "Skip" Koons lost his father, Lucius, a coal company president, to cancer the year before he entered Princeton at the age of seventeen. Skip's mother, Peggy, remarried, but she and her son, her only child, always maintained a close, though sometimes tormented, relationship.

At Princeton, Skip pursued his interest in international relations, studying Russian language, history, and politics, as well as French and Spanish.[1] After two years of college and with World War II raging, Skip left Princeton to join the US Navy's Office of Naval Intelligence. In February 1945, Skip was assigned to the Navy's Oriental Language School at the University of Colorado to study Russian. Skip grew close to a fellow student there, Charles Turner, whom he described in a letter to his mother as his "best friend." The young men also became physically involved before Charles was transferred to the University of Oklahoma with other Japanese-language students.[2]

Skip received his commission as an ensign in the US Navy Reserve as an intelligence specialist in June 1945. That fall, he was assigned to the Office of the Deputy Chief of Naval Intelligence in Washington, DC.[3] Secretary of the Navy James Forrestal asked Skip to work with Forrestal's special assistant, Edward Willett, to perform an analysis of the Soviet government's international strategic ambitions. By this time, it was clear the US–USSR World War II–era alliance was rapidly disintegrating, and the navy secretary wanted to know whether the Soviets were likely to moderate their Communist philosophy or pursue an aggressive attack on Western capitalism. Skip blended easily into the intelligence team, having become friends with Forrestal's son Michael while at Princeton. Forrestal and Willett were also Princeton men. Willett and Skip soon wrote "The Philosophy of Communism," a report that concluded the

Soviets were pursuing a Marxist "messianic goal" of abolishing capitalism and that the United States should build an "invincible defense" and view the Soviet regime as its principal enemy.[4] In mid-January 1946, a week after Willett and Skip submitted their report, Forrestal made some minor changes and forwarded it to President Truman, the Senate Naval Affairs Committee, *Time* magazine publisher Henry Luce, and even the pope. Just nineteen years old, Skip later described this time as "a pretty heady experience."[5] Skip "briefed Willett on the ins and outs of Marxism, and Forrestal on Russia generally." Forrestal invited Skip to discuss Soviet policies at lunches with senior naval officers, and Skip briefed Admiral Chester Nimitz on Soviet financing of its military.

Skip was soon assigned to the operational branch of the Office of Naval Intelligence, a step toward becoming an intelligence operative.[6] On May 22, 1946, Skip and Ed met with Sidney Souers, who had become the first director of Central Intelligence earlier that year.[7] In August, Skip was assigned to the staff of Admiral Charles M. Cooke Jr., commander of the Seventh Fleet, as a Soviet intelligence specialist.[8] The Soviets were aiding Chairman Mao Zedong's Red Army in their civil war with the Chinese Nationalist forces, or Kuomintang, led by US ally Chiang Kai-shek. Skip's duties focused on collecting intelligence on Soviet activities in China. Skip also developed relationships with members of the Russian émigré community who had fled their homeland after the revolution of 1917 and now lived in fear of yet another Communist takeover — this time in China.[9]

The strategic northern Chinese region of Manchuria, with its vital ports of Dairen and Port Arthur — and its proximity to Korea — was a particular focus of US intelligence concerns. In 1945, when Soviet dictator Joseph Stalin met with President Roosevelt and British prime minister Winston Churchill in Yalta, the Allies were on the brink of victory over Germany. Roosevelt and Churchill sought to bring the war in the Pacific to a swift end as well by getting the Soviets to enter the war with Japan. Roosevelt and Churchill signed a secret accord promising Stalin that in exchange for the USSR entering the war against the Japanese, Dairen would be "internationalized" and the Soviet Union would jointly control with China the rail lines connecting Dairen to Soviet territory.[10]

On August 6, 1945, a US plane dropped the atomic bomb that destroyed Hiroshima, and three days after that, another American nuclear device leveled Nagasaki. The weapons were so devastating that from the first blast, it was widely believed the Japanese would surrender. On August 9 — the very same day as the Nagasaki bombing — the Soviet Red Army invaded Manchuria and engaged the Imperial Japanese Army.[11] Four days later, on August 13, Japan surrendered. Two days after that, Stalin and Chiang's emissary signed an accord confirming that Dairen would be a free port open to commerce and shipping of all nations and providing for the withdrawal of Soviet troops from China's northeastern provinces within three months.

With Japan out of the war, the Chinese Communists and the Kuomintang resumed their fierce civil war, and the Soviets rushed to aid their Chinese Communist allies. President Truman threw US support behind Chiang and the Kuomintang, sending planes and other military equipment to bolster the Nationalist army. As the struggle for China unfolded, George Kennan, working from the US embassy in Moscow, pushed the Soviets in March 1946 to permit the Americans to open a consulate in Dairen. Kennan, who a month earlier had written his "Long Telegram" to Secretary of State James Byrnes, warned Byrnes that Dairen would be run by KGB officials who are "bigoted and fanatical men, hostile to and suspicious of foreigners and inclined to keep particularly close watch on [British and Americans]." Kennan predicted that the Soviets would likely take every step to "cut off contact between" the US consular staff in Dairen and the US government.[12]

By May, Consul Merrill Benninghoff set up a consular office in Dairen, but the conditions were extremely tough, with limited supplies of coal for heating. In the following months, American diplomats struggled to communicate with Benninghoff because the Soviets tapped his phone lines and refused to let him use a radio, instead requiring him to send cables via Moscow.[13] Frustrated by the Soviet tactics, General George C. Marshall, whom President Truman had named as his special ambassador to China, began developing a plan in October 1946 to send courier ships to Dairen. Marshall sent the State Department a cable saying that the Seventh Fleet commander, Cooke, proposed sending a courier ship to "the open port of Dairen" once or twice per month.[14]

Soviet military authorities in Dairen claimed that Japanese troops were still active in the area and the streets were unsafe.[15] The Soviet commanding general in Dairen announced that his military would continue controlling Dairen because there was still a state of war in existence between his country and Japan. The Soviet general's suggestion was striking because Japan and the USSR had never been formally at war. The Americans perceived the general's claim as a fig leaf covering the Soviet Union's naked aggression in seizing Dairen.

In December 1946, Admiral Cooke proceeded with his plan to send a navy vessel, the LCI-1090, a landing craft infantry assault ship, to take a US diplomatic courier to Dairen.[16] A representative of an American oil company also joined the mission, the stated purpose of which included opening the port for commerce. To avoid the risk of provoking a military conflict, the vessel, which had a crew of twenty-four men, was stripped of its guns. Cooke also permitted a reporter for the Scripps Howard news service and a photographer for *Life* magazine on board. Cooke also assigned to the mission his Russian-speaking intelligence officer Skip Koons, who was twenty years old at the time.[17]

The LCI-1090 departed from Tsingtao on the morning of December 17 and arrived in Dairen on the morning of December 18, docked at a pier, and requested permission from Soviet authorities to remain in the harbor.[18] A Soviet officer granted the vessel a forty-eight-hour stay and permitted its captain and the US diplomatic courier to go ashore but blocked the journalists and the oil company representative from leaving the vessel.[19] Benninghoff tried to reach the Russian general in charge of Soviet forces in Dairen in a bid to extend the LCI-1090's stay, but the general refused to receive him.[20] Armed Chinese police under Soviet control patrolled the docks and prevented anyone from going ashore without a Soviet pass.

Skip went ashore to gather intelligence, though it is unclear how he managed to do so. He produced an intelligence report that described with military precision Soviet troop strength, gun emplacements, anti-aircraft guns, and bunkers as well as the harbor facilities, piers, shipping activity, city utilities, roads, and even the state of air transport to Vladivostok.[21] "The Intelligence Officer," Skip wrote, apparently referring to himself, "held conversations with six Soviet officers who alternately had charge of the Wharf Guard, and with members of the Staff of General Koshunoff. About half of these officers have been, according to their statements, in Dairen since it was first occupied by the Soviets. The other half had recently arrived from European duty by way of Vladivostok."

Skip described the encounter with Soviet officers, life for ordinary citizens in Dairen, and the challenging circumstances facing Consul Benninghoff in a letter to a favorite Princeton professor later that month. Omitting names, likely for security reasons, he painted a bleak picture of life in Dairen. "The sun shines, people walk on the streets, buy what little food they can, gossip, go to the movies . . . but this is not their life. They live terror, and the sun might just as well not be there, and life might just as well not exist, because the life inside the individual is dead, in its place is pitch blackness which is the nothingness in nothing."[22] He went on to describe a gathering of Americans late on a cold night at the consul's home, wondering whether a listening device was planted in a light fixture. Alcohol was served and a fire crackled in the fireplace, but it was a grim scene. Consul Benninghoff said he felt "expendable."

In a wrenching account, Skip described some five thousand Japanese "repatriates" being held at the end of the pier where the LCI-1090 was docked. Soviet officers claimed American ships were expected to come in early November to take them back to Japan, but the ships never arrived. Confined by the Soviets to the pier, the Japanese had little food and several committed suicide each day, Skip reported.[23]

Skip apparently engaged Soviet officers in conversation in an officers' club. Years later, after another confrontation with Soviet intelligence, he said he was reminded of "the last time I met up, in similar circumstances, with the KGB in a glacial Soviet Officers' Club, in Dairen, Manchuria. That time they nearly killed me . . . though in due course the command-ing Soviet general was authorized to apologize personally for the 'over-zealousness' of the 'security boys' . . . 'After all,' he laughed, 'you know you shouldn't have been there.'"[24] He somehow escaped from the officers' club and returned to the LCI-1090.

Tension filled the air as the LCI-1090's permitted forty-eight-hour stay in port drew to a close on December 20. At about 1:00 PM, a Soviet major, identifying himself as a personal representative of the Russian general, came aboard to deliver an ultimatum. He spoke loudly and aggressively in Russian and, as American sailors and Soviet troops looked on, Skip stepped forward to translate the Russian officer's words.[25] "Unless you leave within twenty minutes," Skip said in translating the major's barely veiled threat, "we will not be responsible for the consequences." With his vessel's weaponry removed, and facing Soviet and Chinese forces on shore, Commander Edgar Yates ordered the LCI-1090 to leave port and return to Tsingtao.

After the courier's return, the US consul general in Shanghai reported to Secretary of State Byrnes via cable on December 23 that the Soviet major had given a "verbal ultimatum" to the vessel to leave port. The consul, Monnett Davis, also told Byrnes that Admiral Cooke had taken the press representatives on the mission without getting Soviet permission first despite being given a warning that doing so would likely "anger Soviet authorities" and imperil the US effort to send couriers to the consulate in Dairen. Davis also said that the *Life* photographer had taken photos from the vessel and warned that "steps should be taken to prevent" publication of the photos in *Life*.[26]

On December 24, 1946, four days after the vessel departed from Dairen, the Scripps Howard reporter's account of the confrontation appeared on the front page of *The New York Times*, and the story quickly reverberated around the world. "Ensign Tilghman B. Koons of Plainfield, N.J., who speaks Russian, interpreted for the Senior Navy officer on board," the story said.[27] In Washington, a State Department spokesman, Lincoln White, downplayed the intensity of the encounter and the ultimatum translated by Skip. White said it was "not in any sense a fist-shaking affair." In Moscow, the Soviet government news agency Pravda denounced the news story as "the invention of an American correspondent." Two US naval officers on the mission, however, gave subsequent interviews backing up Koons. One of them said Skip had the Russian officer repeat his statement, perhaps as many as three times, to ensure a "perfectly accurate translation." In addition, Commander Yates reported to Cooke that the Russians had issued an ultimatum, and Cooke himself cabled the navy in Washington to say the news story that ran in the *Times* was accurate.[28]

The New York Times editorial board jumped into the fray, arguing that the troubling — and uncontested — point was that a Russian military officer was ordering the US to leave a port in China that was supposed to be open. It also noted that the Chinese Nationalist government,

America's ally, was eager to take over the administration of Dairen.[29] "We think that our own State Department, instead of apologizing for the action of the Dairen Russians, would be better advised to help China achieve this proper and reasonable object." *Time* magazine suggested the US government had failed to stand up for itself.[30] "If a similar incident had happened to a Russian ship in a US-controlled port, Soviet indignation would have blown the turrets off the Kremlin."

The navy, possibly at the behest of the Truman White House, later banned reporters from traveling on navy vessels to Soviet-controlled ports, and Dairen dropped out of the headlines. *Life* magazine never published the photos.[31] Yet the incident at Dairen was not forgotten. It later became a focal point of the Republicans' politically explosive charge that the Truman administration had lost China to the Communists due to pro-Communist sympathies within its own ranks. In June 1951, Senator Joseph McCarthy, who was then ratcheting up his anti-Communist campaign, took to the Senate floor to attack Marshall. He cited Dairen repeatedly and charged that at Yalta Roosevelt had surrendered to Stalin what he called the "historic levers of power over China — the ports of Dairen and Port Arthur and the Chinese Eastern and South Manchurian railways."[32] In McCarthy's conspiratorial worldview, Marshall had been "at Roosevelt's elbow" at Yalta urging the president to entice Stalin into the war against Japan, and later Marshall — as Truman's special ambassador to China — failed to take more aggressive action when the Soviets closed Dairen, consolidated their hold on Manchuria, and helped secure the Chinese Communists' ultimate victory. After Eisenhower and other Republican leaders jumped into the fray defending Marshall, the furor died down, though bitter charges over the loss of China to the Communists persist to this day.

The month following the Dairen incident, in January 1947, Secretary of the Navy Forrestal asked Kennan to review the report Skip had written with Ed Willett a year earlier, "The Philosophy of Communism." Kennan found the report to be alarmist and prepared an essay featuring his own more moderate recommendation as to how the United States should respond to Soviet aggression.[33] Kennan's essay, published in July 1947 in *Foreign Affairs* with the title "The Sources of Soviet Conduct" and under the mysterious byline of "X," called for a "long-term, patient but firm and vigilant containment of Russian expansive tendencies." Kennan's paper established "containment" as the precept that would influence American diplomatic policy toward the Soviets for years to follow.

Skip's intelligence activities took him far beyond Dairen. In Shanghai, he worked with Colonel G. K. Bologoff, chairman of the Russian Emigrants Association, considered an anti-Communist group. Back in Washington, the Central Intelligence Group, the predecessor organization to the CIA, was tracking the activities of Bologoff and other Russians in China.[34] In a letter to Skip in July 1948, Bologoff cryptically promised to assist Skip with a request the young intelligence officer had made. "I will do my best in selecting candidates who would answer your requirements both in their qualifications and political and personal qualities," Bologoff wrote. "I do hope that this work will be completed by me in a week's time and then I will immediately inform you of the results."[35] The exact nature of the project these "candidates" would perform remains secret.

Skip made regular trips to Nanking, the Philippines, Singapore, and Hong Kong. In August 1948, the naval attaché in Nanking (now Nanjing) requested that Skip be named assistant naval attaché in that city, but instead Skip was ordered back to Washington to serve again in the Office of Naval Intelligence.[36] He returned to Washington but soon resigned his commission to return to Princeton to complete his studies.[37]

In 1949, Skip graduated with honors from the university's Woodrow Wilson School, having written a senior thesis on the failure of US policy in China. In his thesis, Skip argued that Truman's State Department and Marshall had failed to react to obvious signs that the Soviets were supporting the Chinese Communists and had withheld crucial military support from Chiang Kai-shek, thus ensuring a Communist victory. He provided an account of the Dairen incident, saying that the State Department's assertion that the Soviets had not issued an ultimatum was "obviously at variance with the facts." As for General Marshall, Skip cast him as repeatedly turning a blind eye to Soviet assistance to the Chinese Communists.[38] Skip's views mirrored those of McCarthy and other Republican critics of Marshall and the Truman administration, though Skip's writing lacked the vitriol and unsupported accusations that were McCarthy's hallmarks.

Following his graduation from Princeton, Skip entered a doctoral program at the Sorbonne in Paris and obtained a Fulbright fellowship to support his study of the Russian émigré community in Europe, its political activities, and its potential usefulness to the United States in the struggle against Communism.[39] In June 1950, he was in Nice working on his dissertation at the home of a friend, Madame Miki Paronian, when he took a break from his work one night to visit nearby Cannes. He ventured into a well-known gay bar, Les Trois Cloches, on the same night that Steve Benedict also happened to be there alone.[40]

Benedict recalled:

> I sat at the end of a long, curved bar. At the far end, distinguished by his golden blonde hair, large lips and broad smile, was Skip Koons . . . We eyed each other at once and in no time were sitting side by side telling each other about ourselves, the whys and wherefores of our presence in Europe and our forthcoming plans . . . It was clear from the beginning that we would leave together and so we did before long, returning to my hotel. Our sexual encounter that first night was warm, affectionate, if not especially memorable. It seemed more important that we had each found a new and excitingly sympathetic friend, perhaps lover, whom we wanted to know and please.

Steve and Skip spent the next few days together in Cannes and Nice, and they reunited later in the summer for the last part of an auto trip Skip took with his mother, Peggy, and stepfather, Howard Lutz, in France and Italy. In Rome, the two young men made a day trip that followed in the footsteps of Gore Vidal, who had visited philosopher George Santayana at the Convent of the Blue Nuns in Rome. Skip and Steve went to the convent and had a wide-ranging conversation with the philosopher.[41] Steve and Skip reunited in Paris, where Skip had been living in servant quarters at the top of an apartment building on Avenue Paul-Doumer in the well-to-do 16th arrondissement. The two young men lived in the tiny apartment as lovers.[42] Skip resumed work on his dissertation for the Sorbonne, and Steve began helping him revise his Princeton thesis on China to prepare it for possible publication.

The decision to follow in Vidal's steps to Santayana's door was not pure happenstance. In June 1949, a year prior to his meeting Skip, Steve had met Vidal by chance in Paris as the two were checking into the Hotel de l'Université. For Steve, the encounter was momentous. Reading Vidal's *The City and the Pillar* had been transformational for him, illuminating his own experiences as a young gay man. Before his departure for Europe, Steve had even written Vidal a fan letter. Vidal's room turned out to be just a few steps from his own, and the next day he worked up the courage to knock on Vidal's door. They dined together several times at the hotel over the next week.[43] Several days into their acquaintance, Vidal introduced him to Charles "Chuck" Turner, a young man whom Vidal had picked up at the American Express office who, by extraordinary coincidence, was the same Charles Turner whom Skip had met four years earlier at the navy language school in Colorado. Turner, a violinist and composer, had come to Paris to study with Nadia Boulanger, a grande dame of French classical music. Steve found Turner musically knowledgeable, witty, intelligent, and attractive. They quickly made plans to play tennis the next day. "Hot and sweaty we returned to his room and almost immediately tumbled into bed together in a sexual encounter that was simple but satisfying," Steve recalled. "He was quite short, broad-shouldered and muscular with, Gore Vidal remarked to me later, a 'voluptuous' physique. I was quite smitten by him."

During that summer, Vidal spent time in Paris with his close friend, playwright Tennessee Williams, and also found time to squire Turner around the City of Light. Ned Rorem, a composer and memoirist living in Paris at the time, noted seeing Turner "on the arm of" Vidal.[44] Yet Vidal soon set Turner up with another man, the famous American composer Samuel Barber, who was Vidal's friend. For a decade, Barber had been companion and lover of Gian Carlo Menotti, a revered classical music composer, but both Barber and Menotti had now begun romantic relationships with other men.[45] In July 1949, Vidal told Steve Benedict that Barber had been struggling with a mental block in his composing, and so he intended to introduce Turner to Barber because he thought "Chuck Turner might be the person to get Sam out of his funk." Turner returned to the United States in the fall, met with Barber, and they soon became lovers.[46] Barber arranged for Turner to perform as violin soloist in recordings of Barber's music and in a series of performances in European capitals.

The cultural scene in Paris in the early 1950s was heady, particularly for American gay men who sensed liberation in the wake of publication of Vidal's *The City and the Pillar* and Kinsey's study of male sexuality. Just as Paris had beckoned to African American writers and artists eager to escape the brutal climate of discrimination in the United States, it offered relief to gays seeking to escape America's restrictive attitudes toward their sexuality. Ever since the audacious African American performer Josephine Baker had danced nude across the Parisian stage in the 1920s, Paris had been a beacon for sexual liberation to many Americans. Beyond Vidal and Williams, another gay writer at the time in Paris was the African American novelist, essayist, and social critic James Baldwin. At the same time, French intellectuals Albert Camus, Jean-Paul Sartre, Simone de Beauvoir, and Jean Genet all explored questions about race, class, and gender. Genet depicted the lives of homosexuals in his novels and plays. Sartre had explored the dilemmas faced by gays coming out of the closet in his 1943 existentialist tome, *Being and Nothingness*. These open discussions of homosexuality owed a debt to André Gide, whose 1902 novel, *The Immoralist*, was considered a brilliant portrait of homosexuality, shockingly open for its era. After Gide won the 1947 Nobel Prize for Literature, *The Immoralist* was reissued in English. The excitement of Parisian cultural life was palpable. Sartre and other writers sometimes gathered at cafés, like the famed Les Deux Magots on the Boulevard Saint-Germain, also frequented by Picasso and other artists.

Still, Benedict insisted that French openness toward homosexuality had nothing to do with his decision to move to Paris — he merely wanted to be with his lover, Skip. Finding the Parisian winter grim, the pair returned to sunny Cannes and rented an apartment overlooking the Mediterranean. Skip bought a Lambretta motor scooter, which they used for daily trips to the market and occasional getaways along the coast. They drank inexpensive wine packaged in skins from Morocco. They had a group of friends in Cannes, Nice, and elsewhere along the French Riviera who made life interesting. Foremost among them was Miki Paronian, an Armenian émigré and classical pianist who was a close friend of Nadia Boulanger.[47] Paronian also knew many other figures in the French musical and arts worlds. Steve played the piano for "Madame P" and once accompanied her to a concert by her friend pianist Alfred Cortot in Cannes.[48] Skip, meanwhile, continued to work on his dissertation for the Sorbonne. Despite their bohemian lifestyle, Skip hewed to his military responsibilities. In February 1951, he traveled to the US Navy base in Bremerhaven, Germany, for a fourteen-day active training duty in naval intelligence.[49]

He remained a navy reserve officer, regularly met with navy officers, and considered returning to his career in naval intelligence.

The idyll on the French Riviera was short-lived. Steve felt a need to resume his career and get on with his life back home in the United States. In September 1951, he left Cannes to return to New York in search of work, possibly with the US Information Agency and its Voice of America radio service. The two lovers had not broken up; yet each gave the other freedom to pursue relationships with other people. In New York, Steve resumed his relationship with Chuck Turner, and he detailed their romantic and sexual interludes in letters he sent back to Skip in Cannes.

With Steve gone, Skip stopped work on his dissertation and sank into what he would later call a minor nervous breakdown. "At night I lay awake until exhaustion as thoughts of you spun through my head," Skip wrote in a letter to Steve in October 1951.[50] "In any case, the crisis stage is past. It was that week that you spent in New York enjoying yourself living with Chuck and during which you did not have time to write . . . I have gone through the feeling of losing you a million times a day anyway . . . I told you it would be OK if you played around before you left. I knew you would." He signed the letter, "I love you, Skippo."

As he sought to pull himself out of this breakdown, Skip continued to see old friends and make new ones, such as Richard and Sheila Yates. Richard Yates, a fiction writer later known for his novel *Revolutionary Road*, had been a boyhood friend of Steve's at the Scarborough School, and Steve introduced Skip to the Yateses from a distance after he returned to New York.

Soon Skip recovered his energy. He sold the Lambretta, gave his vinyl records to the Yateses, and moved into a hotel room in Paris's 6th arrondissement. "Now about my sex life," he wrote Steve in November. "Now sex statistics show that the average desire is once or twice a week. But gay people, by their nature are much more promiscuous, due to many factors . . . Guy came on Tuesday per schedule and was quite happy to. Didn't mind being screwed and didn't give any indication of wanting to screw." Three days later, Skip met a Swedish boy at a bar and "decided to give that a try . . . It was rather a dirty trick too. After screwing him, he wanted to do same to you know who, and I of course would have none of it."[51]

Back in New York, Steve had begun seeking employment with Voice of America, the federal government's radio agency. For Skip and Steve, both interested in positions in government service, the threat of exposure loomed. As an intelligence officer, Skip was all too aware that letters could be opened, revealed carelessly, or otherwise cause significant problems for gays. In one letter, Skip warned Steve about security: "I certainly hope you are burning these letters."[52]

The idea of living life openly as a gay person caused Skip considerable unease, and he felt he and Steve diverged on this important point. He was particularly concerned about Steve's friendships with Turner, Barber, and Menotti. "What makes you think I will want to know Sam, Gian-Carlo, or even Chuck in the intimate friendly way you have accepted, in joining their 'group'?" Skip asked in a letter in December 1951.

> Just as it is natural that you get on better with Chuck than he with me (you are both musicians) so it is natural that my interests do not lead me primarily into close friendship with a musical group of people — and least of all, internationally known "gay" people. Are those the circles we are going to be known in? To you it seems very natural, I see. To me, it is not. Nor am I sure that my "best interests" are served by circulating in such groups. Or do you want me to make an absolute choice and let the State Department be able to put down "KH," known you know what, by my name?[53]

Skip needed to avoid being branded a "Known Homosexual" to remain active in government and the struggle against Communism, so he concluded that the days of his gay trysts in Europe must draw to a close. One tactic he adopted to ensure he could continue to pursue his career in government service was to play the role of a heterosexual, including with a young woman named Monique. In January 1952, Skip wrote Steve that Monique had come over on a Wednesday evening.[54] "She came after I had had dinner, flopped herself down on the bed clearly showing she had come expressly for that . . . was able to screw her twice, and that way I hope definitely reestablish my reputation as a 'male.'" Then he added: "While I was doing it was reminded of all the Chinese and Philippine whores I have gone through the act with. The whole process seemed — rudimentary, unsubtle, and mechanically animal. I used rubbers, I hasten to assure you." In early February, he noted that his prior weekend included sex twice with Monique, but also twice with an "English boy." While Skip suggested his sex with Monique was merely intended to hide his homosexuality, he indeed pursued this ruse vigorously.

Despite his worries that Steve's circle of gay friends would derail his career, Skip was still a music fanatic — and this led him directly into contact with Steve's musical friends. Nearly every missive he sent to Steve included an account of some opera, classical concert, or other live performance he had attended, often with a critique for this or that performer. Skip also could not resist a chance to meet with Barber when the famed composer visited Paris in March 1952. Barber called Skip's hotel room and asked him to have a drink at Les Deux Magots, an invitation Skip readily accepted. "Soon there was a whole flock of artists (and their little boys, or other hangers-on) about us, and the crowd kept growing," Skip wrote Steve. "Doda Conrad [the singer] showed up, and — oh yes, true to form — started pestering Barber to write some songs dedicated to him. Ugh."

Meanwhile, back in New York, Steve learned from a friend that the research director at Citizens for Eisenhower, the group seeking to build support for Eisenhower to run for president, was looking for an assistant. Steve got an appointment to see Gabriel Hauge, an economics writer on leave from *Business Week*, at the McGraw-Hill building on West 42nd Street. Hauge asked Benedict if he knew of anything that might embarrass the campaign, and Benedict unhesitatingly lied and said no. The interview went well, and Hauge hired Benedict to be his assistant shortly thereafter.

Skip continued to lay the groundwork to be sure Steve and he could survive security checks. He went to visit a former landlady who knew the relationship between the two young men to discuss the possibility that FBI investigators might ask her questions. "She gave the impression of complete loyalty and meaning well, so that's covered." Skip also defended his having sex with Monique as helpful in building a cover story. "You should not be bothered emotionally by Monique, other than a certain amount of natural jealousy. What is most important now is that my reputation be snowy white in the FBI investigation — and as you certainly know, Monique contributes greatly towards that result. You sometimes forget, or undervalue, how much of me is tied to serving the cause I believe in, in the way I feel I must — through the govt. I cannot permit myself to be barred that means of service." He added that his relationship with Monique "also gives me a sexual outlet . . ."

In New York, Steve and Chuck were in their final rehearsals for a violin and piano recital they were to give at the Scarborough School on February 15, 1952. Chuck's relationship with Samuel Barber had intensified personally and professionally, and it soon became clear that Chuck and Steve could no longer continue their romantic trysts. "The erotic aspect of our relationship went out with a bang, so to speak, with a passionate encounter on the stage floor of the Scarborough School theatre after we had gone through our recital program the day before the concert," Benedict said.[55] The next evening, Barber and Menotti came to watch Chuck and Steve perform. Debussy's Violin and Piano Sonata was the climax.

Shortly after the recital at the Scarborough School, Steve began working as Hauge's assistant in the Citizens for Eisenhower offices at the Hotel Marguery on Park Avenue at 47th Street. When Skip got the news, he sent Steve a congratulatory note and added that he "wouldn't mind doing something in that line myself later." Yet for all his interest in national security issues and the struggle against Communism, Skip was still enjoying a freewheeling and occasionally reckless Parisian lifestyle. "Alright, alright!" he wrote to Steve:

> At 6 PM I went into the Montana, sat at the bar, next to me was a very nice young English boy, in the designing business. It turned out he had been in town for just a night, was flying back on the 7 PM plane . . . He was interested though, so rushed him up and then rushed him out to a plane. It all took only 30 minutes. I couldn't have cared less whether I had any energy left for Monique or not, as it turned out I did. Hence, the comical nature of Skippo's actions that day.[56]

This was Skip's last epistle to Steve on his sexual adventures. Henceforward, as Skip approached his reentry into the world of US intelligence and national security activities, his letters omitted references to any sexual conduct with men or women and were tight-lipped in discussing any gay friends.

Within the next two weeks, Skip successfully defended his dissertation at the Sorbonne, received his doctoral degree, and boarded a ship to New York. He spent time with his mother and stepfather in Pennsylvania, traveled to Washington for job hunting, and visited Steve in New York. He then traveled to Munich as an employee of the American Committee for the Liberation of the Peoples of Russia Inc., known as AMCOMLIB, a CIA front organization that was preparing to broadcast anti-Communist radio programming in Russian to the Soviet Union.

AMCOMLIB, with support from figures such as George Kennan, Frank Wisner, and Charles Bohlen at the State Department, was created to fight Soviet propaganda and provide information to people in the USSR, where freedom of speech was suppressed and the crimes of Stalin's regime remained hidden. The broadcasts, it was hoped, would nourish a yearning for freedom and undermine the Communist lock on political power. With support from the CIA and the State Department, AMCOMLIB had been launched in 1951 with the intention of having Soviet dissidents take the lead in creating broadcasts.[57] Yet this mission proved daunting, as exile groups had their own internal disputes that made collaboration challenging. Even the name of the organization, with its reference to "the peoples of Russia," proved a challenge, as various nationalities voiced objections to Russian domination.[58]

Skip and his AMCOMLIB colleagues sought to build an émigré group to carry out the broadcasts. In October 1952, Skip wrote Steve, "Ten days ago, after two years of quarreling and failure, the majority of the parties we have been dealing with finally managed to formulate enough compromises on their view of what the future of Russia should be to enable them to form a Political Center, baptized the Political Center of Anti-Communist Struggle."[59] He added that the disputes were briefly interrupted by the "good news" that Eisenhower had won the presidential election. The challenges facing AMCOMLIB dragged on, however, and the Russian-language broadcasts did not commence until March 1, 1953.[60] Decades later, these broadcasts into the Soviet Union would be credited with contributing significantly to the demise of Soviet Communism.

Steve, who had worked closely with Hauge on the Eisenhower campaign, was asked soon after the election to join him in the White

House as his assistant. In December, the month before Eisenhower's inauguration, Steve wrote Skip that, in the hope of finding him a job, he had given an outline of Skip's manuscript on China to Hauge, who promptly forwarded it to secretary of state designate Foster Dulles. Steve's efforts to interest Bobby in Skip Koons led Bobby to offer Skip a post at the center of the White House national security apparatus.

8

REFORMING AND RUNNING THE NSC

On January 20, 1953, before a large crowd gathered at the west front of the US Capitol, Dwight D. Eisenhower was inaugurated as the thirty-fourth president of the United States. After taking the oath of office, and surrounded by political leaders of both parties, he uttered a prayer to God calling for the ability "to discern clearly right from wrong."[1] Then, sounding an alarm over the dawning threat of nuclear war, he said that science was poised to give us "the power to erase human life from this planet."

The first order of business the following day was the swearing-in of Ike's executive assistants: first Sherman Adams, then Bobby Cutler, spokesman James Hagerty, economic adviser Gabriel Hauge, and speech-writer Emmet Hughes. Ike had made clear a few weeks earlier that Bobby would restructure the National Security Council and then lead it, but for now his title was simply "Administrative Assistant to the President."[2] Two hours later, Secretary of State Foster Dulles and other cabinet members were sworn in.

Cold War conflicts topped the new president's agenda. Ike had pledged to end the bloodshed in Korea. He wanted to quickly find a resolution to the war, shore up the South Korean government, and head off Chinese threats against other US allies. The Soviet Union was advancing its production of nuclear weapons and sought to spread Communism across Eastern Europe and elsewhere around the planet. In Iran, a popularly elected premier had nationalized a giant English oil company, and seething British officials were urging the United States to overthrow Iran's government. The CIA was concerned about the spread of Communism into the Western Hemisphere, as Guatemala's democratically elected government began showing signs of a leftward shift.

Bobby's role in the new administration came quickly to the attention of Joseph Alsop, who published a syndicated column with his brother Stewart. Bobby had been friends with Joe since 1930, when

Alsop joined the Porcellian Club at Harvard. Both men also served on the Harvard Board of Overseers and saw each other at meetings.[3] One morning shortly after the inauguration, Joe stopped by Bobby's office in the Executive Office Building and asked him to provide information about the administration anonymously.[4] Bobby refused. "I was to be exclusively engaged in the most sensitive matters in Government," he told Joe. "If the national interest required that any matter in that area should be disclosed, the President (or someone he should select) should make the disclosure."

Joe, a relative of both Presidents Theodore and Franklin Roosevelt, already had many sources across Washington. He was close friends with key CIA figures like Richard Bissell and Frank Wisner, for example. Yet he wanted a source inside the White House, and he was not easily put off.[5] The day after Bobby refused his request, Alsop sent him a letter warning that Truman's secretary of state, Dean Acheson, paid dearly for taking such a stance. "A very large part of Dean Acheson's troubles derived from his refusal to have anything to do with reporters," Joe wrote. "If an administration wants to explain its policies and to gain dependable support for them, the press is the only recourse. A man in your position can make an invaluable contribution to this end."[6] Unmoved, Bobby replied a few days later in a letter defending his "passion for anonymity" and again refusing to leak information: "An Administrative Assistant must occupy a strictly confidential relation to the President." Still, Bobby signed off with a friendly flourish referring to their mutually admired Porcellian Club, "Yours in P.C."

Bobby showed Alsop's letter to Ike and said to the president, "I told him that, under the arrangement I have with you as your Special Assistant, I couldn't possibly do what he asked. In fact, I told him I could not talk with him again about a matter of this kind." Ike replied, "That goes for me, too."[7]

"My dear Mr. Cutler," Director of the FBI J. Edgar Hoover began a January 28 letter to Bobby, offering assistance and outlining the FBI's work with the NSC. Hoover also invited Bobby to the next meeting of the Interdepartmental Intelligence Committee, which had recently developed the proposed rules identifying "sexual perversion" as a factor in security risk investigations.[8] Thus began a relationship that would take many twists in the years ahead. "My dear Mr. Hoover," Bobby responded two days later, thanking him for the "very able assistance" of the FBI liaison officer to the NSC, J. Patrick Coyne. Hoover soon began sending a stream of letters to Bobby regarding secret FBI investigations and an array of subjects related to national security.

While Bobby was eager to reform the NSC, the rush of international developments commanded immediate attention. Under Truman, the NSC held its meetings on Thursdays, and Eisenhower's NSC would do the same, beginning on Thursday, January 29. Prior to the meeting's start, Bobby and NSC executive secretary James Lay met privately with Eisenhower to prepare. Once the meeting started, retired army general Walter Bedell "Beetle" Smith, who served as Truman's CIA director and still held that position, delivered an oral briefing on world developments. The NSC also reviewed Ike's first cautious steps toward ending the Korean War — he had approved a request by the Joint Chiefs of Staff to activate two more divisions, raising the troop ceiling to 460,000 soldiers on the peninsula.[9]

Smith, an old friend of Eisenhower's who had been his chief of staff during World War II, had the president's ear. Eleven days later, Eisenhower named Smith undersecretary of state, leaving the CIA director's post empty. Ike was still hesitating over his choice to replace Smith as CIA director, and he had received opinions that gave him pause about one candidate, Allen Dulles, the current CIA deputy director and Foster's younger brother. After President Truman named Smith director of the CIA in 1950, Smith had recruited Allen to be its "deputy director of plans." After seeing Allen operate for two years, Smith was uncomfortable with the idea of his taking over as CIA director, as he considered Allen likely to pursue extravagant covert actions.[10] He "worried what Allen would do with the expanding resources of the CIA without a cool hand to guide him," as one historian noted.

After graduating from Princeton in 1914, Allen worked for the State Department as head of intelligence at the US embassy in Bern, Switzerland. After World War I ended, he obtained a law degree from George Washington University and joined Foster's firm, Sullivan & Cromwell, in 1926. Allen joined the new spy agency that President Roosevelt established during World War II, the Office of Strategic Services (OSS). In late 1942, he traveled to Switzerland, where for the next three years he orchestrated espionage against German forces.

Perhaps his greatest wartime success was Operation Sunrise, in which he secretly negotiated with an SS commander in Italy to arrange the surrender of German forces in that country in May 1945. After the war ended, Allen returned to Sullivan & Cromwell. Following the CIA's creation in 1947, Allen took temporary leave from the firm to help direct a covert ten-million-dollar campaign by the agency to help Italy's Christian Democrats win election over the Communist Party.[11]

In the end, however, Eisenhower concluded the two able and energetic Dulles brothers could dramatically reshape US foreign policy, as he had promised American voters he would do. Yet he also put in place a plan to ensure that the new Eisenhower foreign policy would be just that — *his* foreign policy, not theirs. Ike had embraced Bobby's ideas about reforming the NSC and related bodies, and these strengthened policy mechanisms would help him maintain control over covert actions proposed by the Dulleses — or anyone else.

Eisenhower surrounded the Dulles brothers with people who were more moderate than they were. Most significantly, in naming Smith undersecretary of state, Ike placed him in a post from which Smith would work closely with the secretary of state. Then there was Bobby, a moderate Republican with a record of reaching compromises with Democrats. Eisenhower nominated Henry Cabot Lodge Jr., Bobby's old friend who was central to Ike's decision to seek the presidency, to act as US representative to the United Nations. The president also chose Charles Bohlen, a career diplomat who had a track record of communicating effectively with the Soviets, to be ambassador to the Soviet Union. In the end, Eisenhower created a team of men with the expectation that the structure Bobby helped design for setting policy would forge their differing views into a single powerful national security strategy. The approach echoed Ike's leadership style in World War II, where he abided headstrong leaders like General George Patton and Field Marshal Bernard Montgomery, who at times seemed erratic or haughty, because they were effective and he was confident he could manage them through the general staff procedures he created.[12]

Ike perceived the NSC as having a special role in running the government. After Admiral Charles Cooke wrote the president a letter urging more effective use of the NSC, Ike replied on February 18 expressing full agreement:

I look upon the Council as the most important single agency in the Executive Department and, like you, I do not believe it has had the staff and prestige to do its job in the past. With this in mind, I gave a good deal of thought to finding a man to head the senior staff who would have the stature, experience and ability to energize the operation and command the respect and cooperation of the Cabinet and the military services. I think we have such a man in Robert Cutler, who is presently assigned as my personal assistant for National Security Council matters. I am in close daily touch with Cutler and, despite our newness here and the complexities of the security field, I feel that he is getting hold of the situation quickly and well.[13]

The Senate confirmed Allen Dulles's appointment to be the new CIA director on February 26, and he would soon work with Bobby and others as the Eisenhower team faced a dramatic turn of events. At about 2:00 AM on March 4, Allen called Bobby to inform him that Soviet dictator Joseph Stalin had apparently had a stroke and was near death. The CIA director asked whether he should wake the president, and Bobby said no, noting that Eisenhower woke typically at six thirty. "As I waited, sleepless, I became convinced that here was a moment in time that should be seized upon and not allowed to slip by. The President should speak out for the Free World. He should speak for our American people to the Russian people," Bobby wrote.[14] "Not a message to provoke trouble. Just what an ordinary citizen of our country would say, if he could, to a citizen of the other."

That morning, the president met in the Oval Office with Bobby, Allen Dulles, spokesman Jim Hagerty, and C.D. Jackson, Ike's advisor on psychological warfare. Bobby offered a draft statement for the president to make. Jackson, seeing Stalin's apparent demise as a unique opportunity for a propaganda blow, wanted a longer statement. Later that day, when the NSC met, Foster Dulles opposed releasing any comments, voicing concern that it might be seen as an attempt to foment rebellion in the Soviet Union. Secretary of Defense Charles Wilson also warned that a statement that sought to "go over the heads of the bosses of Soviet Russia" and appeal to the people to "overthrow their masters" could "boomerang."[15]

Ultimately, the NSC endorsed the idea of making a statement, blending the drafts proposed by Bobby and C. D. into the president's words released later that day.[16] "At this moment in history when multitudes of Russians are anxiously concerned because of the illness of the Soviet ruler, the thoughts of America go out to all the people of the USSR — the men and women, the boys and girls — in the villages, cities, farms, and factories of their homeland," the president's remarks began. They continued in a similar respectful tone, a solemn break with the hostile verbal volleys that had come to characterize the Cold War.

Bobby soon presented to the president a secret twenty-page report outlining his proposed reform of the NSC, accompanied by a four-page summary letter. Among other things, Bobby's March 16 report proposed creation of a new position, the "Special Assistant to the President for National Security Affairs," who would serve as the "principal executive officer" of the NSC and would ensure that the president's "views as to policy-planning are carried out."[17] Prior to Bobby's proposal, there had been no position identified as the principal executive for the NSC and no person designated as responsible for setting the agenda for NSC meetings. Now, under Bobby's proposal, the new special assistant for national security affairs would have specific authority to work with the president to set the agenda for council meetings and to brief the president prior to the council's meetings.

Bobby's proposal replicated a system that had worked effectively for him in his years with Stimson and Marshall: Rather than being a decision maker, he preferred to make his contribution behind the scenes as the adviser, analyst, and top assistant to the decision maker — in this case, the president. Bobby did not propose himself — or anyone else — for the position of special assistant for national security. Yet it was evident that he was creating his own position.

Bobby also proposed that the special assistant for national security affairs serve as the chairman of a new staff for the NSC, which was to be called the Planning Board. The Planning Board was to analyze and debate policies before they were placed before the NSC itself. The board would be "composed of top-flight personnel to be appointed by the President from the departments and agencies," Bobby wrote. These staff members were expected to straddle both worlds — their own executive agencies and the Planning Board, with their primary responsibility being to the latter.

Prior to Bobby's reform, the NSC had played a limited role in development of national security policy since its creation under the 1947 National Security Act. President Truman placed little value in the work of the NSC and attended only twelve of its fifty-one meetings prior to the outbreak of the Korean War in June 1950.[18] Typically, national security policy was developed by a single agency, advanced to the president's office, perhaps reviewed briefly by the NSC, and then adopted by the NSC. This was the case with one of the Truman administration's most significant national security policies, NSC-68. Truman asked the State and Defense Departments in early 1950 to prepare a policy on how to respond to aggression from the Soviet Union. In response, Paul Nitze, who replaced George Kennan as the State Department's director of policy planning, chaired a committee that developed a fifty-four-page report and delivered it to the NSC in April. The policy, which called for a rapid buildup in American military forces, received little attention until after North Korea's invasion of South Korea in June 1950. Three months later, President Truman approved the report as NSC-68.[19] Bobby knew from his experience with the Psychological Strategy Board that too often national security policies conflicted or favored one agency over another. In Bobby's view, the national security policy process was flawed, and this undermined America's security.

Bobby's reform was aimed at establishing the NSC as the president's primary mechanism for formulating national security policy. This included extending the NSC's authority over the CIA. His plan noted specifically that the National Security Act placed the CIA "under the direction of" the NSC. Bobby would later describe this preeminent place of the NSC as being at the "Top of Policy Hill." He wrote: "I was convinced that the procedures we developed were the Chief Executive's best protection against pressure for *ex parte* decisions, against special pleading, imprecise guidance, and suppression of conflicting views."[20]

When it came to the president's role, Bobby trod lightly, not wanting to restrict him. Under law, the president was not required to use the NSC at all, and he could work with the NSC in any way he wished. Yet Bobby also knew from many conversations with Ike that he fully intended to use the NSC to set national security policy and steer his administration. Bobby proposed that the president, designated as chairman of the NSC, take a lead in managing its meetings. "The President as Chairman should lead the discussion at Council Meetings. He should exercise that leadership by asking for views around the table so as to bring out conflicts and so as to create a sense of team participation among those present in making the policy which they must later carry out."[21] That was the vision. In practice, in the months and years to follow Bobby often introduced agenda items and asked for comments, though final decisions on policy were always the president's alone.

On March 17, just one day after Bobby delivered his report to Ike, the president approved Bobby's reform of the NSC in a one-page letter addressed to him. "I approve both your letter and the recommendations, and direct that they be circulated promptly to the Council for information and guidance."[22] He told Bobby the people nominated for positions on the Planning Board were first to be "approved by you," and then "I can decide on their appointments."

The following Sunday, Bobby went to the White House to meet with Eisenhower for an hour and a half before going to church. Ike told Bobby he was going to appoint him as the special assistant for national security affairs. The next day, Monday, March 23, barely two months into the new presidency, the White House issued a news release announcing the president's "attention to strengthening and improving the operations of the National Security Council." The release said the president, vice president, secretary of state, secretary of defense, and other senior cabinet officers would regularly attend NSC meetings. The release also announced Bobby's appointment as special assistant for national security affairs.

Two weeks after the White House announcement, *Time* magazine profiled Bobby, mentioning his novels, his career as a banker, his love of bicycling, and his reputation for energetic management of the NSC.[23] "He probably carries more top secrets in his head than any other man in Washington," it said. Asked about the subject of his novels, Bobby replied, "Love, love. What else does a young man write about?"

As Bobby began hiring the staff for his revamped NSC, his young friend from the campaign train, Hauge's assistant Steve Benedict, saw an opportunity to locate a job in the White House for his former lover, Skip Koons. Skip was still in Munich developing anti-Soviet radio broadcasting for the CIA front organization, AMCOMLIB. On March 30, Steve wrote Skip a letter describing an open NSC position for which he might be an ideal candidate. Two days later, Steve wrote to Bobby describing

Skip as a Princeton graduate, a former Office of Naval Intelligence officer who spoke Russian and worked under Forrestal, a Republican, and a hard worker.[24] He even mentioned the Dairen incident. When Steve spoke with Bobby about Skip, Bobby said Skip seemed "absolutely perfect for the job he envisaged," a staff assistant post.[25]

Steve also sent Bobby a memo attaching Eisenhower's news release about the reform of the NSC, adding, "It strongly confirmed my opinion that Koons is your man."[26] On April 7, Bobby sent Skip a letter offering him a post on the NSC staff. "On the basis of recommendations recently furnished me, I would like to invite you to join the staff of the National Security Council pending clearance by the Federal Bureau of Investigation . . ." Bobby had already obtained approval for hiring Skip from AMCOMLIB's president, Admiral Leslie Stevens, and he expected Koons, who was still in Munich, to report the week of May 11.[27]

While the new administration placed emphasis on security and background investigations by the FBI, there is no evidence that the FBI ever probed Skip's background and completed a background report — the very sort of scrutiny Skip had been so worried about.[28] It may be that his experience at the CIA and in naval intelligence enabled Skip to avoid a formal FBI background check. On April 28, Skip signed a "personal history statement," which he forwarded to Bobby. Bobby soon put him to work on one of the most comprehensive Cold War strategy planning sessions of the Eisenhower administration.

In early May, Foster Dulles invited his brother Allen, Bobby, Beetle Smith, and C. D. Jackson to his home in Washington on a Sunday afternoon. The secretary of state outlined a plan for holding a secret conference to settle on a strategic policy toward Communism. Foster Dulles proposed that this conference be held within the framework of the NSC, recently revised under Bobby's reform. Foster Dulles proposed consideration of three core concepts: (1) a general goal of containment of Communism, as had been the policy of President Truman; (2) drawing a sharper line around the USSR, with a threat of attack if the Soviets violated that line; and (3) aggressively moving to roll back Communism in countries where it could be attacked.[29] Beetle Smith proposed the idea of using three teams, each advocating for one of the three strategy alternatives, and recommended that Bobby draft an outline of the mechanics and take it to the president.

Foster Dulles proposed this idea at a time when the administration was awash in competing approaches to the Soviet Union. For years he had called for a more aggressive policy to roll back Communism, charging that Truman, Secretary of State Dean Acheson, and others in Truman's administration had appeased the Soviet and Chinese Communists. Yet President Eisenhower, who had benefited from anti-Truman rhetoric during the campaign, was nonetheless a proponent of moderation, as shown by his willingness to appoint Bohlen as ambassador to Moscow and his well-known defense of General Marshall. Now Bobby's reform of the NSC created a new hurdle for the Dulles brothers: The NSC was dedicated to ensuring that all opinions be brought into the White House's national policy discussions. Under these circumstances, Foster Dulles knew he would need to channel his efforts into the new NSC framework, which he now embraced.

The next day, Bobby entered the president's office and laid out with excitement Foster Dulles's idea. "Mr. President, it was the most eloquent unfolding of the worldwide scene I ever heard," Bobby said. "His plan seems a fine way to crank up our first comprehensive basic national security policy operation for the Council."[30] Eisenhower replied, "Sounds like a conspiracy! But not a bad one." The president went on to propose meeting the following Thursday with Foster Dulles and Smith in the Solarium, a small sunlit room on the roof of the White House.

At the meeting, Foster Dulles laid out his concept of the three alternatives to be considered, and Smith proposed that the task forces meet in a place where they would draw little attention, the National War College in Washington. He also recommended that General James Doolittle, famed for leading a secret mission to bomb Tokyo in April 1942, be placed over one of the task forces. "I tell you what, get Jimmy Doolittle to head up such a group. He's tough-minded and gets things done," Bobby recalled Eisenhower saying.[31] As the men left, Bobby asked whether the plan might be called Operation Solarium, and Ike agreed.

As the plan moved forward, Ike privately formulated his views about Foster Dulles, which he recorded in his diary on May 14. "I still think of him, as I always have, as an intensive student of foreign affairs. He is well-informed and, in this subject at least, is deserving, I think, of his reputation as a 'wise' man,'" the president wrote. "He is not particularly persuasive in presentation and, at times, seems to have a curious lack of understanding as to how his words and manner may affect another personality."[32] Ike, who had long understood that his lieutenants had qualities good and bad, showed balance in his appraisal of the secretary of state and other administration officials. He mentioned Bobby among a second tier of officials who he said are "likewise important in the administration."

Bobby prepared a top-secret memorandum summarizing the concept for Operation Solarium's three teams, naming a series of candidates for participation in a panel that would write the "terms of reference" — the framework — for each of the Operation Solarium teams. An NSC working committee composed of Bobby, Allen Dulles, and Beetle Smith would plan the project.[33] Bobby also designated Skip, just days into his employment with the NSC, executive secretary of the committee and the three teams.

Ultimately, Doolittle led a group that oversaw selection of the three task forces with assistance from Bobby and Skip.[34] George Kennan led Task Force A, which was to advocate the thesis of maintaining the sort of containment policy Kennan had originally supported within the Truman administration. This, in itself, was a dramatic selection. The Truman administration had reacted with increasing vigor to the spread of Communism and in 1950 adopted Paul Nitze's hard-line approach with NSC-68. Kennan felt Truman overreacted and continued to urge the Truman administration to moderation in its efforts to contain Communism. Selecting Kennan to lead Task Force A signaled that the Eisenhower administration respected his views and was interested in at least exploring a moderate alternative to Nitze's approach to containment.

Indeed, Kennan's selection came at the end of a behind-the-scenes struggle in the Eisenhower administration over Nitze and Kennan. Secretary of State Dulles did not offer Kennan a position in the new administration, effectively forcing Kennan to resign. But Bobby opposed Nitze as the State Department's representative on the Planning Board. Bobby made his feelings clear in notes that wound up in NSC files: "Not acceptable to RC as State Dept PB member."[35] As an alternative, Foster Dulles nominated Robert Bowie to be State's representative on the Planning Board, which Bobby and then Ike approved.

The next Solarium group, Task Force B, was to advocate the thesis that the best response to Soviet aggression was more rigorous enforcement of the containment policy — with a threat of military response. Major General James McCormack, an early proponent of the development of thermonuclear weapons, led this task force.

Task Force C advanced the strategy of an aggressive approach to fighting Communism — Foster Dulles's call for a "rollback" of Soviet expansionism — through a variety of methods. Admiral Richard Conolly, whose wartime responsibilities included commanding US Navy destroyers in the Pacific Ocean, was its leader.

The three task forces met secretly for a full day on July 16, 1953, at the War College to present their cases. Eisenhower, Vice President Nixon, Bobby, Smith, Foster and Allen Dulles, the Joint Chiefs of Staff, and numerous cabinet officers along with Skip and other NSC staff members were in attendance. At the end of a question period, Eisenhower addressed the participants: "The American people have demonstrated their reluctance after a war is ended to take the necessary action to properly occupy the territory conquered in order to gain our legitimate ends. What would we do with Russia, if we should win a global war?" he asked. The rhetorical question must have fallen like a heavy stone in the room. Many of those present hungered to wipe out Communism, and yet Eisenhower's question made it clear that starting a war for that purpose would be senseless. Next, the president suggested that it would require not just military force, but diplomacy and persuasion, to free the Soviet Union from Communism: "The United States has to persuade her allies to go along with her, because our forward bases are in the territories of our allies."[36]

Ike set the tone for policy toward the Soviet Union, yet after he left the meeting, the three teams remained in "strong disagreement" over an array of issues. "When I reported this back to the president, he seemed very put out and left it to me to work what I thought best," Bobby wrote in a memo. Ike told Bobby to instruct Nixon not to prepare a presentation of the facts "and left me the working out of the other details." In the following weeks and months, Bobby, assisted by Skip, worked with the three teams and the NSC Planning Board to prepare a new NSC policy on national strategy toward the Soviet Union.

The resulting statement of basic national security policy came before the NSC on October 29, 1953. The policy stated that the major deterrent against a Soviet attack on Western Europe was the "manifest determination of the United States to use its atomic capability and massive retalia-

Bobby Cutler at age 2 in 1897. *Courtesy of the Eisenhower Library*

Mary Cutler and her sons in 1904 at the Cutler family log cabin in New Brunswick, Canada. Top row, from left: John, George and Roger. Bottom row, from left: Bobby and Elliott. *Courtesy of the Eisenhower Library*

Bobby in costume as Sir Harcourt
Courtly in the Volkmann School
production of the play, *London
Assurance.* *Courtesy of the Eisenhower Library*

Cutler family home at 61 Heath Street in Brookline, Massachusetts. *Courtesy of the Eisenhower Library*

Bobby and his mother Mary
Wilson Cutler, in about 1913.
Courtesy of the Eisenhower Library

18-year-old Bobby and an
unidentified friend, June 1914.
Courtesy of Stephen Benedict

Bobby's father, George C. Cutler, ensured the family remained tied to its Maine heritage and the outdoors life.

Courtesy of the Eisenhower Library

The five Cutler brothers with their father, George. Bobby is in the front to the right of his father.

Courtesy of the Eisenhower Library

Bobby at US Army training camp in Plattsburgh, NY, 1915, front row first from right. *Courtesy of the Eisenhower Library*

Bobby on the *Harvard Law Review* Board of Editors, 1921, front row second from left. *Courtesy of the Eisenhower Library*

Bobby and Nell Sears on the beach in the Bahamas in 1928. *Courtesy of the Eisenhower Library*

Bobby, his brothers and other friends playing nude on a Bahamian beach in 1928. *Courtesy of the Eisenhower Library*

Bobby helps Nell Sears over a low wall in the Bahamas in 1928. *Courtesy of the Eisenhower Library*

Bobby, William S. Patten and Chandler Bigelow crossing the Atlantic in 1930. *Courtesy of the Eisenhower Library*

Jean Sears, Emily Sears Lodge, Chan Bigelow, Bobby and Henry Cabot Lodge Jr. on a Caribbean cruise in 1933.

tory striking power if the area is attacked." It also called for normalizing nuclear weapons "as available for use as other munitions." The policy statement, eventually called NSC 162/2, also warned that excessive government spending would harm national security by weakening the US economy and called for balancing the budget of the federal government.[37] Treasury Secretary George Humphrey described the new policy as a "revision of our whole military strategy." Ike cautioned that abrupt changes could cause "political and morale problems," but he wanted to look forward to this "new concept" for US defense. The policy statement became the basis of what was called Eisenhower's "New Look" defense strategy.[38]

9

IKE'S PECULIAR BAN ON GAYS

Eisenhower won the 1952 presidential race partly by tapping into the same fears over Communist subversives that McCarthy had exploited. Once in office, the new president set out to follow through on his campaign pledge of getting subversives out of government. Ike also understood that taking a firm stand on improving security would neutralize any attacks McCarthy might launch against him or his administration. Shortly after taking office he said he wanted to make it unnecessary for "another branch of the government" to police the executive branch, a thinly veiled reference to McCarthy's drumbeat of investigations and allegations.[1]

Ike instructed Attorney General Herbert Brownell to develop new rules for federal hiring aimed at tightening security. On January 20, Inauguration Day, Brownell wrote a letter to the president recommending that he issue an executive order, which Brownell had drafted. It was a simple two-page order titled "Strengthening Security Requirements for Government Employment," which would extend an existing security law to all federal agencies and require security investigations of all prospective hires.[2] Brownell recommended that the president issue the order quickly, and had even prepared a press release.

Bobby Cutler, however, recommended a different course. The day after the inauguration, Bobby urged the president to implement the broad overhaul of security rules developed under President Truman. In marked contrast with Brownell's proposal, the Truman rules cited "sexual perversion" as a factor for investigators to consider when determining whether a federal employee posed a security risk. These were the rules developed by the Interdepartmental Committee on Internal Security.[3] Bobby told Ike that Truman had held off issuing the rules as an executive order because they would only take effect under Ike's presidency. Bobby endorsed Truman's plan, calling it a "rational complement" to other security measures in place, and noting: "It has been exhaustively reviewed by elements of government."[4]

Truman's draft rule provided no definition of the term *sexual perversion*, but in the charged atmosphere of the day — amid McCarthy's allegations, the State Department's testimony about firings, the Hoey report, and Hoover's investigations targeting homosexuals — the rule's target was clear: homosexuals. In recommending Truman's draft order to Ike, Bobby urged that Attorney General Brownell review it to "recheck possibilities of loopholes and the general criteria." Ike wrote to Brownell, "You will notice that Mr. Cutler has suggested that I submit this memorandum to you in order that you may propose it in any way that you think most appropriate," and he had Bobby hand-deliver his memo to Brownell that same night, January 21.[5]

Ike's team soon took another major step toward appeasing McCarthy's drive to rid the State Department of Communists and homosexuals. Secretary of State Foster Dulles hired Scott McLeod, a former FBI agent from New Hampshire who was close to McCarthy, to lead security investigations and background checks as head of the Bureau of Security and Consular Affairs.[6] McLeod kept a photograph of McCarthy on his desk, inscribed by the Wisconsin Republican, TO A GREAT AMERICAN. In a newspaper interview, McLeod boasted about his relationship with McCarthy: "He used to call me up and ask my advice." McLeod made it clear that he intended to spearhead the purge of Communists and gays from the State Department. In testimony shortly after he took his new position, he said, "The campaign toward eliminating all types of sex perverts from the rolls of the department will be pressed with increased vigor. All forms of immorality will be rooted out and banished from the service." Within two weeks of his appointment, the department announced the termination of twenty-one people, sixteen identified as "moral deviates" and five as "security risks."[7]

A tense debate over how to tighten federal employee security rules had begun before the inauguration. Ike had asked Nelson Rockefeller, the Republican heir to the Rockefeller fortune who had served as an assistant secretary of state under Roosevelt and Truman, to lead a study of government efficiency. Rockefeller's group recommended that a commission — composed of both citizens and officials like the attorney general — "handle the problem of Government employees' security and the prevention of subversive activity." The idea drew a blast of criticism from Milt Hill, the Republican who a month earlier had informed the FBI of the arrest of Arthur Vandenberg Jr.'s friend. Hill sent a memo on January 12, 1953, to General Jerry Persons, Eisenhower's liaison to Congress, saying that the commission concept was backed by a variety of left-wingers and would face opposition from Congress.[8] He added that the commission would be a "direct affront to the investigating committees of Congress" and that FBI director J. Edgar Hoover was "diametrically opposed to the idea of a presidential commission" — but was also ready to discuss the matter with Ike. And indeed, after Ike took office, Hoover soon became closely involved in developing the executive order that Bobby had recommended. From January 23 to April 10, the FBI director sent Attorney General Brownell or his assistants seven memorandums commenting on, or recommending revisions of, drafts of the order.[9]

The president, meanwhile, contended with allegations of homosexuality against two of his key appointees. Arthur Vandenberg Jr.'s withdrawal in January 1953 demonstrated that a threat of allegations of homosexuality becoming public could have a powerful impact. Vandenberg finally wrote a letter to the president on March 2 definitively declining any role in his administration. The next day, Ike responded with sympathy, thanking Vandenberg for his support: "I clearly understand the part you played in bringing about my election. Your dedication to the task of giving me that role constitutes, of course, the highest compliment that one man could pay another. I shall be eternally grateful to you."[10]

The second homosexual smear would become a much larger public dispute involving a respected career diplomat who Ike hoped would serve as the American ambassador to the Soviet Union. Ike had nominated Charles E. Bohlen in February to be the ambassador in Moscow. The ambassadorship had been vacant since the Soviets declared the previous ambassador, George Kennan, persona non grata in September 1952. Bohlen, a good friend of Kennan's, shared many of his views and supported his efforts to moderate US policy. Bohlen had served in the embassy in Moscow in the 1930s, acted as translator for Roosevelt at the Yalta Conference in 1945, and then served in the State Department. Eisenhower had met Bohlen while serving as supreme NATO commander in Paris in 1951, where he saw Bohlen's "tough, firm but fair attitude" and came to admire him as "one of the ablest Foreign Service Officers I had ever met."[11] Yet Bohlen's approach toward containing Communism would make him a target for those advocating a more aggressive posture.

McCarthy blamed Bohlen for his role in the "betrayal" of the Chinese Nationalists under the Yalta agreement and charged he was among those responsible for "losing China." In public remarks that the media carried nationwide, McCarthy also condemned Bohlen as a "security risk." He did not specify the basis for the claim but rather cited the existence of a confidential security report on Bohlen by the State Department. Heightening tensions, McCarthy charged that Secretary of State Dulles had misled the Senate Foreign Affairs Committee about the security report.

The first sign that a homosexual smear loomed over Bohlen arose in early February, when Hoover met with Bobby and Undersecretary of State Beetle Smith regarding Carmel Offie, a suspected homosexual who was seeking a position in the State Department.[12] Offie, who had been arrested on a morals charge in Lafayette Square in 1943, had resigned from the CIA under pressure after McCarthy publicly highlighted his case — without naming him — in 1950.[13] Now, Hoover warned, key State Department officials were supporting Offie. Six days later, on February 11, Hoover sent Bobby and Brownell a report showing that Offie's friends and contacts in the State Department included Bohlen.

The FBI soon generated its own background report on Bohlen, which bristled with allegations, some of them anonymous, that the diplomat appeared to be gay along with claims that his politics leaned toward appeasement of the Soviets. Hoover sent the secret report, dated March 16, 1953, to Foster Dulles. Remarkably, the FBI report gave a long explanation of charges against Offie and then quoted Offie as saying Bohlen was an "extremely attractive and intelligent fellow," but also saying Bohlen was loyal to the United States and of good character. Another man — identified as a former employee of the State Department who was an admitted homosexual — said "Bohlen walks, acts and talks like a homosexual." However, that man also "admitted that he has had no relations with Bohlen, but strongly believes Bohlen to be a homosexual."[14] A female former employee of the State Department said Bohlen's "manner of speech indicated effeminacy and she is of definite belief he has strong homosexual tendencies." An employee in the State Department's Security Office, noting that the office had been gathering information on employees suspected of homosexuality, said the office "has an index card on Bohlen in this regard and Bohlen was associated with sexual perverts."

The report also said that while Bohlen was working at the Moscow embassy in the 1930s, he "shared a room" with a young vice consul, Charles W. Thayer. Thayer, who had come under investigation by both Hoover and McCarthy in 1950 over allegations that he was gay, was again under scrutiny by McCarthy after being named US consul general in Munich. Bohlen had married Thayer's sister, Avis H. Thayer, in 1935, and the brothers-in-law roomed together a few years later in Moscow, where housing was extremely limited. But those facts were not enough to shield the two brothers-in-law from being smeared by the absurdly ominous finding that they "shared a room."

Thayer was a swashbuckling figure in the American diplomatic corps. The scion of a prominent Philadelphia family, he graduated from West Point and went on to learn Russian and work in the Moscow embassy. Among other achievements, he introduced the Red Army to polo in 1934. During World War II, he served in the US Army and then transferred to the Office of Strategic Services, where he supported Yugoslav Communist forces undermining Nazi control of southern Europe. After the war, he returned to the State Department to lead the Voice of America (VOA) from 1947 to 1949.[15] In 1950, he published *Bears in the Caviar*, a memoir that managed to find humorous moments amid his often grim years in the State Department from 1933 to 1942. On March 11, 1953, the FBI delivered to McCarthy a report stating that Thayer had fathered a child out of wedlock with a Russian woman who worked for VOA, and revealing confidential allegations from a State Department employee that Thayer was gay.[16] In addition to having become a target in his own right for Hoover and McCarthy, Thayer was now being used to smear Bohlen.

Former ambassador William Bullitt, who had become staunchly anti-Communist after his service under Roosevelt as ambassador to Moscow, also attacked Bohlen. Bullitt told the FBI that Bohlen was "drinking excessively" in the 1930s and his "conduct became intolerable." Bullitt said he had no evidence that Bohlen was gay, although he asserted Bohlen was unfit for the job because of his willingness to placate the Soviets. Remarkably, the FBI's investigative methods, which vacuumed up and repeated unsubstantiated claims, also pilloried Bullitt. The FBI report on Offie a month earlier said, "During 1950, Offie stated he was the recipient of a substantial monetary gift from Bullitt. A reliable source of information advised that he understood the payment by Bullitt to Offie was similar to payments bestowed upon mistresses."[17]

For all its ill-founded allegations, the FBI's report on Bohlen also included a long list of prominent figures in government who made no unfavorable comments about him. The list included three prominent members of the new administration: Allen Dulles, Beetle Smith, and an assistant to the president — Bobby Cutler. Ike himself soon reacted firmly to McCarthy's smear of Bohlen. When Secretary of State Dulles called Ike on March 16 to discuss the Bohlen affair, Dulles noted: "The President indicated he had not the slightest intention of withdrawing Bohlen's name."[18]

The next day, Foster and Allen Dulles went together to Hoover's office to review the findings of the FBI's report on Bohlen. Hoover seemed intent on bolstering McCarthy's smear. An FBI memo of the meeting read: "The Director would not be inclined, if he were passing on the question of security, to give Bohlen a complete clearance. The Director pointed out that there was no direct evidence that Bohlen had engaged in homosexual activities, but it was a fact that several of his closest friends and intimate associates were known homosexuals."[19] Allen Dulles suggested giving Bohlen a lie detector test, but Hoover demurred. "The Director pointed out that he did not attach very much credence to this."

The next day, March 18, 1953, McCarthy called Hoover to confer on the Bohlen situation. Hoover recounted their conversation in a confidential memo to his longtime top assistant Clyde Tolson and two senior agents. Hoover did not report a single question by McCarthy regarding Bohlen's official duties or diplomatic matters; the senator was focused only on Bohlen's sexual orientation. "Senator McCarthy asked whether I thought he was a homosexual and I told him I did not know," Hoover wrote.[20] "I told the Senator it was very difficult to prove a charge of homosexuality; that he did associate with such individuals and certainly normally a person did not associate with individuals of that type."

Nonetheless, Hoover seemed reluctant to give McCarthy the support he was seeking. "The Senator stated that this was a matter he was almost precluded from discussing on the Floor [of the Senate]; that it was so easy to accuse a person of such acts but difficult to prove," Hoover recounted in his memo. "I agreed and stated it was often a charge used by persons who wanted to smear someone."

That same day, Foster Dulles and Bohlen went to testify before a Senate committee. The secretary of state asked Bohlen to ride in a separate car so they would not appear in photographs together, leaving Bohlen to suspect that Foster Dulles did not support him and did not have "the courage to stand up to the McCarthyites."[21] Secretly, Foster also had gotten his brother, Allen, and one of his top assistants at the CIA who was a friend of Bohlen's, Frank Wisner, to urge Bohlen to accept a deal: Thayer would have to resign for Bohlen's nomination to win approval.[22] It was a brutal request, asking Bohlen to sacrifice his brother-in-law so he could continue his career.

Five days later, on March 23, McCarthy continued to fulminate over Bohlen on the floor of the Senate. He accused Bohlen of appeasing Communists and hinted at homosexuality rumors by saying the concerns about him were "of such a nature that we cannot discuss it on the floor of the Senate."[23] To resolve the matter, the Senate proposed that one Republican senator, Robert Taft of Ohio, and one Democrat senator, John Sparkman of Alabama, be permitted to see the raw FBI files — documentation that went beyond the FBI summary memo — and then report back to the Senate before a final vote on the nomination. Hoover opposed the request but was overruled by Ike himself, who ordered Hoover to provide the two senators access to the full FBI files.[24]

The same day that McCarthy was ranting over Bohlen in the Senate, Thayer arrived in Washington from his post in Munich and unobtrusively slipped into the State Department to meet with his brother-in-law, who informed him that the State Department's security office — ruled by McCarthy's ally McLeod — had shown Thayer's complete file to McCarthy. He told Thayer "the battle was lost" when they "put his man [McLeod] in charge of security and personnel files."[25] Thayer agreed to resign, but he wanted it to be on the record that it was because of his relationship with the woman, not because of homosexuality. Undersecretary Smith, worried that McCarthy would subpoena Thayer, told him to return promptly to Munich, which he did, leaving the matter unresolved.

Bohlen's agony over this tortuous nomination process gave rise to what columnist Joseph Alsop later called the "tea-table episode." Bobby was an old friend of Bohlen because they were both Porcellian Club "brothers." Bohlen, who went by the nickname Chip, invited Bobby and Alsop, also a Porcellian brother, to his house for tea one day before his confirmation vote in the Senate. Chip and his wife, Avis, lived on Dumbarton Avenue in Georgetown, just down the street from Alsop.[26] "On a personal level, Bobby Cutler was a nice enough man, but he brought with him from Boston a well-established reputation for what the eminent English historian Edward Gibbon called 'incorrect tastes in love,'" Alsop later wrote, alluding to rumors that Bobby was gay. As tea was being poured, Bobby raised the subject of the attack on Bohlen by McCarthy, who "was suggesting to anyone who would listen that Chip, too, of all people had incorrect tastes in love," Alsop continued. "It was a charge incredible to anyone who knew him. Chip was a married man, closer to his wife than almost any man I knew, with a well-deserved reputation, before he met Avis in Moscow, as one of the most successful ladies' men in Europe." Bobby went on to suggest that Eisenhower and Secretary of State Dulles "were showing nobility by staying steadfast behind Chip's nomination." But, Alsop continued, "While it was true President Eisenhower had offered Chip continued public support, Dulles had, in fact, done the exact opposite. Bohlen was enraged by this exhibition of self-righteousness, as I could tell from the muscle in his cheek, which used to announce his anger by bouncing detectably. As his face hardened, . . . I could see that Chip was about to remind Bobby of his own incorrect tastes and that, in the upshot, unforgivable things were likely to be said." Just then, Avis Bohlen "saw the same signs and took the rather drastic measure of a sudden movement that knocked the tea tray off its precarious perch on the coffee table. Amid the broken tea cups and the general need for tidying up, the conversation mercifully changed and the meeting ended amicably enough." If Alsop's account is to be believed, Bobby was widely rumored to be gay by the time he joined the Eisenhower administration, and Avis Bohlen artfully sacrificed her tea set to avert a confrontation with Bobby over the tumult engulfing her husband and her brother.

On Thursday, March 26, the day before the confirmation vote was set, three FBI agents delivered a secret letter in person from Hoover to Undersecretary of State Smith, while a copy went to Bobby.[27] Allen Dulles received a copy, too, and Wisner was informed of its contents. Hoover's letter remains classified, but it may have spelled out the bargain that was struck to clear the way for Bohlen to become ambassador. Bobby's low-profile role suggests he was quietly helping Ike arrange a settlement of the imbroglio. That same day, the US consulate in Munich announced that Thayer had resigned to pursue a writing career. McCarthy snarled to the press that Thayer had been called home "to be discharged" and "his activities are well-known to the Senate."[28]

With Thayer ousted and the FBI files unsealed to the two senators, the logjam in the Senate broke. Amid a last fiery debate on March 27, Senators Sparkman and Taft announced that there was no evidence Bohlen posed a security risk — they breathed not a word of the homosexuality allegations — and the Senate approved the nomination by a vote of 74–13. The lopsided vote was immediately hailed in the media as a victory for Eisenhower and a defeat for McCarthy. Eisenhower had forged an alliance with Taft and won support from Democratic senators, severely outnumbering McCarthy and his allies.

Ike managed to win the day with the Bohlen nomination, but the battle with McCarthy had taught him a hard lesson about the politics of homosexual smears. Ten days before the final vote, he privately told Foster Dulles, "Let's never mention another name until we have all of these clearances before us and know that we aren't going to get into this again." Foster Dulles replied that he was already "operating on that basis."[29] Politics aside, Ike also apparently believed that homosexuality posed a risk to national security. He later wrote in his memoir, *Mandate for Change*, "It is important to realize that many loyal Americans, by reason of instability, alcoholism, homosexuality, or previous tendencies to associate with Communist-front groups, are unintentional security risks."[30]

In early March, Attorney General Brownell circulated a draft of the personnel security executive order. Bobby made no comment on the inclusion of the "sexual perversion" provision, though he objected to the draft order's requirement that the NSC oversee federal agencies' performance of their duties to investigate and reject job candidates considered threats to national security. He sent Brownell a memo on March 9 arguing that the NSC did not have sufficient staff to carry out such a function. Bobby also warned that charging the NSC with such duties would place the NSC and the president at the center of "legal actions as well as public attacks."[31] After discussing the matter with Eisenhower, Bobby called Brownell on March 11 and told him Eisenhower was "strongly opposed" to the NSC having administrative duties.

Brownell eventually produced a draft of the executive order that removed those offending provisions, and the draft executive order was sent to numerous executive agencies and a union for federal employees for review. In comments sent in response, no one objected to the inclusion of "sexual perversion" as a standard for refusing to hire an employee on national security grounds.

On April 27, Ike signed the rule as Executive Order 10450. The eight-page order required *every* federal agency to investigate new hires and existing employees in search of information on connections to groups seeking to advocate Communism or to overthrow the government, and also on criminal behavior, drug addiction, and "sexual perversion." Previously, only the State Department and military agencies conducted such background checks. The White House publicly announced the plan the same day, and McCarthy swiftly rewarded the president with glowing words to the press about the new security program: "I think it is a tremendous improvement over the old method. Altogether it represents a pretty darn good program. I like it. It shows that the new administration was sincere in the campaign promises to clean house."[32]

McCarthy's praise did not halt his investigations, however. On the very day that Eisenhower announced his new security order, one of McCarthy's investigators called the NSC to launch an inquiry that had the hallmarks of a homosexual smear.[33] The investigator, Donald Surine, asked whether an Ohio labor leader had been given access to classified information as part of his work for an NSC advisory board. (Surine had been fired from the FBI over improper conduct with a prostitute during a prostitution investigation, but Hoover had recommended him to McCarthy, who quickly hired him.[34]) According to Surine, an anonymous caller had told McCarthy's office that David Robertson, the president of a labor union in Cleveland, had "certain personal weaknesses," code sometimes used in smearing people as homosexuals. Robertson was unique among the civilian consultants the president had invited to review the NSC policy-making process in that he was the only union representative. All the others were corporate executives, financiers, or lawyers.

Bobby disclosed Surine's call the following day, April 28, in an NSC meeting, and said that he proposed sending a letter to McCarthy in response. Eisenhower, however, objected. The president spoke bluntly and categorically: "What went on in the National Security Council and what advice the president sought from consultants to the National Security

Council was solely the President's business and the President's responsibility. If Senator McCarthy proposed to take on the National Security Council, he was taking on the President."[35] Eisenhower instructed Bobby to do no more than call McCarthy and explain the president's position on the matter.

Bobby reached McCarthy by phone late the next day and told him the president had asked seven citizens to serve as consultants to the NSC and had used government agencies to check and clear them. McCarthy claimed he was unaware of Surine's call. "He seemed to have no interest in the matter or in pursuing it; gave me the impression that this was a routine check by one of his office staff." Bobby said McCarthy "was very friendly in tone and conversation." He "called me 'general,' and ended up by inviting me 'sometime to come and have that beer we talked about'" during the campaign. The minor skirmish with McCarthy was over.[36]

Executive Order 10450 expanded investigations of homosexuals across the federal government. Agencies had to establish their own security regulations to implement the order, sometimes comically so at agencies with little or no national security exposure. In January 1954, for example, the National Gallery of Art in Washington was put on notice that its regulations failed to comply with the executive order.[37]

In addition, the order abolished the requirement under Truman's rules that a person be found "disloyal" in order to be dismissed as a security risk. Eisenhower's order gave agencies authority to dismiss employees suspected of homosexuality whether or not they had done anything disloyal. The order set the stage for inquiries into the private lives of thousands of suspected gays, many of whom were fired or resigned to avoid the pain of an investigation. Some who came under investigation suffered depression or even committed suicide. By October 1953, the US Civil Service Commission reported that the order had led to 58,791 new investigations, with 50 job applicants rejected, 843 employees fired, and 2,283 employees resigning.[38]

J. Edgar Hoover and Senators McCarthy, Hoey, and others already had made it clear that homosexuals were not wanted — and indeed were considered equivalent to Communist enemies in the federal government. Yet, Steve Benedict said that he and Skip Koons, flying quietly under the radar as gay employees in the White House, did not consider the executive order a sign that Eisenhower was launching a drive to rid the government of gays, and it didn't prompt them to take any additional precautions to hide their homosexuality. "I knew well that McCarthy and others had been on the war path for homosexuals in government well before Ike was in office. I think I regarded 10450 simply as part of a continuum, not as something that made any basic changes in what was already going on . . . I never had a reason to believe that Ike would use his capital to make a fight in this particular area."[39] Steve said Skip shared these views. Bobby also showed no sign of concern over 10450's impact on gays and instead remained focused on national security, nuclear weapons, and the struggle against Communism.

10

THE PASSION OF OPPENHEIMER

The brilliant physicist J. Robert Oppenheimer directed the Los Alamos National Laboratory in its secret design and creation of the atomic bomb for the US Army during World War II. After two of the laboratory's atomic bombs were dropped in August 1945, forcing Japan's surrender, Oppenheimer became a widely recognized hero of American scientific and military prowess. Yet after the war, he became profoundly concerned about the devastating power of nuclear weapons, the danger of radioactive fallout, and the threat to humanity posed by nuclear arsenals being developed by the US and USSR under a blanket of secrecy. Urging President Truman to pursue nuclear disarmament, he told him privately in the Oval Office, "I feel I have blood on my hands."[1]

Oppenheimer had a history of friendships with Communists, which was intensively investigated by the FBI but tolerated by the military during the war because Oppenheimer was critical to the bomb project and he insisted he had cut his ties with Communist friends.[2] Oppenheimer's connections to Communists eventually became public knowledge. His brother Frank, a physicist who also worked at Los Alamos, admitted to being a Communist in open testimony before the House Un-American Activities Committee in 1949. By early 1952, Oppenheimer's earlier Communist associations and his public warnings about the nuclear arms race made him controversial, though he still had the respect of important Democrats, including Secretary of State Dean Acheson.

In April 1952, seeking new ideas for disarmament talks with the Soviets, Acheson appointed Oppenheimer to a "Panel of Consultants on Disarmament," whose other members included then deputy CIA director Allen Dulles and military technology innovator Vannevar Bush. The panel selected Oppenheimer as its chairman. McGeorge Bundy, a former World War II intelligence officer and academic who had written a book about Acheson, was named the panel's secretary.[3] Granted security clearances and provided with top-level briefings, the panel worked through the year. Oppenheimer retained his post as director of the Institute for Advanced Study at Princeton, taking periodic trips to Washington for panel meetings. Oppenheimer and Bush had opposed development of the hydrogen bomb, and the panel considered the issue briefly before the US exploded the world's first hydrogen bomb on November 1, 1952. Measured at ten megatons, it was more than five hundred times more powerful than the bomb dropped on Hiroshima.

The Oppenheimer panel delivered its top-secret report to Acheson shortly before he was to leave office in January 1953, as the Eisenhower administration was taking over. The report was a blunt assessment of the arms race, projecting that with the Soviets likely to have five thousand atomic weapons within a several years, both countries would very soon have enough weapons to destroy each other. Noting that the American people were unaware of the large numbers of nuclear weapons in both countries' arsenals, the report's first recommendation was to "adopt a policy of candor toward the American people" by informing them of the facts of the arms race.[4] The report went on to make four other recommendations for the government to pursue: communicate more effectively with allies about the arms race, enhance the "continental security" of the United States, disengage from the fruitless United Nations disarmament talks, and seek to build a direct channel for continuous communications with the Soviet leaders.

The Oppenheimer panel's report could easily have fallen into obscurity since the man who requested it, Acheson, had clashed bitterly with Eisenhower over the Korean War and had been blamed widely by McCarthy and other Republicans for losing China to the Communists. Despite all this, the secret report — and Oppenheimer's ideas — found new life. On February 17, Oppenheimer went to the offices of the Council on Foreign Relations in New York to give a confidential talk titled "Atomic Weapons and American Policy."[5]

More significantly, Bobby Cutler placed the Oppenheimer panel's report on the agenda for the NSC meeting of February 25. Bobby knew Oppenheimer personally because they served together on the Harvard Board of Overseers. Bobby started the discussion by explaining the background of the paper. He then read its five principal recommendations and asked the council members to comment. President Eisenhower immediately weighed in with the observation that it seemed "strange that two eminent scientists had been put on the Panel and that they had immediately moved out of the scientific realm into the realms of psychology and policy." Ike continued by saying, "He could see no sense in this and in his experience, notably as President of Columbia [University], most scientists concerned with atomic problems had no real grasp of the security issue and were generally anxious to reveal what they knew to any and all their fellow scientists."[6]

Allen Dulles, a member of the Oppenheimer panel, responded in its defense, saying it had not been tasked with a scientific approach to the problem. Its members had been tremendously impressed by the question of "enough-ness." This is "the problem that would exist when the Soviet Union possessed a stockpile sufficient to deal the United States a damaging blow, regardless of the fact that the United States might itself possess a much larger stockpile of weapons." Bobby then said that the panel was "very greatly disturbed by the public apathy and lethargy about the atomic problem," adding that this was the reason it recommended candor in revealing to the public the "enough-ness" conundrum. Eisenhower was unmoved. "The President expressed his opposition at this stage to indicating to the American people anything about the size of our stockpile of weapons, and Secretary [of Defense Charles] Wilson joined him by stating that it seemed foolish to scare our people to death if we don't need to and can't really do anything about this problem."

This led to a series of challenges to the proposed policy of candor. Treasury Secretary George Humphrey argued there was no use in "blowing hot and cold with the public on the atomic situation, frightening them one day and reassuring them the next," and expressed concern about the fiscal impact of increased expenditures. Atomic Energy Commission (AEC) chairman Gordon Dean noted that Congress had recently approved a major expansion of the nation's nuclear weapons production capacity after the AEC argued it was necessary for atomic preparedness. President Eisenhower then said, "It would make us look very silly if at this stage we reversed the field and called off the expansion program which had been approved," and pointed to an upcoming "open" nuclear test planned for the Nevada desert. In short, asked the President, "isn't it a plain fact that the information which the members of the Panel were so anxious to give to the American people was indeed already getting out to them?"

At that moment, just as serious doubts about the report were erupting, Bobby steered the conversation back to the panel's recommendation of openness with the American people about the reality of the nuclear arms race:

> Mr. Cutler broke in to say that according to his understanding the Panel was making a strong recommendation that the people of the United States be informed about what was called the "enough-ness" problem and its significance for them. "I read in the report," continued Mr. Cutler, "that the people of the United States are mature and should be informed in so far as compatible with security."
>
> The President agreed with Mr. Cutler's statement as to the maturity of the American people, but remained unconvinced of the desirability of the first recommendation. He then inquired as to the next move.
>
> Mr. Cutler suggested that the Council turn the Panel report over to the Senior NSC staff to come up with a study of ways and means of carrying out its five major recommendations.

Without further questioning or debate, the NSC then referred the matter to the NSC staff to work with Bush and report back to the council. Despite the president's deep misgivings, the Oppenheimer panel's proposed policy of candor had found a safe harbor at the NSC with Bobby's support.

To pursue the Oppenheimer panel's recommendations, the Planning Board named an Ad Hoc Committee on Armaments and American Policy, drawing on representatives from the State Department, Defense, AEC, CIA, and Psychological Strategy Board (PSB). William Bundy, McGeorge Bundy's brother and also Dean Acheson's son-in-law, represented the CIA. The Bundy brothers were the sons of Bobby's friend Harvey Bundy, who also was a friend of Allen Dulles. In the spring of 1953, Allen Dulles appointed William Bundy to serve as liaison to the NSC, just as that body was taking up the Oppenheimer panel report prepared in part by his brother. William Bundy and other members of the ad hoc committee met and worked with Bush to prepare a report on a policy of "Candor Toward the American People," identifying the types of information that should be shared with the public. Their secret report was designated NSC 151 and forwarded to the full NSC for consideration.[7]

Meanwhile, across Washington — in the offices of Senator McCarthy, Senator Stuart Symington, the FBI, and the AEC — wheels had been set in motion against Oppenheimer. On Sunday, May 10, McCarthy aide Roy Cohn was in Miami with the senator when he called FBI assistant director Louis Nichols. Cohn said that Symington, the Missouri Democrat who sat on McCarthy's subcommittee and was a key proponent of expanding the air force and its nuclear capabilities, had become extremely concerned about Oppenheimer.[8] Cohn wanted to know what Nichols thought about the idea of "calling in Oppenheimer and launching an investigation." Two days later, McCarthy and Cohn visited J. Edgar Hoover at the FBI offices in Washington to discuss the idea further. McCarthy "stated he had been giving this matter quite some thought and was wondering what my reaction would be to his Committee looking into the activities of Oppenheimer," Hoover wrote in a memo.[9] "I told the Senator that I thought that he had a number of problems to consider before embarking on this project. I pointed out that there were several other committees in Congress which probably might resent his taking on this investigation unless he first cleared with them." McCarthy replied that he understood this would need to be addressed before he undertook an investigation of Oppenheimer.

In another sign of brewing trouble, *Fortune* magazine published an article in its May issue called "The Hidden Struggle for the H-Bomb," which suggested Oppenheimer had undermined the project to build the hydrogen bomb even after President Truman had ordered the project to proceed. The article, riddled with inaccuracies, had been published with assistance from Admiral Lewis Strauss, who had repeatedly clashed with Oppenheimer over nuclear security.[10] Strauss, an assistant to the president whom Eisenhower was now considering appointing as chairman of the AEC, was a fierce opponent of Oppenheimer.

Oppenheimer, meanwhile, was taking steps to advance his ideas for limiting the risks of nuclear war. He wrote an article that he hoped to publish in *Foreign Affairs*, the influential publication of the Council on

Foreign Relations, outlining his proposed policy of candor. The article, to be called "Atomic Weapons and American Policy," repeated some of the key points in the secret paper delivered to Acheson, although Oppenheimer omitted information considered classified. Oppenheimer wanted the president's approval to publish the article, and so he sent it to Bobby. On Sunday, May 24, Bobby forwarded the article to Ike, with a handwritten note saying, "This article seems to me very fine and goes along with Planning Board recommendation to be presented next Wednesday [May 27]. I see no reason Oppenheimer shouldn't publish it, whatever the Council decides or you approve."[11] Bobby reported to Oppenheimer that there was no reason why he could not proceed with publishing the article after the NSC considered the policy recommendations of the Oppenheimer panel.[12] Oppenheimer was scheduled to attend the May 27 meeting at which the NSC would take up the ad hoc committee's NSC 151 report.

Bobby arranged for Oppenheimer to arrive two hours before the meeting so that he could read the NSC 151 document in Bobby's office.[13] After the NSC met secretly in the Cabinet Room, Oppenheimer, ushered into the room for the discussion of NSC 151, addressed the NSC at "the invitation of Mr. Cutler," a meeting memorandum says.[14] Oppenheimer again made an appeal for a policy of candor in revealing to the American people the nature of the threat from the nuclear arms race. While the US Army had made four atom bombs in 1945, "Today we could make a thousand," Oppenheimer said. The power of the weapons is doubling every few years, and the Soviets will be "pressing us hard," he said. "Whatever steps we took to create a defense against this threat would still leave us vulnerable. The public does not realize the true facts of the situation, and it was crucially important to enlighten them." In sharp contrast with the questions and doubts Eisenhower raised in February, the president responded by saying he "certainly agreed in principle" with Oppenheimer's recommendation of candor, yet he remained concerned about the security implications of providing information to the public. The president asked Oppenheimer: How can we determine which information it is "safe and wise to release"? The physicist responded that the United States should not release *any* information concerning technological aspects of nuclear weapons. "But a release on the general problem of the atomic race and the atomic equation, far from inciting the Russians, might even deter them by bringing home to them the fact of our enormous atomic power," Oppenheimer said.[15] He added that the situation was so dire that the "highest voice in the land," meaning the president, must address the nation. President Eisenhower agreed with this idea and asked C. D. Jackson, his psychological warfare expert, to write a speech for him to make in carrying out this new policy of "candor." The NSC also directed Jackson to have his Psychological Strategy Board determine specific steps that should be taken to carry out the policy. In an about-face from February's meeting, President Eisenhower had set "Operation Candor" in motion.

Strauss learned of the president's decision and became worried about Bobby's relationship with Oppenheimer — and he conveyed his concerns to the FBI. On June 4, Strauss asked to review the FBI summary file on Oppenheimer, and when agent Charles Bates brought it to him, Strauss suggested that Bobby might be protecting Oppenheimer. "This acquaintanceship is on a 'first name basis,'" FBI assistant director Milton Ladd quoted Strauss as saying about Bobby and Oppenheimer.[16] "Strauss stated that General Cutler was the type of individual who did not like to hear criticism of his 'friends.' Strauss intends to talk with General Cutler in the near future and to 'lay the cards on the table' concerning Oppenheimer." It is unclear whether Strauss ever took this step with Bobby, and Strauss's doubts about Bobby's relationship with Oppenheimer would persist through the tumultuous months ahead.

Strauss met with Hoover on June 22 and raised the alarm over Bobby's relationship with Oppenheimer. Asking Hoover to keep the information in "strictest confidence," Strauss said columnist Joseph Alsop had written a seven-page letter "appealing to Cutler to take steps to prevent an investigation of Oppenheimer by Senator McCarthy."[17] Alsop sat on the Harvard Board of Overseers with both Oppenheimer and Bobby. Hoover was sympathetic to Strauss, responding that he had his own concerns about Bobby. "I then outlined to Admiral Strauss some of the problems which we have been confronted with along the same lines," pointing to three "cases" of individuals whom Bobby had recommended for positions in the government. Hoover also noted that Bobby had blocked a request for the attorney general to attend NSC meetings.

Tension between the Eisenhower administration and McCarthy was building on a number of fronts. McCarthy made headlines by sending his aides, Roy Cohn and David Schine, to European capitals to conduct an investigation into books written by Communists in libraries at US embassies. Ike responded by telling the graduating class at Dartmouth College on June 14, "Don't join the book burners . . . Don't be afraid to go in your library and read every book as long as any document does not offend our own ideas of decency."[18]

The tension escalated on the morning of Thursday, July 9, when Cohn called the CIA and said McCarthy wanted William Bundy, the CIA's liaison to the NSC, to testify later that same morning before his committee. Allen Dulles had recommended that Bundy obtain a top-level "Q" clearance from the AEC so that he could review secret nuclear documents, and Cohn told a CIA lawyer "we wonder whether that should be approved."[19]

McCarthy's inquiry posed a threat. McCarthy might question Bundy about the Oppenheimer panel as well as Bundy's contribution of funds to the defense of Alger Hiss. As the CIA team debated how to respond to Cohn, Allen Dulles called the White House and discussed the matter with Bobby. After hanging up with Bobby, Dulles ordered Bundy to "get out of town." Dulles suggested that Bundy visit his parents at their summer house in Manchester, Massachusetts.[20] Bundy left the agency and quickly took a flight to Boston.

The standoff with McCarthy boiled over. Cohn sent a subpoena that afternoon ordering the CIA attorney, Walter Pforzheimer, to appear before McCarthy's subcommittee. McCarthy went to the Senate floor and publicly accused the CIA director of a "most blatant attempt to thwart the authority of the Senate." McCarthy said he wanted Bundy to appear before the subcommittee so that he could question him about his new position as liaison to the NSC. McCarthy noted pointedly that Bundy was the son-in-law of Acheson and had given four hundred dollars to the Hiss defense.[21] McCarthy charged that Bundy "suddenly disappeared from the CIA" and the agency claimed it didn't know where he was. Ultimately, McCarthy said on the Senate floor, Pforzheimer had said that he "had talked to Allen Dulles and that the policy of the CIA was to refuse to allow any employee to appear before any Congressional committees."

Seeking to avoid an explosive conflict with McCarthy, Allen Dulles met with Ike, Bobby, Nixon, and other senior administration officials. It was agreed that Nixon, who as a red hunter in his own right had a long-standing relationship with McCarthy, would meet with McCarthy over the weekend to negotiate, which the two men did. On Tuesday, July 14, McCarthy announced the matter had been resolved, and his subcommittee's investigation would proceed without Bundy's testimony.[22]

As McCarthy appeared to gear up for a Communist probe targeting the Eisenhower administration, Ike's embrace of Oppenheimer's policies surged into public view. With approval from Bobby and Ike, Oppenheimer's article calling for candor on nuclear armaments appeared in the July issue of *Foreign Affairs*. The article included Oppenheimer's striking metaphor for the nuclear stalemate between the United States and the Soviet Union: "We may be likened to two scorpions in a bottle, each capable of killing the other, but only at the risk of his own life." The policy of candor was reported in the press, and the Alsop brothers wrote a column supporting a policy of openness concerning the threat posed by the nuclear arms race. The president himself publicly endorsed the policy at a July 8 press conference at the White House. "I think the time has arrived when the American people must have more information on this subject, if they are to act intelligently," Ike said. "I think the time has come to be far more, let us say, frank with the American people than we have been in the past."[23]

Strauss, however, seethed over the *Foreign Affairs* article, and he believed Oppenheimer was leading a campaign to reveal critical data on nuclear weapons, such as their rates of production, to the Soviets.[24] Strauss brought his concerns to C. D. Jackson, and the PSB soon developed a series of ideas for the candor campaign that steered away from blunt revelations about the nuclear arms race. Strauss and Jackson met regularly over breakfast to discuss the plan, but the prospects for sharing information under Operation Candor dimmed after the Soviets confirmed on August 19, 1953, that they had exploded their first hydrogen bomb.[25] Newspapers headlines blared: "Reds Test H-Bomb."

Strauss intensified his efforts to discover what Oppenheimer may have been doing to build his relationships with Bobby, Ike, and others in the administration. After learning that Oppenheimer was to visit the White House on September 1, Strauss asked the FBI to place him under surveillance during his trip from Princeton to Washington. The FBI reported back that Oppenheimer had spent the afternoon in the men's bar of the

Statler Hotel with columnist Marquis Childs.[26] However, Oppenheimer's calendar for that day — revealed years later — shows a meeting with "General Cutler" at 4:00 PM, then with Childs at 5:00 PM.[27] With Strauss waging war on Oppenheimer's candor policy, it is possible that Bobby and Oppenheimer felt it wisest to meet away from the White House, but the FBI surveillance did not identify Bobby at the hotel that day.

Eisenhower soon voiced concern that too much focus on the Soviet nuclear threat under Operation Candor would undermine the confidence of Americans and their allies in Europe and around the globe. Yet he continued to seek a way to turn a frank discussion about the nuclear peril into a diplomatic and policy initiative that would gain the US an advantage. At this point, Eisenhower came up with a breakthrough. On September 10, 1953, Ike and Bobby were reviewing discussion of arms control in the NSC the previous day, when Ike had an idea for a policy initiative along the lines of Operation Candor: He suggested that both the United States and the Soviet Union provide radioactive material to the United Nations for "peaceful" purposes. Yet the president also suggested a twist intended to make it difficult for the Soviets to join the effort, Bobby wrote in a memo to Strauss and Jackson.[28] "The President suggested that you might consider the following proposal, which he did not think anyone had yet thought of. Suppose the United States and the Soviets were each to turn over to the United Nations, for peaceful use, X kilograms of fissionable material. The amount X could be fixed at a figure which we could handle from our stockpile, but which it would be difficult for the Soviets to match."[29]

Strauss soon replied to Bobby's memo, saying that the idea "is novel and might have value for propaganda purposes." But he added, "It has doubtful value as a practical move . . ." because, among other reasons, the United States had insufficient intelligence to know the level of Soviet stockpiles of fissionable materials.[30] Nonetheless, Strauss recommended that the idea be explored by a special group that the NSC had designated for studying atomic disarmament. Bobby showed Strauss's memo to the president, and an internal debate soon began on the president's proposal.

Strauss won C. D. Jackson to his side and succeeded in killing the series of public messages planned for Operation Candor, but the president's idea of a speech about the nuclear threat and sharing nuclear material for peaceful uses survived. Jackson continued drafting the speech, which the president was set to make before the United Nations General Assembly on December 8, 1953.

Behind the scenes, the prime author of the policy of candor, Oppenheimer, soon became the center of a searing political drama. On November 7, a former congressional staffer wrote a detailed letter to Hoover charging that Oppenheimer had extensive ties with communists, was in contact with Soviet espionage agents, hired communists to work at Los Alamos, and worked to suspend the American H-bomb program. The author of the letter was William Borden, a former staff member of Congress's Joint Committee on Atomic Energy who had long held doubts about Oppenheimer's loyalty.[31] Borden's letter concluded that "more probably than not J. Robert Oppenheimer is an agent of the Soviet Union."

Hoover sent Borden's letter to his top aides, who reviewed whether it provided any new information or analysis of the mass of investigative information the FBI already had on Oppenheimer. The aides concluded that while Borden had relied heavily on a 1952 FBI summary report on Oppenheimer, Borden's conclusions were not always supported by that report and "are not factual in each instance."[32] The FBI agents found a series of faults in Borden's letter. For instance, where Borden asserted that testimony by Austrian atomic spy Klaus Fuchs implicated Oppenheimer, the aides found that Borden was wrong about Fuchs's testimony. Yet the aides' memo also confirmed that in the early 1940s Oppenheimer met with a Communist leader, Steve Nelson, who was a friend of Oppenheimer's wife, Kitty; and it noted that a "reliable informant has advised" that a student of Oppenheimer's, Joseph Weinberg, gave Nelson atomic secrets. Yet criminal charges against Weinberg were dismissed in court earlier in 1953 because they relied on illegal FBI wiretaps.[33]

On November 27, Hoover forwarded Borden's letter to Bobby, but he also took another step. Perhaps convinced by Strauss that Bobby was biased in favor of Oppenheimer and so might block the letter from getting to the president, Hoover additionally distributed Borden's letter to Strauss, Allen Dulles, and other top officials, including the secretaries of state and defense.[34] The letter was accompanied by a sixty-nine-page summary memorandum on the results of earlier FBI investigations of Oppenheimer. Secretary of Defense Wilson responded by calling Hoover on Wednesday, December 2, saying he was "shocked" by the

FBI report. Hoover said he had "suspected [Oppenheimer] since the Manhattan Engineer days." Hoover also said this is a "politically delicate case," adding that scientists considered themselves "sacrosanct," and Oppenheimer was "very prominent in the scientific world," according to a memo Hoover sent Tolson and other aides that day.[35] "I stated for this reason I thought any move which was made ought to be taken up with the AEC, General Cutler, and other parties interested for their opinions, to be certain that they are aware of all the aspects." That same day, Wilson called the president and asked if he had seen Hoover's latest report on Oppenheimer. When Ike responded that he had not, Wilson said Strauss had called him to warn that "McCarthy knows about it and might pull it on us."[36] Wilson was warning of a major political threat against the president. Ike replied that he was not worried about McCarthy but that the Oppenheimer case should be brought to the attention of Attorney General Herbert Brownell.

By the end of the day, December 2, Ike had made up his mind. "Tomorrow morning before the security council meeting, I intend to call into my office the secretary of state, the secretary of the treasury, the secretary of defense, General Cutler, and Allen Dulles and inform them that until this matter is definitely settled all access to sensitive information is to be denied to Dr. Oppenheimer," the president wrote in his diaries.[37]

Bobby and others, however, were still debating the reliability of the accuser, Borden. Coyne, the FBI liaison to the NSC, sent Bobby a one-page memo on December 3 summarizing the concerns of an AEC security officer who said Borden was terminated by the congressional committee because of his role in the loss of nuclear secrets earlier in the year. Coyne said the agent reported that Borden "doesn't know anything about the subject of security."[38] Bobby told Sherman Adams about Coyne's memo. "Very interesting. P also read it," Bobby said, referring to the president, in a note to Coyne. Bobby asked Coyne to get a copy to Hoover. Yet Ike had made his decision about Oppenheimer.

That same morning, Ike met with Strauss, Wilson, Bobby, and other members of the administration in the Oval Office to discuss how to handle the Oppenheimer case.[39] In the meeting, which has been recounted variously by participants and historians, Ike did what he'd indicated he would do the day before: issued instructions that

Oppenheimer be denied access to classified information.[40] In addition, Ike said he wanted the attorney general and FBI to investigate the case closely and consider whether criminal prosecution was appropriate, and he asked Bobby to summarize his instructions in a memorandum. Ike was preparing to depart the following morning to Bermuda for a meeting with British prime minister Winston Churchill, and he wanted to be sure his orders were carried out.

That afternoon, Bobby went to Attorney General Brownell's office to meet with Brownell and Hoover, informing them of Ike's instructions regarding Oppenheimer and giving them two copies of the memorandum he had prepared.[41] Bobby also informed them that Strauss was revoking Oppenheimer's Q clearance, which might cause Oppenheimer to request a hearing. Hoover worried that a hearing could pose problems. "Both the Attorney General and I raised the question with General Cutler as to the advisability of proceeding with a hearing in this matter," Hoover wrote in a memorandum. Brownell suggested that simply abolishing the committee Oppenheimer was serving on might resolve the matter and avoid an open hearing. Hoover warned that some information could not be produced in a hearing because of the "confidential sources from which it had been obtained," possibly a reference to illegal wiretaps. The question of how to proceed — through an open hearing, an administrative solution, or criminal charges — was debated for the next two weeks while Oppenheimer was out of the country.

With Oppenheimer officially cut off from the nation's nuclear secrets, and a national security investigation into his conduct now set in motion, his policy of candor nonetheless took a giant leap forward. On December 8, 1953, President Eisenhower went before the United Nations General Assembly and delivered a speech that had stemmed in part from the NSC's discussion of the Oppenheimer panel's report. While C. D. Jackson was the speech's chief writer, it had evolved through discussions with Bobby, Strauss, the Dulles brothers, and other senior officials, and Ike himself had made extensive revisions. Dubbed "Atoms for Peace," the speech was broadcast on national television. Ike revealed that the United States had conducted forty-three nuclear tests since 1945, that nuclear bombs now were twenty-five times more powerful than the first bombs, and that all branches of the US military were capable of nuclear strikes. The president also said bluntly that, with the Soviet Union now in possession of nuclear weapons, there was no security in numeric superiority. "Even against the most powerful defense, an aggressor in possession of the effective minimum number of atomic bombs for a surprise attack could probably place a sufficient number of his bombs on the chosen targets to cause hideous damage," he said. This was a muted paraphrasing of Oppenheimer's "two scorpions" metaphor, though of course the president made no mention of Oppenheimer.

Ike's depiction of the nuclear dilemma facing the world was bleak. Yet, speaking in a calm voice from the dais before the General Assembly, the president offered a plan to guide the world out of the gloom: "My country wants to be constructive, not destructive. It wants agreements, not wars, among nations. It wants itself to live in freedom and in the confidence that the people of every other nation enjoy equally the right of choosing their own way of life." Eisenhower called for the United States and Soviet Union to contribute nuclear materials to a new agency to be called the International Atomic Energy Agency, which would seek to provide for peaceful use of nuclear materials in fields such as medicine and electric power.[42] "It is not enough just to take this weapon out of the hands of the soldiers. It must be put into the hands of those who will know how to strip its military casing and adapt it to the arts of peace." The speech boosted Eisenhower's reputation globally as a man who could make peace, not just war. Ike had taken a bold step toward openness with the American public and the world on nuclear weapons.

However significant it was, the Atoms for Peace speech did not halt the debate raging secretly within the administration over the Oppenheimer security case. Bobby reviewed the case further and discussed it with the president on the morning of December 12. Bobby proposed that if the attorney general concluded no criminal charges should be brought, it would be possible to have a "friendly scientist" like Bush explain to Oppenheimer why his security clearance was revoked, and the physicist might accept a quiet resolution.[43] The president agreed that Bush would be a "good intermediary" to approach Oppenheimer. But the idea of Bush serving as a mediator was abandoned.[44] On December 21, Strauss met with Oppenheimer, informed him of the suspension of his security clearance, and gave him time to consider whether he would demand a hearing. The next day, Oppenheimer sent Strauss a letter refusing to accept the suspension, saying, "This course of action would mean that

I accept and concur in the view that I am not fit to serve this government . . . This I cannot do."[45]

The AEC then sent Oppenheimer a letter informing him of the formal allegations against him: He associated with Communists; he contributed to the Communist Party of California; he failed to report a plot to obtain information about the atom bomb project in 1943; and he opposed the American hydrogen bomb project and sought to convince other scientists not to participate in it.[46] The letter, by AEC general manager Ken Nichols, said the AEC was taking the action under federal personnel security rules, Executive Order 10450. Strauss appointed former PSB director Gordon Gray to head a three-member personnel security board to preside over the hearing. Strauss named a federal prosecutor, Roger Robb, to present the evidence against Oppenheimer behind closed doors at AEC offices in Washington.

The investigation swirled behind a wall of national security secrecy. Bobby held to his own code of absolute secrecy, even when he dropped by Joe Alsop's home in Georgetown shortly before Christmas to mend fences with his old friend. Joe gave Bobby a bourbon and water, and they sat by a fire. Bobby knew Alsop would want to learn of the investigation, but he made no mention of it. When Bobby declined another bourbon, Joe said, "I suppose you think that, if you took another, you'd tell me some of those top secrets?" Bobby replied, "Yes, Joe, that's part of it, certainly. But thank you and Merry Christmas."[47] Despite his friendship with both Bobby and Oppenheimer, Joe Alsop was not the one who broke the story of the Oppenheimer security investigation.

As Oppenheimer's April 12 hearing date approached, agents in the Newark FBI office set up a wiretap at the physicist's home and monitored his movements. On March 12, the FBI picked up an alarming call from Lee DuBridge, a physicist and friend of Oppenheimer's who had worked at Los Alamos and then became president of the California Institute of Technology. DuBridge asked Oppenheimer whether anything could be done to speed up the AEC hearing process. Oppenheimer answered, "Well, I saw Cutler at Harvard Monday, but I think that there are things that the White House might do if they wanted to, but I don't think they are ready to . . ."[48] FBI agents scrambling to understand what Bobby and Oppenheimer had discussed found a confidential informant who verified that both men were at Harvard when a board of overseers meeting took place on March 8.[49] A report by the Newark FBI office on Oppenheimer's remarks about Bobby ignited FBI concerns that the physicist might be trying to get Bobby and the White House to interfere with the AEC hearing.

Hoover, informed of Oppenheimer's recorded comments about Bobby, sent letters on the matter to the attorney general and to Strauss on March 25.[50] Hoover also sent a memo to Bobby outlining the potentially explosive charge. Hoover omitted the fact that the tip came from a wiretap and instead falsely suggested that the information came from a "reliable informant." Hoover said that Oppenheimer asserted he had "conferred with Mr. Cutler on March 8, 1954, regarding procedures which have been established by the Atomic Energy Commission."[51] Bobby responded to Hoover days later with a letter denying that he discussed procedures for the AEC hearing with Oppenheimer, although he acknowledged seeing him at the board of overseers meeting. "I remember very clearly shaking hands and greeting Dr. Oppenheimer and made a point to do so, because at the January 12, 1954, Overseers Meeting he avoided me," Bobby wrote. "I know and will take oath that I did not speak to him regarding procedures established by the Atomic Energy Commission or whether the White House would or would not interfere in connection with 'the case' or with such procedures."

On the morning of March 30, Strauss raised the issue with Bobby at the White House, according to an FBI report quoting an assistant to Strauss, David Teeple.[52] Teeple asserted that Bobby told Ike that Oppenheimer was a "G.d. liar." Strauss, however, was apparently unconvinced by Bobby's denial and asked the FBI to put Bobby under surveillance. FBI assistant director Alan Belmont, however, refused. "I see nothing to be gained," he said in a memo. "They are making a mountain out of nothing."[53]

The Oppenheimer hearing began as planned on April 12 behind closed doors at AEC offices, with a three-member board appointed by Strauss presiding. The next day, *The New York Times*, which had obtained the formal allegations and Oppenheimer's response from the scientist's lawyers, published a story at the top of its front page about the case, instantaneously transforming the proceeding into a major event of the McCarthy era. McCarthy responded by saying the suspension of Oppenheimer "was long overdue — it should have been taken years ago."[54] Scientists from across the nation responded by supporting Oppenheimer, many of them viewing the case as a persecution of Oppenheimer for his political beliefs, including his opposition to development of the hydrogen bomb. Support also came from figures such as John J. McCloy, Truman's former assistant secretary of the army who had gone on to serve as chairman of Chase Manhattan Bank. McCloy wrote President Eisenhower, "I am very distressed, as I assume you are, over the Oppenheimer matter." The president replied that he hoped the board would exonerate Oppenheimer.[55]

Strauss remained out of the hearing room, although he continued to communicate with both Robb and Gray. On April 14, the hearing's third day, Strauss sent a letter to Gray enclosing Bobby's account of his conversation with Oppenheimer at the Harvard Board of Overseers meeting and urged Gray to read a report by J. Edgar Hoover on Oppenheimer's "conference" with Bobby. Three days later, an AEC attorney reported back to Strauss that Gray had read the material. Gray "commented (with a smile) 'obviously someone is lying.'"[56] Strauss's letter was an example of his efforts to sway Gray against Oppenheimer — and underscored Strauss's continuing suspicions of Bobby.

As an administrative hearing, and not a judicial court trial with rules of evidence, the proceeding afforded limited rights to Oppenheimer. Gray repeatedly issued rulings that sided with the prosecutor, Robb, on questions of procedure. For instance, Gray permitted Robb to meet privately with the three-member board to review the contents of the vast FBI file on Oppenheimer, without Oppenheimer and his attorney, Lloyd Garrison, being present. When Garrison requested a similar opportunity, Robb opposed the request, and Gray agreed with Robb. *American Prometheus*, the authoritative biography of Oppenheimer by Kai Bird and Martin J. Sherwin, described the hearing as a "veritable kangaroo court in which the head judge accepted the prosecutor's lead."[57]

Evidence of Oppenheimer's past associations with Communists was extensive. Oppenheimer's wife, Kitty, her friend Steve Nelson, his brother Frank, and Robert's former girlfriend Jean Tatlock were or had been Communists. Robb also presented evidence that Oppenheimer had hired Communists to work at Los Alamos. In addition, General Leslie Groves, who had led the Manhattan Project with Oppenheimer, testified about Oppenheimer's statements regarding a Communist friend of Oppenheimer's, Haakon Chevalier, who allegedly asked the scientist in 1943 to provide information to the Soviets about the bomb project. Oppenheimer had said he rebuffed the request, but his account of the approach by Chevalier changed over the years. Groves testified that Oppenheimer had said Chevalier approached his brother Frank, which differed from accounts Oppenheimer and others gave the FBI. Finally, Groves testified that while he believed it was right to grant Oppenheimer security clearance in 1943 to work on the atom bomb project, the law had changed and, as a result, "I would not clear Dr. Oppenheimer today."[58] As Robb shifted the hearing to take up the H-bomb claims, Vannevar Bush testified about his own opposition to the H-bomb and said many scientists around the country believed Oppenheimer was "being pilloried and put through an ordeal because he had the temerity to express his honest opinions."[59] Yet physicist Edward Teller, a strong proponent of the H-bomb since the early days of the Manhattan Project, took a different view. Teller testified at length about Oppenheimer's opposition to the H-bomb and then deftly supported terminating Oppenheimer's security clearance saying, "If it is a question of wisdom and judgment, as demonstrated by actions since 1945, then I would say one would be wiser not to grant clearance."[60]

The hearing ended, after summary arguments by both sides, on May 6, 1954. On May 23, the AEC personnel security board delivered its verdict, finding by a vote of 2–1 that Oppenheimer's security clearance should remain revoked. Board member Thomas Morgan joined Gray in the majority finding, which concluded that Oppenheimer's conduct regarding the H-bomb had been "sufficiently disturbing as to raise a doubt as to whether his future participation . . . would be clearly consistent with the best interests of security."[61] Board member Ward Evans dissented, saying, "There is not the slightest vestige of evidence before this Board that would indicate that Dr. Oppenheimer is not a loyal citizen of his country . . . I personally think that our failure to clear Dr. Oppenheimer will be a black mark on the escutcheon of our country." The matter then went to the AEC itself, where chairman Strauss authored a majority opinion dated June 29, with a 4–1 vote, finding that Oppenheimer was loyal but nonetheless a security risk, so his security clearance should not be restored.

With Oppenheimer largely removed from important scientific and military debates over nuclear weapons, the way was clear for the US nuclear weapons arsenal to grow rapidly over the next seven years of the Eisenhower administration. Yet Bobby, who had supported Oppenheimer's passion for candor as a way to reduce the threat of nuclear holocaust, would later wage his own battle to urge the US military to step back from its strategy of building a massive nuclear strike force.

11

THE IRAN COUP

Soon after taking office, Eisenhower had turned to the NSC for help managing a major international crisis. In Iran, the giant British oil company, Anglo-Iranian Oil, had controlled the country's oil production under a concession that a weak Iranian government granted in the early 1900s. But in 1951, the country's parliament passed a bill nationalizing Anglo-Iranian, which Prime Minister Mohammad Mossadeq signed into law. The company's owners, the largest of which was the British government, launched a campaign fighting the seizure of its facilities and waging a diplomatic and legal battle around the globe to prevent Iran from selling any of the oil it produced. President Truman had maintained neutrality in the dispute. On January 9, not long before Ike's inauguration, Mossadeq sent a cable imploring the president-elect to "give most careful consideration to the Iranian case so that Iran would be able to attain its just aspirations in a manner which will strengthen the cause of world peace and will renew confidence in the determination of the United States to support with all its power and prestige the principles of the charter of the United Nations." Eisenhower replied within twenty-four hours, assuring Mossadeq that he would continue the US policy of neutrality. "I hope you will accept my assurances that I have in no way compromised our position of impartiality in this matter and that no individual has attempted to prejudice me in the matter."

For months, British intelligence officials had been waging a secret campaign to convince the CIA to join them in a coup to remove Mossadeq from power.[1] It was a challenging time for the English royal family. King George VI had died a year earlier, leaving his daughter, Queen Elizabeth II, to take the throne at age twenty-five. Yet the queen was supported by her shrewd prime minister, Winston Churchill, who sought American help in regaining control of Anglo-Iranian. This campaign intensified after Eisenhower and his aggressively anti-Communist secretary of state, Foster Dulles, took office. In early February 1953, agents from the British

Secret Intelligence Service, or SIS, more commonly known as MI6, came to Washington for a meeting with both Dulles brothers. They recommended that Kermit Roosevelt, chief of the CIA's Near East and Africa Division and grandson of President Theodore Roosevelt, serve as the "field commander" for a coup against Mossadeq. Iranian general Fazlollah Zahedi was identified as the coup's Iranian commander.[2] On February 18, British intelligence secretary John Sinclair arrived in Washington and met with Allen Dulles to continue pressing the US to support Mossadeq's overthrow.[3]

On the same day as Sinclair's visit, the Dulleses brought their concerns about Iran before the NSC. In the meeting in the White House Cabinet Room, Allen told the NSC that the Mossadeq government was on the verge of collapse. He said "a showdown was imminent, either as a result of an attempt by the shah to take over the government, or as a result of attempts to get rid of Mossadeq by his rivals."[4] The president asked what points of contention remained between Iran and the UK in the negotiations over Anglo-Iranian. Allen Dulles said compensation for future profits from the lost oil concession were in dispute but that Mossadeq "could not afford to reach any agreement with the British lest it cost him his political life." The discussion ended without the NSC recommending any action, and there was no sign that Ike had shifted from the neutrality he had vowed to Mossadeq a month earlier.

The CIA soon raised concerns that the Communist Tudeh Party, which held seats in the parliament, could try to grab power. In a secret report to the president, the agency asserted the "Tudeh Party may be expected to capitalize on, and increase, the tension in every possible way. The Tudeh Party, which has always been anti-shah, will probably back Mossadeq for the time being."[5] The report also projected that the shah would likely appoint the fanatical Muslim speaker of the Majlis, or the lower house of parliament, Abol-Ghasem Kashani, to be prime minister if Mossadeq were ousted. Kashani was pro-shah, but anti-American. The CIA drew the pessimistic conclusion that "the present situation offers the shah an opportunity which he has not as yet seized. His past record does not suggest that he will act."

The shah, Mohammad Reza Pahlavi, had a deep-seated resentment of the English. After all, it was the English who signed a treaty with the Russians in 1907 dividing Iran in two, and who in 1919 took control of

Iran as a protectorate.[6] And after World War II, Britain and the Soviet Union occupied Iran militarily, though both ultimately withdrew their forces. The shah's distrust even extended to suspecting a British hand in an assassination attempt against him in 1949. "The British had their fingers in strange pies," he wrote. "They were always interested in forging links with diverse groups in nations they wished to control, and they had long exercised a good deal of control over Iran. There is little doubt that London was involved with the Tudeh in various ways and of course the British had ties to the most reactionary clergy in the country."

Eisenhower continued to hold to his neutral position. At its next meeting, on March 4, the NSC again addressed the situation in Iran. Secretary of State Dulles sounded the alarm over a possible Communist takeover of the country and its tremendous oil production facilities and petroleum reserves. "Worse still, Mr. Dulles pointed out, if Iran succumbed to the Communists there was little doubt that in short order the other areas of the Middle East, with some 60% of the world's oil reserves, would fall into Communist control."[7] Foster Dulles laid out options for the US that included disassociating from the English in an effort to regain popularity in Iran, purchasing oil from the new Iranian national oil company, and lending material support to Mossadeq's government. The Iranians were seeking assistance in restarting the massive refinery in the city of Abadan. Eisenhower said that given the situation in Iran, the British themselves might agree to a US policy that was independent of British policy. However, the president also noted that recent British settlement offers to Iran, "unlike earlier ones," had been reasonable.

Bobby, perhaps sensing a critical shift in policy was afoot, broke with his usual posture of neutrality and urged an independent US policy that would hinge on a bold move — purchasing Anglo-Iranian. "Mr. Cutler again pleaded the wisdom of an American policy in Iran independent of the British, and suggested it might even be wise for the United States to buy out the British oil company," meeting notes show. "The President replied that he had long believed that this should be done, but he could see no way of convincing Congress it was the part of wisdom for the United States Government or any American oil company to buy the bankrupt Anglo-Iranian."

After further discussion of the Iranian military and other Middle East matters, Bobby again argued for an independent US policy toward Iran:

Mr. Cutler again inquired of the Secretary of State whether it would not be possible, in the forthcoming conversations with the British, to induce them to waive their claims and let the United States proceed to negotiate unilaterally with Iran. The British had lost their investment in Iran in any case, and a unilateral course of action by the United States was about the only thing which had not been tried. The President was impressed with this argument, and informed Secretary Dulles that he ought to try to work out a position with the British that would save their face but actually give the United States control of the situation and freedom to act along the lines suggested by Mr. Cutler.[8]

Secretary of State Dulles, however, tried to dampen the push for a separate US policy toward Iran, saying he had already raised the issue with British foreign secretary Anthony Eden. Dulles also backpedaled from the concerns he expressed at the NSC's previous meeting about the imminent crisis in Iran, suggesting the situation was in fact no longer urgent. He said the British "did not anticipate any real crisis in Iran for a long time to come." Ike retorted that the British had too often been wrong in assessing how much time they had to react to developments, and he warned that if the Soviets moved into Iran, the discussion at the NSC table would concern full mobilization of US troops. "If," said the president, "I had $500,000,000 of money to spend in secret, I would get $100,000,000 of it to Iran right now." Eisenhower again returned to the proposal — advocated by Bobby — for an independent US policy, asking the secretary of state how soon he could discuss the matter with Eden. The foreign secretary was already in Washington for a series of meetings. "Would it be possible this evening?" Ike asked. "We must find out immediately how the British really feel — whether they are ready to concede to us on this situation, or whether they are going to be stiff-necked."

That night, March 4, Eden met at the White House with Eisenhower and Secretary Dulles, and their conversation ranged over subjects from Egypt to a new strategy, proposed by Dulles, to create a security organization called the Middle East Defense Organization as a bulwark against Communism. During the meeting, Ike "suggested the United States might have to exercise a freer hand with relation to Iran and the oil situation."[9]

Even though the president himself had floated the idea with Eden, Dulles did not push for an independent US policy as Ike and Bobby had urged. Dulles's top priority in America's relationship with the UK was its ongoing support in the battle against global Communism. In a meeting on March 6 at the State Department, Eden warned Dulles that sending technicians to help Iran resume oil production would endanger US–UK relations and suggested that the best approach would be for the US not to render any assistance to Iran's oil industry. Dulles replied that "he thought this probably would be the proper course."[10]

Likely encouraged by Dulles's remarks, Eden firmly opposed US assistance for Iran's oil industry when he and Dulles met with Eisenhower at the White House later that day. He urged that any measures the US took to stabilize Iran "be in terms of aid unrelated to any purchase of oil or activation of the refinery." Eden added, "The presence there of any American technicians would arouse very bitter resentment in the United Kingdom and be apt to create serious parliamentary difficulties."[11] He was indeed being stiff-necked, as Eisenhower had put it.

When Mossadeq met with US ambassador Loy Henderson in Teheran three days later, he said he was disappointed by the latest British proposal and was prepared to take the Anglo-Iranian case to the International Court of Justice in The Hague. He also asked whether the United States would buy Iranian oil and help Iran restart the Abadan refinery.

Two days later, on March 11, Bobby briefed the NSC on Mossadeq's expected rejection of the latest British settlement offer and his plea for US assistance. Secretary of State Dulles flatly declared: "Any proposal that the United States purchase Iranian oil at this time would constitute a terrific blow to the British." Eden had drawn a line in the sand, telling Foster that if the US sent technicians to help reopen Anglo-Iranian's vast refinery at Abadan, Eden would be unable to survive as foreign secretary." Bobby, however, again questioned the wisdom of standing with Great Britain, citing market economics. He said that if the Iranian government were to slash the price of oil, "the effect would be chaotic on the world price of oil."[12] Charles Wilson, the former General Motors chief executive whom Eisenhower had named defense secretary, argued that Iran's action might undermine contracts that companies had with other countries. He said if the US bought oil from Iran, that would "destroy what was left of the idea of sanctity of contracts," and that "if we entered into an agreement to purchase oil from Mossadeq we ourselves would quickly be swindled."

Bobby asked Secretary Dulles to explain the latest British terms that Mossadeq "was about to turn down." Dulles did so, and then "explained at some length the Iranian fear that if they submitted the issue of compensation to arbitration at The Hague, they would undergo a protracted economic bondage to Great Britain." Now Eisenhower spoke up. "The President said that he had very real doubts whether, even if we tried unilaterally, we could make a successful deal with Mossadeq. He felt that it might not be worth the paper it was written on, and the example might have very grave effects on United States oil concessions in other parts of the world." After hearing from the Joint Chiefs of Staff about the challenge of defending Iran from a Soviet military attack, the NSC moved quickly to its final action. It agreed that no proposal to buy Iranian oil should be made at the present time. The prospect of an independent US solution to the Iran dilemma was dimming.

Meanwhile, the CIA and State Department had begun working with the British on contingency plans in the event of an overt Communist attempt to take over the Iranian government. Undersecretary of State "Beetle" Smith told the NSC on March 20 that the CIA and British intelligence operatives had met in February to discuss "joint activities in Iran in the event of a Tudeh coup."[13] Political operations in Iran to influence political, military, and religious leaders to speak out against Tudeh were already under way. The operations were also designed to instigate "physical attacks on Tudeh facilities" and to build relationships with anti-Tudeh tribal groups in southern Iran. In the event of an attempted Communist takeover, the CIA could supply weapons and demolition material, stockpiled in Tripoli, sufficient "to supply a 10,000-man guerilla force."

In the ensuing weeks, the NSC made no change in its policy on Iran, and there is no official record of a US policy shift. Yet top-secret plans were under way to remove Mossadeq with a CIA-backed coup. On April 4, CIA director Allen Dulles "approved a budget of $1,000,000 which could be used by the Teheran Station in any way that would bring about the fall of Mossadeq."[14] In this secret move, far from the strategic debate of the secret NSC meetings, and with no known record of approval by President Eisenhower, a course was charted to change the history of US relations with Iran and indeed the entire Islamic world.

Remarkably, while the Iranian drama was unfolding, the US Department of Justice had been conducting a major anti-trust investigation into the practices of the oil industry, a probe that had begun under the Truman administration. Federal prosecutors were pursuing an investigation into charges that Anglo-Iranian had conspired with Standard Oil and four other American oil giants to control prices. But in December 1952, Eden had filed a memo in federal court in Washington arguing that as a sovereign company owned primarily by the British government, Anglo-Iranian should be immune from litigation in US courts and should be exempted from the anti-trust investigation. The judge ruled in the company's favor.[15]

While Anglo-Iranian was now legally exempt, the investigation could nonetheless impugn the actions of Anglo-Iranian and American oil companies in Iran and other countries. The State Department had argued, in a secret paper submitted to the NSC in January, that the investigation posed a threat to US national security interests by offering a propaganda victory to enemies of the United States.[16] The Dulles brothers' former firm, Sullivan & Cromwell, had been representing Standard Oil of New Jersey for more than a year in an effort to terminate the investigation.[17] Bobby placed a discussion of the anti-trust probe on the NSC's agenda for April 8, 1953. In the secrecy of the NSC meeting, Secretary Dulles moved to kill the anti-trust investigation. The secretary of state "stated flatly that he could not conceive of any decree issuing from this civil suit which would not wreck the oil companies' arrangements outside the United States and therefore redound to the disadvantage of United States national security." Attorney General Brownell firmly opposed Dulles. When President Eisenhower asked what the oil companies had done to require such legal action, Brownell spoke forcefully: "There was no reasonable doubt that they had combined in restraint of trade within the meaning of the anti-trust laws and that indeed some of the companies had admitted this and consented to produce their documents."[18] In the end, however, Brownell agreed to a compromise, one with vast benefits for the oil industry. He would not pursue criminal charges against the oil companies but recommended that Justice file a civil suit. Despite Dulles's objections, Eisenhower approved proceeding with the suit.

The Justice Department filed suit on April 21 alleging that twenty-five years earlier, in 1928, five oil companies had started an international conspiracy to control oil production. The defendants included Standard Oil Company of New Jersey, Socony-Vacuum Oil Company Inc., the Texas Company, the Standard Oil Company of California, and the Gulf Oil Corporation. Three of the five were descendants of John Rockefeller's Standard Oil Company that had spun off as independent entities after the US Supreme Court ruled in 1911 that Standard Oil was an illegal monopoly. In the 1953 case, the Justice Department claimed that Anglo-Iranian had joined the five defendants in forming the international cartel. However, the judge's earlier ruling had released Anglo-Iranian as a defendant.

Shifting to a new phase of its coup plotting, the CIA directed Donald Wilber, a Princeton-trained archaeologist specializing in Persian history who was a covert CIA agent in Iran, to draft a coup plan with British intelligence.[19] In May, Wilber traveled to Cypress to meet with the MI6 chief for Iran, Matthew Darbyshire. They concluded that "the shah would act only with great reluctance but that he could be forced to do so," and that the only military leader they could rely on to lead the coup was Zahedi, the general identified by SIS in Washington three months earlier. They also agreed that the operation should be "made to appear legal or quasi-legal instead of an outright coup."

The agents then moved their operation to Beirut, where Kermit Roosevelt and Roger Goiran, the Teheran CIA station chief, joined Wilber and SIS agents to refine the plan.[20] On June 14, Roosevelt and Wilber took the revised plan from Beirut to London, where they went to SIS headquarters for meetings. The coup plan — which extensively detailed actions to be taken against Iran's military, police, parliament, and media — called for using the shah's sister to convince him to take action against Mossadeq.[21] "We consider Princess Ashraf, his forceful and scheming twin sister, to be the person most likely to be able to induce the shah to play his role. We are certain that Ashraf will eagerly cooperate to bring about the fall of Mossadeq."

The plan called for the shah to name General Zahedi the "chief of staff" of the Iranian military, whereupon Zahedi would establish a military secretariat and order his troops to arrest Mossadeq.[22] The plan also called for paying bribes to lawmakers to support Mossadeq's removal and the naming of Zahedi as prime minister. "To prepare for the change of government, a number of the deputies will be approached and purchased."[23]

Once in power, Zahedi was to seize control of the homes of Mossadeq and his entourage, police departments, telephone exchanges, and the parliament and national bank. "Arrests will include the key figures of the Mossadeq government, key army officers cooperating with Mossadeq, and selected newspaper editors."[24] The plan also called for a targeted assault on the Tudeh Party: "At the time of the coup at least 100 party and front group leaders and journalists must be arrested." The British, CIA, and Zahedi would provide names of people to arrest.[25] Finally, the plan called for a "massive propaganda campaign against Mossadeq and his government but with Mossadeq himself as the principal target." The campaign, with a budget of $150,000, would discredit Mossadeq by asserting he favored Tudeh and the USSR, was an enemy of Islam, and was leading the country to economic collapse. In its breadth and detail — with its combined use of military force, bribery, and political subterfuge — the plan was poised to be a stunning assault on one of the few parliamentary democracies in the Middle East.

On June 25, Roosevelt took the plan to the State Department for a meeting with the Dulles brothers, Undersecretary of State Smith, Secretary of Defense Charles Wilson, Ambassador Henderson, and others. Secretary of State Dulles began the meeting by saying, "So this is how we get rid of that madman Mossadeq." He ended the meeting with: "That's that, then; let's get going."[26] Ike and both Dulles brothers approved the "operational plan" for Mossadeq's ouster on July 11, 1953, Wilber wrote in a top-secret history of the coup that was leaked to *The New York Times* in 2000.[27] Eisenhower's official appointment book shows separate "off the record" meetings on July 11 with each of the Dulles brothers.

By late July, the NSC was no longer engaging in vigorous policy discussions on Iran as it had in February and March when Bobby and Ike pushed for a strategy of an independent US policy. At the July 31 NSC meeting, for example, Allen Dulles said that "in Iran another crisis was approaching. A plebiscite was due to be held on August 5 to give Mossadeq the right to get rid of Parliament. The shah had locked himself in his palace, and the Tudeh party was supporting Mossadeq . . . the situation remained serious." There was no further discussion of Iran, and the NSC moved on to consider Soviet containment strategies being analyzed under Operation Solarium.[28] The NSC's official policy on Iran remained unchanged while the coup plotters proceeded.

With the CIA and MI6 teams moving forward on the ground in Iran, Roosevelt crossed into the country from Iraq on July 19 under a pseudonym and arrived in Teheran.[29] He worked with other CIA agents to ensure that Princess Ashraf agreed to her role. She traveled from France to Teheran on July 29 to meet up with her brother. Asadollah Rashidian, an MI6 agent, prepared the shah for a meeting with US general Norman Schwarzkopf, who had developed a friendship with the monarch during his time as chief of the US Military Mission to the Iranian Gendarmerie from 1942 to 1948.[30]

On the evening of August 12 the draft orders, or "firmans," for the coup were taken to the shah at the royal palace in Ramsar, on the Caspian Sea. Late the next evening, the firmans, signed by the shah, were delivered to Zahedi in Teheran, according to Wilber.[31] Early on the morning of August 16, pro-Zahedi colonels tried to arrest Mossadeq at his home but were themselves arrested by soldiers loyal to the sitting prime minister. Fearing the coup had failed, the shah and his wife fled to Baghdad, where he could expect kind treatment from his friend, Iraq's King Faisal.[32] Soldiers loyal to Mossadeq secured Teheran, and pro-Mossadeq nationalists and Tudeh Party members began denouncing the coup publicly. Zahedi was moved to a safe location.[33]

The coup appeared on the verge of failure, but Roosevelt believed it might yet succeed if the shah would make a radio broadcast from Baghdad with statements the CIA had prepared for him. On the morning of the seventeenth, the shah took to the airwaves announcing he had issued orders for the dismissal of Mossadeq and his replacement as prime minister by Zahedi.[34] Rather than rely on bribed parliamentarians to vote against Mossadeq, the shah declared he had constitutional authority to remove him. The CIA station, meanwhile, continued to seek support from Islamic religious fundamentalists and used gangs of ruffians posing as Tudeh supporters to ransack businesses.[35] By the end of the day on August 18, pro-Mossadeq forces still controlled the capital, and the CIA considered abandoning the coup, though Roosevelt refused to flee.[36]

Then the tide turned suddenly. Residents of Teheran awoke on the morning of the nineteenth to multiple newspaper accounts of the firmans naming Zahedi prime minister.[37] Massive pro-shah crowds gathered and proceeded through the city, sacking offices of Tudeh newspapers along the way. A colonel involved in the coup obtained a tank and appeared in front of parliament hall, and by ten fifteen truckloads of pro-shah soldiers took up positions at all the main squares. Pro-shah royalists had seized Radio Teheran by midafternoon, and Roosevelt met with Zahedi to prepare the final steps. Mossadeq went into hiding, but soldiers under Zahedi's command arrested him the next day.[38] The shah returned to Teheran and images circulated of him greeting Zahedi as the new prime minister. The new regime was in power.

A military tribunal later convicted Mossadeq of treason and sentenced him to three years in prison.[39] Anglo-Iranian Oil Company was returned to its English owners, who soon renamed it BP. Under pressure from the NSC and State Department, the Justice Department in January 1954 agreed to grant immunity from anti-trust laws to major oil companies so they could form a consortium to buy Iranian oil, which the NSC deemed critical to prevent the Soviets from gaining control of Iran's oil production. With the shah's approval, the consortium — owned 40 percent by BP, 14 percent by Royal Dutch Shell, and the remainder mostly by Exxon and other major American oil companies — began oil purchases later that year.[40] The grant of immunity forced the Justice Department to drop significant parts of its anti-trust claims against the oil companies — a sacrifice to what one historian called "the conceived exigencies of national defense and security" in the Cold War.[41] Most of the oil companies eventually settled the case, and the department dropped its remaining claims in 1968, making it one of the nation's longest-running anti-trust cases.

Eisenhower never publicly acknowledged that he ordered the coup that overthrew Mossadeq. In his published memoirs, Ike denied there was a military coup in Iran and instead portrayed the US role as merely supporting the shah of Iran in his efforts, permitted under Iran's constitution, to appoint Mossadeq's successor.[42] Yet in his personal diary, just weeks after the coup, he appeared to acknowledge that the US role was a secret transgression against the people of Iran: "The things we did were 'covert.' If knowledge of them became public we would not only be embarrassed in that region, but our chances to do anything of like nature in the future would almost totally disappear."[43]

In his memoirs, Bobby quietly admitted the CIA's role when he attributed the outcome partly to "the initiative of young Kermit

Roosevelt."[44] Bobby also cast the coup as a success for the United States and suggested Mossadeq had conspired with Communists. Bobby wrote: "In Iran, it was not necessary to send American troops to sustain the established government of the young Shah from the frenzied, weeping, Red intrigue of Premier Mossadeq."

12

MYSTERY MAN

As Ike's special assistant for national security affairs, Bobby ran the reformed NSC and also handled classified information for the president from the FBI, CIA, and defense agencies, all while keeping a low profile at the White House and refusing to talk to the press. This role, on top of the fact that he was a close confidant of Ike's, soon earned Bobby the title in the press of "Mystery Man." *The Saturday Evening Post*, then one of the nation's most widely circulated and influential magazines, headlined a February 1954 profile of Bobby: "Mystery Man of the White House." The story said, "Cutler, always impeccably dressed in restrained grays and blues, seems the prototype of the Proper Bostonian. Many a person, though, has done a double-take on hearing his Oxford-by-way-of-Harvard accent employed in telling smoking room stories . . . Cutler invariably acts as the gay master of ceremonies at informal White House parties, usually reciting a witty poem he has written for the occasion. But if Bobby seems the closest thing to an unofficial court jester in the Eisenhower entourage, he is also a dynamo of energy with a keen mind and a fierce devotion to duty."[1] The double entendre of the phrase "gay master of ceremonies" might have struck a chord for those who had heard the rumors cited by Joe Alsop of Bobby's "incorrect tastes in love." Published at a time when Senator Joseph McCarthy was at the peak of his power, the story said Bobby "tends to dislike Sen. Joe McCarthy."

A month later, the *St. Louis Post-Dispatch* ran a profile of Bobby under the headline "White House Mystery Man Is the Top Secret Keeper of Eisenhower Regime." The story began by saying, "The President's insistence on extensive staff work for important policy decisions has changed a gregarious, fun-loving Boston Banker and civic leader into a monastic 'mystery man . . .'"[2] This story and others noted that Bobby dealt in high-level secrets, refused to talk about his work for Ike, and often included the personal detail that he was a bachelor.

"'Untouchable, unreachable and unquotable': That sums up Robert Cutler, the President's alter ego on the National Security Council, where 'Cold War' policy is hammered into shape," a *New York Times* Sunday magazine feature asserted in January 1955.[3] The article deemed Bobby "one of the most elusive men in Washington. The description is apt both because of the nature of Bobby's job and the nature of the man. Cutler knows virtually as many secrets about the problems of our security and the proposed solutions to those problems as the president himself."

The *Times* also noted Bobby's passion for cycling, a somewhat unusual form of exercise in Washington in the 1950s, particularly for a man of his age. "At 59, cycling is his only outdoor recreation. He has registered 935 miles on his bicycle gauge since last May."

Some press coverage, particularly when it devolved into conspiracy theories about Bobby, irritated him. In January 1954, Drew Pearson wrote in his influential and widely syndicated column that Bobby was part of a coterie of liberal advisers guiding Eisenhower to the left after conservative policies hurt his popularity in 1953. Pearson described Bobby as a "Boston banker with liberal Republican ideas" and a "close friend of Justice Felix Frankfurter who masterminded his appointment."[4] In another column, Pearson claimed Frankfurter had arranged for Bobby to join Eisenhower's campaign train. Bobby later noted, "So crass an error led Mr. Justice Frankfurter in January, 1954, to pen me a humorous note: 'Dear Bobby, Can't you get divorced from me, especially since we were never engaged? F. F.'"[5] Bobby had upon occasion praised Frankfurter, a Harvard graduate who achieved prominence under President Franklin Roosevelt, as an example of what a man can achieve through hard work, but there is no evidence he played any role in Bobby's joining the campaign train.

While Bobby's realm was the NSC, he also regularly attended cabinet meetings. Still, despite Bobby's broad role, and despite the press's perception of Bobby as the administration's keeper of secrets, there were plenty of important national security secrets in which Bobby played no role. For instance, when Ike approved a proposal to build a super-secret high-altitude surveillance jet in November 1954, Allen and Foster Dulles, Secretary of Defense Charles Wilson, Ike's aide Andrew Goodpaster, and others were present but Bobby was not.[6] Dulles's special assistant, Richard Bissell, developed the jet, dubbed the U-2, in offices directly across from the Metropolitan Club near Bobby's residence at The Family, and yet there is no record of Bobby's involvement.[7]

One area that did keep Bobby embroiled in secret information was his duty as a conduit for FBI director J. Edgar Hoover to communicate with the president. In September 1953, less than a month after the CIA's coup ousted Mossadeq, Hoover sent Bobby a top-secret memo saying the USSR was obtaining information from the offices of British prime minister Churchill and foreign minister Eden. Citing unidentified informants, Hoover also said that Eden was gay, and so was his undersecretary of state for foreign affairs, Anthony Nutting. "According to the informant, Mr. Nutting is known as a homosexual and his unexpected rise to a high position was due to his peculiar relations with Mr. Eden. It was alleged that continued leniency toward Communists and fellow travelers in the Foreign Office is explained by the fact that Mr. Nutting is, mildly speaking, a fellow traveler."[8]

Hoover also wrote that, according to an FBI source, Lord Louis Mountbatten, a member of the British royal family and at the time an admiral in command of Great Britain's Mediterranean fleet, "is a homosexual and this fact has been allegedly known for many years." The memo went on to say that Mountbatten had a "peculiar relationship" with his former private secretary, Peter Murphy, a member of the Communist Party and former manager of a Communist bookshop. Murphy "was said to be an extremely good looking man and a talented musician. He reportedly had a most undesirable influence over Mountbatten." However, Hoover closed his secret memo with a caveat. "In view of the unknown reliability of the source, I am unable to place any evaluation whatsoever on this information. Sincerely yours, J. Edgar Hoover."

In the margin of Hoover's letter, Bobby made a handwritten notation using "P," his standard abbreviation for the president. "P would not give any credence to it at all." Bobby had discretion over how to respond to the stream of secret letters and memos that Hoover directed to him for the president's consideration. In this case, Bobby's notation was ambiguous. He may have shown the letter to the president, and Ike told him he would not give it credence. Or Bobby may have chosen not to show it to Ike because he knew the president's views of Hoover's rumored allegations of homosexuality. Ultimately, there is no evidence that Ike saw or responded to the allegations.

Eisenhower had been a friend of Mountbatten's since World War II, when Mountbatten, then the British chief of combined operations, worked with Ike to plan the 1942 invasion of North Africa.[9] As supreme Allied commander, Ike then appointed Mountbatten supreme Allied commander for the Southeast Asia Command, a position in which he led the recapture of Burma from the Japanese in 1944 and 1945. Mountbatten's longtime personal secretary, John Barratt, revealed his own homosexuality years later but denied Mountbatten was gay.[10]

Hoover's handling of allegations against Chip Bohlen, Anthony Eden, and Lord Mountbatten made it abundantly clear that the FBI director was willing to seize on and spread even the most unsubstantiated claims of homosexuality. As a bachelor, Bobby would likely face questions about whether he was gay, and Alsop and others reported that Bobby was trailed by rumors that in fact he was. As a result, it would have been reasonable for Bobby to feel at risk that such claims could target him, too.

Yet there is one account that raises questions about Bobby's discussions with Hoover about homosexuality, suggesting that Hoover may have sought to shield Bobby from investigation. The two men at some point had a conversation about the Chicken Hut, the well-known gay bar adjacent to Bobby's residence on H Street. Stephen Benedict said that at some point in the mid-1950s, Bobby revealed the conversation to him. "My recollection is that in some setting, Bobby mentioned to Hoover the noise being generated in the gay bar below him and outside it by the patrons," Benedict recalled.[11] "Bobby said that Hoover indicated he knew about the bar and that it and others like it were being closely monitored by his [FBI] people." The exact reasons for which Hoover discussed the gay bar with Bobby, and when and where their conversation took place, remain unknown.

Bobby had become a gatekeeper of Hoover's secrets, deciding which of them the president needed to see and which were merely political information to be safely filed away. The secret flow of information from Hoover to Bobby included items such as a report in April 1953 that a "highly confidential source" had said that Supreme Court justice William O. Douglas, who had taken a very public stance in support of Premier Mossadeq of Iran, was seeking a meeting with the Soviet ambassador to the US. Bobby noted in the margin: "told to P and W[illiam] Jackson." Then in June 1953, Hoover sent Bobby a series of letters saying supporters of Julius and Ethel Rosenberg, the husband and wife convicted of conveying nuclear secrets to the Soviets, were organizing protests and calls to the White House in a bid to stop their execution. Bobby merely initialed these letters; the Rosenbergs were executed on June 19. When the FBI reported back to Bobby on the results of its security investigation of CIA official William Bundy in February 1954, Bobby made no notation as to whether he informed the president. When Hoover reported a few years later, in December 1957, that Communists were building a campaign around widely respected black scholar W. E. B. Du Bois "to embarrass the United States internationally," Bobby noted simply, "not shown to P, RC."[12] According to one account, Bobby was once so enraged by one of Hoover's reports that he threw a pair of scissors across the office, causing them to stick in a leather couch.[13]

Bobby vigorously guarded his independence as a judge of what was in the president's interest. This is reflected in his relationship with the Dulles brothers. Bobby was strongly anti-Communist but did not always share the brothers' aggressive, hard-line positions. He maintained cordial social relationships with the brothers but diplomatically steered clear of too close an association with them. In November 1953, after Allen Dulles invited him to join the Council on Foreign Relations, Bobby declined politely.[14] "I regret that I do not feel in a position to accept this invitation at this time," Bobby wrote, without elaborating. "May I express the hope that at some later, and more feasible, time this invitation may be renewed for I should like to take part in the fine work accomplished by the Council." Bobby never became a member.

While staying out of the public eye, Bobby welcomed attention from Eisenhower's staff, who knew Bobby for his humorous toasts at parties, quick wit, poems on special occasions, and celebration of birthdays and anniversaries. Bobby's poems often had a hint of bawdiness or gender play, such as the one he wrote for Dwight and Mamie's wedding anniversary on July 1, 1953, making reference to the male staff and Ike's secretary, Ann Whitman:

> *For thirty-seven years of marital bliss*
> *Each of us offers a great big kiss!*
> *Not for Ike (except for Ann)*
> *But all for Mamie, man by man.*

We who dwell in the halcyon calm
That surrounds our Chief like a healing balm,
With sweetness and light pervading our lives
As we slave mid that quiet on which he thrives,

We can readily grasp all the reasons why
Mamie stays young and pleases the eye.
Nothing to worry her — nothing to fret:
Just resting at ease with "Ma" and her "Pet."

We come to salute, then, the Happy Pair
In their nest set apart from the public's stare,
To let them look, through their rose-colored glasses,
At the men and women of the working classes.

Whether at Camp David or at Burning Tree
Or at the Gettysburg Farm (but NOT, no certainly NOT, at Sea)
Many, many more days of connubial joys,
To Mamie and Ike . . . from Ann and the Boys!

He signed this bit of doggerel from "Bobby," identifying himself jokingly as "The Oliver Wendell Holmes of the Cold War," a phrase that *Fortune* magazine had used to describe him.[15]

Ike's friendship with Bobby remained strong as the NSC mechanism helped Ike wrestle with issues ranging from nuclear strategy to Iran and the Oppenheimer affair. Bobby had enormous quantities of secret information to manage, and Ike did not hesitate to show his gratitude to Bobby and concern for his well-being. When Bobby fell sick in late November 1953, Ike dictated a message from Augusta, Georgia, where he was on a golfing vacation, to be delivered with flowers to Bobby at Walter Reed hospital: "Dear Bobby: One thing I am thankful for today is that you are obeying doctor's orders and staying in bed. I do hope that you won't make your principal companion a flock of Security Council papers. Take it easy!"[16]

Under Bobby's hand, the NSC had become a high-pressure operation that produced many policy papers, circulating drafts to Planning Board members for comments, and identifying — and trying to solve — disputes among agencies. Yet Bobby was not beyond poking fun at bureaucracy and, by extension, the policy machinery he had created. In September 1954, he prepared a mock policy statement on a draft of President Lincoln's Gettysburg Address, replete with objections from an array of agencies — the Defense Department said its reference to the "honored dead" was too morbid, and the Commerce Department said it was seeking 253 editorial changes.[17] In the end, the draft speech was referred to an interagency committee for further revision, a likely grave for Lincoln's oratorical masterwork. Bobby read the humorous report to the NSC on August 18, 1954, reportedly prompting laughter from Ike and others.[18]

Bobby's impact on the White House continued to grow as he sought to improve the president's control of psychological warfare and covert military and political actions. In June 1953, a committee led by former CIA deputy director William H. Jackson and whose members included Bobby and C. D. Jackson, recommended abolition of the Psychological Strategy Board.[19] The committee concluded that the PSB suffered from a "basic misconception" that some policy actions had psychological implications while others did not. The committee also said the PSB had adopted "psychological" plans that conflicted with State Department plans. To improve the president's ability to implement national security policy, the committee recommended the creation of a new organization, the Operations Coordinating Board, or OCB. The OCB's mission was to ensure that the president's policies were executed effectively by CIA, State, Defense, and other federal agencies.[20]

On September 2, 1953, Bobby flew to Denver, where President Eisenhower was on vacation, staying at the home of Mamie's mother, Mrs. Elivera Doud. Bobby and the president met that night at the Doud home, and Ike signed the executive order creating the OCB immediately and abolishing the PSB.[21] The new board was to report to the NSC, and Bobby was to have the right to attend any OCB meetings he wished. Two years after Bobby had experienced the bitter paralysis of the PSB's work under President Truman, he had abolished it and established the NSC as the predominant body for setting national security policy.

The OCB held its first meeting, on September 17, in C. D. Jackson's office with Bobby in attendance. The board's members included Director of the CIA Allen Dulles and Undersecretary of State Smith. C. D. Jackson was its acting executive director. The OCB coordinated its work closely with the NSC staff and circulated its papers to Bobby. In addition, Bobby designated Skip Koons of the NSC staff to maintain standing liaison with Jackson's deputy on the OCB staff.[22] Thus, Bobby and his assistant, Koons, would maintain a finger on the pulse of the covert actions that the OCB was coordinating.

Despite Bobby's efforts to keep up his health through bicycling and other activities, the work took its toll on him. On March 20, 1954, he wrote a letter to Ike offering to resign if the president felt it was necessary. What exactly drove Bobby to write the letter is unclear, but he pointed to the stress of work. Bobby said the job "was a real back-breaker . . . There have been many times when I thought this 10–11 hour schedule couldn't be kept up any longer. But you set such a high standard and you repose so much undeserved confidence in a fellow, there is no other way but to keep on. There must be someone who could perform better than I. If we could find and train him, he could run for you this Juggernaut we've developed much better than my poor powers can."[23] By the end of his letter, however, Bobby offered the president an opportunity to keep him on staff through the November 1954 midterm elections: "But if you want me to stay until after the election, I will keep on working my head off until then."

In a reply three days later, Ike rejected the notion that Bobby should resign. "Dear Bobby," the president wrote:

> I think my blood pressure would have shown less violent variation had you reversed the order in which you expressed the thoughts contained in your March 20th letter. Throughout the entire first part, I had the sinking feeling of "Et tu, Brute!". But your sentence, "But if you want me to stay until after the Election, I will keep on working my head off until then," restored me to some-thing like normal. By which I mean I am selfish enough to want you to keep doing just that, even though I do most seriously urge that you, for one, practice a modicum of malingering.[24]

The president continued:

When I try to deal with the sentiments of personal appreciation you express toward me I am completely helpless. Perhaps I should just say that I lean on you far more than you can possibly know — and with far greater reason.

My most profound thanks and appreciation for your offer to continue your tiring task — and I accept it without any further words.

As ever,

If Bobby was exhausted, his workload showed no sign of letting up. Ike soon sent him on a secretive mission that seemed suited to his "Mystery Man" moniker. From July 3 to 15, Bobby visited US military installations and met with US generals and diplomats in England, France, Germany, Canada, Italy, Morocco, and Portugal. Those Bobby met with included General Alfred Gruenther, the supreme allied commander in Europe, and the US ambassadors to Great Britain, France, and the Soviet Union. On July 20, after returning to Washington from the whirlwind tour, Bobby delivered to Ike his top-secret ten-page report on deployment of nuclear weapons in the allied nations and a range of other subjects.[25] He began by outlining Gruenther's views on the problem of Soviet conventional military superiority in Europe: Gruenther believed willingness to use atomic weapons was critical to defending Western Europe, and Gruenther wanted to have greater authority "to determine on the spot the priorities needed under this 'New Approach.'" Bobby noted that the New Approach called for "instantaneous use of nuclear weapons. Atomic weapons do not supersede ground forces, but supplement them to make up the deficiency."

Bobby's report to Ike also reviewed the likelihood that the allies would permit the use of nuclear weapons, saying, "there is no problem at all with Turkey, Greece, and the Benelux countries, which understand and will side with us on the 'New Approach.'" He continued, "The British like to wait as long as possible, but when the chips are down, they will certainly be on our side." David Bruce, an experienced US diplomat with whom Bobby met in Paris, "thinks the French will probably agree to let the US use the bomb from bases in France." Bobby also reviewed an array of issues including significant progress in the racial integration of US armed forces, poor housing conditions for soldiers and dependents in some countries, and the deteriorating relations between France and its colony Morocco.

Bobby's visit to Morocco drew a rave review from Major General Frederic Glantzberg, commander of the US 17th Air Force in Morocco. Glantzberg wrote Ike, "I feel that someone should tell you about the activities in Morocco of your emissary of goodwill, Brigadier General Robert Cutler. I have no doubt that he has done a superior job as your Special Assistant, but after having seen him operate here for two days, I think he is presently miscast and should be 'Ambassador at Large.' He has completely captivated the entire French colony here and left with the entire Air Force in Morocco in his pocket. After he announced that he wanted a ride in a jet and then took one in a T-33, the 45th Fighter Interceptor Squadron made him an honorary member of the squadron. We have thoroughly enjoyed having him . . ."[26] Please send him back again." Ike added a note to Secretary of State Foster Dulles across the bottom of Glantzberg's letter: "Please note and return. Possibly we have got Bobby in the wrong place!" Dulles replied, "Dear Mr. President, Noted. I will take him any day anywhere."

Yet Bobby would remain in his post behind the scenes at the NSC, where he quickly dove into an array of national security issues awaiting him. Since December of the previous year, the CIA had been moving matériel and personnel into Central America in preparation for another coup against a democratically elected government, this time in Guatemala. The new OCB was coordinating the effort, with oversight from Bobby and the NSC.

13

THE GUATEMALA COUP

Guatemala was approaching a crisis, Allen Dulles warned the NSC in the White House Cabinet Room on February 18, 1953. "It was quite possible, Mr. Dulles thought, that Guatemala's neighbors might take military action to protect themselves from the Communist infection in Guatemala."[1] A month later, a coup attempt, backed by the CIA and the United Fruit Company, was launched from Honduras. Guatemalan government forces intercepted the invaders in the town of Salama, killing four rebel fighters and crushing the coup attempt.[2] This was just the opening salvo of a CIA strategy to overturn Guatemala's young democracy and stamp out the perceived threat of Communism.

With operations across Latin America, United Fruit had grown so powerful that it became known as El Pulpo, the octopus. The Boston-based enterprise began in the late 1890s buying land in Guatemala to grow bananas for export to the US. It developed close ties with Guatemalan military leaders and used its political power to avoid paying property taxes. United Fruit's operations grew rapidly, and it became the second largest employer in Guatemala after the government. It also acquired the country's only railroad, used to transport bananas to a port it ran on the Caribbean Sea, and built the Great White Fleet shipping line to transport bananas to the US. It also developed operations in Cuba, Honduras, Panama, and other Latin American countries. As bananas became increasingly available in American grocery stores, United Fruit sold shares to the public and became a hot stock on Wall Street. In 1930, after the start of the Great Depression, the company purchased one of its few competitors for $31.5 million worth of United Fruit stock.[3]

In the early 1940s, teachers and labor organizers in Guatemala led a reform movement calling for replacement of the country's repressive dictator, General Jorge Ubico. In 1944, Guatemalan voters elected Juan José Arévalo, a schoolteacher who called for agrarian reform and stronger labor rights, as the country's president. Arévalo's reforms for the first time permitted banana workers to join labor unions. In November 1950, Guatemalan voters elected Arévalo's defense minister, former army officer Jacobo Arbenz, to succeed him as president.

In his inaugural address in March 1951, Arbenz said he wished to "transform Guatemala from a backward country with a semi-feudal economy into a modern capitalist country."[4] A land reform law enacted in June 1952 required that all privately held, uncultivated land in lots of more than 672 acres be expropriated for distribution to impoverished peasants. The owners of the expropriated land were to receive compensation based on valuations of their property that they themselves had provided for tax purposes.[5] Arbenz, a large landowner, had some of his own land expropriated. The expropriation law, coupled with strikes by banana workers, threatened United Fruit's production, and its stock price dropped.

United Fruit moved swiftly to oppose the Arbenz land reform and government-mandated wage increases for banana workers. United Fruit supported rightist generals who left Guatemala and formed opposition forces in Nicaragua and Honduras.[6] The company hired a well-connected lobbyist in Washington, Tommy Corcoran, who pressed the Truman and then Eisenhower administrations to carry out a coup removing Arbenz. The company also hired a Madison Avenue public relations expert, Edward L. Bernays, who began planting stories in the press charging that Arbenz was a Communist and that his government posed a threat that could lead to Communism engulfing Latin America.

There were few voices in America defending Arbenz or the Guatemalan peasants working for United Fruit. One exception was Gore Vidal, who had lived in Guatemala and whose 1950 novel, *Dark Green, Bright Red*, was a thinly veiled critique of United Fruit's domination of the country. It tells the story of a US fruit company that abuses its workers only to find they turn to Communists for protection. The company helps a deposed dictator mount a coup d'état to regain power, an uncanny prophecy of events soon to take place.

United Fruit's ties to the new Eisenhower administration were numerous and deep. Prior to taking his post at the NSC, Bobby Cutler served for seven years as president of Old Colony Trust Company, which had managed issuance of bonds and provided other financial services for United Fruit since the early decades of the century. Old Colony's parent company, First National Bank of Boston, and United Fruit still maintained their "interlock" arrangement in which a president or other executive of each company served on the board of the other, a practice dating back to 1907.[7] Bobby remained friends with United Fruit chairman T. Jefferson Coolidge, his colleague from Old Colony and the Tavern Club, and helped him make contacts in the new administration. In April 1954, Tommy Corcoran told Assistant Secretary of State for Inter-American Affairs Henry Holland that Bobby would be calling to invite him to dinner with Coolidge.[8]

Others tied to United Fruit included Secretary of State Foster Dulles, who had been managing partner of Sullivan & Cromwell for decades while United Fruit was a client. In 1936, Foster negotiated an agreement with Guatemalan dictator Jorge Ubico that gave United Fruit control of one-seventh of the country's arable land for ninety-nine years and control of its only port.[9] His brother, Allen, also did work for United Fruit while he was a partner at Sullivan & Cromwell. Allen also represented the J. Henry Schroder Banking Corporation, a part owner of the railway company controlled by United Fruit.[10]

Among a number of Bostonians connected to the company was Henry Cabot Lodge, whose family owned United Fruit stock.[11] In 1949, Lodge went onto the Senate floor to accuse the Guatemalan regime of unfair restrictions on Boston-based United Fruit. The company's connections even extended to the president's secretary, Ann Whitman, who was the wife of United Fruit advertising executive Edmund Whitman. She later acknowledged that she made connections for her husband, and he "reveled in" them and used them "quite freely."[12]

United Fruit's practices had come under an anti-trust investigation by the Truman Justice Department in 1951. By mid-1953, under Eisenhower's attorney general, Herbert Brownell, the Justice Department completed its review.[13] Justice officials concluded the company had engaged in price fixing, controlled domestic markets, and blocked competitors from shipping bananas to the US. The department recommended filing suit and seeking penalties that included forcing United Fruit to divest overseas assets.

Once again, as with the oil cartel case two months earlier, the State Department warned that the United Fruit anti-trust case would interfere with US interests. The NSC Planning Board, chaired by Bobby, took up the issue. The Planning Board's report, delivered to the NSC on June 1, recommended that anti-trust action against United Fruit be postponed for six months so that a settlement could be negotiated. The report warned: "Institution of the action would provide a propaganda weapon generally to Communists and leftists in Central America. Moreover, to the degree that it would promote government seizure, it would assure the placement of extremists in charge of the former Company properties, and would thus increase the power of elements opposed to the United States in Central America, possibly including Panama, and make uncertain the cooperation of governments of the area with the United States."[14] In an alarmist tone, the report argued the suit might prompt the Guatemalan "example" to spread, provoking nationalization of five billion dollars' worth of properties owned by US companies across Latin America.

The NSC gathered in the Cabinet Room on June 4, 1953, with Eisenhower, the Dulles brothers, Nixon, and other NSC members present. After discussions of Korea and Soviet nuclear weapons, Bobby turned attention to the third item on the agenda — the Planning Board's proposal to postpone the anti-trust suit against United Fruit — and then made a striking announcement.[15] "Mr. Cutler explained that, owing to the connections between the Old Colony Trust Company, of which he had formerly been President, and the United Fruit Company, he thought it inappropriate for him to be present at the Council's discussion of this item. He accordingly left the Cabinet Room." Bobby's action marked the first time that a national security advisor left a meeting to avoid a conflict of interest. Others in the room, including the Dulles brothers, did not respond to Bobby's announcement, a meeting memo shows.

After Bobby left the room, President Eisenhower immediately recommended that the anti-trust suit be postponed a full year. "Not only would this longer period be useful in negotiating with the fruit company; it would give us an opportunity to strengthen our position in Central America in the event that the negotiations failed and it proved necessary to proceed with a civil suit," the president told the NSC.[16] Foster Dulles underscored his opposition to anti-trust cases, pointing to "the terrible repercussions which suits like this had on our foreign policy objectives."

Attorney General Herbert Brownell did not oppose the delay, though he noted that a shorter delay would "instill a greater sense of urgency" in the settlement negotiations with the company. Ike retorted that he saw "no reason to tell the United Fruit Company of the interval of time which was to be agreed to." The NSC quickly agreed that the Justice Department should postpone legal action for a year and seek to resolve the dispute through negotiations with United Fruit. The president later formally approved the NSC action.

The Psychological Strategy Board soon took up a revised plan for Arbenz's removal, which the CIA had given a code name: PBSUCCESS. On August 12, the PSB met and approved the CIA's plan to proceed with PBSUCCESS and to take "principal responsibility" for the operation.[17] The next day, with President Eisenhower absent and Vice President Nixon acting as chairman, the NSC authorized the PSB to move ahead with "overthrowing the present regime in Guatemala."[18]

Not everyone in the State Department agreed with the push to remove Arbenz. State Department official Raymond Leddy compared the plan to the 1948 Soviet coup that ousted a democratically elected government in Czechoslovakia and installed a Communist regime. "Were it to become evident that the United States has tried a Czechoslovakia in reverse in Guatemala, the effects on our relations in this hemisphere, and probably in the world at large, could be as disastrous as those produced by open intervention," Leddy wrote in an August 19 memo.[19] However, there is no record that Leddy's memo was ever forwarded to the NSC.

PBSUCCESS picked up steam after Allen Dulles secretly approved a three-million-dollar budget for the operation on December 9, 1953.[20] The CIA began moving weapons, aircraft, and operatives into Honduras in support of the coup to be led by a Guatemalan rebel general, Carlos Castillo Armas. News of the buildup of forces in Honduras leaked out, and Guatemalan officials grew concerned. On January 16, Guillermo Toriello, the Guatemalan ambassador to the United States, went to the White House to meet with Eisenhower and John Cabot, the assistant secretary of state, whose brother Thomas had been president of United Fruit. Toriello directly denied that Communists would take control of the Guatemalan government and urged respect for his country's young democracy.[21] Eisenhower stated his concern bluntly: "We certainly had the impression that the Guatemalan government was infiltrated with Communists, and we couldn't cooperate with a government that openly favored Communists." Toriello attacked United Fruit as a monopoly, displaying a map that showed "United Fruit's stranglehold on ports, railways, etc." Toriello also pointed to the ties of administration officials to United Fruit, noting that Sullivan & Cromwell, the secretary of state's former firm, represented United Fruit. The meeting ended after President Eisenhower suggested that the Guatemalan claims against United Fruit might be resolved through an "international judgment," a suggestion that went unexplored. Toriello's bold effort to appeal to Ike yielded no resolution.

In Honduras, the CIA prepared instructions for the Castillo Armas forces on use of death squads for killing opponents and sent them rifles with silencers.[22] CIA training activities included assassination teams, and a briefing prior to the invasion called for the teams to eliminate Communists after the invasion began. PBSUCCESS also included a political propaganda campaign led by CIA official E. Howard Hunt, who managed a team in Florida producing materials aimed at convincing the people of Guatemala that Communists controlled the Arbenz government.[23] CIA planes dropped leaflets carrying anti-Communist and religious messages in rural areas of the country.

The CIA's coup in Iran had come dangerously close to failing, and Ike wanted to improve control over CIA covert actions. On March 15, the president signed a top-secret NSC directive requiring the CIA to coordinate covert operations with the Departments of State and Defense. Called NSC 5412, the directive made the newly created Operations Coordinating Board "the normal channel" for achieving coordination by State, Defense, and CIA.

Bobby immediately sent the 5412 directive to Allen Dulles with a letter bluntly laying out the president's concerns. Bobby told Allen that Ike was "emphatic" that he wanted to have "an overall knowledge of the major elements" of covert operations. In a gentle warning to Allen that he needed to keep Ike informed of important covert actions, Bobby said Ike "tended to brush aside the possibility that he would ever be in a position to disown responsibility for major undertakings."[24] Bobby also told the CIA director that Eisenhower wanted Allen to appear "quarterly or so" in the president's office to give an oral report to NSC members and others whom the president might invite, such as the chairman of the Joint Chiefs of Staff. Allen responded in a letter to Bobby the next day, vowing to comply with the president's and Bobby's instructions. "I stand ready to make an oral report to the statutory members of the

NSC, and others the President may wish to include, whenever you deem it appropriate."[25]

At this time, Allen was aggressively pursuing a wide array of clandestine programs — MK-Ultra, for example, was subjecting humans to tests of LSD and other drugs in an effort to achieve mind control. The CIA also had begun using American news reporters to publish stories supporting the agency's views; hundreds of journalists, including both Alsop brothers, eventually wrote stories at the behest of the CIA.[26] Yet NSC 5412 was specifically aimed at coordination of international covert operations, the kind that would topple elected governments like Guatemala's. If the CIA's role in Guatemala were exposed, it would reveal that Ike had made a very sharp break with the promise of non-intervention that President Roosevelt made in his "Good Neighbor" policy.

The United Fruit public relations machine, meanwhile, had fueled concerns in the United States about Communism in Guatemala. In April, Congressman Charles Kersten, a Wisconsin Republican, wrote a letter to Bobby outlining his plans to hold hearings on Guatemalan Communism. Bobby's assistant, Skip Koons, forwarded a copy to the CIA, where Kersten's proposed hearings set off alarm bells. An assistant to Allen Dulles sent a memo back to Koons noting that "unfriendly propagandists would attempt to create hostility toward the [Kersten committee's] investigation and might well establish a frame of mind in Latin America in which the investigation would be considered a unilateral interference in Latin American affairs . . ."[27] Bobby soon took the issue up with Kersten personally, convincing him to put off the hearings until July.[28] By then, the coup would be over.

A few weeks later, the Arbenz administration handed the CIA an unexpected political windfall — a connection with a Communist regime that bolstered claims Guatemala was entering Moscow's orbit. On May 15, the Swedish freighter *Alfhem* docked in Puerto Barrios, Guatemala, and began unloading crates of military equipment from Communist-controlled Poland. The State Department issued a statement condemning Guatemala for importing arms from the Soviet bloc.[29] Guatemala's leaders claimed the country was merely attempting to defend itself, noting that the United States had refused to sell arms to it since 1948 and also blocked other countries from doing so.[30] Toriello, in a front-page *New York Times* story, proclaimed that Guatemala "is not a colony of the United States nor an associated state that requires permission of the United States Government to acquire the things indispensable for its defense and security."[31]

On May 26, Foster Dulles called Bobby and started the conversation with a simple question: "The Sec. asked if he didn't have pretty close relations with the United Fruit Company," notes on the call show. Bobby replied, "Yes, and the Sec. asked if they could talk about it."[32] Foster's appointment book that day shows "Gen Cutler (United Fruit)" was at Foster's office for a four forty-five appointment.[33] The substance of their conversation was not recorded. As the CIA's covert action unfolded over the next months, United Fruit kept a low profile, while General Castillo Armas took center stage as the coup leader.

Meanwhile, sporadic domestic protests arose against the US role in Guatemala, including a street demonstration in New York City. The Labor Youth League, an organization of the Communist Party, distributed a pamphlet titled "Who is Dulles Kidding?" It jeeringly quoted the secretary of state as saying, "The United States never interferes in the affairs of other countries." It charged that United Fruit's connections in Washington included "Robert Cutler — administrative assistant to President Eisenhower."[34] When FBI director J. Edgar Hoover obtained a copy, he forwarded it to Bobby.

On June 17, when the NSC met secretly in the White House Cabinet Room, Bobby announced that the issue of the anti-trust suit against Guatemala was up for consideration because a year had passed since the NSC first recommended a one-year waiting period.[35] Just as he had a year earlier, he told the NSC he wished to be excused from the discussion, "in view of the connections of the Old Colony Trust Company with the United Fruit Company." With Bobby absent, Attorney General Brownell reported that United Fruit had rejected a settlement and that the Justice Department wanted to proceed with the suit.

With coup forces advancing toward Guatemala, Secretary of State Dulles changed tack and recommended permitting the anti-trust suit to proceed. In a Machiavellian twist, Dulles said "that on balance it might be positively advantageous to US policy in Latin America if the suit were instituted." He noted: "Many of the Central American countries were convinced that the sole objective of the United States foreign policy was to protect the fruit company. It might be a good idea to show them that this was not the case by instituting the suit." Allen Dulles concurred. The NSC agreed the suit should proceed, and the president approved.

Later that same day, Castillo Armas's forces — about five hundred soldiers in all — crossed the border from Honduras into Guatemala. Castillo Armas himself crossed the border the next evening, June 18.[36] On June 19, rebel planes blew up a railroad bridge at Gualan, and the next day, Castillo Armas's soldiers overcame a small police force and captured a large town, Esquipulas. After these early minor successes, the coup forces suffered a series of setbacks. A Guatemalan military unit engaged 122 rebels at Gualan, killing or capturing all but 30 of them in the course of thirty-six hours. On the Caribbean coast, 20 rebels landed by boat at Puerto Barrios and another 150 joined by land from Honduras, but a combined force of policemen and hastily armed dockworkers captured the amphibious force and drove the remainder back to Honduras, where they dispersed and refused to return to the fight.[37] Castillo Armas called for the CIA to provide "heavy bombardment" by planes or else he would be "forced to abandon everything."

As the coup forces faltered, Henry Cabot Lodge, Ike's ambassador to the United Nations, fought accusations by Guatemalan officials that its sovereignty was being violated. Guatemala demanded action by the UN Security Council, but Lodge argued the dispute should be heard instead by the Organization of American States.[38] After Secretary General of the UN Dag Hammarskjold implored Lodge to set a hearing before the Security Council, Lodge finally relented, but he delayed the hearing until June 25. By the time that hearing took place, Foster Dulles had induced the United Kingdom and France to abstain from voting, and a motion for a UN investigation failed to pass.

On June 22, Foster Dulles asked Eisenhower to approve two additional fighter-bombers for the rebel forces. Dulles contended that without the planes, the rebel forces would have "about zero" chance of success. Assistant Secretary of State Holland recommended against the step, saying it would expose the US to charges of intervention in the affairs of a sovereign state.[39] Eisenhower, however, decided to send the two P-51 fighter-bombers. "On the actual value of a shipment of planes, I knew from experience the important psychological impact of even a small amount of air support," Ike later wrote.

Once the new CIA planes arrived on June 23, they bombed targets including the military barracks in Zacapa, and they strafed the town of Chiquimula, where a total of seventeen soldiers on both sides died. The next day, Castillo Armas took control of Chiquimula and announced it was the headquarters of his provisional government.[40] On June 25, the planes strafed the town of Zacapa and bombed oil reserves at Guatemala City.

The Guatemalan army chief of staff, Colonel Carlos Enrique Díaz, told Arbenz on June 27 that military officers were prepared to demand Arbenz's resignation. Within hours, after discussions with US ambassador John Peurifoy, Arbenz went on the radio to announce he was resigning and turning over the presidency to Díaz. He denounced the "cruel war" that had been waged against Guatemala. "The United Fruit Company, in collaboration with the governing circles of the United States, is responsible for what is happening to us . . ."[41] On the same day, Guatemalan secret police began arresting Communist leaders.

The following day, Díaz irritated Peurifoy by speaking of Arbenz and his reforms in respectful terms, and also announcing his support for an amnesty for political prisoners, including Communists just arrested. Peurifoy quickly made it clear that the Arbenz policies and an amnesty were not acceptable to the United States, and a rebel plane dropped two bombs in the parade ground of the Matamoros fort in Guatemala City. Under pressure and threats against his life, it was now Díaz's turn to resign, and another military officer, Colonel Elfego Monzon, took over as president.[42] After negotiations in El Salvador on June 30 and July 1, Castillo Armas and Monzon formed a ruling junta.

On July 2, in federal court in New Orleans, the US Justice Department filed its anti-trust case claiming that United Fruit had built a monopoly by controlling nearly all banana-growing properties in Latin America, preventing competitors from using ship and rail transport facilities and threatening customers with loss of products in the future. The suit asked that the company be broken up. United Fruit quickly denied the suit's claims, saying they were based on "incomplete or unreliable information."[43] The company battled the suit for years, ultimately agreeing to a settlement in 1958 that required it to sell some operations.[44]

In Guatemala, the new regime returned expropriated lands to United Fruit. Many Guatemalan Communists disappeared and were never heard from again, although the CIA later claimed there was no evidence its

The five Cutler brothers often lined up in birth order, such as at Harvard's tercentenary celebration in 1936. From left to right: John, Elliott, Roger, George and Bobby. *Courtesy of the Eisenhower Library*

Boston's Democratic mayor, Maurice Tobin, hired Bobby as the city's attorney, and the two men became friends and political allies. *Courtesy of the Eisenhower Library*

Secretary of War Henry Stimson presents the Distinguished Service Medal to Bobby, September 19, 1945. *Courtesy of the Eisenhower Library*

Bobby's country house, called Fair Harvard, which he shared with his friends Bill and Ruth Sullivan. *Courtesy of Stephen Benedict*

Ike, Mamie and Bobby descend the steps of St. Paul's Chapel at Columbia University in New York.

Crew and passengers of the LCI-1090 during an early Cold War conflict in December 1946 in the port of Dairen, China. Skip Koons is fifth from the left in the first row. *Photo by Mark Kauffman/The LIFE Picture Collection via Getty Images*

Skip Koons in his US Navy uniform. *Courtesy of Stephen Benedict*

View of Soviet soldiers on pier in Dairen. *Photo by Mark Kauffman/The LIFE Picture Collection via Getty Images*

Skip on the balcony of the apartment he shared with Steve Benedict in Cannes, France, 1951.
Courtesy of Stephen Benedict

Steve Benedict in Cannes, 1951.
Courtesy of Stephen Benedict

Gaylord Hoftiezer, shown in a photo that Bobby included in his autobiography, *No Time for Rest*.

Chuck Turner and Steve Benedict at rehearsal before their recital in 1952. *Courtesy of Stephen Benedict*

Ike and Bobby during the 1952 election campaign. © *Getty Imagess*

Ike and Bobby riding in a car through Harvard Square Oct. 21, 1952. Christian Herter, later Ike's Secretary of State, is in the front seat to the left of Ike. © *Associated Press*

assassination teams actually executed anyone. Castillo Armas would eventually take over as the president of Guatemala — only to be assassinated in 1957 and replaced by a right-wing military officer. Shorn of its democracy, Guatemala sank into a military dictatorship.

When Ike wrote his memoirs, he retold the story of his crucial decision to send the additional fighter-bombers to support the coup and boasted, "By the middle of 1954 Latin America was free, for the time being at least, of any fixed outposts of Communism."[45] Bobby, without mentioning details of the covert action or his potential conflict of interest in the anti-trust case, also sang the coup's praises: "In Guatemala indirect and very minor help to Castillo Armas preserved that Latin republic from the clutching hand of Communist takeover."[46]

14

THE DR. DICK HOUSE, JOE McCARTHY, AND "SEXUAL PERVERSION"

One day in late April 1954, Skip Koons and Steve Benedict drove to Alexandria, Virginia, a sleepy town on the Potomac River about eight miles south of Washington. Its leafy, brick-paved streets were lined with eighteenth-century colonial homes, some down-at-heel. The two young men toured a three-story rental property known as the Dr. Dick House, named after its former owner, Dr. Elisha C. Dick, a physician who cared for President Washington on his deathbed.[1] The two young men decided that the elegant yet modest brick home located at 209 Prince Street, far from prying eyes in the capital, would be perfect for them.[2] Skip and Steve needed to keep their homosexuality secret, and the Dr. Dick House soon became their refuge.

After Skip and Steve moved into the house in May, Bobby visited for cocktails on a number of occasions. His warm friendship with Steve had begun on the Eisenhower campaign train, and he had developed a close relationship with Skip working with him at the NSC on matters like Operation Solarium and the Guatemala coup. Skip had even introduced Bobby to his mother, Peggy Lutz, to whom Bobby had written in a letter in January 1954, "I have become very fond of Skip, and think he is a remarkably talented young man."[3]

Soon, Skip brought into the house a new boyfriend, twenty-three-year-old Gaylord Hoftiezer, who went by Gayl. A South Dakotan, Gayl had served in the US Marine Corps but was recently discharged.[4] He soon began sleeping regularly in Skip's room on the second floor, and Bobby became friends with Gayl, too.

Steve and Skip knew they needed to be discreet if they wanted to avoid trouble in McCarthy-era Washington, so they kept reasonable hours, didn't have parties, and didn't frequent gay bars. Their work life was routine, although their differing roles at the White House meant they had different schedules.[5] Each morning, Skip and Steve would get in their separate cars — Skip, his black Thunderbird convertible, and Steve, his dark green Studebaker — and drive north along the Potomac, cross the bridge to Washington, and park in the White House parking lot.

Shortly after moving into the house, on May 24, Steve's career took an astonishing turn when Eisenhower chief of staff Sherman Adams appointed him to be the White House security officer.[6] His duties as security officer, to be performed in addition to his other duties as assistant staff secretary, chiefly entailed reviewing FBI background reports on potential appointees and reporting on them to Adams. A year had passed since Ike signed Executive Order 10450, which in effect had banned homosexuals from *any* federal job, let alone the position of White House security officer. Months after Steve took his new White House security post, FBI director J. Edgar Hoover invited him to a cocktail party at the Army and Navy Club in Washington for new officials whose work brought them into contact with the FBI. Steve shook Hoover's hand as they exchanged a polite greeting.[7]

Hoover had sent Steve's confidential FBI background report back in January 1953 to Adams. The report contained eight pages about Steve's interest in world federalism, including detailed accounts of connections between his world federalist associates and alleged Communist organizations. The report said, for instance, that Elisabeth Mann Borgese, who served with Steve as co-editor of a world federalist magazine in Chicago in 1947 and 1948, was involved with an array of Communist or subversive organizations.[8] Citing confidential informants, the FBI report said that Borgese — the daughter of German writer Thomas Mann — and her husband were listed as prospective students of the Workers School of Chicago, considered a Communist organization. The report also said that in June 1942 Borgese had spoken at a meeting of the German American Anti-Axis League, labeled by the FBI as a Communist front. The report also delved into the activities of the Foundation for World Government and its president, Stringfellow Barr, who employed Steve in 1948 and 1949. It said Barr had on several occasions called for dismissal of criminal charges against an array of Communist leaders, including an appeal printed in the *Daily Worker*, a Communist newspaper. It also noted that Steve had subscribed to *Alternative*, the magazine of the Committee for Nonviolent Revolution, which sought to advance "equality" and opposed the use of nuclear weapons. The FBI had interviewed Barr and others who asserted that Steve was anti-Communist and a loyal citizen — but the report did not draw any conclusions on the accuracy of those claims.

The FBI report also revealed, "From September, 1950, to about October, 1951, Benedict was employed as an Editor and Research Assistant to Tilghman B. Koons, Cannes, France." The report said Skip had been "interviewed abroad by another Governmental agency" in 1952, apparently a reference to Skip's interview with the CIA about his work broadcasting to the Soviet Union.[9] The FBI report quoted Skip as saying the two men "had met through mutual friends in Paris." Evidently, Skip had lied to conceal his first passionate meeting with Steve at Les Trois Cloches in Cannes and their ensuing affair in Paris and southern France and had instead cast their relationship as strictly professional. "Koons knew nothing derogatory regarding Benedict," the report noted.

Given Steve's connections with world federalism and people who espoused radical causes, why would Sherman Adams choose him to be White House security officer? It was an odd selection, given McCarthy's fearsome reputation for latching on to a wisp of fact and blowing it up into a full-on case of subversion. Steve was considered an intelligent, reliable, and likable young man, yet Adams may have regarded his left-of-center political orientation as a strength. It meant, for one thing, that Steve would not likely funnel information to McCarthy or Hoover. In contrast, McCarthy's ally Scott McLeod, the chief of State Department security, had leaked information to McCarthy concerning Bohlen and other cases that had led to red-baiting and homosexual-targeting, which caused deep frustrations for the president and others in the administration. Steve's presence in the security post would help keep McCarthy from digging into White House matters. As it turned out, Steve said he seldom found anything seriously objectionable in the FBI background reports he reviewed. "If there was anything at all questionable, I noted it. I don't remember any case of Adams not going ahead with the appointment. Ike's appointments, for the most part, were squeaky clean."[10]

Steve's own FBI background report would have given McCarthy fodder for hours of questioning about Communist infiltration of the White House. One can only imagine what McCarthy might have done had he known that the new White House security officer espoused world federalism, associated with people linked to alleged Communist organizations, *and* was gay.

At the State Department, McLeod had created an investigative branch called the Miscellaneous M Unit for the purpose of investigating an array of morals cases, the vast majority of which involved suspicions of homosexuality. The unit reported that in 1953 its work led to the departure of ninety-nine employees, with a backlog of hundreds of cases it still planned to pursue.[11] Its investigative techniques went beyond merely interviewing suspected employees; polygraphs, or lie detector tests, were administered. Investigations typically went like this: An M Unit investigator would contact an employee suspected of being gay and offer him a chance to confess, or submit to a lie detector test, usually resulting in the employee's resignation. Eighty percent of homosexual interrogations ended in confessions, a special agent in charge of sexual perversion investigations said in 1953.[12]

Gays and lesbians in the State Department and other federal agencies worked in a climate of fear. Investigators routinely pressured their targets to name others with whom they associated, causing a chain of departures. State Department security agent Peter Szluk dismissed the need for the most basic due process protections, such as holding hearings. "Hearings . . .what the hell for? That was a waste of time! No, I was the hatchet man. Szluk says the son of a bitch is queer, out he goes!"[13] In some cases, employees under investigation left the agency and committed suicide. In a frank acknowledgment years later, Szluk said he felt bad about the suicides, as recounted in David K. Johnson's book *The Lavender Scare*:

> The only thing I regret in my campaign to rid the State Department of that type of individual . . . was when within minutes, and sometimes maybe a week, they would commit suicide. One guy, he barely left my office and he must've had this thing in his coat pocket — and boom! — right on the corner of 21st and Virginia. Of course, nobody knew that he had been in to see me. It remained a mystery except to me and the security people.

While fanning the flames of anti-gay hysteria, McCarthy had been burned by his own conflagration. In October 1952, the *Las Vegas Sun* had printed an accusation that he spent the night in a hotel with a Wisconsin

Republican and "engaged in illicit acts" with him.[14] In a subsequent column, the *Sun*'s publisher, Hank Greenspun, called the senator "the queer that made Milwaukee famous."[15] McCarthy had even gotten into an angry shouting match with Greenspun in a Las Vegas campaign event where he denounced the *Sun* as "the local Daily Worker."[16] Desperate to stop Greenspun, McCarthy met with J. Edgar Hoover in May 1953 to ask for advice on how to handle the Greenspun allegations and whether he should sue Greenspun for libel. Hoover advised it would be best to have Senator William Jenner's Senate Internal Security Subcommittee subpoena Greenspun and question him on "whether it was part of a Communist plot to smear the reputation of the senator."[17] But McCarthy found another way to try to counter the rumors. He married his secretary, Jeannie Kerr, on September 23, 1953.

In his State of the Union speech in January 1954, Eisenhower said his new employee security program had caused twenty-two hundred employees to be "separated" from the federal government. "Our national security demands that the investigation of new employees and the evaluation of derogatory information respecting present employees be expedited and concluded at the earliest possible date. I shall recommend that the Congress provide additional funds where necessary to speed these important procedures."[18] His brief comments on the program, which included no mention of homosexuality or "sexual perversion," suggested Ike had no interest in pursuing McCarthy-style witch hunts.

McCarthy and his right-wing allies, however, seized upon the president's number — twenty-two hundred federal employees already found to be in violation of the security rules — as vindication for their cause and a way to lay the foundation for new political broadsides. McCarthy said in a radio program that 90 percent of the security dismissals were for "Communist connections and activities of perversion." Vice President Richard Nixon used the same tactic, asserting publicly, "We are kicking the Communists and the fellow travelers out not by the hundreds but by the thousands."[19] That statistic blurred reality by blending the relatively large number of people who lost their jobs due to concerns over their sexual orientation with the much smaller number of dismissals related to Communist activities.

This numerical charade soon drew criticism, as news organizations began reporting that people were being swept up in a wave of dismissals that had no legitimate national security justification. Joseph and Stewart Alsop charged in a column that the administration had been "palpably dishonest" in its use of numbers in reporting the results of the security program. "In the vast majority of these cases there was no question whatsoever of disloyalty or pro-Communism. In about 19 out of 20 cases, the reason, if any, for the firing was heavy drinking, temperamental unsuitability, or the like," the brothers wrote. "In short, there was not a single case of actual subversion in all the State Department's security firings — and it is doubtful there was one such case throughout the government."[20] *The Washington Daily News* published a seven-part series on the security program's inflated numbers, including the case of a navy worker who was terminated only to later be reinstated and receive an apology from the secretary of the navy. The series also revealed that some heterosexuals were being dismissed under the security program, as in the case of a female State Department employee who had a child out of wedlock and was discharged for immorality.[21]

McCarthy, meanwhile, had begun investigating alleged Communists in the US Army. In a public hearing on February 18 in New York, McCarthy harshly questioned General Ralph Zwicker, who had served with distinction in the invasion of Normandy in World War II, about the discharge of an army dentist whom McCarthy suspected of being a Communist. When Zwicker was unable to answer some of the questions, McCarthy told him he did not have "the brains of a five-year-old child" and "should be removed from any command."[22] The verbal assault on a war hero highlighted McCarthy's tactics, causing an uproar. On March 9, CBS newsman Edward R. Murrow profiled McCarthy on his television show, *See It Now*, devoting an entire program to a review of the methods McCarthy used to attack Zwicker and others. Murrow closed his report: "The actions of the junior Senator from Wisconsin have caused alarm and dismay amongst our allies abroad, and given considerable comfort to our enemies. And whose fault is that? Not really his. He didn't create this situation of fear; he merely exploited it — and rather successfully."

Meanwhile, the stage had been set for a dramatic confrontation between McCarthy and the Eisenhower administration. The army had drafted David Schine, McCarthy's young assistant, in the summer of 1953. McCarthy's top assistant, Roy Cohn, repeatedly sought to have Schine commissioned as an officer, even during some of the same meetings when he pressed the army on allegations that the army was harboring Communists. Ike sought to keep out of the dispute, but entanglement was unavoidable as the press sought the White House's view on McCarthy's allegations that there were subversives in the military. As the battle became heated, syndicated columnist Drew Pearson named Bobby, C. D. Jackson, and Sherman Adams as the leading "anti-McCarthy" White House staffers.[23] Another McCarthy opponent, UN ambassador Henry Cabot Lodge Jr., warned Ike in a February 23 "Eyes Only" letter that McCarthy's attack on the army was "part of an attempt to destroy you politically."[24] Two days later, an old friend of Ike's, retired general Lucius Clay, told the president in a phone call that McCarthy had gotten "too powerful" and people were "scared to do anything about him."[25] Clay warned that McCarthy might have information on honorable discharges that were given to Communists when Ike was army chief of staff.

Ike had avoided direct confrontation with McCarthy throughout 1953, but he had taken strategic action against him by putting in place a trusted aide, Fred Seaton, to assist Defense Secretary Wilson in dealings with Congress. Behind the scenes, Ike apparently ordered Seaton to prepare a document listing — in chronological order — the demands McCarthy and Cohn made for Schine's benefit.[26] The chronology was leaked to the press on March 11, 1954, making headlines nationwide.[27] The lengthy document, which had the legal tone of an indictment, listed multiple threats that McCarthy and Cohn had made against the army in an attempt to help Schine receive posts at certain army bases and favorable treatment.[28] McCarthy responded by denying the army's claims and accusing the army of releasing the chronology to undermine his anti-Communist probe of the army. McCarthy quickly arranged for hearings into his charges against the army to be held by his own Subcommittee on Investigations.

On Sunday, March 14, Roy Cohn went on the attack on live national television, making an explosive charge. Appearing on NBC's *Meet the Press*, Cohn accused the army's general counsel, John G. Adams, of trying to terminate McCarthy's probe of Communists in the army by offering Cohn information about "sex deviates" in the air force. Cohn said a "specific proposal was made to us that we go after an air force base wherein Mr. Adams told us there were a number of sex deviates and that would make excellent hearings for us."[29] The army quickly denied the claim, but the swirl of charges and countercharges garnered headlines nationwide. Homosexuality, innuendo, and threats of exposing homosexuals — in both McCarthy's committee offices and the military — fueled the furious debate.

As the hearings approached, C. D. Jackson became concerned that McCarthy, the chairman of his subcommittee, would act as "both investigator and investigated" in the upcoming hearings. So on March 20, Jackson persuaded Bobby to join him in raising the issue with Ike.[30] In their presence, Ike called another member of the subcommittee, Senator Karl Mundt, Republican of South Dakota, to raise the objection. Four days later, after a meeting with Bobby and Press Secretary Jim Hagerty, Ike gave a press conference that exemplified his measured approach in undermining McCarthy. First he denied he was talking about a "particular situation." Then he said, "I am perfectly ready to put myself on record flatly, as I have before, that in America, if a man is a party to a dispute, directly or indirectly, he does not sit in judgment on his own case." There was little doubt about who "he" was. Ultimately, McCarthy recused himself as chairman of the subcommittee, though he would nonetheless participate fully in questioning witnesses.

Political tensions soared in advance of the hearings, dubbed the Army-McCarthy Hearings, as the media cast a spotlight on the showdown. In March, *Time* magazine carried on its front cover a photo of Cohn and Schine, under a banner headline that read, "McCarthy and His Men." The picture showed Cohn, then twenty-seven, speaking into a microphone at a table as Schine, twenty-six, sits close at his side. From the first day of testimony on April 23, ABC television would provide gavel-to-gavel national coverage.

The army's counsel, Joseph Welch, went on the attack on April 30, trying to link McCarthy, Cohn, and Schine with the taint of the homosexuality rumors that had been circulating in Washington. Cohn had acknowledged in his testimony that he had a photo doctored, removing another officer to show Schine alone with Army Secretary Robert Stevens. Cohn said the photo of the two men showed that Stevens, who had charged he was being threatened by McCarthy and Cohn over Schine, was in fact solicitous about Schine and had even asked that his picture be taken with Schine in November 1953.[31] Welch, however, sought to highlight the use of falsified evidence by Cohn, and when McCarthy aide James Juliana testified on April 30, Welch probed exactly how the committee acquired the doctored photo in a question laden with homosexual innuendo.[32]

"Did you think this came from a pixie?" Welch asked.

Before Juliana could answer, McCarthy returned fire with suggestive language of his own: "Will counsel for my benefit define — I think he might be an expert on that — what a pixie is?"

"Yes. I should say, Senator, that a pixie is a close relative of a fairy," Welch shot back, prompting laughter from the chamber.[33] "Shall I proceed, sir? Have I enlightened you?"

"As I said," McCarthy replied, "I think you may be an authority on what a pixie is."

Adams, the army general counsel, leveled an explosive charge during his testimony on May 12. He said that during a break in a meeting in 1953 to discuss Schine's military service, Cohn had followed him to the men's room where he threatened to remove Army Secretary Stevens from his post and "wreck" the army. Cohn denied making such a statement, but Adams insisted that Cohn's denial was "false."[34] Adams also denied that he had offered to provide McCarthy's investigators evidence about homosexuals in the air force if they would drop their investigation of the army.

Eisenhower sought to remain above the fray, but as the hearings dragged on the president finally saw an opening to attack McCarthy. On May 31, while on a visit to New York City, he told reporters he hoped the hearings would "drive from the temple of freedom all who would seek to establish over us thought control, whether they be agents of a foreign state or demagogues thirsty for power."[35] The punch landed squarely; there was no question about whom he was calling a demagogue.

On June 1, Senator Ralph Flanders, a Republican from Vermont with a prominent position in his party leadership, took to the Senate floor to denounce McCarthy's tactics and to call for his removal from his committee chairmanships. Flanders charged that the Army-McCarthy hearings — now more than a month old — had failed to dig into the "heart of the mystery," namely, the nature of the relationships among McCarthy, Cohn, and Schine. Flanders said Cohn had an "almost passionate anxiety" to keep Schine on the staff, and asked specifically whether the private had some "hold on the Senator." Flanders offered no solid evidence of homosexual conduct, but the three men were again getting a dose of their own medicine.[36]

Flanders denounced McCarthy's tactics in hunting Communists, saying, "his anti-Communism so completely parallels that of Adolf Hitler as to strike fear into the heart of any defenseless minority." He further asserted, "Were the junior senator from Wisconsin in the pay of the Communists he could not have done a better job for them." Yet Flanders justified his call for the removal of McCarthy from his committee chairmanships on a simpler claim: McCarthy had refused for two years to appear before a Senate committee looking into alleged financial improprieties by McCarthy.

As the hearings dragged on, Welch used McCarthy's own tactics to suggest there was a homosexual relationship between Cohn and Schine. Under questioning by Welch on June 9, Cohn admitted that he repeatedly picked up Schine from the army base where he was stationed, New Jersey's Fort Dix, and drove him to hotels, cafés, and even the posh Stork Club in New York. Cohn insisted the meetings were for work on their investigation into Communists in the government. Welch relentlessly badgered Cohn for details about the meetings with Schine, and Cohn was repeatedly unable to explain what work they had actually done at the meetings. Welch pressed Cohn about a meal in December 1953 at a hotel in Trenton, but Cohn could not recall whether Schine had been with him that evening, even though the total cost of the tab suggested more than one person had been dining. "Let's say the big, strong, hungry, silent man was with you," Welch said.[37]

Cohn did not respond to the remark, but McCarthy soon went on the attack, linking a former member of the army legal team, Fred Fisher, with the National Lawyers Guild, which he described as an "arm of the Communist Party." Welch acknowledged that while attending Harvard Law School, Fisher had joined the guild, an organization that had provided legal defense to accused Communists. Welch also noted Fisher was a member of the Young Republicans League. Welch said that prior to the hearings, when he learned of Fisher's association with the guild, he removed Fisher from the army legal team in an effort to avoid having McCarthy make an issue of it.[38] As McCarthy pressed on, Welch responded with what became perhaps the most recognized lines of the hearings: "Let us not assassinate this lad further, Senator. You have done enough. Have you no sense of decency sir, at long last? Have you left no sense of decency?"

The tables were suddenly turned on the Wisconsin senator, who had held the nation spellbound with fears of Communists and gays since his West Virginia speech in February 1950. The hearings, which McCarthy had launched in an effort to attack the army, had become the vehicle for his downfall. As prominent Republicans criticized McCarthy, emboldened Senate Democrats also went on the attack. Senator Stuart Symington of Missouri, who sat on the investigative committee and had challenged McCarthy repeatedly, called for the Wisconsin senator to testify about the personal financial dealings cited by Flanders, including a ten-thousand-dollar payment he received from a corporation that had obtained a federal loan.

On June 11, Flanders dramatically approached McCarthy as he testified and handed him a formal notice that he intended to ask the Senate to remove McCarthy from his committee chairmanships unless he responded to the financial charges against him. On June 17, the thirty-sixth and final day of the hearings, Senator Charles Potter, a Michigan Republican who sat on the committee but had remained mostly quiet during the hearings, announced that he believed there might be perjury prosecutions in store for officials on both sides of the dispute. Potter also called for the dismissal of Roy Cohn, McCarthy's right hand man.[39]

McCarthy deflected by pivoting to a new target. He announced that he would soon reveal significant charges against an unnamed Democratic senator who had tried to apply improper influence over another governmental agency. His threats against the unnamed senator appeared in newspapers on the morning of Saturday, June 19. That same morning, Senator Lester Hunt, a Wyoming Democrat, went to his Capitol Hill office and shot himself in the head with a .22-caliber rifle and died.[40] Press accounts of the suicide noted the senator had been suffering from depression, but behind the scenes lay a tragic story. Hunt's son, Lester Hunt Jr., had been arrested in October 1953 by the Washington, DC, Metro Police vice squad for allegedly soliciting an undercover officer in Lafayette Square. It was a first offense for young Hunt, and the charges had been quietly dropped. However, two Republican senators allied with McCarthy, Styles Bridges of New Hampshire and Herman Welker of Idaho, got wind of the charges and used that knowledge to press Senator Hunt to resign from office. Welker informed Hunt through intermediaries in Wyoming that if he resigned, charges would not be pressed against his son.[41] Hunt let it be known that he would not resign.

Shortly thereafter, Lester Hunt Jr. was charged formally in court and then found guilty after a trial, which his parents attended. It was a grueling experience that left the senator's wife unable to eat for a week. Senator Hunt privately told a journalist, "If the opposition brings this up in the Senate race . . . I shall withdraw."[42] In early June, he announced that he would not run for reelection, citing a kidney condition. Then came McCarthy's threat from the Senate floor that he would make the accusations against a Democratic senator. After Hunt walked into his office and shot himself, McCarthy did not name the lawmaker he had threatened to attack.

After Flanders failed to advance his effort to strip McCarthy of his chairmanships, the Vermont senator introduced a censure motion accusing McCarthy of a variety of misdeeds, including his abuse of General Zwicker and other witnesses and sending Cohn and Schine on a trip to Europe that embarrassed the United States and the Senate.[43] Cohn, who had been threatened with a perjury prosecution and shown to have an obsessive devotion to Schine, resigned from his committee job on July 20 and returned to New York. McCarthy and his allies fought the censure motion, but a revised version ultimately passed on December 2, sealing McCarthy's loss of power and influence.

It was in the midst of the Army-McCarthy hearings on Capitol Hill that Steve Benedict was appointed White House security officer while he, Skip, and Gayl were settling into their new abode, the Dr. Dick House. By the end of the summer of 1954, McCarthy, Cohn, and Schine were under fire from Republicans and Democrats alike for their tactics, but life did not become any easier for gays working in the federal government, a point underscored by the fact that the mighty McCarthy's opponents had sapped his political strength partly by questioning his sexual orientation and that of his two young male assistants. In the Dr. Dick House that summer, Steve, Skip, and Gayl maintained their low profile. Skip and Gayl took some time off in July to go sailing. They also sought assistance from Bobby, who wrote a letter to the director of the US Information Agency in support of Gayl's application for a job there.[44]

Nearly a month after the Army-McCarthy hearings concluded, a senior intelligence official took an interest in knowing more about the new White House security officer, Steve Benedict. On July 15, Ermal P. Geiss, the deputy director of the CIA's internal Office of Security, came to the White House to review the FBI's background report on Steve. Geiss spent the next hour and a half studying the seventeen-page document.[45] No one knows what inspired Geiss's interest, and nothing ever came of his visit, but if rumors of Steve's homosexuality had spread to the CIA, the crew living at the Dr. Dick House had dodged a bullet.

A strange climate of paranoia and dishonesty permeated Washington, where vicious hunts for homosexuals were led by men themselves suspected of being gay, where people laughed as Welch and McCarthy sparred maliciously over the words *pixie* and *fairy* during a nationally televised hearing, and where senators practiced the art of gay blackmail against political foes. Officially pilloried as "sexual perversion," homosexuality was simultaneously everywhere but nowhere, suspected but not proved, concealed but then revealed, loathed and labeled a security risk — but then giggled about. Amid it all, from their posts deep inside the NSC and the White House, Bobby and Skip were doing their best to serve President Eisenhower and fight Communism.

15

EXPLOITING SOVIET VULNERABILITIES

On January 15, 1954, Skip Koons sent CIA director Allen Dulles a top-secret draft report titled "US Policy on the Exploitation of Soviet Vulnerabilities." The report said there was no "comprehensive statement of US policy" on how to attack weaknesses in the Soviet system, and the absence of such a policy had the effect of "inhibiting action."[1] Prepared by Koons in collaboration with Bobby Cutler, the report called for Bobby, Allen Dulles, Undersecretary of State Walter Bedell Smith, and psychological warfare adviser C. D. Jackson to select members for a new special committee to develop a policy steering US efforts to undermine the Communist regime.

Long-simmering divisions between Russians and other nationalities were Soviet vulnerabilities, and Skip knew well that disputes over how to attack those vulnerabilities could lead to paralysis. At AMCOMLIB, he had seen firsthand how the launch of the CIA's anti-Soviet radio program stalled amid disputes between Russian nationalists and minority nationalities such as Ukrainians. While Radio Liberation finally aired its first program in March 1953, officials remained concerned that pro-independence sentiment expressed by minority nationality groups in broadcasts would inhibit Russians from embracing anti-Communist views. Now Skip was recommending to CIA director Dulles that the US government address these issues and decide how best to attack Soviet vulnerabilities.

Discord over how to exploit Soviet vulnerabilities had surfaced after labor unrest and riots broke out in East Germany in June 1953. Seeking to capitalize on the unrest, Jackson recommended that the US government prepare a battery of radio broadcasts to spread the word if new strikes or protests occurred in East Germany in the cold months ahead, exploiting what he called a "Winter of Discontent."[2] But CIA political warfare specialist Tracy Barnes objected to the idea, warning that "sponsoring active opposition" to the Soviets would be "contrary to our best interests."[3]

To avoid such disputes in the future, the plan proposed by Koons and Cutler called first for the committee, operating under NSC auspices, to have "full and free access" to CIA operations to assess the agency's current activities. Dulles's special assistant, Richard Bissell, quickly warned that the plan would launch an unwanted review of CIA secret operations. "The description of the scope of this study indicates that the people working on it would have to have access to knowledge of all of our most sensitive operational activities and assets," Bissell wrote in a top-secret memo to Dulles. "I am inclined to believe that the sort of major new project originally proposed by General Cutler would be a waste of intellectual and executive resources and should be discouraged."[4] Bissell recommended that Dulles narrow the scope of the committee's review and ensure a CIA official would monitor its work. Bissell also said someone — evidently from CIA, though the name remains classified — "discussed this sort of arrangement with Koons who saw no objection to it."

The Solarium Project had established that neither a nuclear nor a conventional attack on the Soviet Union was a rational option, but many other ways to attack Soviet Communism remained: radio broadcasts, clandestine political support of opposition groups, covert military action, and the constant war of words in public between the two foes. The Dulles brothers, as heads of the State Department and CIA, had pushed hard for covert actions against governments like Iran's that appeared vulnerable to Communist encroachment. Eisenhower often supported those efforts. Yet there was another side to Eisenhower's political views, that of the former general who sought to bridge the divide with the Soviets, the experienced warrior who wanted to avoid a renewal of the horrors of war. Bobby and Skip now were seeking to develop a policy that would ensure the US exploited Soviet vulnerabilities in a way that was both effective and in accord with the president's political and strategic views.

Anticipating the CIA's objection to a broad examination of its anti-Soviet projects, Bobby sent a letter to Dulles proposing that the Operations Coordinating Board staff first undertake a limited study of the need for a policy on Soviet vulnerabilities. He also made a pitch for his protégé on the NSC staff to be involved, crediting the suggestion to C. D. Jackson.[5] "C. D. suggested that Skip Koons work with the Group, which he can do within the limits of his normal work over here."

In a letter on February 10, 1954, beginning "Dear Bobby," Allen Dulles sounded a friendly note and supported the idea but sought to clamp down on the review, saying he expected the OCB staff to perform "a summary study of existing documentation, such as NSC papers, research projects, etc. and not to contemplate a survey of existing covert operations."[6] He didn't object to Koons's role, but asked that the OCB special staff "coordinate their work through Mr. Richard Bissell (or an assistant of his) who will be following the further developments of this project for me."

As the "Soviet Vulnerabilities" study took shape, Bobby was also shepherding the work of a panel of scientists and consultants studying the inadequacies of the technology used by US strategic nuclear forces. Called the Technological Capabilities Panel (TCP), it was headed by James R. Killian Jr., president of the Massachusetts Institute of Technology. The panel presented its report, "Meeting the Threat of a Surprise Attack," in the White House Broadcast Room on February 14, 1955.[7] "General Cutler had carefully orchestrated all the plans for the presentation of the report," Killian later recalled. He said Bobby "recognized the importance of independent thinking about national security problems on the part of people outside of the agencies of government, and he welcomed inputs that resulted from this independent thinking." The TCP report recommended that development of intercontinental ballistic missiles be given the highest priority, that an early warning system to detect Soviet missiles be developed, and that major efforts be made to enhance intelligence gathering about Soviet forces. It was during his work for the TCP that scientist Edwin Land, later famed for inventing the Polaroid camera, developed the idea of the U-2 aircraft that would fly at extremely high altitudes and use a powerful photographic system to capture images of enemy forces.

World events also underscored the need to find ways to weaken the Soviet regime. In early 1954 in Vietnam, the Soviet-backed Communist Viet Minh army encircled a French fort at the village of Dien Bien Phu, and heavy fighting began on March 13.[8] The Viet Minh launched the assault just as its leader, Ho Chi Minh, went to Geneva for an international conference to negotiate a formal peace in Korea and to work toward restoring peace in Vietnam, Laos, and Cambodia. The timing of the Viet Minh attack on Dien Bien Phu sent a clear message to the diplomats in Geneva — the Communists were negotiating from a position of power. Almost each day brought news of French fatalities and of French defenses collapsing.

In a speech on March 29, Foster Dulles publicly denounced Russian and Chinese determination "to dominate all Southeast Asia" and called for "united action" to stop the Communist takeover. Admiral Arthur Radford, chairman of the Joint Chiefs of Staff, had extended a broad offer of support to the French, but Ike considered the effort to save Dien Bien Phu — in a valley, with Viet Minh artillery firing down on it — practically an unwinnable battle, as he wrote in his diary.[9] In an NSC meeting April 6, Ike asked rhetorically, "Why had the French ever committed resources to a remote area where these forces could not be reinforced?"[10] Radford said US assistance could be provided, but Ike put off a decision, knowing that neither he nor Congress embraced the idea of another conflict like the one in Korea.

As the Viet Minh continued striking French forces at Dien Bien Phu, Ike met with Nixon and Bobby at the White House on the morning of April 30 and discussed the question of giving nuclear weapons to the French for use in Vietnam. In a memo of the meeting to Beetle Smith, Bobby said Ike and Nixon doubted whether the weapons, obliquely called "new weapons," could effectively assist the French in the confined jungle conditions around Dien Bien Phu and thought napalm would "be more effective." Nonetheless, he said the two men raised for consideration the idea of telling the French that if they "wanted some 'new weapons' . . . *now* for possible use, we might give them a few."[11] The French foreign minister, Georges Bidault, later said that, in April, Foster Dulles had offered the French two atomic bombs to drop on Dien Bien Phu, but the French declined the offer.[12]

As talks unfolded in Geneva, the United States refused to negotiate with Ho or recognize the Communist government of China, and Secretary of State Dulles ordered the US delegation not to speak with any Chinese representatives. Under intense pressure, fissures divided the Western allies. Dulles fell out with his UK counterpart, Foreign Secretary Anthony Eden, who had endorsed a compromise with Ho. Frustrated, Dulles abandoned Geneva on May 3, turning over leadership of the US delegation to Smith.

Back in Washington, at the NSC meeting of May 6, Foster Dulles reported that Bidault had asked the United States to send jets from aircraft carriers to launch air strikes against the Viet Minh. Without the airpower, Dien Bien Phu would be lost, Bidault said.[13] But Dulles said the US should not send assistance until the French agreed to coordinate operations and remain in the war, which seemed unlikely.

Eden, meanwhile, was advocating for a "Five Power" agency — the UK, US, France, Australia, and New Zealand — to study the threats to peace in Vietnam and the rest of Southeast Asia, Dulles reported. On May 7, President Eisenhower met privately with Secretary Dulles and Bobby and reconfirmed his decision to push Eden to accept a coalition with a broader membership than just the five countries he had named, hoping for the swift creation of an international force. Bobby wrote in a memo the next day summarizing the president's position for the secretary of defense and the Joint Chiefs of Staff: "The United States will not agree to a 'white man's party' to determine the problems of the Southeast Asian nations."[14] Time had now run out. On the same day that Bobby wrote the "white man's party" memo, the Viet Minh commander at Dien Bien Phu, General Vo Nguyen Giap, ordered a final assault on the fort, which fell swiftly. More than ten thousand French soldiers were taken prisoner.[15]

The collapse of the French forces catapulted the Geneva Conference into a new phase of negotiations. In July, France and the Democratic Republic of Vietnam, the government created by the Viet Minh, agreed to a cease-fire that divided the country into north and south sectors, designated a demilitarized zone along the 17th parallel, and called for elections. The Soviet Union, China, and the United Kingdom also signed the agreement, dubbed the Geneva Accords, but the United States and the state of Vietnam abstained. The defeat of the French left the US as the chief ally of the new nation of South Vietnam, and Secretary of State Dulles picked Ngo Dinh Diem, a Catholic from North Vietnam who had lived in the US, to be the new country's prime minister.

As the turmoil in Southeast Asia unfolded — and the CIA coup effort in Guatemala ramped up — the OCB completed its "Soviet Vulnerabilities" study, delivering it to Bobby on June 8. The report, prepared by Skip and two OCB staff members, concluded that the NSC had no "detailed formulation of US policy" on the exploitation of Soviet vulnerabilities.[16] As a result, some US programs challenged the "internal authority" of the Soviet government, while others did not. In addition,

US policy was unclear on whether programs seeking to attack Soviet vulnerabilities should support deviations from Communist orthodoxy such as Titoism, the philosophy of Yugoslav leader Josip Broz Tito, who had split with the Soviets.[17] The report also concluded that the NSC had failed to provide guidance in regard to whether US-backed broadcasts to the Soviet Union should exploit nationalism among the non-Russian peoples of the Soviet Union.[18] After reciting these "inadequacies," the report recommended that the NSC set a uniform policy for exploiting Soviet vulnerabilities.

Following that recommendation, Bobby asked Max F. Millikan, chairman of the MIT Center for International Studies, to serve on a committee along with Skip, Bissell, and representatives of the State and Defense Departments to recommend a Soviet vulnerabilities policy.

By this time, rumblings had grown over Allen Dulles's handling of the CIA, and President Eisenhower had asked General James Doolittle to prepare a report on Dulles's performance. Ike had asked Allen in a letter in July to cooperate with the investigation, saying, "You will kindly extend to General Doolittle the facilities necessary to enable him and his associates to carry out this study including access to any and all information relating to the covert activities of CIA."[19] Doolittle interviewed a broad array of officials in intelligence and national security, including Bobby and Skip. In a meeting on October 19, Doolittle told the president that Dulles was guided by "emotionalism . . . far worse than it appeared on the surface." The CIA itself had "ballooned out into a vast and sprawling organization" that was uncontrolled because of the "family relationship" between the two Dulles brothers.[20] "It leads to protection of one by the other, or influence of one by the other," Doolittle asserted. Ike replied that he could not remove Dulles because of the agency's unusual nature, and "it probably takes a strange kind of genius to run it . . . I'd rather have Allen as my chief intelligence officer, with his limitations, than anyone I know."[21] Ike also knew that Bobby's revitalized NSC and the newly created OCB served as checks on Dulles.

Bobby received the final "Soviet Vulnerabilities" report on November 30, 1954. The top-secret document called for a "political warfare strategy" that would take advantage of such Soviet weaknesses as popular discontent with its police state, low standards of living, suppression of religion, and poor treatment of minorities. The report said, "In the event of intercontinental atomic warfare, should we effectively destroy from the air the centers of Soviet control and wish to negotiate a settlement with separate widely scattered groups in Russia, our chances of doing this quickly would be materially improved by a history of support for the minorities."[22] However, the report also warned, in chilling language, that such a strategy could backfire:

> Consider the situation after an atomic bombardment which knocked out the nerve centers of Party control in the cities but left intact large armies in the field. In this event it would be the military with whom we would be negotiating a cease fire. Their willingness to come to terms would be influenced by whether they thought they could salvage intact the Russian federation. A prior commitment on our part to independence for the minority groups might hold things up seriously.

Ultimately, after reviewing the risks of exploiting an array of Soviet vulnerabilities, the committee concluded that the nation's political warfare strategy must be in essence a "scissors" with two blades: The first blade ensures that the Soviets know that any Soviet military expansion would be met with a swift military response from the United States, and the second encourages members of Soviet society to make decisions that would achieve a "gradual evolution of the system over time to something less menacing."[23] This strategy of gradualism set aside any bid to overturn the Soviet government or encourage national minorities to break it up.

Bobby placed the proposed Soviet vulnerabilities policy directive, designated as NSC 5505, on the agenda for the NSC meeting of January 27, 1955. In the secrecy of the Cabinet Room that day, he provided a detailed briefing on the report and said that he was inserting one change resulting from a conversation the previous evening with Nelson Rockefeller. Bobby recommended placing a committee, to be headed by Rockefeller, in charge of devising strategy for exploiting Soviet vulnerabilities through both overt and covert means.[24] He said Rockefeller's committee would be considering covert actions, such as those in Guatemala and Iran, and those programs should not be considered before the full NSC. President Eisenhower quickly voiced support for the policy, saying that the US was not in a position to state that it would promote revolution in the USSR. "What we must try to do is 'win these guys' over," he said.

Hawkish NSC members who favored covert and military actions to roll back Communism balked, however. Vice President Nixon inquired whether the new policy would prevent actions like those in Guatemala, where he said a "revolution" supported by US efforts had ousted Arbenz. "Mr. Cutler answered that such methods would not necessarily be ruled out if they were likely to achieve success."[25] President Eisenhower added that the Rockefeller committee controlling covert actions would not merely "carry out this policy slavishly," but would report back to the NSC on "unforeseen possibilities" or "measures that had turned out wrong." The Dulles brothers said they did not want NSC 5505 "to destroy all possibility of seizing opportunities for exploiting a different type of strategy if such opportunities clearly presented themselves." Bobby replied that NSC 5505 would not exclude this possibility.

President Eisenhower approved the policy with a few minor amendments. Soon thereafter, he appointed Nelson Rockefeller to chair the Planning Coordination Group, the committee that would approve political warfare programs and covert actions following the new policy.[26]

Ike's declaration in the NSC — that US policy must be to "win these guys over" — exemplified the president's moderated approach to undermining Communism, which can also be seen in his comments on Stalin's death, Operation Solarium, and NSC 161, all of which bore Bobby's subtle imprint.

As the administration developed its gradualist psychological warfare policies, it deployed an array of cultural events to sway public opinion in the Soviet Union and around the world in America's favor. The State Department arranged for cultural figures such as jazz great Louis Armstrong and Nobel Prize–winning novelist William Faulkner to go on tours around the world and, in some cases, behind the Iron Curtain.[27] The State Department's Voice of America, which broadcast into the Soviet Union, found that its programs featuring a distinctly American form of music — jazz — garnered a huge audience behind the Iron Curtain.[28]

The overall impact of this gentler approach to undermining Communism is difficult to assess. Whatever the impact was, a new generation of Soviet Communist leaders soon launched their own attack on Stalin and his rigid and brutal ideology. In February 1956, behind closed doors at the Soviet Communist Party's 20th Congress, General Secretary Nikita Khrushchev made his now-famous denunciation of Stalinism, calling the dead dictator a "supreme egotist and sadist, capable of sacrificing everything and anybody for the sake of his own power and glory."[29]

16

"LOSING MY RIGHT ARM"

In the White House Cabinet Room on Thursday, March 3, 1955, Bobby Cutler led the NSC through a sobering Cold War reality: a new national plan for civilian warnings and evacuations — and for survival of the federal government — in the event of a Soviet nuclear attack. Bobby had chaired a committee that worked for three months on the plan with representatives from the CIA, the Joint Chiefs of Staff, the Federal Civil Defense Administration, and other agencies. This was the first time the NSC had tried to forge a comprehensive national strategy for surviving a nuclear attack. After a lengthy discussion, President Eisenhower said he was "gratified" by the plan and approved it as NSC 5513.[1]

The following Tuesday, Bobby wrote a letter to the president asking to step down as his special assistant for national security affairs effective April 1, 1955. Bobby wrote, "You are familiar with the reasons for my resignation. They are wholly related to my personal and private concerns. For no other reason, so long as my duty was satisfactory to you, would I consider leaving your service." After remarking on the reform of the NSC as a mechanism for formulating national security policy, Bobby turned to expressing his gratitude toward Ike:

> Being quite human, I have to say what these many months of close, personal association have meant to me as a person. You have given me more courage, direction, and appreciation of the right course in life than anyone I ever knew. Any fellow who works closely with you comes away a debtor for the rest of his life. I shall always carry in my heart and mind the imprint of your warm humanity, your broad judgment, and your inner strength.[2]

This time, Ike did not rebuff Bobby's resignation. He responded in a letter the same day:

Dear Bobby,

It is almost worth losing my right arm — which I am doing in your departure — to receive such a glowing personal tribute as is paid me in your letter of resignation. I truly feel a high sense of distinction in knowing that our association over the past two and a half years has meant as much to you as it has to me.

Your tireless energy and your dedication to hard work have been so complete as constantly to astonish and even bewilder me. Everyone in the Cabinet and your other associates in the Executive Branch of Government will share my feeling of loss in your going. More especially, those of us who have participated in the work of the National Security Council will not fail to remember that you have breathed into its work new life and effectiveness, and that you have been the real mainspring responsible for the accomplishment of many of its tasks of vital importance to the entire nation.

All of this, of course, is merely a feeble attempt to give expression to the great debt of gratitude that I shall always owe you.

May a full measure of health, happiness and prosperity be yours, and may you often find compelling reasons to bring you to Washington to see the friends who will sorely miss you.

With warm regard.

Although Bobby's resignation appeared to be abrupt, there are indications that it was part of a transition that he and Ike had agreed upon. After Bobby had written his first letter offering to resign in March 1954, he wrote a second letter in August 1954, proposing that he return to Old Colony Trust in January 1955. In August, Bobby had given a series of reasons for wishing to do so — others could do the job better, he was exhausted, and more time away from Old Colony was jeopardizing his promised position as chairman of the trust company. He also voiced bitter disappointment in the Republican Party, likely a reference to McCarthy. "Because of the conduct of certain Republican Senators, I do not have one inner satisfaction that comes from such hard work. A 'Party' which relies upon these untrustworthy men makes me sick at heart."[3] He also recommended in August that Dillon Anderson, the Texas Democrat who had worked with him to help Ike win the Republican nomination in July 1952, take over his position. Ike appointed Anderson as Bobby's replacement.

Media accounts of Bobby's departure lauded his work and did not hint at any hidden motives for his stepping down. *The Washington Post* called him "one of the president's closest friends and confidants" since the early days of the 1952 presidential campaign.[4] In an editorial on March 11 calling Bobby "one of the most important and least known men in Washington," the paper said:

> As assistant to the President for national security affairs, he has had a preeminent part in giving the National Security Council the new meaning and prestige which Mr. Eisenhower has sought for it. The Security Council has all but eclipsed the Cabinet on questions of broad strategy. This shy, witty Boston banker has been the ideal staff agent for the president — quiet, unobtrusive and completely dedicated, and with a singular ability to cut through nonessentials in keeping attention focused on the major problems in following through on decisions. Through his own choice, he has led a virtually monastic existence in the Capital, shunning social engagements and contact even though previously in private life he had been known as the life of the party. Whether this self-enforced seclusion has helped build proper appreciation of the work of the Security Council is debatable, but it certainly has served to keep the council staff out of embarrassing controversy.

At FBI headquarters, the *Post*'s coverage of Bobby's departure was routed to Tolson and Nichols. FBI director J. Edgar Hoover sent Bobby a friendly note. "I was indeed sorry to learn of your plans to resign as Special Assistant to President Eisenhower, and I wanted to take this opportunity to let you know that it was a real privilege to cooperate with you during the past months."[5]

Ike and Mamie threw a farewell dinner party for Bobby on the evening of Saturday, March 12, at the White House. Guests included United Fruit chairman T. Jefferson Coolidge, Harold Vanderbilt, Henry Cabot Lodge Jr., Foster Dulles, Beetle Smith, Sherman Adams, Sinclair Weeks, Gabriel Hauge, and Dr. Howard Snyder, most with their spouses. Bobby sat between Mamie and her mother, Elivera Doud, while Ike was on the other side of Mamie. Friends and family members included William Sullivan, Chandler Bigelow, and an array of Bobby's nieces and nephews, including Patricia Cutler Warner and Mary Cutler. During the dinner, Ike, who enjoyed painting in oils, presented Bobby with one of his own paintings, a depiction of a mill and waterwheel.[6] After dinner, the party went upstairs for coffee and liqueur in the president's private rooms.

Bobby was ecstatic with this send-off. "Saturday night was RC's apogee or apotheosis or transfiguration, or some wonderful and happy thing that occasionally happens to some unworthy fellow to remind him why life is really worth living," he wrote in a thank-you note to Ike and Mamie. "Really, my dear friends, it was 'la nuit de gloire est arrivé.' Ulysses' old dog 'Argus' is on his toes. Affectionately, Bobby."[7]

Ike replied with the gentle teasing about Bobby's linguistic skills that had by now become their patter:

> Dear Bobby:
> Mamie and I together read your note. We must admit that your knowledge of $5 words, of mythology and of the French language is such as to require a number of conferences in the Eisenhower family in order to reach agreed conclusions as to the exact meaning of such a missive. On one point, however, there was no need for discussion. We both enthusiastically agree that it was a great pleasure to meet your relatives and good friends, and that we could not remember an evening that had been so thoroughly enjoyable for the two of us. We are truly grateful you gave us the opportunity of meeting such nice people.

Skip Koons did not attend the party, though by this time he had become a close and trusted assistant to Bobby. Before leaving the White House, Bobby sought to advance Skip's career, asking Secretary of State

Dulles to find him a State Department position in Europe. "Dear Foster, I am writing you about an able, attractive, and gifted young member of my staff at the National Security Council, who after two years in Washington, following several years overseas, desires to return to Europe for more training and experience," Bobby wrote.[8] "Personally, I like Mr. Koons a great deal, and we have become friends in our work together. He has a studious, keen mind, an agreeable disposition, and an attractive personality." The effort failed, and Skip remained at the NSC.

On March 30, just prior to Bobby's departure, Skip wrote Bobby a letter expressing deep fondness for him and suggesting an intimate bond. "I have also seen an everpresent and serene rightmindedness, sure in every touch while always warm and human — and much more," he wrote.[9] "So as you depart, temporarily, from the Washington scene, I hope you will permit the lasting admiration and affection of one young man to accompany you. Your friendship has been his finest possession during these years — he would like to guard it."

The White House party was not the only festivity to mark Bobby's departure. Secretary of State Dulles hosted a dinner at the Alibi Club, a private men's club in Washington whose members have included presidents, senators, and other members of the political elite. There was another at 1718 H Street, and one at the Cosmos Club.[10] The White House staff also gathered together at their mess to wish Bobby farewell over lunch. The NSC began its March 31 meeting with a private ceremony in which Secretary of Defense Charles Wilson read a commendation presenting Bobby with the Medal of Freedom, the nation's highest civilian honor.[11] "His broad grasp of the security issues confronting the United States and his great devotion and tireless energy in seeking their solution have been important factors in the formulation of national security programs for the security of our country and that of the Free World," it said. That evening, Ike and Mamie attended another farewell party for Bobby at the home of Secretary of Commerce Sinclair Weeks.[12]

On April 1, his last day in office, Bobby delivered to the president a ten-page report summarizing the operations of the NSC and its transformation since the Truman administration. The report showed that since the Eisenhower administration had taken power more than two years earlier, it had held 113 NSC meetings, nearly the same number of meetings that the NSC had during the more than the five years it operated under President Truman.[13] The rate of official actions by the NSC also sharply increased. "Today, the National Security Council is a smooth-functioning and high-speed mechanism, available to aid you in formulating national security policy," Bobby wrote.

Bobby would remain in contact with the White House through Skip. Before his departure, he had asked presidential assistant Nelson Rockefeller to let Skip attend meetings of the Planning Coordination Group, the committee that Rockefeller chaired and that was to approve covert actions and ensure that Soviet vulnerabilities were exploited in accord with the policy adopted in January.[14] Rockefeller agreed to let Skip attend PCG meetings "as your representative," even though his note was dated April 2, by which time Bobby was no longer a White House employee.[15]

There is no documentary evidence that the FBI was investigating rumors of Bobby's homosexuality at the time of his resignation. However, it is possible that documents relating to such an investigation were in FBI files that were destroyed.[16] Bobby was an astute practitioner of the political arts; he understood very well what in today's political parlance is called optics. Eisenhower had won the 1952 election largely by promising clean government and removing the stain of subversives in Washington. A report that one of Ike's closest confidants, a man entrusted with extraordinary national security secrets, was gay would have been a windfall for any Democratic challenger. If rumors were circulating at this time that Bobby was gay, as an FBI document would later assert, this might explain the "personal and private concerns" he mentioned obscurely in his March 1955 resignation letter. It is possible that Bobby left the White House to avoid the risk of a scandal that would harm Ike's chances of reelection.

Liberated from his White House post, Bobby took a trip to the Caribbean to relax. Staying at the Mill Reef Club in Antigua, British West Indies, he swam in the ocean, bicycled, and wrote letters. He jotted a friendly note to Vice President Richard Nixon:

> Dear Richard,
> Now that I have recovered from the initial shock of "freedom," which sent up my temperature for two days to nearly 102°, I want properly to thank you for your many kindnesses and continuous consideration while I was doing my part for the President. It was mighty nice of you, with

all you have to do, to come to Foster's dinner for me last week. I appreciated it. You have always made me feel that I can rightly sign myself — your friend Bobby Cutler.[17]

The next day, he wrote a nostalgic letter to Ike. "Mr. President — Today is the first Council Day in 27 months that I shall not have been there to bring you into the Cabinet Room and, when you are seated, say: 'Sir, the first item is . . .'" Bobby continued with praise for Dillon Anderson, his replacement as special assistant for national security affairs. "The pang of leaving your side at such a time is ameliorated by my strong belief that Dillon will do magnificently."[18]

Bobby next went to Palm Beach, Florida, to stay with his friends Harold and Gertrude Vanderbilt at their oceanfront estate, Eastover. Harold, the great-grandson of shipping and rail magnate Cornelius Vanderbilt, was a railway executive, a yachtsman, and the inventor of the card game known as contract bridge. He also was a Harvard graduate, a Porcellian Club member, and a friend of Bobby's brother Roger. At Eastover, Bobby took long bicycle rides and spent time painting by the pool. He had the Vanderbilts' butler send one of his paintings to the president as a gift. Bobby called the painting *Old Foggy Bottom*, a reference to the part of Washington where the State Department is located, though the title also undoubtedly had a double entendre in keeping with Bobby's naughty wit. Bobby remained in regular contact with the White House. In an April 21 letter to Ann Whitman from Eastover, Bobby said — with concern, even sounding a note of disdain — that he had spoken with Dillon Anderson via telephone the previous night: "He seems to be getting things under control — says he's tired. After three weeks?"[19]

Bobby soon assumed the post of chairman of Old Colony Trust, living again in his Somerset Club apartment. He plunged back into Boston life, continuing his position on the Harvard Board of Overseers and being named president of the board of Peter Bent Brigham Hospital. On June 2, he was elected to the board of Raytheon Manufacturing Company, a manufacturer of missiles for the US government founded by Vannevar Bush. Ike also called Bobby back to the White House for a meeting, and on June 4, just two months after Bobby's resignation, the White House announced that the president had engaged Bobby as consultant to the NSC. "It is gratifying to know that, although you have returned to private life, you will be able on occasion to give the Council the benefit of your wealth of experience in national security matters," Ike said in a letter to Bobby.[20]

Bobby also began making a series of speeches touting the Eisenhower administration's achievements. In September, he spoke before the national convention of the American Bankers Association in Chicago, saying that a strong economy was critical to national security and praising the work of Secretary of the Treasury George Humphrey.[21] Bobby also noted that one of the innovations adopted by the NSC under Eisenhower was a fiscal impact report accompanying any policy that the NSC was considering so it could know the cost of implementing the policy. "He firmly believes that the vitality of the free world is dependent, for the nearby years at least, upon a strong American economy," Bobby said.

Now speaking publicly and outside the confines of White House secrecy, Bobby became a bigger target for journalists. In a speech at Harvard, he underscored the importance of keeping classified national security information secret, drawing fire from brothers Joseph and Stewart Alsop. In a column titled "'Security' vs. Democracy," the brothers attacked Bobby in June 1955. "Our system, although Cutler forgets it, is a democracy . . . And any democratic government will surely fail if its masters, the people, are successfully kept in the dark about the national situation. The facts that Cutler would withhold from the people, on the ground that they are classified, are almost all the facts which define the national situation of this republic," the brothers wrote in their column in *The Washington Post*, which was carried in other newspapers as well. "In short, the Cutler system, which is also the Eisenhower Administration system, is not merely antidemocratic. Worse still, it is plain silly, unless its real purpose is to prevent those political embarrassments which officials of all governments have always wished to avoid."[22] Bobby brushed off the criticism and continued giving his speeches in support of Eisenhower. He had shifted back into his role as a campaign strategist, and he soon began to focus on preparations for the 1956 presidential election, still a year away. In late August, he hosted Richard Nixon during a visit to Boston, where Nixon met with the Catholic archbishop and was the guest of honor at a dinner Bobby threw at the Somerset Club. "I think the visit to the Archbishop was a ten-strike, as it worked out," Bobby wrote Nixon later.[23]

After Ike had a severe heart attack on September 24, 1955, Bobby maintained contact with Mamie and top White House officials, and she sent him a letter informing him that she had read Ike Bobby's letter wishing the president a happy birthday. Mamie wrote, "We were so heartened to know a good friend like you is remembering us daily with your prayers and good wishes in this time of anxiety."[24] In early November, Bobby flew to Denver to visit the president and Mamie while the president convalesced in a hospital. Even though the president was in weakened health, the two men discussed the idea of Bobby's returning to work at the White House for the reelection campaign. In a letter to Bobby following this visit, the president, by this time back in Gettysburg, wrote, "You may resent being called 'medicine', but you are just that, in the best sense of the word, for all the members of the Eisenhower family."[25]

At the end of November, Ike was back at the White House, and Bobby wrote him a letter pointing out that he — Bobby — had made thirty speeches since May 1. One event he spoke at was a Republican campaign dinner that raised $460,000, an extremely large sum for that era.[26]

Bobby's delight in writing poems for the president and Mamie continued and was met with appreciation. On December 20, 1955, Ike wrote Bobby a personal note from the Gettysburg farm:

Dear Bobby:
Mamie and I have decided that if we can't have, this year, the Bobby Cutler Christmas poem delivered in person (you see we are still hopeful that there will be a poem), we like best the smiling, verbal, handsome Cutler.

Many thanks, and the hope that despite your brother's illness, the many Cutlers, big and small, have a wonderful Christmas holiday.

As ever,
DE[27]

If Bobby did not have a Christmas poem for the Eisenhowers written by that time, he likely would have completed one forthwith, though it is not among the many Cutler poems at the Eisenhower Library.

Bobby also wrote articles to support the administration. At the request of CIA director Allen Dulles, he wrote an essay on the NSC for *Foreign*

Affairs. The April 1956 article described the reform of the NSC under Eisenhower: "General Eisenhower transformed the Council into a forum for vigorous discussion against a background of painstakingly prepared and carefully studied papers. He likes nothing more than the flashing interchange of views among his principal advisers."[28]

Bobby shuttled back and forth between Boston and Washington. In June 1956, he had dinner in the capital with Treasury Secretary George Humphrey and Commerce Secretary Sinclair Weeks. He also visited with Mamie and Ike, who was recovering from an attack of ileitis in his room at Walter Reed hospital. He brought two orchids for the president and First Lady's wedding anniversary. "When he gave me his large hand, I took it in both of mine; and then laid one of the orchid sprays on the bed's coverlet for his fortieth wedding anniversary," Bobby wrote later.[29] "I came away encouraged and fortified," Bobby wrote in a letter to Skip, adding that he believed Ike would indeed run for reelection despite his recent illness.[30] Bobby also told Skip he would come to Washington for the "campaign months of September and October," staying at 1718 H Street. "So we'll have opportunities to see each other and relax occasionally. This I look forward to, as I hope you will. Your letter encourages me to hope we'll be working together again, which I would like — Affly Bobby."

That same month, on June 18, 1956, a Senate investigator named John Mitchell made an allegation that Bobby was gay to FBI assistant director Louis Nichols.[31] Mitchell worked for the Senate Internal Security Subcommittee (SISS), which had led many high-profile anti-Communist investigations during the McCarthy era. Mitchell told Nichols that the former US ambassador to the Soviet Union, William Bullitt, was his source. "Bullitt told [Mitchell] that Robert Cutler who formerly was the President's assistant for intelligence matters was engaged in a homosexual incident at Harvard University in his young days . . . [and] that he believes several hundred people know of Cutler's sex deviation activities. Cutler finally left the government when the stories began circulating about him," Nichols recorded in an internal memo that he sent the next day to FBI deputy director Clyde Tolson. It is highly likely that Tolson would have discussed the issue immediately with Hoover. Executive Order 10450 and Hoover's "Sex Deviates" program both required investigations of alleged "sexual perversion." When the Arthur Vandenberg Jr. case blew up in December

1952, it began with a memo from Nichols to Tolson, and Hoover discussed Vandenberg personally with Eisenhower soon thereafter. When the investigation of the Bohlen homosexuality claims erupted two months later, Hoover, Tolson, and Nichols all were involved.

Mitchell's report raised the risk that the FBI would launch a "sex deviate" investigation of Bobby, but three other threats loomed over Bobby. First, Mitchell and the Senate Internal Security Subcommittee could independently pursue Bobby. SISS was a powerful force driving the Red Scare, and its chairman, Democratic senator James O. Eastland of Mississippi, had often joined forces with McCarthy and other right-wing Republicans in attacking Democrats and others as Communists or being Communist-influenced. Perhaps most famously, it was SISS that led the investigation of former Truman Treasury official Harry Dexter White. Mitchell, identified at the time as a magazine journalist, had testified in the SISS probe of White in 1954, suggesting that White believed capitalism was destined to fail and that Treasury Secretary Henry Morgenthau was under White's influence.[32] By 1956, Mitchell was still helping SISS investigate what was called the Morgenthau Diary, thousands of pages of diary entries by Morgenthau during his tenure in office, in a bid to identify subversives in the Roosevelt administration. Mitchell was reporting his findings on the Morgenthau Diary to Nichols at the FBI when he revealed Bullitt's homosexuality allegations against Bobby.

Another potential peril for Bobby stemmed from Bullitt's role in spreading these allegations. Bullitt launched a secret homosexual smear campaign during the Roosevelt administration against a political enemy, Undersecretary of State Sumner Welles, who played a key role in crafting Roosevelt's foreign policy. Welles had quietly resigned in 1943. Thirteen years later, in May 1956, the scandal magazine *Confidential* revealed that Welles resigned because Bullitt had threatened to publicize allegations that Welles had made sexual advances to a male steward on a railroad dining car.[33] "Bullitt threatened to expose the fact that Welles was a man morally ill," *Confidential* reported. "The Roosevelt regime couldn't afford the scandal, and F.D.R. had to sacrifice his old friend on the altar of respectability."

Finally, there was the possibility that *Confidential* would be tipped off to the homosexuality allegations against Bobby and publish a story. With the 1956 election approaching, a smear alleging that one of President Eisenhower's closest advisers was gay would have been explosive. *Confidential's* risk-taking and controversial editor, Howard Rushmore, had joined the Communist Party as a young man in 1933 in St. Louis, Missouri.[34] He was working for the Communist newspaper, the *Daily Worker*, when he wrote a positive review of *Gone with the Wind*, which he said led to his firing because his review conflicted with Communist Party tenets. Amazingly, Rushmore then went to work for the conservative *New York Journal-American* newspaper, where he built a reputation as a Communist hunter. In 1947, he testified before the House Un-American Activities Committee naming movie stars, including Edward G. Robinson, as supporters of Communist front groups.[35] Rushmore then went to work as a staff member for McCarthy's investigating committee, though he left in spring 1953 after clashing with Roy Cohn and David Schine, whom he described as "bumbling publicity seekers."[36] Rushmore moved on to become editor of *Confidential*, where he benefited from a friendship with anti-Communist radio personality Walter Winchell. Winchell sometimes used his broadcasts to tout upcoming issues of *Confidential*, as in June 1953 when he announced Rushmore's article in the magazine's next issue would be about *New York Post* editor James Wechsler, a former Communist Youth League member.[37] Wechsler also had been under investigation by FBI director Hoover and had been subpoenaed to testify before McCarthy's committee.

The intertwining relationships among *Confidential*, Winchell, McCarthy, and Hoover created an echo effect in which anti-Communist charges reverberated across the political landscape. As the controversy over Oppenheimer's security case had unfolded, *Confidential* ran a story in November 1954, "The Strange Death of J. Robert Oppenheimer's RED Sweetheart." It told the story of Oppenheimer's former Communist girlfriend Jean Tatlock, who committed suicide in 1944 while under FBI surveillance, noting in typical titillating detail that she was found nude in her bathtub in her San Francisco apartment. However, Rushmore's extreme tactics eventually soured his allies. In 1955, when Rushmore staged his own kidnapping as part of a plan to investigate claims that Communists had assassinated James Forrestal in 1949, Hoover had grown leery of the erratic editor. "Rushmore must be a 'nut.' We should have nothing to do with him," Tolson wrote Hoover. "I certainly agree,"

Hoover replied.[38] Still, *Confidential* continued publishing, and tales of homosexuality and political scandal were grist for its mill.

As the 1956 election approached, some Republicans grew worried that Nixon's association with the disgraced Joe McCarthy undermined Eisenhower's chances for reelection. Harold Stassen, the former Minnesota governor whom Eisenhower had appointed as his special assistant for arms control in 1955, launched a campaign to force Nixon off the ticket. Stassen's effort failed and, in August, at the Republican National Convention in San Francisco, Nixon was again nominated for the vice presidency. Senator Adlai Stevenson of Illinois was again the Democratic nominee for president, and once again Republicans sought to depict him as weak on Communism and to exploit rumors that he was gay.

In September 1956, the White House announced that Bobby had joined the president's campaign as a speechwriter.[39] Skip and Steve Benedict, meanwhile, had continued their practice of low-profile living, avoiding overtly homosexual establishments or revealing their gay relationships in public. Of course, they still had friends from their earlier, more carefree and open days. "Dear Boys," Chuck Turner began a letter from Rome to Skip and Steve at the Dr. Dick House. Chuck went on to describe his life in Europe, including tidbits of news about Samuel Barber and Gian Carlo Menotti, and a planned trip to Milan with another well-known gay couple, the writer Christopher Isherwood and artist Don Bachardy.[40]

Chuck, Sam, and the others were left unmentioned on September 26, when Bobby and NSC staff member Bromley Smith went to the Dr. Dick House for cocktails. As the evening unfolded, Steve turned on his reel-to-reel tape recorder, as he often did when friends gathered, and captured a conversation that provided unusual insight into the turmoil that had gripped the NSC in advance of Dillon Anderson's resignation the month before. Smith explained that during the 1955 conference in Geneva, Anderson had run into a "buzz saw" of opposition from the State Department when trying to advise the president. "In his frustration, I think he felt his only outlet was to advance his own personal policy view, and this soon became known around town. And that in itself has an effect that is quite disastrous," Smith said.[41] In revising the structure of the NSC, Ike and Bobby had set an expectation that the special assistant for national security affairs would act as a neutral adviser to the president, an honest broker — not an advocate for specific policy recommendations. Bobby had periodically deviated from this principle, advancing his own views or ensuring a voice for someone controversial like Oppenheimer. Bobby had the stature to stray from the principle of neutrality, which he himself had devised for the position, yet he always returned skillfully to neutral ground, restoring the appearance of balance and impartiality. Smith suggested that Anderson had deviated from neutrality so much that he had become known for doing so — and had been unable to recover. Anderson would later say he left the post to return to his home state of Texas to work for Ike's reelection.[42]

On September 1, Ike had appointed William H. Jackson, a trusted hand at intelligence and national security matters, to replace Anderson as his special assistant for national security. Nonetheless, Bobby expressed confidence that soon he would return to the NSC post. The tape recording reveals Bobby predicting, "I should tell you frankly, if I haven't told you before, that if the president is elected I have an almost certain feeling — so certain that it's higher than Ivory soap — that he's going to ask me to come down two or three days after the election and say, 'Now I want you to do this again.'"

At the time, Eisenhower was in the midst of two major challenges — the Suez Canal crisis and the Soviet Union's suppression of a democratic reform movement in Hungary. In Egypt, President Gamal Nasser had nationalized the Suez Canal, and three US allies — Great Britain, France, and Israel — threatened to take action against Egypt. Eisenhower supported Egypt, arguing that respect for the country's sovereignty over the canal was critical to building alliances with Muslim countries against Communism, but the three allies secretly conspired to formulate a plan of attack. Israel's invasion of the Canal Zone and French bombing raids that destroyed the Egyptian air force on October 29 caught Eisenhower and Secretary of State Foster Dulles by surprise. The British-French-Israeli attack raised the possibility of Soviet intervention in support of Egypt, possibly with nuclear weapons. Eisenhower and Dulles denounced the allies' attack, and Cabot Lodge introduced a resolution in the United Nations General Assembly calling for withdrawal of all foreign forces from Egypt. The resolution passed on November 4 by a vote of 57–0.[43]

On Election Day, November 6, Eisenhower swept to victory, winning his second term in a landslide. Securing forty-one of the forty-eight states, with 457 electoral votes to Stevenson's 73, Eisenhower became the first Republican president to win reelection in the twentieth century. Yet there was little time for jubilation at the White House. Both crises — in Hungary and in Egypt — were still evolving. The boot of the Soviet military had come quickly down on Hungary, but Ike was still working to compel the British, French, and Israelis to withdraw their forces from the Suez Canal Zone, which they ultimately did.

The president emerged from the two crises with changes he intended to put in place. Eisenhower had used the NSC repeatedly throughout both crises to analyze intelligence and possible policies, strategies, and tactics. Yet he questioned Foster Dulles's decision in July 1956 to precipitously withdraw US funding from Egypt's Aswan Dam construction project. Ike had concurred in Foster's decision after only a brief discussion. The decision created an opening for the Soviets to strengthen their ties to Egypt, contributing significantly to the Suez Canal crisis.[44] In addition, US intelligence had not served Eisenhower well at several instances throughout the ordeal.[45] Now the president sought to reinvigorate the NSC in an effort to improve his administration's national security decision-making processes, and he once again turned to Bobby to make the changes.

On November 23, Bobby met with the president and William H. Jackson at the White House to discuss Bobby's return to the position of special assistant for national security affairs and the changes Bobby would implement. Later that day, Bobby sent the president a memorandum summarizing their discussion, including changes to improve the Operations Coordinating Board. Ike responded the next day, thanking Bobby and saying, "I am delighted that you are again to be a valued member of the Administration team."[46] Reports of Bobby's resumption of his White House position appeared in newspapers that day.

The timing of Bobby's return to the White House bolsters the idea that concern about a homosexual smear had prompted him to step down. He resigned in March 1955, twenty months before the election, and his return was announced just weeks after the election, so his resignation removed him from the White House during the politically sensitive campaign period. His frenetic level of activity and engagement shortly after his resignation — becoming chairman of Old Colony; sitting on university, hospital, and corporate boards, writing for publications; giving speeches; and advising the Eisenhower campaign — belies his claims of exhaustion. Still, whether Bobby interrupted his tenure at the NSC to remain several steps ahead of those who might smear him as gay is a matter of speculation. But there is no question that following his return he was vulnerable should the FBI or Eisenhower's political enemies decide to go after him.

On November 28, Hoover sent a congratulatory letter to Bobby that appeared to underscore this vulnerability. "Dear Bobbie," he wrote, "I was pleased to learn of your plans to return as special assistant to the President for National Security Council affairs. Your many friends in this Bureau want to welcome you back, and we do hope you will not hesitate to let us know whenever we can be of aid. Sincerely, Edgar."[47] Although Bobby had signed at least one letter to Hoover as "Bobby," Hoover had spelled his name "Bobbie," commonly considered the spelling for a girl's name. Was it merely a slip, or was Hoover signaling that he had learned things about Bobby? A copy of Hoover's letter in FBI files includes additional typed notes stating there was "an alleged homo-sexual incident involving Cutler while at Harvard University" and that "Cutler left the Government when stories relating to this incident began circulating about him." Hoover inscribed his initials below these typed notes, indicating he had read them.

Hoover may have felt as if he were playing a high-stakes card game, facing his quarry across a table. Bobby, however, was expert at this game. On December 6, he replied to Hoover using the Old Colony Trust Company letterhead, which featured the image of a Puritan with a wide-brimmed black hat and the bank's motto, "Worthy of Your Trust." "Dear Edgar," he began. "Thank you for your thoughtful letter about my return to Washington as Special Assistant to the President. It was good of you to write and I look forward to renewing old associations, beginning January 6, 1957. Sincerely yours, Bobby." After Bobby's letter landed on Hoover's desk, the FBI director forwarded it to Tolson and Nichols.

Twenty months had passed since Bobby last occupied the post of special assistant to the president for national security affairs. Some might have demanded that the FBI perform a new background report on Bobby. Had such a background check been performed, the resulting report might well have included the homosexuality allegations by Bullitt, the memo to Tolson, the Oppenheimer wiretap, and anything else in FBI files on Bobby. However, searches of Eisenhower administration documents and requests to the FBI have turned up no reference to a second background check, and it appears none was performed. The way was clear for Bobby to take office one more time as Ike's top national security assistant.

17

THE RETURN

The Suez Crisis had given President Eisenhower new perspectives on how to create peace and security in the Middle East, and he proclaimed his new strategy for achieving these goals in a speech to Congress on January 5, 1957. This "Eisenhower Doctrine," as it became known, underscored Ike's view of the region as a key Cold War battleground. "The reason for Russia's interest in the Middle East is solely that of power politics. Considering her announced purpose of communizing the world, it is easy to understand her hope of dominating the Middle East," he said. The president called upon Congress to approve economic and military aid to Middle Eastern countries seeking to maintain their "national independence." The Eisenhower Doctrine posed a challenge to the non-aligned countries, such as Egypt, India, and Indonesia, whose leaders had proclaimed they wished to ally themselves with neither the Soviet Union nor the United States. Their movement coalesced in a global conference held in April 1955 in Bandung, Indonesia, where twenty-nine countries from around the world embraced a ten-point declaration that included support for national self-determination, the protection of human rights, an end to racial discrimination, and peaceful coexistence. Secretary of State Foster Dulles had shunned the conference. Now the Eisenhower Doctrine appeared to urge Middle Eastern countries to pick a side — the United States' side.

The day after Ike's speech, on January 6, Bobby resumed his post as special assistant to the president for national security affairs, taking charge of an NSC that faced many challenges. The Suez Canal remained closed, and tensions were high. The Egyptian president, Gamal Nasser, was continuing to expand his Arab nationalist political movement and was drawing closer to the Soviet Union as an ally. The Soviets had militarily suppressed the Hungarian Revolution and were continuing to advance Communist and anti-colonialist movements around the world. They also continued to build their nuclear arsenal while at the same time waging a global propaganda campaign that blamed the United States for failure to reach a disarmament agreement.

Having served as the nation's first national security advisor, Bobby was now the fourth, and he moved swiftly to reestablish the NSC's mission and his own. On his second day back in the office, he sent Secretary of State Foster Dulles and CIA director Allen Dulles letters saying that the president had approved a memo outlining key steps for effective operation of the NSC, including these:

- The NSC "should be the channel through which recommendations for national security policy reach the President for his decision."
- Except in special cases of urgency, security policy recommendations should be based on written papers shared with NSC members prior to meetings and discussed at meetings chaired by the president.
- The Operations Coordinating Board should be brought under the NSC structure, and the president's national security advisor — Bobby — should be its vice chairman.[1]

Foster Dulles raised concerns that Bobby's enhanced role at OCB would interfere with State Department operations, but in February Ike issued an executive order making the changes anyway.[2] In an effort to ensure that Bobby had the latitude he needed, the president also gave him authority to attend any meetings of the cabinet or other groups he felt necessary.

Bobby soon began meeting with a top-secret group set up to approve and coordinate covert actions. Nelson Rockefeller's Planning Coordination Group, which previously had that authority, had struggled to achieve a working relationship with the State Department and CIA.[3] Rockefeller himself recommended abolition of the Planning Coordination Group in December 1955. Ike agreed and signed NSC 5412/2, a directive that required the CIA to provide advance notice of covert actions to "designated representatives" of the president, the secretary of state and the secretary of defense.[4] Once Bobby returned to his NSC post in January 1957, he began serving, evidently as Ike's representative, in the small secret group under 5412/2 that came to be called in secret documents simply the "Designated Representatives."[5] Their mission was to approve and coordinate covert actions designed to defeat Communism such as propaganda, sabotage, demolition, aid to underground resistance groups, and related types of actions that the US government could "plausibly disclaim responsibility for."

In Syria, leaders of the Ba'ath Party had joined with army leaders and the Communist Party to overthrow the country's military strongman ruler three years earlier. CIA director Allen Dulles had begun sounding alarms about Syria's ties to the Soviet Union. On January 10, Bobby and other OCB members met to consider the Middle East situation. Allen Dulles and others argued that the United States should do whatever it could to strengthen defenses of countries bordering Syria. Gordon Gray, assistant secretary of defense for international affairs, urged providing radar systems to Iraq. At the end of the meeting, some OCB members left so that a meeting of the 5412/2 Designated Representatives — Dulles, Bobby, Gray, and Undersecretary of State Hoover — could be held.[6] Their discussion — and any possible covert action decisions they made that day — remain classified. In the coming months, the Eisenhower team would devise a secret plan, this time in collaboration with the British, to depose the Syrian government in a coup.

The NSC meeting the next day, January 11, focused on a subject that would dominate much of Eisenhower's second term — US ballistic nuclear missile programs. The programs had made technical advances, but all were still in development and testing phases.[7] E. V. Murphree, an assistant to Defense Secretary Wilson, began by discussing the intercontinental ballistic missile, or ICBM, intended to strike Soviet targets from the continental United States. The air force was pursuing two different ICBMs, Atlas and Titan, and they were hoped to be operational by 1959, he said. Next he reviewed the intermediate range ballistic missile, or IRBM, intended to travel roughly fifteen hundred miles. Two different IRBMs were also under development, Jupiter for the army and Thor for the air force, and they were expected to be operational by 1958. A test firing of a Jupiter missile was expected in the following month, February 1957. Finally, the navy's IRBM, the submarine-based Polaris, was under development and would not be ready for operation until 1962, the NSC was told. The missiles were being developed by companies including General Dynamics, Lockheed, Douglas Aircraft, and Chrysler.

Bobby said it was his understanding that all of the missile programs were only in testing and development stages, and there had been no decision by the president on how many missiles would ultimately be deployed. Eisenhower "stated this was also his interpretation."[8] Wilson, however, argued "that it would be very difficult for the planners to proceed with the development of the missiles if they were to have no reasonable assurance that these missiles would enter our weapons inventory at some future date. Moreover, he was sure that before long we should have to face squarely the question of creating a real operational capability for the ballistic missile."

The NSC then plunged into a sobering discussion of the federal government's fiscal condition and budget expectations. Bobby called on Treasury Secretary George Humphrey to comment, and Humphrey expressed frustration at getting reliable projections on tax revenue and military costs. "We must admit that neither the military on their side nor the Treasury and Budget on theirs, really knew very much what they were talking about. Defense is hard put to it to produce reliable information as to what this country needs at any given time for an adequate national defense," Humphrey said. "Here we were, engaged in spending billions of dollars to achieve a ballistic missile. At the same time we were spending other billions to produce aircraft like the B-52, early warning systems, etc., etc.; yet if these ballistic missiles really work, the early warning network would be overflown by the enemy and rendered useless." The treasury secretary's remarks set off a freewheeling discussion, with Defense Secretary Wilson, Secretary of State Dulles, disarmament negotiator Harold Stassen, and Bobby all pitching in. It was finally Eisenhower's turn, and he pointed to the level of armaments and said that "there was already in the world all the deterrent power that could be used. That is, there was enough deterrent power so that each side could destroy the other side completely. The concept of deterrent power has gone as far as it can. In view of this incredible situation we must have more fresh thinking on how to conduct ourselves . . . [O]ver the long run this country must get to a point where we can stabilize at least on a percentage basis of the gross national product to be devoted to our defense. Everyone who professes to be seriously concerned with the future of our country must do some fresh thinking. We cannot continue along our present line of thinking and acting without 'busting' ourselves."[9] The president's remarks, which drew the meeting to a somber close, revealed his frustration with his policy-making team and his concern about the rapid growth of the nuclear arsenals.

Stassen, Ike's special assistant for disarmament since 1955, had made limited progress in discussions with the Soviets. He helped develop the president's "Open Skies" concept, which would provide for both sides to perform aerial inspections as part of a disarmament accord,[10] yet direct talks with the Soviets stalled. A key sticking point was that the Soviets supported a ban on nuclear bomb tests, while the president and his advisers opposed a test ban unless it was part of a broader disarmament agreement. Stassen's failed bid to unseat Nixon as the vice-presidential nominee in 1956, coupled with disputes with Secretary of State Dulles, had diminished Stassen's status within the administration. With Eisenhower's backing, Stassen was instructed in early 1957 to report to Dulles, and his office was moved out of the White House and into the State Department building.[11] Criticism of both the United States and the Soviet Union for failure to make advances on disarmament continued to mount globally.

At the March 6 NSC meeting, Stassen laid out his plans for discussions with the Soviets in a new round of UN-sponsored negotiations in London. Stassen said he proposed to speak with his Soviet counterparts about a disarmament plan that would include aerial and land inspections. Foster Dulles warned that the inspection system and other aspects of his plan went beyond proposals approved by the NSC and the president. As a result, Stassen would have to outline his proposal only on an informal basis. "If such views are advanced and discussed, the discussion must be explicitly made on a purely personal basis, unless, again, we here back home provide approval in advance," the secretary of state said.[12] Bobby said none of Stassen's disarmament ideas were to be binding on the government, and the president underscored that the proposals were to be made by Stassen on a "personal basis." With these orders, Stassen and his staff departed for London.

As the nuclear arms race intensified, US nuclear policy often appeared contradictory, with conflicting policies advancing on separate tracks. While disarmament talks were progressing, expansion of nuclear weapons continued, as was shown two weeks later when the NSC reviewed US policy toward Turkey. Bobby summarized for the NSC a policy recommending at least one hundred million dollars per year in economic aid for Turkey through 1960, with Turkish and US military forces in Turkey continuing to grow. A State Department official representative noted that the United States was permitting Turkey to "get away with murder," as the country "welshed on all their promises to us that they would under- take necessary internal economic reforms." President Eisenhower said the low educational level in Turkey would make it difficult to create an elite force. Bobby chimed in jokingly that "what was lacking in Turkey were the advantages of a Harvard education." Other council members retorted that that was precisely what made the Turks such tough fighters. "The President expressed strong agreement," and laughter erupted.[13] When the chuckles subsided, General Nathan Twining, the air force chief of staff, said the military planned to provide Turkey with "atomic capable forces." The strategy of placing nuclear weapons in Turkey, on the Soviet Union's southern border, would later have momentous consequences.

One country that drew close scrutiny by the Dulles brothers was Indonesia, whose president, Sukarno, had been a leader of the non-aligned bloc of nations. Sukarno publicly expressed admiration for America and embraced democracy in his own country. Yet US intelligence officials worried that Sukarno's tolerance for Communists in the Indonesian government posed a risk that Communists would seize control of his nation. In 1955, the NSC secretly had authorized government agencies to undertake "all feasible" overt and covert actions to prevent a Communist takeover.[14] Sukarno, meanwhile, pushed for a better relationship with the United States. In 1956, he charmed many Americans when he traveled to Washington and attended a state dinner at the White House. He then spoke at a joint session of Congress, calling for Indonesia and America to have "the best friendship which has ever existed between nations." While in New York, he received a ticker-tape parade. Sukarno traveled to historic sites across America, such as Mount Vernon, and he visited Hollywood, where Marilyn Monroe sang at a party in his honor.[15] By early 1957, the Communist threat in Indonesia appeared to have ebbed, but now anti-Communist army generals were threatening to break away and fragment the country. In an NSC meeting on March 14, 1957, Allen Dulles explained that the Indonesian central government controlled only the main island of Java, while military leaders controlled all of the country's other large islands. The US military had prepared plans to take action in support of the rebel generals, and now an admiral of the

US Navy's Pacific Fleet was asking what steps he should take in light of the NSC's 1955 directive, Dulles said. Bobby responded by saying that the NSC's 1955 directive was issued at a time when the government was worried that Communism would spread from Indochina to the south, but "the developments in Indonesia at the present time were quite different." President Eisenhower said the admiral should be informed of "our view of what is actually happening in Indonesia." The president went on, "We would be up against a very tough problem if we ever had to face the contingency of recognizing several governments in the Indonesian area." The NSC concluded that the situation in Indonesia required no military action.[16]

By the time Bobby returned to his White House post, Joseph Alsop, who had attacked Bobby's penchant for secrecy, had moved to Paris to continue his journalism from an international vantage point. Soon it was Alsop's turn to keep a secret, this time in an excruciating Cold War episode. In early 1957, Alsop traveled to the Soviet Union for a journalistic tour. At a dinner in Moscow in late February 1957 he met a young man, Boris, whom he later described as "an athletic blonde, pleasant-faced, pleasant-mannered fellow" from Leningrad (now St. Petersburg). The young man offered praise of dissident Russian writers like Anna Akhmatova and Boris Pasternak and identified himself as a homosexual.[17] As Alsop explained later, "When I did not appear shocked, this in turn merged into an invitation." After the dinner was over, Alsop went to Boris's hotel room and spent an hour with him there. Boris invited him to come back the next day at 4:00 PM. After Alsop returned to the hotel room the next day, he was in for a shock — the door burst open and a police officer and two other men entered the room. Alsop, secretly gay, had been caught in a sting. Soviet interrogators told him he had broken Russian law and showed him photographs they said they had taken of him with Boris. The Soviet agents suggested the charges against Alsop might be dropped if he agreed to advocate for Soviet views in his articles. Alsop's old friend Chip Bohlen, the US ambassador in Moscow, scrambled to help him, and Alsop soon was allowed to leave the Soviet Union.

At some point, possibly at the instruction of his friend Frank Wisner, the CIA deputy director, Alsop wrote a nine-page memorandum describing the sting, including the alleged photos and also encounters with a number of other men in Russia prior to the fateful meeting with Boris.[18]

With an ironically clinical tone, Alsop wrote: "This is the history of an act of very great folly, unpleasant in itself but not without interest for the light it casts upon our adversaries in the struggle for the world. It must begin with a personal confession. I have been an incurable homosexual since boyhood."[19] Alsop insisted that a photo the investigators showed him was a "singularly brilliant fake," yet his confession suggested that a sex act had taken place in the hotel room. He also said that at the time of the sting he had considered suicide and later contemplated revealing the story to the world as a warning. Ultimately, though, his secret was not made public. Safely back in Paris, Alsop resumed writing articles with his brother.

Alsop's written confession, however, soon spread throughout high-level offices in Washington. CIA director Allen Dulles sent it in a secret transmittal to FBI director Hoover.[20] On April 17, Hoover informed Ike's chief of staff Sherman Adams, as the FBI director noted in a memo:

> Today following a conference in Governor Adams' office at the White House, I remained behind and told Governor Adams briefly of the developments in the Joseph Alsop case. He had not previously been advised of this situation, and I told him that as I understood it, the information had been held quite closely and that I knew that the Secretary of State and the Under Secretary of State had been advised of this by Mr. Allen Dulles, the Director of CIA, and that I, in turn, had advised the Attorney General and the Deputy Attorney General about it.[21]

Hoover sent his memo to Clyde Tolson and other FBI officials and placed it in his file on Alsop in his Official and Confidential Files, a secret filing system that he kept in his own office. An FBI report prepared for Hoover cited an informant's claim that he had homosexual relations with Alsop in Germany in 1954.[22] That report also resided in Hoover's Official and Confidential file on Alsop.

Alsop, however, appeared to escape further investigation by Hoover. The journalist had often taken left-leaning positions in his writing, for instance when he published, with his brother Stewart, the book *We Accuse* in defense of Oppenheimer. He had testified against an anti-Communist informant, Louis Budenz. Yet Alsop was not a government employee, and his liberal politics were balanced by a wartime record of supporting the Chinese Nationalist leader, Chiang Kai-shek. Hoover kept Alsop's homosexual confession in his Official and Confidential Files for the next two decades while Alsop remained a nationally prominent columnist.

Even as Hoover spread the Alsop story, a potentially more explosive scandal had quietly erupted — and was threatening to engulf Bobby Cutler. On the evening of April 11, White House correspondence clerk George A. Dame went to the men's bathroom in the library at George Washington University. He went to a toilet stall and slid a message asking for a "blow job" through a hole in the partition of the stall to a man on the other side.[23] When Dame opened the door, he found that the man waiting outside was a member of the Washington, DC, Metro Police vice squad. Dame led vice squad investigators to two other male clerks in the White House Correspondence Office, Kenneth E. Blaska and Joseph L. Halter. Blaska denied being gay, but all three men quickly resigned their White House jobs.

Andrew Goodpaster, the White House staff secretary, and Roemer McPhee, an attorney for the president, asked the Secret Service to investigate whether the three men knew of other homosexuals in the White House and whether they had violated security regulations. Dame had admitted in a signed statement that he had asked for oral sex by passing the note in the bathroom. Now the Secret Service conducted a polygraph examination, which "conclusively showed that Dame had had homosexual relations with an employee at the White House" and that he'd had sex with Blaska.[24] Halter, who had been working as a secretary for Bobby, told the Secret Service he believed he should not work for the NSC, giving a reason that impugned Bobby. "His principal reason for declining to work full time with the National Security Council was his belief that General Robert Cutler is a homosexual and his fear that continual association with General Robert Cutler would eventually place him in a position that could result in extreme embarrassment for the White House," the Secret Service investigative report said.

Halter's charge against Bobby took a more ominous turn when he said he had seen a document alleging British prime minister Anthony Eden was a homosexual. Sherman Adams quickly informed Hoover about Halter's claim, and the case was turned over to the FBI because there had been an apparent breach of security. On the afternoon of April 17, Hoover went to the White House and plunged into the investigation himself. Later that day, Hoover said in a memo that Halter admitted that he had seen a "confidential report on Anthony Eden indicating similar activities on the part of the former Prime Minister of Great Britain and that he had told Dame about this. Halter has been taking dictation for General Cutler."[25] Hoover continued, "General Goodpaster stated that General Cutler and other assistants of his in his office have checked and have been unable to find any such report on Anthony Eden and they believe that if, in fact, Halter did see such a report, it possibly was one passing through his office from CIA or the FBI."

Hoover soon reported that his agents checked the FBI's own files and quickly found its own copy of the missing document — the very letter that Hoover had sent Bobby nearly four years earlier alleging Eden, Mountbatten, and Nutting were homosexuals. The next day, April 18, Hoover called Bobby on the phone to inform him that the missing document was the letter "addressed to him, Cutler, dated September 16, 1953." Hoover recounted his conversation with Bobby in a memo to Tolson, Belmont, and Nichols, the same FBI officials who had been informed of the prior homosexuality allegations against Bobby.[26]

The fact that the 1953 letter had been sent to Bobby appeared to put Bobby's own conduct in question. Had he shown Hoover's letter to Halter? If Bobby did show it to him, why and when? If Bobby did not show the letter to Halter, how had Halter seen it? Why did Halter think Bobby was homosexual, and why did he think continuing to work with Bobby would lead to an embarrassment for the White House? These questions would have been fairly logical to ask, yet Hoover's memo ends abruptly without mention of further investigative steps.

For years, Hoover had positioned himself as vigilant in ferreting out "sex deviates" from the federal government, yet there is no documentary evidence he pursued Bobby further. It is possible to speculate that Hoover decided to overlook the allegations of homosexuality against Bobby because Bobby was a general, an unquestionably loyal American, a devout Christian, a vigorous anti-Communist, and a key member of Eisenhower's inner circle. Perhaps most significantly, an investigation of Bobby would likely have caused severe damage to Hoover's relationship with Eisenhower.

Hoover also may have recognized in Bobby a kindred soul — a powerful, aging bachelor who had intense relationships with men. Each was vulnerable to, and could ill afford, an allegation of homosexuality levied against him publicly. Ultimately, Hoover may have rushed to make that phone call to Bobby with two competing motives — first to investigate the case and gain leverage over Bobby, and second to protect Bobby as a friend and ally. Hoover himself may not have known which of these two competing motives he would give free rein to later.

Whatever his reasons, Hoover soon dropped his probe of Bobby's handling of the Eden letter and of Halter's allegations that Bobby was gay. There are no additional investigative reports in Hoover's Official and Confidential file on the matter, titled simply "White House Employees — Homosexuals." On April 19, Hoover noted that Goodpaster asked the FBI to return the Secret Service investigative report to the White House. Hoover, however, had a photostat copy of the Secret Service report placed in his confidential "White House Employees — Homosexuals" file.[27] There also was no mention of Halter's allegations in the other FBI file on Bobby — the one that held Bullitt's allegations. A few weeks later, in a memo to Tolson and the other agents, Hoover said he had informed the attorney general that "our investigation had not in any way substantiated the original allegations against General Cutler."[28]

Hoover also gave no sign of losing confidence in Bobby. The FBI director continued his practice of sending secret intelligence and security reports to him for the president. A week after the White House homosexuals probe arose, he sent Bobby a letter about the civil rights movement, beginning, "I thought the President and you would be interested in the information in the enclosed memorandum . . ."[29] Hoover's agents had discovered that the Communist Party was supporting a civil rights march called the "Prayer Pilgrimage for Freedom," planned to take place in Washington on May 17, 1957, the third anniversary of the Supreme Court's *Brown v. Board of Education* school desegregation ruling. Martin Luther King Jr. and other civil rights leaders had called for Eisenhower to urge southern officials to move more swiftly to desegregate schools. They also were urging Congress to pass a civil rights act. The FBI memo sent by Hoover cited information from confidential informants asserting that the Communist Party was supporting the march, and that King had "orally and unofficially asked the CP for support in this mobilization." Paul Robeson and W. E. B. DuBois, two prominent figures of the civil rights movement whom the FBI said were associated with subversive groups, were expected to attend, the report said. Bobby noted that he relayed the "substance" of the memo to the president on May 1.[30] The president, as he often did when informed of Hoover's stream of information about alleged Communists, considered the information and took no action, although he declined to meet with King while he was in Washington for the march. For the most part, the intense debate over civil rights involved the US attorney general and remained out of Bobby's NSC realm. Ultimately, the May 17 event, a milestone in the civil rights movement noted for King's famed "Give Us the Ballot" speech at the Lincoln Memorial, took place without incident.

For all of his secrecy and desire to recede into the shadows at the White House, Bobby was again highlighted in the press when on May 24, *The New York Times* profiled him in a story under the headline "Puritan — Up to a Point." The article, with a photo of Bobby at his desk captioned "One of the legends of the Eisenhower Administration," included a description that captured the air of mystery surrounding him:

> No man in the Government, with the possible exception of the President, knows so many of the nation's strategic secrets.
>
> Yet no other man so high in the Administration is so little known outside the President's immediate circle. Even to that circle, Bobby Cutler is something of a paradox.
>
> Mr. Cutler is a proper Bostonian, tall and spare of frame, with the unadorned features of the New England Puritan. He is a Rabelasian with a salty vocabulary and such a repertory of bawdy stories as only a very proper man could afford to tell.
>
> He is an earnest Episcopalian, who might be mistaken for a successful preacher. And he is a man who can move so quickly from ribaldry to piety and back to ribaldry again as to leave his friends with an uneasy feeling that they laughed in the wrong place.
>
> He is, as a government official, a "slave driver" who can force his staff to work as hard as he works himself. As his subordinates have learned, he can be at the end of the long day, with a bourbon old-fashioned in hand, a charming and generous friend.

Finally, Mr. Cutler is a bachelor's bachelor, but a bachelor who has had a lifelong love affair. It is a love affair with the city of Boston — "The loveliest city in the world." As a fundraiser for Boston charities, he has no peer.

A Boston editor once quoted these lines about Benjamin Franklin as equally descriptive of Mr. Cutler:

"He enjoyed himself among the girls and loved women all his life, but no woman, however charming she was, could completely capture his mind and imagination. He loved politics, too, and the struggle of commerce. But he never considered his enterprises in these fields, picturesque and intoxicating as they were, as ends in themselves. Nothing could satisfy him entirely but the feeling that he was serving men by leading them."

In the Eisenhower Administration, Mr. Cutler has been leading men by serving the President.

At FBI headquarters, copies were routed to Tolson, Nichols, and Belmont, and a copy was placed in the FBI file on Bobby that held the report on Bullitt's homosexuality allegations.[31]

In late May, disarmament negotiator Harold Stassen again appeared before the NSC, outlining progress in his discussion with the Soviets at the United Nations disarmament talks in London, noting in particular Soviet receptivity toward the use of aerial inspections to verify an arms accord. Stassen also reported other progress — the Soviets had dropped demands that all nuclear weapons be banned and that the US abandon all overseas bases. The Soviets, fearing encirclement by American nuclear bases, now called for nuclear weapons to be based only in the USSR, the United States, and the United Kingdom.[32] Stassen displayed a map showing regions of the Soviet Union that the Soviets had expressed willingness to open to aerial inspection. With additional meetings planned for the following days to resolve specific negotiating positions, President Eisenhower closed the meeting by telling the NSC he wanted to express one thought: "This thought was the absolute necessity of some kind of a halt in the arms race."[33]

Two days later, on Saturday, May 25, the president met at the White House with Stassen, Secretary Foster Dulles, Atomic Energy Commission chairman Lewis Strauss, Deputy Secretary of Defense Donald Quarles, Joint Chiefs of Staff chairman Arthur Radford, and Bobby. Stassen argued in support of a test ban agreement as the first phase of a comprehensive agreement, proposing a dramatic shift in policy. Ike expressed support for the plan and gave Stassen permission to present his ideas to the Soviets as an "informal memorandum," but only after clearing those ideas with the NATO allies.[34] Stassen then returned to the talks in London with other members of the US delegation and on May 31 presented his plan, which he called an "informal memorandum," failing to heed the president's requirement that the allies be consulted first. Upon learning of Stassen's actions, the British were incensed. Prime Minister Harold Macmillan sent Eisenhower a cable saying, "I would have hoped that we could have examined together the consequences of these proposals before they were put forward."[35] The French indicated they would not accept a ban blocking tests unless both major powers agreed at the same time to stop making nuclear weapons.

Secretary of State Dulles was furious over Stassen's failure to consult the allies. On June 4, he chastised Stassen in a cable, instructing him to correct the situation with his Soviet counterpart, Valerian Zorin. "You will notify Mr. Zorin at the earliest possible moment that the memorandum you submitted to him was not only informal and unofficial, but had no approval in its submitted form, either by the President or the State Department . . . Therefore, you will request that Mr. Zorin return the memorandum."[36] Zorin, however, had already forwarded the memo to Moscow. Meanwhile, the White House rushed to revise the memorandum and submit the revision to the allies, and Bobby was pulled into the effort. On Saturday, June 8, Bobby sent Ike a letter attaching a revision of the disarmament policy based on a Stassen memo of May 9 and incorporating changes sought by the president. The revision had been drafted by the State Department working with Bobby and representatives of Defense, the AEC, and the CIA. Bobby offered to discuss the matter with Ike, saying, "Except for Church and a walk, I'll be available all Sunday if I can be useful. The switchboard will know."[37]

The revision was soon complete. "Mr. President," Bobby wrote the president four days later. "The interagency working group last night agreed upon a final draft of the . . . guidance for the US Delegation."[38] It proposed a twelve-month nuclear test ban but reverted to the position that it would only be implemented if the Soviets and other nations agreed to a broad disarmament plan, including a ban on production of radioactive materials for weapons, the establishment of a system for both aerial and ground inspections, and reduction of troop forces to 2.5 million by both the United States and the Soviet Union. The revised position spelled the end to Stassen's efforts to finesse a test ban. Enraged by Stassen's missteps, Foster Dulles assigned an assistant to make sure Stassen didn't stray from the plan, and in July Dulles himself took direct control of the talks with the Soviets. In August, the Soviets rejected the revised plan and the talks collapsed.

Even as the disarmament talks played out, Eisenhower's team was working assiduously not only to increase the nation's atomic forces but also to deceive the Soviets into thinking those forces were more devastating than they actually were. Bobby and CIA director Allen Dulles began discussing a proposed operation identified as the "Deception Plan" as part of the review of proposed covert projects by the 5412/2 Designated Representatives.[39] On June 6, Bobby sent the CIA director documents prepared by the Joint Chiefs of Staff and classified "Eyes Only." Two weeks later, on June 19, the 5412/2 Designated Representatives met in the offices of Christian Herter, who had replaced Herbert Hoover Jr. as undersecretary of state. Also attending were Allen Dulles, Assistant Secretary of Defense Mansfield Sprague, and General Graves Erskine, who headed special operations for the Department of Defense. A top-secret memo by Bobby on the meeting sketched the outlines of the Deception project: Dummy missiles would be deployed to suggest that the US had successfully stationed IRBM missiles in the United Kingdom, possibly with the assistance of a "double agent" to convey false information that would bolster the credibility of the ploy.

Doubts about the strategy arose at the meeting. "Herter stated that, on balance, he and the Secretary (Foster Dulles) thought the project involved a greater risk of damage if it were unmasked, which seemed likely."[40] Bobby questioned whether the plan — if in fact it succeeded — would have an adverse impact on the United States. "If the deception succeeds, will it not also deceive the American people and Congress, — with possible inquiries and hurtful results?" Finally, Bobby questioned the entire premise of the plan — that Soviet fear of US nuclear missiles would yield some positive benefit — and wondered whether another outcome was possible: "Will the effect on the Russians be to deceive them in being scared of the US and deterred, or feel impelled to act more quickly to fight in order to get ahead?"

Allen Dulles urged deferring for at least six months "any use of dummies or working with the UK," Bobby's memo reported. "It was left that Allen Dulles and Erskine would confer on writing out a minute as to the assets that were available (double agent) for carrying out such a deception project, and report back before any further action was taken. At least we would then know what could be done in the way of planting papers, etc. There was no decision as to the basic policy and there was a unanimous feeling that the use of dummies, etc., should not be undertaken for six months after further consideration." Further details of the proposed Deception project remain classified, and it is unclear whether it was later implemented.

Bobby's young friend Skip Koons, meanwhile, had decided he wanted to leave the NSC and return to Europe, and he found a position with the US Information Agency at the US embassy in Paris. Since May he had begun discussing this change with Bobby, who immediately began helping him consider other options. When at last it was clear that Skip was set upon the Paris position, Bobby wrote a letter to Arthur Larson, the agency's director, praising Skip at length. "Mr. Koons is industrious, devoted to the performance of his duty, and capable of preparing reports of an informative and highly intelligent content. He has been of maximum personal help to me in my duties as Special Assistant to the President."[41] With Skip preparing to leave his NSC post in early August, Bobby began asking Skip to spend time with him outside the office. Bobby's fondness for Skip had grown over the years, but his emotions always had been held in check by a dam of professionalism, propriety, and secrecy that he himself had built. Now, as the anxieties and pressures of the NSC weighed on him, and with Skip preparing to depart for Paris, that dam was about to break, releasing a torrent of emotions.

18

"THE GREATEST ADVENTURE OF MY LIFE"

On Saturday night, July 13, 1957, Bobby and Skip went out to see a movie, and after the show Skip drove Bobby home in his Thunderbird. Skip pulled the black convertible up in front of The Family, Bobby's residence a few blocks from the White House. The stark age difference between the two men — Bobby was sixty-two, and Skip was thirty-one — did not impede the sharing of affection. The moment came rushing back to Bobby, as he poured out his feelings of love for Skip in a secret diary:

> He brought me home from a movie in the Thunderbird and when to say goodnight outside #1718 H ST I took his hand our fingers for a moment interlaced. It was at that moment the greatest adventure of my life began: the best, the purest, the most penetrating emotion I ever knew. God keep this spirit always so; wearing his cross, thinking of his happiness, remembering every minute of his serenity and serious charm, wanting nothing of life but to have a part of his life.[1]

By the time Bobby wrote this glowing diary entry a year later, he was wearing a gold cross that Skip had given him. In an earlier diary entry, Bobby wrote, "The brilliant light of my love for him throws all the rest of this world in shadow."[2]

The Thursday after they went to see the movie, and after an NSC meeting at which CIA director Allen Dulles warned of the dangers of a possible military dictatorship in the Soviet Union, Bobby and Skip spent the evening at Skip's apartment in the Crestview building in Washington. Bobby would also recall this time fondly in his diary. "This day is the anniversary of our wonderful love evening together at Crestview 6 PM to 1:30 AM."[3]

The next day, Friday, July 19, Bobby and Skip dined together. Bobby's passionate feelings for Skip were alloyed by his sadness over Skip's impending departure to Europe. Bobby wrote Skip on Sunday from Fair Harvard, the home outside of Boston that he shared with Bill and Ruth Sullivan, "Your appreciation of another's feelings make these last weeks together, instead of sadness, a shining promise of what can be ahead," he wrote.[4] He mentioned the Greek myth of Damon and Pythias, two male friends who are deeply loyal to each other.[5] "The real Damon wants what makes Pythias happiest. May I be to you, — as you are being to me, — a resource for all our tomorrows. B."

The next weekend, Bobby and Skip went to Dumbarton Oaks, a mansion with elegantly landscaped grounds owned by Harvard in Georgetown, where they swam in an elegant pool and had a picnic.[6] They then drove to Haverford, Pennsylvania, to stay with Skip's mother, Peggy, and stepfather, Howard Lutz. On Sunday, Skip said something that fueled Bobby's emotions. "On July 28 he said he thought of me constantly," Bobby scrawled on the back of one of Skip's letters.[7] In a thank-you note to Peggy days later, Bobby playfully expressed his feelings for Skip. "I have voted him the young man whom I would first choose to be with me were I to be castaway on a desert island."[8]

Skip would travel to Europe from New York via ocean liner on August 3. The day before, Friday, August 2, he traveled with Bobby from Washington to Boston. They went to the Country Club in Brookline, where Bobby was a member, and strolled around the golf course before dining together. At the evening's end, Bobby returned to his apartment at the Somerset Club.[9] The next day, Skip traveled by plane to New York, where he would board the SS *Constitution* for his Atlantic crossing.

Before they parted, Bobby had handed Skip two White House stationery envelopes, one with his name and the words "open on the plane" on it, and another addressed to Skip aboard the ship. In the envelope for the plane, Bobby placed a pair of cuff links that his brother Elliott had given him four decades earlier.[10] "And now, as there is nothing more precious that I can give — I give them to you, little brother. When you wear them, think that with them come all the thought and hope and confidence and love that one man can have for another who is his friend. God bless you and keep you until we are together again. B."

Two days prior, on August 1, Bobby had written Skip an impassioned letter that went into the envelope to be opened aboard ship. "It seems odd to be writing an au revoir to one whom, God willing, I will be with tomorrow night. But there will be many letters in these dark months ahead," Bobby wrote.[11] "In gaining your friendship, I have gained all I can ever wish: a responsive companion, gentle, sympathetic, profoundly understanding, filled with discerning maturity nourished out of surmounted pain, true valuer of things beautiful and intellectually satisfying, still also a laughing comrade — a person to share life with in the spiritual being together which transcends words and acts. Nothing can break this golden chain."

Bobby went on to implore Skip, "Always remember this: I am waiting, around the corner, always — to help in whatever way I can. That is what friendship is for. In your joy, in your sickness, in your unhappiness: ask me to bring the solace of unselfish love." He then wrote what he called a prayer for friends, beginning, "O God, we would fain be near them who are not here with us. We would fain be near them to shield them from harm and to touch them with the tenderness of love."

Bobby's letters danced along a fault line: He described his feelings for Skip alternatively as love — and friendship. To stop short and say simply that he loved Skip, omitting the mention of friendship, might reveal the strength of his emotions too nakedly.

Aboard the SS *Constitution*, Skip wrote Bobby thanking him for the cuff links. "Your letters, both on the plane and to the boat, meant a great deal to me, and touched me deeply. The prayer, I am afraid, made me cry, from a mixture of feelings," he wrote. Commenting on Bobby's prayer for a friend, Skip referred to the biblical Books of Samuel, in which the story of David and Jonathan is considered by some observers to be a paradigm of homosexual love.[12] "I have read Samuel, and I thank you for the pledge, yet it is rather for me to turn to Him to whom you pray and ask Him that His will be done. Skip." Skip appeared to be trying to dampen Bobby's ardor. An imbalance had formed in their relationship: Bobby was obsessively passionate, while Skip deflected that passion and held Bobby at a distance, though never fully rejecting him.

Bobby wrote a letter to Skip at the home of Miki Paronian in Nice, where Skip was to stay before starting his new job in Paris. Bobby recalled their last evening together:

Dear Skip,

I am still so impregnated with last Friday night, the *nox mirabilis*, again, — not at all as might be feared (knowing myself), a *nuit des larmes* [night of tears], but thanks to your sensibility a *nuit d'espoir* [night of hope], that I must write once more in a vein which I hope will not infringe your "rationality," to catch you at Nice . . .

Could there have been a more wonderful setting for our talk than that 10th tee at the Country Club? The gathering dark of evening making mysterious the green reaches of the golf course; the last flush of day in the western sky; the bright half moon and a few stars in the clear soft sky of summer . . .

My wish is that you found an equal satisfaction. For this has been, I feel, a great turning point in my emotional life. In other times, Friday would have been an evening of grief and sharp doubts: to be losing so much for awhile, which I had just found! In other times, my heart would have been vexed with selfish, unconstructive, saddening concerns: how much I meant to you? Whether others meant more? And so on. But thanks (I think) to your gentle under-standing, I came away with a radiant conviction: grateful to Providence that I had a sure place in your heart, a place that you wanted to hold and maintain and keep always; a place that would be there, warm and welcoming, if I could make myself worthy of it.[13]

He closed his letter with a plea:

Let me hear often from you, those "little winning words of love" that obliterate time and distance and can put us once more on the 10th tee in the August night, tying our lives together with invisible but unbreakable bonds of affection. B.

Skip, meanwhile, wrote Bobby again from the SS *Constitution* as it plied the waters from Genoa to Nice. He transcribed a passage from a book he was reading, *In the Wake of Ulysses*, by Finnish writer Goran Schildt: "The greater the tension between, for instance, the lust of the flesh and the soul's demand for purity, between a logical striving for clarity and emotional ecstasy, to quote one or two common antitheses — the nobler the classicism that succeeds in bringing them harmoniously together."[14] Skip selected an apt passage, as both men were living with the tension between their own unmentionable desires and society's expectations of heterosexual purity. He signed the letter, "Affectionately, Skip."

As nuclear weapons issues consumed his work in the NSC in early August, Bobby took the train back to Boston and traveled again to Fair Harvard, with a lake nearby and Mount Wachusett rising above the gently rolling landscape. The house was Bobby's retreat, and here he gave full expression to his emotions. In a letter to Skip on Monday, August 12, Bobby recalled his failed romance with Nell Sears and described the transformation that Skip had inspired in him:

> A sweeping change has come over my life and thinking. For years since the cruel heart-blow in 1928, work and duty have filled the nooks and crannies of my life. The terrible momentum of that drive rushes on in my work, hour after hour after hour. But there is another well in life, that has been dry and is now gushing forth. Strange how this came about. Through the intervention of a man, young in years but full grown in sensible understanding that can be learned only from personal griefs overcome. Intervening in a moment in time he wished to push outside our lives. But intervening, in this fragile moment, with deep caring, with the only sword that destroys all foes: loving understanding.

He resumed the letter the next day, giving voice to worries that Skip did not love him enough. He cited Ralph Waldo Emerson's reflections on unrequited love — "It is thought a disgrace to love unrequited. But the great love will see that true love cannot be unrequited."[15] Bobby wrestled with what he deemed inadequate expressions of affection from Skip, trying to understand Skip's need to be with other people. "And so I shall be sensible enough not to grieve that my friend has other affections and ties to monopolize some of him, so long as I am sure my caring is related — not to *my* happiness, but to *his*." Two days later, he noted that he'd received a letter that Skip sent from Algeciras, Spain. "It was like a hand squeezing my heart to open the envelope — delight, anticipation, unreasonable fear that you might have changed your mind." Recalling the cuff links he had given Skip, Bobby wound gently around to a subtle expression of love. "I rejoiced that you liked the cufflinks; and, though you were cool and temperate in your judgments of ourselves, that is your temperament I take it and, being a part of you, I love it too." Yet Bobby also plunged headlong into doubts of their relationship, wondering whether Skip was breaking his bonds with Bobby. "You are not forming a new self overseas that will disown and discard the association so luminously formed in our lives? O, do not say or intimate such things. It is not so." He finishes: "You are the best thing in my life, remember that. Always B."

Traveling in France, Skip sent a postcard from Honfleur in Normandy, then a brief letter from Nice making no mention of their relationship. He mentioned a visit with friends and noted disappointedly that the weather was too bad to sail. Bobby was undone by Skip's lack of emotion. On August 18, he wrote Skip in care of Madame Paronian in Nice:

> Dear Skip —
> Your second letter, from Nice, is here. The gods must smile at the strange antiphony of our correspondence. My letters charged with subjective response to the emotional explosion in my life, pouring molten lava over everything, — each word, each action, each lyric poem, each philosophic concept, — self-centered, "without skin," as Rousseau was described; and your replies roaming calmly the stratosphere of philosophy — Finnish appraisal of true classicism, the influence of the wine-dark sea — in objective balance, as if the explosion were not in our lives, but only somewhere nearby. Yet it was just 30 days ago tonight that we talked for eight hours at Crestview and three weeks since our picnic at Dumbarton and our Thunderbirding adventure to Haverford and back: days that shook the world in which we two live . . .

Skip pleaded with Bobby not to read too much into his letters. Writing from the beach at Cannes, he explained on August 27 that he had been traveling to London and the French Riviera.

> You must not, as the French say, *'Casser la tête'* in pulling my letters apart for if you do, you will only go through exercises of the imagination — whether in a negative or positive sense — which are neither necessary, nor particularly healthy — it seems to me. I am a poor correspondent, you will see. As far as what I have said before goes, yes I do think the classical, rather than the romantic, approach to life is the better of the two. Furthermore, I think your life has beautifully expressed the classical approach to date, and I would expect it to continue to do so. I will pass over your other *"interpretations de texte,"* with the gentle request that you not dissect my poor phrases with too sharp a scalpel — Skip.[16]

Skip reveled in his travels, spending time at Miki Paronian's home in Nice and meeting members of the arts world whom she knew. He and Miki listened to music and discussed Schubert, Beethoven, and other composers, he said in a September 1 letter to Bobby, written at twilight from Miki's terrace overlooking Nice's Mediterranean bay, the Baie des Anges. He met Marc Chagall and the mistress of Fernand Léger. Finally, after driving to Paris, Skip began his new job at the American embassy on September 9:

> I am lucky. My office, in the right wing of the Embassy gives on the front, and therefore, from the third floor I have a fine view of the Place de la Concorde, the Bridge and the Chamber of Deputies. Below in the Cours la Reine, through which the Champs Elysees runs, the trees are beginning to be touched with faint hues of yellow and orange. It is 6:15. The sun is setting and the Dome of the Invalides glitters in the golden rays. Later as the leaves fall, the other buildings on the Left Bank from the Quai d'Orsay north to opposite the Grand Palais will come into view.[17]

Bobby by this time had begun writing a stream of letters to Skip, sending five in September. They often contained snippets of information about NSC matters or meetings with the president. In a September 13 letter, he said he'd participated in a two-hour meeting on the previous Saturday with President Eisenhower on the Middle East, was burdened with work on both the NSC Planning Board and the OCB, and was taking "a briefcase bulging with work" back to Boston. "Monday at 8 I see the President at Newport, after flying down the night before in a helicopter." He added a reproachful note about the distance he sensed between them. "Let me have more like the letter from Nice at twilight — like the you that I thought to know and care for."

Skip replied on September 18, expressing concern about Bobby's penchant for overworking himself. "I wish I was on hand to try to cajole you into a more reasonable attitude towards the necessity of letting up a bit . . ." Bobby responded, referencing Skip's wish to be with him: "Now we are both wishing the same thing. O happy day when it could be true, for though I live with it, I miss you constantly, all the time, and think of you at all kinds of odd moments."[18] Bobby also explored the idea of a bicycle trip with Skip on the French Riviera, noting that the previous evening he had dinner with Secretary of Commerce Weeks and his wife and the Viscount and Viscountess Harcourt from England, and Betty Weeks said weather on the Riviera was "divine" in April, "so let us think on it." He continued with news of the NSC. "Tomorrow we have a Council Meeting, the P coming in from Newport to preside . . . We take up Formosa, Indochina also." Bobby also included in the letter his own handwritten copy of a nineteenth-century French poem about a secret unrequited love.[19] The poem, "My Secret," was translated by Longfellow:

> *My soul its secret has, my life too has its mystery,*
> *A love eternal in a moment's space conceived;*
> *Hopeless the evil is, I have not told its history,*
> *And the one who was the cause nor knew it nor believed.*

Bobby's letters appeared at times to careen from one extreme to another, first a soaring expression of emotional attachment to Skip, then deep despair over perceived inadequate affection from Skip, and then regret over his own possessiveness toward Skip. Equanimity was rare.

Bobby bikes along the Potomac River in Washington, December 3, 1953. This photo hung near the small door entering President Eisenhower's Oval Office with a caption: It's not young Lochinvar, of course, But Bobby on his iron horse.

Bobby, in a swim suit, sits near a pool with, from left to right, Eisenhower Administration Budget Director Joseph Dodge, Treasury Secretary George Humphrey, Defense Secretary Charles Wilson (standing) and Attorney General Herbert Brownell at Quantico, Va. *The Saturday Evening Post* published the picture with its profile of Bobby on February 6, 1954, entitled, "Mystery Man of the White House." *Saturday Evening Post/AP Images*

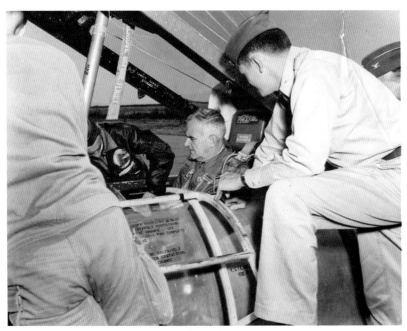

Bobby in cockpit of a jet during his July 1954 tour of US military bases overseas. *Courtesy of the Eisenhower Library*

Bobby Cutler with Ike and Mamie Eisenhower, Mamie's mother Elivera Doud, standing at left, and an unidentified woman at right, Christmastime 1954. *Courtesy of the Eisenhower Library*

Bobby, flanked by Ike and Mamie, at his farewell lunch in the White House Mess, March 29, 1955. *Courtesy of the Eisenhower Library*

Bobby during a light moment while Ike golfs in New Hampshire, June 1955. *Courtesy of the Eisenhower Library*

New Year's Eve 1956 at the Dr. Dick House, with Steve Benedict in the center and Skip Koons to his right. *Courtesy of Stephen Benedict*

Skip, behind the wheel of his Thunderbird, with Gaylord Hoftiezer in front of the Dr. Dick House in Alexandria, Virginia, 1957. *Courtesy of Stephen Benedict*

Skip and Bobby at the pool at the Dumbarton Oaks mansion, in Washington, DC, July 1957. *Courtesy of Stephen Benedict*

Bobby in Venice on the trip he took with Skip in May 1958, in a photo Bobby taped into his diary. *Courtesy of Stephen Benedict*

President Eisenhower signed this photo for Skip after his departure from the NSC staff: "For T.B. Koons with appreciation of long and efficient service on the White House staff and with best wishes."
Courtesy of Stephen Benedict

Ike and Bobby share a laugh after Bobby is sworn in as American executive director of Inter-American Development Bank. *Courtesy of the Eisenhower Library*

Bobby and Skip in Trouville,
France, 1958. *Courtesy of Stephen Benedict*

Skip and Bobby on a sailboat, likely the Chaika, which Bobby financed for Skip. *Courtesy of Stephen Benedict*

Tony Favello in a photo taken by Bobby on their European tour in 1968. *Courtesy of Anthony Favello*

Steve Benedict with Bobby Cutler's diary, which he found at Skip's home after Skip's death in 2005. *Courtesy of Peter Shinkle*

On September 28, Bobby wrote Skip from Cleveland, where he was visiting his friends Treasury Secretary George Humphrey and his wife, Pamela:

> Perhaps I do not understand you yet. Why should I? In the actual 6–8 weeks we had before you left, I found in you all kinds of qualities and excellences that I rejoiced to find, wanted to find. This all swept over me like a Bay of Fundy tide. But did I ever get to know you as you really were? Your letters present a new Skip — friends everywhere, late hours, no sleep, running to keep up. Somehow this was not my idea of you: who had seemed to me so gentle and tender and compassionate and full of intellectual and artistic appreciation to share. I had forgotten or not thought of all the rest. So, with receding time these half seen little snapshots alarm me lest you, the you I have, is disappearing. This I cannot bear and will never willingly allow. (There I go boring you again, I suppose, and will be dismissed with a postcard. Please, no. Your friendship is most important to my life, my friend.) 8 weeks ago we swam in the sun at Dumbarton and Thunderbirded to Haverford. An anniversary of a kind. Do you ever think of such things? I wonder. Is it "mutual aid" that we have, or something else? Give us the true word and God watch over you every minute with my best love B.

Skip reacted tartly to this chiding and questioning. "Dear Bobby," he wrote in response October 2:

> So much interrogation of my poor, lacerated personality! An interrogation — how shall I say it — which seems to show a rather pained concern on your part about facets of my character you may not be entirely familiar with, or perhaps just about activities I must now undertake which, because they seem new and different to you, take on a disquieting aspect. We all have many sided personalities, you do too, you know. And there is no person on earth

who we can ever know, or "possess" entirely, because they would have to be copies of ourselves. Nor is such possession desirable. I have in the past been devoured by possessiveness myself in personal relations, and it has brought nothing but pain, sorrow and destructiveness with it.

He then recounted a recent rendezvous in France with Steve Benedict, including a visit to the opera and tour through the countryside to the cathedral of Chartres. He signed the letter simply, "Skip."

Before Skip's letter could reach Bobby and wreak its inevitable emotional havoc on him, Bobby would confront an event that posed an ominous threat to US national security: the Soviet Union's launch of the Sputnik satellite.

19

SPUTNIK, TURMOIL, AND LOVE

The US missile programs were experiencing cost overruns and techni-cal challenges, and President Eisenhower had asked Defense Secretary Charles Wilson to recommend streamlining them. Bobby scheduled the NSC to take up the issue in its meeting in the White House Cabinet Room on August 1, 1957. There, Wilson proposed cutting costs by combining the two IRBM programs: Thor, managed by the air force, and Jupiter, managed by the army. Seeking to avoid a stalemate between the two branches, Wilson proposed that a three-person committee, with one representative each from army, air force, and Defense Department, review engineering and scientific information and decide which program would be kept. The NSC minutes show it was a blunt, terse discussion: "Secretary Wilson said that the United States had a 'mess' of Jupiter and Thor missiles. The president said these missiles wouldn't be a mess if they worked. Secretary Wilson said we had a missile that went 1500 miles, but it had no guidance and the re-entry problem was not solved."[1] Bobby asked how long it would take the committee to complete its work. Wilson replied that he did not know. The council then turned to the ICBM programs, Atlas and Titan. Wilson proposed advancing with the Atlas program "at the highest priority" but cutting efforts on the Titan program in order to make "substantial economies." The president approved the recommendations swiftly in the meeting.

Other nuclear issues crowded the agenda that day. Bobby briefed the NSC on the "human effects of nuclear weapons development," includ-ing a report about the possibility that an attack might kill fifty million Americans and disable the US government. The Joint Chiefs of Staff had recently agreed with a draft plan to inform Americans gradually about this risk through discussions with groups such as the American Assembly, the organization Eisenhower formed when he was at Columbia University. Eisenhower supported this approach: "If we attempted to inform the public on the human effects of nuclear weapons by dramatic actions, we could create hysteria instead of spreading information . . . He favored the gradual approach."

Public concern was already spreading about the dangerous effects of radioactive fallout from both Soviet and American tests. The Eisenhower administration had announced a series of nuclear bomb tests in Nevada from June through September, and tourists had been flocking to see the blasts. In late July, J. Edgar Hoover had sent Bobby a confidential memo saying that the American Friends Service Committee, a Quaker organization dedicated to nonviolence, was advancing a petition calling for a test ban.[2] The Soviet Union also had announced that it hoped the two countries would agree to a test ban, scoring a propaganda win in the world press.

On August 7, Bobby sent President Eisenhower a memo pointing out potential flaws in the military's strategy of pursuing a massive buildup of nuclear weapons. Spending on nuclear weapons was depriving the United States of forces it needed to fight smaller or "limited" wars that might erupt, Bobby warned. He noted that the nuclear arsenal had become so tremendously powerful that both US allies and the Soviets had begun to doubt the United States would ever use this supposed deterrent threat. Bobby summarized and transmitted to the president a memo prepared by a participant in NSC Planning Board meetings — General Thomas Farrell, who had played a key role in the Manhattan Project and was now an adviser to the Joint Chiefs of Staff. Farrell warned that if the US military focused too much on nuclear weapons, "we are leaving ourselves open to piecemeal aggression against which we will have only weapons which are too powerful to use, except under exceptional circumstances."[3] Bobby also forwarded the president a memo by Captain Jack Morse, a navy officer who was an observer of the NSC Planning Board for the Atomic Energy Commission. Morse argued in the memo that the massive US nuclear force had become, in essence, a threat to destroy the world. "If we use our deterrent (as we now think of it) to protect all allies, we must promise to invoke world holocaust whenever they are threatened. This is the reason I am appalled to hear high Government officials propose that we fight no more local wars, but depend entirely upon our big deterrent." Morse argued that the US must develop tactical nuclear weapons that could be used in limited wars. Bobby urged Ike to consider how best to deal with limited hostilities short of general war with the Soviet Union.

Yet the drive for nuclear firepower surged forward. On August 9, the president met privately with Bobby, Foster Dulles, and Atomic Energy Commission chairman Lewis Strauss regarding a series of twenty-five nuclear test blasts, called Operation Hardtack, which the Joint Chiefs of Staff proposed to conduct in the Pacific Ocean in 1958. Strauss was urging that a large blast, considered "clean" because it would have relatively low levels of radioactive fallout, be included in the tests. Expressing caution, Ike "indicated our statecraft was becoming too much a prisoner of our scientists," Bobby wrote in a memo about the meeting. Ike warned that the blasts would leave the United States vulnerable to the criticism that it was acting in bad faith because it also was planning to propose a ban on nuclear weapons tests. He said he would like to curtail the length of the testing period and the number of test shots. Still, despite his concerns that nuclear scientists were dominating diplomacy, Eisenhower agreed to let Operation Hardtack proceed.

On September 12, Allen Dulles reported to a meeting of the NSC in the Cabinet Room that the Soviets had announced their first successful launch of an intercontinental ballistic missile. He had earlier informed the council that the Soviets had constructed a missile testing range that stretched thirty-five hundred miles from Tyuratam in the Soviet Republic of Kazakhstan to the Kamchatka Peninsula on the Pacific Ocean. "We are currently re-examining our previous estimate that the Soviet Union could have an operational ICBM capability in 1960 or 1961. We may have to change this estimate. We consider this question to be one of the highest possible priority."[4]

Recent electoral gains by Communists in Indonesia, meanwhile, spurred renewed concerns at CIA and State about the Sukarno government. In the NSC meeting on September 23, Bobby briefed the council in detail on a report by a special committee formed to study the issue, which concluded Sukarno "has become increasingly identified with" the Indonesian Communist Party.[5] The report said ominously: "Communist control of Indonesia would split off Australia and New Zealand from Southeast Asia and would sever sea lines of communication and hinder air communication between the Pacific and Indian oceans." Allen Dulles told the NSC that the island of Sumatra was recently found to have a reserve of twenty billion barrels of oil. Three oil companies, two American and one British, were operating there.[6] The NSC concluded that it was "neither feasible nor appropriate" to use US forces under current conditions, but planning should proceed for "concerted military action" if the Communists seek to gain control over Java or the outer islands. Yet the CIA was already building its ties with anti-Communist forces, as a CIA agent gave an anti-Sukarno colonel fifty thousand dollars in rupiah, the Indonesian currency, two weeks later.[7]

Amid this tumult of national security events facing the NSC, the Soviet government announced the launching of Sputnik, the first artificial satellite to orbit the earth, shocking the world as the Soviets appeared to soar past the Americans in the race for missile technology.[8] The launch of Sputnik on October 4, 1957, was a technological achievement by the Soviets that suggested the enemy might have the capability to drop nuclear weapons on any target in the United States. The tiny satellite, with its flashing red beacon, could be seen in the night skies by Americans and others around the planet, and the new space wonder sent tremors through the Eisenhower administration and US national security agencies. Because delivery of nuclear bombs via missiles was the focus of the arms race, this achievement of the Soviet missile program was ominous. American officials quickly said that the launch of the small satellite did not mean that the Soviets could deliver missiles carrying nuclear weapons to targets in the United States and announced that US rockets would carry a satellite aloft soon, but to many these comments looked like pale excuses. It was a stunning propaganda coup for the Soviets, as news media around the world proclaimed they had moved ahead of the United States in the arms race. The Soviets even announced instructions to enable shortwave radio operators around the world to pick up Sputnik's telltale "beep" as it passed overhead at eighteen thousand miles per hour, making fifteen orbits of the planet per day.

When the NSC met on October 10, Sputnik dominated the agenda. Allen Dulles provided a briefing on Sputnik, noting that the Soviets had timed the satellite launch to coincide with the announcement of a successful test of an ICBM and the recent test of a large-scale hydrogen bomb. The Soviets also announced they would launch as many as thirteen satellites, he noted. Dulles underscored that the Soviet Union "was making a major propaganda effort which was exerting a very wide and deep impact."[9] When Bobby called on Deputy Secretary of Defense Donald Quarles to address the Sputnik issue, Quarles said he would be stating information already familiar to the NSC, and Ike quipped about the wave of Sputnik-related information that he was "beginning to feel somewhat numb on the subject of the earth satellite."

Quarles went on to note that the earth satellite concept arose in 1954 as scientists gathered in Rome, Italy, preparing to mark 1957 as the International Geophysical Year. President Eisenhower had announced a satellite program in 1955, stressing the supremacy of scientific objectives for the US program, known as Project Vanguard. Quarles said the US government had never regarded it as a "major objective" to be the first to launch a satellite; yet, he added, "We have always been aware of the Cold War implications of the launching of the first earth satellite."

Bobby confided his Sputnik torments to Skip. "This has been a horrid week. First, the American hysteria over the Russian moon. Every morning, a page-wide 3-line spread in the *Washington Post*. Most people seem to have gone nuts," he wrote Skip after the NSC meeting on October 10:

> The problems facing us, as a free people struggling against a tyranny, will get worse instead of better. Freedom can't fight a cold war because her side is full of free-press sieves. Everybody gets in the act. Oil is poured on fires that could and should be put out. Meanwhile, the Soviet quietly in the dark does what he wishes until ready to spring. There is no question in my mind we could have had a satellite up last year if we had married weapon rockets to scientific accomplishment and downgraded the latter.[10]

The media soon laid blame on US intelligence for failing to anticipate Sputnik. *The New York Times* noted that as recently as three months before Sputnik's launch, the *Times* had reported that Russia was believed to be trailing the United States in the development of missiles, but that information now appeared to be "completely mistaken."[11] That original *Times* story identified no sources, stating instead that the information was from Washington and "accepted here as authoritative." The *Times* noted that the assertion about the Soviets trailing had been made despite an "authenticated report" that the Russians had fired a test ballistic missile twelve hundred miles. Now, in the wake of Sputnik's launch, the *Times* concluded that the US intelligence was faulty. The *Times* story suggested that a "tendency to underestimate Soviet capabilities" stemmed from attitudes that assumed Russians were ignorant and primitive, that the wealth of the United States ensured that it would be first, and that the Communist system was inferior. Ultimately, it was "key decision makers" in the federal government, facing conflicting intelligence reports, who evaluated the intelligence on the basis of their "own preconceptions." While Bobby was not specifically named in the report, the *Times* faulted the government's national security apparatus generally.

US stock market prices fell as doubts over US missile capabilities rose. President Eisenhower flew to New York on Tuesday, October 22, to give a speech urging the American people to be confident and to banish "morbid pessimism." In an apparent recognition of national concern about Sputnik and the Soviet missile program, Ike said, "I have unshakable faith in the capacity of informed, free citizens to solve every problem involved."[12] Bobby had flown with Ike to New York and worked on all fifteen drafts of the speech, Bobby told Skip in a letter the next day:

> The P did a hell of a good job. I had dreamed up the night before 3 excellent opening paragraphs to give a wider context to the narrow subject, because America is on its ear over Sputnik. Those paragraphs made the headlines and the applause. In substance, they said he was going to talk to the people of the serious issues which were in his heart and mind. The stock market went up 10 points today. America has got her confidence badly shaken by Sputnik. It is part of our mercurial temperament. We shall take steps to restore that confidence. This last week I have been working with the P in the field of . . . better scientific cooperation, in the field of steps he should take to rebuild confidence.[13]

While Ike publicly expressed optimism, Washington's powerful syndicated columnists soon turned their fire on Eisenhower's advisers. Joseph and Stewart Alsop wrote a column asserting that defense officials had raised serious concerns about Soviet progress on its missile program but that Bobby and other advisers had failed to inform the president of this danger. "It is quite obvious that the president was never told of the black despair of the American experts who saw the American missile effort lagging behind the Soviet effort for the lack of a few millions of dollars," the Alsop brothers wrote in a column published in newspapers across the country on October 24. "There is plenty of evidence, in short, that the President is being wrapped in cotton wool and saved from 'bother' by the usual persons — Gov. Adams, Security Council Secretary Robert Cutler, Press Secretary Hagerty and the rest." The solution, the brothers suggested, was for Ike himself "to take personal charge, full time."

Bobby, as usual, said nothing publicly but shared his anger with Skip. "The Alsops say this morning I 'shield' him — Adams, Herter and Hagerty. Well, *I* don't. I *tell* him. You know that. I have breakfast with him and Adams tomorrow morning at the WH. We are working on a scientific procedure of highest importance," Bobby wrote Skip.[14] He added notes about a visit by the young Queen Elizabeth of England to the White House. "When Mamie telephoned I had to go to the State Dinner. Orders, of course," he wrote. "Everyone was won over by her [the Queen], and the Prince is quite a stunner, too." Bobby also provided some news about his efforts to get a visa for Xavier Fourcade, a young Parisian friend of Skip's with an interest in art galleries. He also confided that during these stressful days he was taking an amphetamine, Dexedrine, to wake up and get to work, and a barbiturate, Seconal, to sleep. "I do hope to continue to improve in health. These days with Dexedrine and nights with Seconal are not good for the long haul." He closed, "Truly I miss you more than I can say . . . remember your most loyal supporter. Love, B."

As the criticism intensified, Bobby dismissed it and returned to his favorite subject — his affection for Skip. "Your letter of the 21st was a joy to receive. In your long and checkered career all about the world, I doubt if you ever wrote letters that were so read and reread and stored away like Dead Sea Scrolls," Bobby wrote. Turning to Skip's financial difficulties, he offered to send Skip a check for a thousand dollars, saying he could pay back fifty dollars per month. "If we lived together in an apartment, as I wished we did, this arrangement would be a natural one . . . Well let me know. I am no longer rich. But I can do this — and I am richer when I help someone I love. B."

In November, Democratic US representative John Moss of California publicly blamed Bobby for the government's failure to inform the public of the Soviet plans to launch Sputnik, asserting that the government knew of the plans months in advance.[15] Moss, chairman of a House government information subcommittee that held hearings on the subject, said, "Mr. Cutler's blueprint of secrecy is apparent in the failure to inform the public of the nation's missile-satellite deficiencies until Sputnik sailed across the skies." He assailed the administration for "public-be-damned information policies."

Bobby sent a defiant letter to Skip dismissing the charges. "Yet out of it, like a catharsis — and despite floods of Cong. Moss's attacks on me in the press this AM, stories in all the big papers 2 columns each — I am better in my mind. To hell with it. My views are right: I am for the safety of the republic, and they are for calling newspapers and getting headlines and being big shots," Bobby wrote to Skip on November 25. Then he confided, "But just today, like the fine line that divides dusk from night, the change came," he wrote. "I lie in bed looking at your blown up picture on the other side of the room. It is a pleasure to see its smile, once more — and now I would like to hear your foot on the stair, and hear your solemn gentle thoughtful voice, and take your hand in mine again . . ."[16]

The criticism ratcheted up further after *Aviation Week* magazine ran a story reporting that US radar installations in Turkey had been tracking Soviet missile launches since 1955, but they had not been reported to the public. *The New York Times* had picked up the story and run a front-page article about the radar station at the Turkish city of Samsun, on the Black Sea. Speaking behind closed doors to a business group under the auspices of the Commerce Department, Bobby criticized the *Aviation Week* revelation, and columnists seized on the incident. Drew Pearson said that Bobby told the meeting, without naming *Aviation Week* specifically, that the report was an action "close to 'treason.'" Stewart Alsop launched his own attack:

> WASHINGTON — It does not really matter very much whether Presidential Aide Robert Cutler was silly enough to say that "Aviation Week" was "treasonable" for publishing what the Russians already knew — that our radar installations had picked up sure evidence of Soviet missile progress as early as 1955. But Cutler himself does matter,

as a symbol of what has gone wrong with the American government.

For Cutler has been a key figure in the Eisenhower Administration's "Daddy knows best" policy. And the extent of the Soviet lead in weaponry, which threatens the United States as it has never been threatened before, is a direct outgrowth of that policy.

Remarkably, Alsop also blamed Bobby, along with Lewis Strauss, for killing Operation Candor in 1955.[17] "It might make life simpler for high officials like Cutler if the American people were obedient sheep who unquestionably obeyed the orders of daddy-government. But the United States is not the Soviet Union. It is, instead, a society in which the government derives its authority from the people. And such society is instantly in deadly danger if the essential facts on which to reach a reasoned judgment are concealed by the government from the people." Thus, Joseph Alsop's warning to Bobby shortly after Eisenhower took office — that if he did not provide information to Joe the administration could suffer consequences — had come true in the Alsops' column.

The Washington Post issued a stinging rebuke of Bobby's off-the-record comments about *Aviation Week* in an editorial. "There is something about secret assaults upon the conduct of another that is repugnant to those who believe in ordinary standards of honorable behavior," it said. "Mr. Cutler is well known as an advocate of the most extreme kind of secrecy about government operations."[18]

Sputnik had provoked a crisis of confidence not only in America but in Europe as well, and the European allies expected Eisenhower to address their concerns. British Prime Minister Harold Macmillan came to Washington in late October and issued a joint statement with Ike obliquely downplaying Sputnik: "The free nations possess vast assets, both material and moral. These in the aggregate are far greater than those of the Communist world. We do not ignore the fact that the Soviet rulers can achieve formidable material accomplishments by concentrating upon selected developments and scientific applications, and by yoking their people to this effort. Despotisms have often been able to produce spectacular monuments." The joint statement also endorsed the NATO disarmament provisions calling for inspection of weapons sites, a proposal opposed by the Soviets, and announced a December meeting in Paris of the North Atlantic Council, NATO's principal decision-making body. Eisenhower and Macmillan had named their respective secretaries of state to consult in preparation for that NATO meeting. Ike asked Bobby to play a key role as well by preparing position papers from multiple agencies. "I am asking General Cutler of my staff to assist Secretary Dulles in his effort," Ike wrote CIA director Allen Dulles.[19] Bobby quickly became chairman of a special committee and attended a series of meetings with representatives of State, CIA, Joint Chiefs of Staff, and other agencies to assemble position papers for the NATO conference.[20]

Bobby, meanwhile, also had been preparing for a searing debate on the nuclear arms race in the NSC. At Bobby's recommendation, Ike earlier had created a panel of outside experts to study the nation's preparedness for a nuclear conflict. Headed by H. Rowan Gaither Jr., the panel prepared a top-secret report that called for steep increases in government spending to build nuclear missiles, expand nuclear bomber capabilities, and construct nuclear bomb shelters for civilians nationwide. The Gaither Panel depicted the Soviets as far ahead of the United States in the nuclear weapons race in black-and-white terms — without acknowledging any limitations on US intelligence. The report concluded that the Soviets were building a strong force of ICBMs that within two years could undertake a first strike that would destroy the United States' long-range bombers in the air force's Strategic Air Command (SAC). "By 1959, the USSR may be able to launch an attack with ICBMs carrying megaton warheads, against which SAC will be almost completely vulnerable under present programs," the report said.[21] As a result, the panel recommended dispersing the SAC bombers to air bases around the United States, developing an early warning system, and increasing the United States' planned initial force of ICBMs from eighty to six hundred missiles. The panel called for spending an additional forty-five billion dollars over five years, at a time when the annual military budget was only thirty-eight billion. The Gaither Panel's big spending recommendations posed a challenge to President Eisenhower, who had built his national defense strategy around the concept of cutting government spending in order to balance the budget and spur national economic growth.

By the time the president and other NSC members walked into the secret confines of the Cabinet Room on November 7, 1957, Bobby had distributed the report and asked council members to be prepared to comment. Gaither was unavailable because of illness, but panel members who attended included Paul Nitze, the hawkish former State Department official behind NSC-68 whom Bobby had objected to as State's representative to the NSC, and William Foster, chief executive of a chemical company that made nuclear bomb materials. After the panel members presented an overview of their report, President Eisenhower pointed out that when he recently proposed increasing defense spending from $38 billion to $39.5 billion, even urging the increase in a television appearance, Congress rejected the proposal. Eisenhower said the presentation to the NSC made it "essential that we neither become panicked nor allow ourselves to be complacent."[22] Then he noted that Sputnik, which had prompted fear in Americans, may have laid the groundwork for a change in the nation's thinking. "It was necessary urgently to make an economic, psychological and political survey of what could and should be done. In this context, perhaps the advent of Sputnik had been helpful."

Secretary of State Dulles noted drily that the Gaither Panel "had dealt with one aspect of the problem facing the United States, namely, the military problem, but the military aspect was only one part of the problem and the problem must be viewed in its entirety." If the United States embarked on a massive shelter construction program and our allies could not do the same, he continued, "we could surely write off all of our European allies." It was a startling turn of events, as the secretary of state known around the world for his staunch opposition to Communism was muting the alarms raised by the Gaither Panel that the Soviets were gaining the upper hand militarily. In a personal memo, Dulles said he later told Eisenhower that there was little chance the Soviet leaders would launch a massive surprise attack.[23] Bobby concluded the meeting by calling for various agency heads to respond to sections of the Gaither Panel report by December 15, 1957.

Days later, CIA intelligence officers produced their own report, which underscored a significant lack of accurate information about Soviet missile programs. It noted, for instance, that "evidence was limited" regarding missile testing and made it clear that the CIA's projections were based on a broad array of assumptions about matters such as rocket design, test facilities, rail systems for moving rockets, and effectiveness of guidance systems.[24] Yet on the basis of these assumptions, the report went on to project that the Soviets would have their first ten ICBMs ready in mid-1958 to mid-1959 and that they would have six hundred ICBMs no more than four years later.

Soon, portions of the Gaither Panel report were leaked. An account appeared November 20 in *The Washington Post* saying the panel recommended spending twenty billion dollars to build a vast network of nuclear fallout shelters to protect the US population in the event of nuclear war.[25] Members of Congress called for access to the report, but Ike, Bobby, and others insisted that it remain secret.

As the storm over nuclear weapons swirled, Communists in Indonesia appeared to make political gains in that country's national government, prompting the Dulles brothers to become increasingly concerned. On November 20, a proposed project was brought before the 5412/2 Designated Representatives — Bobby, Undersecretary of State Chris Herter and Assistant Secretary of Defense Mansfield Sprague. "All the Designated Representatives concurred in the project," Allen Dulles noted in a memo.[26] A note in Bobby's handwriting, on a copy of the memo in NSC files, said simply, "Reported to P Nov 21." The government later acknowledged that the Eisenhower administration approved covert action against the Indonesian government in November 1957, although the operation approved that day is one of the many approvals by the Designated Representatives that remains classified.[27] The CIA and other agencies had received their orders, and the Indonesia coup plan shifted into operation.

Amid the strains of the tense days, Bobby wrote a letter to Skip apologizing for "being a bad friend." He lacerated himself for pressing Skip into a relationship for which Skip was not prepared. "Continually I was selfish, thinking only of what I wanted and could not realize. I was pretty bleak. But I am trying to rationalize the situation between us so as to avoid harassing you and so as to give me peace of mind," Bobby wrote in the letter, dated November 10.[28] Then, discussing a series of meetings with the president and denying he ever accused *Aviation Week* of treason, he returned to his affections for Skip. He expressed delight in the pictures of Skip he placed around his room, including a recent photo of him. "Bless your heart for the snapshot. You look terribly well and content, and you know you show as 'handsome.' Steve has given me a blow up of that smiling snapshot of you in a restaurant. It makes me happy to have sights of you about me in my apartment. (Don't worry, no one comes there so you will not be seen)."

As the NATO council meeting approached, Bobby wrote Skip on December 4 saying he expected to join the president's trip to Paris. "Are you still my friend? So I could stay with you. To see you again, a little while, is like strong drink," Bobby wrote.

On December 6, 1957, America's missile program suffered a humiliating setback. A Vanguard rocket exploded in a huge fireball on a launch pad in Cape Canaveral, Florida, an event broadcast globally on television. The Soviets, meanwhile, had launched a second Sputnik satellite a month earlier. By the simple standard of successful launches, the United States appeared to be falling farther behind the Soviet Union, and pressure continued to build on the president and his national security team. To prepare for the NATO meeting, Bobby flew to Paris a day early with Donald Quarles to review the position papers that Bobby's committee had assembled. After Eisenhower arrived, he released on December 15 a statement rejecting Indian prime minister Jawaharlal Nehru's call for the United States and the Soviet Union to cease nuclear tests. Eisenhower warned that a ban on nuclear tests might actually increase the risk of nuclear war.[29] "To stop these tests at this time, in the absence of knowledge that we can go on and achieve effective limitations on nuclear weapons production and on other elements of armed strength, as well as a measure of assurance against surprise attack, is a sacrifice which we could not in prudence accept," the president said. "To do so could increase rather than diminish the threat of aggression and war."

Bobby abandoned the idea of staying with Skip during the Paris trip and joined the rest of the president's team at the Hôtel de Crillon, located close to the American embassy. On the night after Ike's speech in the NATO meeting room, Bobby took Skip out to dinner with Atomic Energy commissioner Lewis Strauss, dining in the restaurant Vefours, where the seats bore silver nameplates recalling its famous patrons. "That night, I was Madame George Sand and Admiral Strauss was Victor Hugo," Bobby noted playfully in his autobiography.[30] Bobby and Skip also found time to have dinner at the Ritz, to spend a late night at the Palace Café, and to visit the medieval town of Senlis, about thirty miles north of Paris. Bobby recalled their time together fondly a week later in a letter to Skip: "Beyond anyone I have known so well, you have more value to offer a friend in intellectual perception, artistic appreciation, depth of human understanding, tenderness and delicacy of feeling, and capacity for fun. All of these you offered to me in our ten days together — in selfless generosity to my selfish demands on your time — enriching my experiences, nourishing my admiration and love for you, giving to the future a golden prospect."[31]

Back in Washington, the administration was hit with more bad news. On December 20, *The Washington Post* broke the story of the remaining findings of the Gaither Panel report, announcing in alarmist terms that a "missile gap" now left the United States vulnerable to Soviet attack:

> The still top-secret Gaither report portrays a United States in the gravest danger in its history. It pictures the Nation moving in frightening course to the status of a second-class power. It shows an America exposed to an almost immediate threat from the missile-bristling Soviet Union.
>
> It finds America's long-term prospect one of cataclysmic peril in the face of rocketing Soviet military might and of a powerful, growing Soviet economy and technology which will bring new political, propaganda and psychological assaults on freedom all around the globe.
>
> In short, the report strips away the complacency and lays bare the highly unpleasant realities in what is the first across-the-board survey of the relative postures of the United States and the Free World and of the Soviet Union and the Communist orbit.
>
> To prevent what otherwise appears to be inevitable catastrophe, the Gaither report urgently calls for an enormous increase in military spending — from now through 1970 — and for many other costly, radical measures of first and second priority. Only through such an all-out effort, the report says, can the United States hope to close the current missile gap and to counter the world-wide Communist offensive in many fields and in many lands. Established as the first, overriding priority is the revitalizing of the American retaliatory offensive force, as principal deterrent to an all-out Russian attack.[32]

The *Washington Post* story, by Chalmers Roberts, enshrined the concept of a "missile gap" though it offered no support for its claim of "complacency" in the government and almost no attempt at balance by reporting the buildup of the US's own nuclear missiles and bombers. On December 28, White House spokesman Jim Hagerty denied that the Gaither Panel report concluded the United States was in a state of peril, saying it found "just the opposite." Speaking with reporters in Gettysburg, Pennsylvania, where the president was at his family farm, Hagerty said congressional committees had all the intelligence that the report was based on, and the president would address the nation's military preparedness in his State of the Union address the next month.

Who leaked the report remains unknown to this day. One respected historian has noted, however, that Roberts's story appeared two days after Nitze and Roberts met for a private lunch. In addition, the Gaither report, with its concern about a missile gap, echoed Nitze's NSC-68, which had identified 1954 as the "year of maximum danger."[33] Some in Congress called for the report to be made public, and some accounts identified Bobby as the one pushing for it to remain classified. Stewart Alsop wrote in a column that Bobby and Sherman Adams were "for a policy of 'top secret' and no comment" and that this "would mean no essential change in policy and continuing on the road to hell."[34] At the other side of the debate was Nixon, Alsop said, praising the vice president. Nixon wanted to release the report in full, or at least release the facts it was based on. "Nixon is said to believe that a policy of candor, even though it clearly entails an admission of past error, would be good politics in the long run — and Nixon is no mean judge of political consequences."

As the nuclear debate became acid at the end of the year, Bobby turned repeatedly for solace to Steve Benedict, who made him feel closer to Skip. Bobby and Steve spent New Year's Eve together — first drinks, then dinner at a restaurant, and finally they sent a cable together to Skip. On January 2, 1958, Bobby wrote to Skip, "Your ears should have burned. From 7–10:30 we talked about you over a pint of bourbon and a lot of Steve's pictures abroad and at Alexandria. How fortunate a youth you are. Here are two people you like who can be happy together just talking about their affection for you. Few people I know encourage such love." The relationship had become triangular: the two former lovers, Skip and Steve, had their longtime bond, and Bobby now enjoyed connections with each of them. "It makes me happy to think of this old time tie between you fine people. How lucky I am to be allowed in, too," Bobby wrote.[35] A week later, he told Skip of a dinner he'd had with Steve, noting, "When I have Steve, I feel as if some of you were there."[36] Bobby acknowledged a certain imbalance in the triangle — he was of an older generation — but he downplayed this aspect of their relationship. "Certainly there are differences between us: some we have worked out and recognized. Our age for example," Bobby wrote in a letter to Skip.[37] He acknowledged the possibility that "I cannot be to you like Steve," but also noted "Steve might not be to you what I can be."

20

CHALLENGING US NUCLEAR STRATEGY

As 1958 began, President Eisenhower and his advisers found themselves in a dilemma: Sputnik, coupled with the leaked Gaither Panel report, had fueled public fears of a "missile gap" and Soviet nuclear superiority. Yet at the same time, critics around the world were calling for the United States and the Soviets to ban nuclear bomb tests. The atmosphere was tense at the first NSC meeting of the year, on January 6. When the Gaither report came up for discussion, Bobby called on James Killian, the president's special assistant for science and technology. Killian said the first question raised by the report was whether the US airborne nuclear force would be "critically vulnerable to a surprise long-range missile attack in the 1959–1960 time period."[1] Killian offered no answer to that question, though he noted the US was on track to deploy 130 ICBMs by mid-1963, while the Gaither Panel recommended producing 600 by that date.

Bobby then called on Deputy Defense Secretary Donald Quarles, who said that the Defense Department had recommended accelerating some areas of weapons production to address the Gaither report's concerns. Quarles said the total expenditures in the proposed package of accelerated programs came to approximately half of the total cost projected by the Gaither Panel. With regard to increasing production of ICBM missiles, he said it would be possible to build six hundred missiles to keep pace with the Soviets, but the problem was building the bases for those missiles. To do so, the department would have to start construction immediately. "By and large, the Department of Defense thought it unwise to undertake this program," he said. No one questioned Quarles or challenged his conclusions.

Secretary Dulles said he would appear before Congress the following week and expected members to ask to see the Gaither report. How should he respond? Bobby replied that he thought no version of the report should be released, as it was a privileged document prepared for the president. When it was pointed out that Senate minority leader Lyndon Johnson had asked earlier that day for the release of a sanitized version, "Mr. Cutler repeated his view that even the issuance of a sanitized version would have catastrophic results."

Vice President Nixon backed release of the report's findings, saying that "what had been published about the content of the Gaither Report was fantastically worse than what the Gaither report actually said. Moreover, most of the recommendations of the Gaither report had appeared in Chalmers Roberts's 'missile gap' story in *The Washington Post*." At the end of the meeting, no plans were made to release the Gaither report.

The next day, Bobby wrote a letter to Skip saying that Ike had taken a "lively interest" in the discussion and the NSC meeting "went off much to my liking." But he also said, "The failure to plan far enough ahead when Russia may be matching our strength worries me deeply."[2] Bobby related his latest evening out with Steve Benedict and another of Steve's young male friends. "My heart goes out to you when I am alone and troubled for you have given me more happiness than I have known in many years. Take care. Your loving brother B."

Skip replied voicing concerns about Bobby's health. He suggested he "perhaps try various tranquilizers to worry less (I mean this seriously, and perhaps you should consult on this), certainly have more planned limitations to your work time . . ." He added, "To be in disagreement with close friends, particularly the President and Secretary of State, is painful and heartrending. It is also frequently one's duty, nevertheless, or at least that is the way I feel."[3] He noted that US information officials at embassies in Europe disliked Foster Dulles. "It is distressing, but all are unanimous in the terrible degree of unpopularity Dulles has (continuing to mount even after NATO), both with governments and peoples."

Pressure on Bobby mounted as he was accused in the press of withholding the Gaither report. "These weeks had been the winter of my discontent," he wrote Skip on January 24.[4] "Somehow I never recovered my health and élan after NATO. Especially the two weeks before this I was in poorest spirit — dexamil by day and sleeping potions at night; driven to the point where I was actually drafting letters to the President about getting out." Bobby even enclosed a typed letter summarizing his views, which he had dictated to a secretary. "If the Russians or the press come, please swallow it," he said, likely half in jest.

He also shared with Skip a January 23 memo he wrote summarizing his malaise. Bobby said that the administration was being damaged by

> repeated press stories that I am a principal person who with-
> holds information from the President. This story appears
> often enough so that, like Hitler's technique of the big lie, it
> comes to be believed by people who should know better or
> who have no way of knowing one way or the other. Nothing
> can be more paradoxical than to accuse me of having withheld
> from the President the information in the Gaither Report
> (as has been stated) when I was the person who caused the
> Gaither Report to be written, caused it to be presented to
> him twice, and caused it to be thrashed out in subsequent
> Council meetings. However, it is not a good thing for the
> American people to be constantly told and come to believe
> that someone close to the President is preventing him from
> receiving information which he should have.

Bobby also expressed deep frustration with Foster Dulles: "Secretary Dulles at the Council Meeting yesterday in referring to our Near East policy said that perhaps the only policy for some time was to continue to try 'muddling through.' We shall lose the Near East if we follow such a policy." And he asserted: "We must somehow find an approach to the Russians to enable us to live together, without annihilating war. So much of US thinking in the Congress today is in military build-up, bent on matching destructive capabilities. So much of what is publicly said is to damn the Russian in terms which can only negate the possibility of negotiation."

The agonizing pressure over the Soviet Union's Sputnik success abated a bit on January 31, 1958, when the United States successfully launched a Jupiter rocket, matching Sputnik's feat by lifting a satellite into orbit. Meanwhile, the uproar over the Gaither report faded as President Eisenhower asked Congress for an additional $1.2 billion in defense spending for new SAC bases and warning systems. Yet the disarmament talks stalled, and international criticism of Foster Dulles mounted.

The secretary of state remained focused on the Communist threat in Indonesia. In early 1958, the CIA's coup planners moved forces into position to aid a rebel group based in the town of Padang. On January 31,

Allen Dulles sent a memo to his brother Foster, Ike, Bobby, and other senior officials saying, "The Padang group probably will develop its ultimatum to the central government on or about 5 February."[5] The coup forces "could probably launch fairly widespread guerilla warfare." Yet there were signs that US covert action would face serious challenges. On February 10, Admiral Charles Triebel, a special assistant to the Joint Chiefs of Staff, sent Bobby a memo warning, "The Indonesians are quick to resent any real or fancied attempts to influence their internal affairs and can be expected to resist sharply under all such circumstances. For this reason, covert activity must be extremely circumspect and by its nature must be limited in size and scope."[6]

Around this time, Bobby concluded he would not be able to remain in his post until the end of the year primarily due to the demands of the job. "During a good many of the last thirteen months — and especially during and after NATO — I have been way below physical par," Bobby told Ike in a letter January 31, 1958. "Several times I thought I would just have to quit. This condition has raised question in my mind whether I will be able to carry on as Special Assistant for National Security Affairs until December 6, as originally promised." He continued: "Then there are other bothersome things (like untrue, but repeated, press stories that I shield you from the facts!), which aren't worth going into." Bobby also said he had some suggestions for a successor.[7] He closed the letter, "Always your affectionate servant . . ." He sent Skip a copy of this letter, with a note saying, "No one knows but you."

The president replied three days later:

> Dear Bobby,
> Take all the leave you want during this year . . . You do not have to ask for permission to go nor do you have to have any concern as to the time you are gone. This is permissive authority that is to be used whenever the spirit moves you and with the knowledge that I would much prefer you here on a half-time basis feeling well — rather than here all the time with the feeling that you are being pushed.

He asked Bobby to come at his convenience to discuss his recommendations for a successor.[8]

Bobby sent Skip a copy of the president's letter and said that sending his own letter to Ike had brought him relief. "I feel easier in my mind. And in our meetings, since he got the letter, we have been in good rapport." Bobby then quickly shifted to discussing his desire to spend time with Skip.

> Long days and nights pass without seeing each other, talking, touching hands, welcoming the responsive smile, sharing a walk — a meal — a ride: the infinite little things that make life precious and not just routine. In seven months, we've been ten days together. Yet out of all the concerns in my world this interest in you and yours predominates. As if some electric current, invisible but sure, pulsed across the sea to communicate between us. I hope this can always be so, and that you will not find I have overidealized. [9]

Recharged, Bobby set to work on the horrific realities of the nuclear arms race. In the summer of 1957, he had brought to the attention of the president thorny questions about the nation's nuclear weapons strategy that had begun to arise in discussions of the NSC's Planning Board. Specifically, doubts had been raised that the US would ever launch a nuclear attack on the Soviets because damages from an all-out nuclear war would be too extreme. These doubts called into question the credibility of US claims that it would use nuclear weapons to defend its allies. Now, in early 1958, Bobby began to prepare the NSC to review its top-secret Basic National Security Policy, which provided objectives for use of the nation's nuclear force in general war with the Soviet Union and other Communist countries.

Adopted in March 1954, the first Basic National Security Policy "assum[ed] that general war has been forced on the United States" and called for a deceptively simple strategic goal: "To reduce by military and other measures the capabilities of the USSR to the point where it has lost its will or ability to wage war against the United States and its allies."[10] This supposedly defensive policy had served as the framework for massive increases in the nation's nuclear weaponry, resulting in a posture that appeared to many people across the world as aggressive.

"I have been living on a razor edge of nervous balance, struggling through each day, lost in a shroud of melancholy, nervous, irritable, low as a whale's knee in morale and confidence," Bobby told Skip in a letter on March 10, 1958.[11] "In part it is due to the appalling world prospect, which is daily borne in upon me, and for which I feel conscientious responsibility without belief in my capabilities to do all I should be doing. The new Estimate of the World Situation is out. It is a shocker, a hair-curler." The estimate was a comprehensive report produced by the CIA and other intelligence agencies. Bobby's intimate letters to Skip provide a candid depiction of the inner turmoil experienced by a senior administration official when, for the first time in history, nuclear arsenals reached the capacity to destroy life on a global scale.

Amid this gloom, Bobby summarized his concerns about nuclear weapons strategy and called for a change in that strategy in a blunt memo he expected to share with the president. Titled "Massive Exchange of Nuclear Weapons," the three-page memo said the nation's military strategy, from the start of the nuclear age, had led to a race to produce as many nuclear weapons as possible to destroy as many enemy targets as possible.[12]

Now this strategy had led to an almost inconceivable world situation due to the threat of global nuclear destruction. A recent exercise indicated that, in fifteen hours of preliminary exchange between the Soviet aggressor and the US, nuclear weapons involving seven million kilotons (over half of it in the first three hours) would be detonated, with the US going on to win with still further detonations against the enemy, Bobby explained in the memo. This exercise contemplated nuclear explosions in North America, Europe, Asia, and North Africa, occurring within a half day, that "were 350,000 times as great in magnitude as the nuclear explosion at Hiroshima (which resulted in over 130,000 casualties — 64,000 killed, 72,000 injured)," he wrote. "The effect of any such exchange is quite incalculable. No one knows what the concentrated explosion of 7,000,000 KTs [kilotons] involving nuclear material would do [to] the weather, to crop cycles, to human reproduction, to the population of all areas of the world (whether or not directly exposed to the detonation). It is possible that life on the planet might be extinguished."

He went on to say that the massive stockpile of nuclear weapons could be assumed to be "reasonable" for purposes of the US launching a "preventive war" — in essence, a first-strike attack designed to obliterate the Soviet military before it could launch its own nuclear attack. However, he reasoned, if the nation's deterrent were based on being able to launch a devastating attack even if the Soviets attacked first, then a much smaller US nuclear force, perhaps aimed at only one-tenth the number of Soviet targets, would be sufficient to provide such a deterrent. Adoption of this new deterrent strategy could enable the US to have far fewer nuclear weapons. In exchange for backing off the headlong rush to nuclear weapon production, Bobby proposed a new target — population centers, rather than military targets — to strengthen the deterrent effect. Bobby theorized "that the enemy would be equally deterred from attacking the US, if the enemy knew we would, in retaliation, destroy their . . . population centers instead of only some of their . . . military installations."

It was a cold calculation, but one that Bobby made in the context of an arms race that posed significant risk of a massive exchange of nuclear weapons that could kill all humans on the planet, whether or not they lived in population centers. Indeed, Bobby argued that the lack of US conventional forces increased the chances of war with the Soviets. Bobby had raised the same concern about the nuclear weapons race that Oppenheimer and numerous other critics had raised. However, Bobby's solution — creating a deterrent by targeting cities with a much smaller number of bombs — was clearly aimed at appealing to the military men who believed the "massive retaliation" deterrent was critical to preventing a Soviet attack.

Finally, Bobby laid blame for the nuclear weapons race at the door of the US military, saying it had failed to properly handle nuclear weapons strategy, and civilian leadership needed to reassert control. "The foregoing commentary suggests military re-examination of hostile targets in the event of retaliatory action and a need for strict civilian control over the objectives upon which 'military requirements' for nuclear weapons and forces are based." He concluded, "It is apparent that there are considerations, other than military, which must control the massive production and use of nuclear weapons and delivery forces."

On the same day he prepared his "Massive Exchange of Nuclear Weapons" memo, March 16, Bobby prepared a second memo laying out the case for development of "clean" weapons, tactical nuclear bombs that could be used in a limited war, thus eliminating a massive nuclear war as the only retaliatory option to Soviet aggression against the US or its NATO allies. All sides had come to recognize the "incalculable devastation" that would be caused by a nuclear conflict, he wrote. "If the US loses its will to retaliate when certain areas other than its own territory are violated, its alliances will crumble and the enemy will be emboldened . . ." Bobby wrote in his memo.[13] Ultimately, he concluded, this meant the United States should continue to conduct nuclear tests until it has "solved the secret" of how to make clean nuclear weapons.

Wrestling with the bleak picture of the world situation, Bobby found his workload had become heavier after Fred Dearborn, an NSC Planning Board officer who had worked with Bobby for years, died in early March. "I was with him at 7:10 PM: he was dead, fallen by his bed at 10 PM: I found him there stone dead, rigid, and blue all over the next morning at 10 AM. A long time to erase that ghastly picture. The P sent me as his representative to the funeral," Bobby wrote Skip without explaining how he came to find Dearborn dead next to his bed.[14] "All of these pressures and despair at inadequacy were the kind of thing which so terribly affected my friend Forrestal," Bobby confided. "There is only one cure, before it is too late: quit Washington, go far away from 70-hour weeks and responsibility and worry over the ghastly future."

Bobby wrote Skip a long letter March 17 unburdening himself of the gloom. "The prospect seems to me incredibly bad — a mutual deterrence coming soon; allies shrinking away because they fear we won't help; everyone becoming more conscious of the incalculable damage of a massive nuclear exchange — I've come to think it might extinguish life on the planet, while we argue about shelter . . . I feel so incapable, so much in the right place to do things and so insufficient to know what to do."[15]

Whether it was due to Oppenheimer's warnings five years earlier, or the simple math of calculated obliteration threatened by the vast nuclear weapons arsenals, Bobby had come to feel that he must abandon his usual posture of neutrality and push for a change in the nation's nuclear warfare strategy. A year later, he would privately acknowledge "my efforts to change policy."[16] On March 18, he prepared a one-page memo for the president urging him to revise the assignment of the Net Evaluation Subcommittee, an NSC body that performed annual assessments of the ability of the United States to survive a nuclear attack. The Net Evaluation Subcommittee was soon to begin its work on a "war-game" report based on the existing "massive retaliation" strategy. Bobby urged Ike to order the game to be expanded for a strategy in which the US nuclear forces would strike only one-tenth as many targets — cities and population centers. Part of this memo remains classified.[17]

Two days later, when the NSC met on the morning of March 20 in the White House Cabinet Room, Bobby gave a dire overview of the Estimate of the World Situation. He distributed an analysis of the report that the NSC Planning Board, which he chaired, had assembled, including a section titled "The State of Mutual Deterrence and the Deterioration in the Western Position." It made some of the same points as his memo to the president a few days earlier: The US and USSR were entering a stage of mutual deterrence, with both unwilling to launch a general nuclear conflict because of the horrific damage it would unleash. As a result, the Western alliance was weakening, and the Soviets would be emboldened to undertake subversion, economic penetration, and limited war. Bobby then presented the estimate's most disturbing aspect: "Should the United States, asked General Cutler, in the face of the estimate's conclusions on mutual deterrence and the deterioration of the western position, continue our existing national strategy? Or should the United States proceed to exert greater pressures on the Soviet Union? Or, finally, should we seek an accommodation with the Soviets by offering them concessions?"[18] Then Bobby asked Foster Dulles to respond to these questions.

The secretary of state said he "could not understand what so concerned General Cutler, inasmuch as we proposed, of course, to protect our allies by invoking our retaliatory capability in the event that their vital interests are threatened." Dulles said the allies were not losing faith that the US would launch a nuclear strike on their behalf, and in any case the allies would have their own nuclear weapons soon. Dulles's hostility to Bobby's views was clear: "Did General Cutler object to this situation? What was wrong with mutual deterrence? Did General Cutler advocate war?"

The air must have crackled with tension, but Bobby responded calmly. "General Cutler replied that he was simply suggesting that once the Russians fully realize the existence of the state of mutual deterrence, they would nibble their way into the fabric of the Free World by small aggressions." When Dulles again objected, President Eisenhower supported the secretary of state, pointing to the US capability to protect Formosa (Taiwan). The discussion quickly broke into an open debate, with CIA director Allen Dulles at one point appearing to side with Bobby — and against his brother — by pointing out that the Soviets had already undertaken military actions in Germany and Hungary. In the end, the NSC took no action that day.

Later that same day, Bobby met with the president in his office to discuss his two memos. Others attending included Atomic Energy Commission chairman Lewis Strauss, Killian, Undersecretary of State Christian Herter, Assistant Defense Secretary Mansfield Sprague, and General Andrew Goodpaster, another of Ike's close advisers. The "clean weapons" memo was not well received for an array of reasons, including the objection that clean weapons would not be used in a general nuclear war, Bobby wrote in a memo.[19]

Bobby's proposal to change nuclear targeting, however, gained support. "It was fairly exciting," Bobby recounted in a March 23 letter to Skip. "I read the memos, commenting as I read, and then the P commented extensively as did others. He vetoed one memo, giving about 7 fully expressed reasons. The other he welcomed, expressed his delight that others were independently raising these questions and gave me directions I have been working to implement today."

Ike soon gave the green light to Bobby's proposal to investigate the idea of changing the nation's nuclear deterrence strategy from a massive strike capability aimed at wiping out the Soviet military to a retaliation force targeting civilian population centers. The next day, March 24, Bobby conveyed the president's position in a top-secret "Eyes Only" memo to Nathan Twining, the air force general who was now chairman of the Joint Chiefs of Staff and also chairman of the Net Evaluation Subcommittee.[20] In clear terms, Bobby stated his challenge to the existing US nuclear strategy: He said that while the massive buildup of weapons "may be reasonable and appropriate for US planning for an attack launching preventive war, it has been questioned whether such a large number of targets would be reasonable or appropriate for US planning for a retaliatory strike following a major nuclear attack on the US." He said that in contrast, it was possible that striking one-tenth as many targets would be just as effective in supporting the concept of deterrence. "That is, the enemy would be equally deterred from attacking the United States, if the enemy knew we would, in retaliation to such attack, seek to paralyze Russia by destroying its . . . population centers instead of some part of a larger number of military installations."

Bobby closed by saying President Eisenhower had asked him to instruct Twining and the subcommittee to base the upcoming 1958 evaluation "upon a targeting plan which would seek immediately to paralyze the Russian nation, rather than upon a targeting plan limited to targets of a military character."

As the debate over nuclear weapons strategy raged deep within the secret confines of the White House, the whirl of politics in the outside world continued. Senator Styles Bridges, the New Hampshire Republican, appeared on the NBC's *Meet the Press* on Sunday, March 23, and warned that a "Palace Guard" in the White House was preventing President Eisenhower from receiving information he needed to make decisions. The criticism, carried the next day by newspapers around the country, implicated Bobby, the mysterious keeper of the White House's national security secrets, though Bridges didn't mention anyone by name. Bobby was outraged by the accusation from a member of his own party, and he dashed off an angry letter to Bridges, saying that the senator, by naming no specific person, had attacked the integrity of the entire White House staff. "For one, I resent this wholesale, and I believe slanderous, indictment. I have not withheld information from [the president]. To the contrary, in performance of my duty, I continuously bring him the sensitive and significant information derived from my national security work."[21] Bobby challenged Bridges either to name the members of this purported "Palace Guard" and the information they had withheld from the president — or else publicly admit he made the statement "without exact knowledge" and express regret. There is no record that Bridges responded to Bobby's letter.

On April 1, President Eisenhower and Secretary of State Dulles, who had both rejected Bobby's arguments during the NSC meeting two weeks prior, changed tack in a private meeting at the White House. This time, Eisenhower and Dulles expressed support for Bobby's concerns. Dulles said that US policy "too much invoked massive nuclear attack in the event of any clash anywhere of US with Soviet forces." Eisenhower said that "he, too, was under the impression that our strategic concept did not adequately take account of the possibilities of limited war."

What exactly caused the two men to shift their views, shortly after they had so vigorously argued against Bobby in the NSC meeting, remains unknown. They may have been compelled not only by the threat of the global nuclear standoff but also by its reliance upon technologies that suddenly appeared unreliable, a fact that Bobby had helped bring to light. At the NSC meeting on April 3, Bobby placed on the agenda a briefing on the so-called Fail Safe system for launching SAC nuclear bombers upon receiving an alert signal. Secretary of State Dulles asked about the communications system that would call the bombers back in case the alert turned out to be false. Dulles also expressed concerns that SAC bomber crews, once launched, would have no idea whether the alarm was "the real thing."[22] "Would not Soviet intelligence pick up the flight of these SAC alert planes, and would they not in turn be uncertain whether these flights portended a real attack on the Soviet Union or not? Being thus uncertain, the Soviets might start their deliveries of nuclear weapons against the United States even though no actual attack by the United States on the Soviet Union was intended."

The SAC commander in chief, General Thomas Power, responded to Dulles's questions, though his reply was hardly comforting. "General Power said that he was well aware of this risk, that a great deal of attention had been paid to it; but that, of course, there was no absolutely sure way to prevent a miscalculation."[23] Later that day, Bobby sent a memo to Deputy Defense Secretary Quarles saying one solution to the false alarm problem, suggested by President Eisenhower, was that bombers, once en route to their preset targets, could wait in a specified area and not proceed on to their targets until they receive "specific orders."[24] Bobby asked that the Defense Department prepare a report on the president's suggestion by May 15.

As Bobby pressed his case for a revision of the nation's nuclear strategy, divisions in the military came into focus. On April 7, Bobby and Foster Dulles met with the Joint Chiefs of Staff, the military service secretaries, and AEC chairman Strauss in the office of Defense Secretary Neil McElroy. "Our allies are beginning to show doubt as to whether we would in fact use our H-weapons if we were not ourselves attacked," Dulles told the group. "It is State's considered opinion that although we can hold our alliance together for another year or so, we cannot expect to do so beyond that time on the basis of our present concept. Accordingly, we should be trying to find an alternative possessing greater credibility."[25] The ensuing discussion quickly broke down along organizational lines. The air force — which Bobby had first seen arguing forcefully for its strategic nuclear bomber force when it squared off against Forrestal a decade earlier — now had thirty-one Strategic Air Command bases. The air force contended that there was already too much focus on tactical weapons. The army and navy, meanwhile, supported an increase in nonstrategic forces, both nuclear and conventional. The contentions between the services persisted, and the meeting ended with no consensus.

Bobby responded to the meeting by writing a memo titled "Some Elements for a Realistic National Military Strategy in a Time of Maximum Tension and Distrust," which he sent to Dulles and McElroy.[26] In this one-page top-secret memo, Bobby stated his warning about the massive nuclear strike strategy and bluntly called for change: "Because US nuclear capability is intended for retaliation, not initial attack, the US targeting plan should be based on paralyzing the Soviet nation through destruction of several hundred population centers and not on knocking out her war-making capabilities (already launched in large part) at several thousand military targets."

Bobby also spelled out his concern that the United States needed the ability to respond to a limited aggression by trying to "stabilize the situation" rather than immediately pressing for outright victory, which could provoke a hostile response and lead to nuclear war. The Operations Coordinating Board, of which Bobby was vice chairman, had recently reported that the US military might place nuclear missiles in Turkey.[27] Bobby asserted that a plan by the United States to increase deployment of nuclear weapons to overseas bases was itself a dangerous "provocation," a startling claim by an administration official. In other words, overseas nuclear weapons deployments could be seen as an act of aggression that might lead to a nuclear conflict.

Bobby's idea of stepping back from building a massive nuclear force — and instead using a small nuclear force to target Soviet population centers — soon drew more objections. Dulles asked Gerard C. Smith, the State Department's director of policy planning, to review the concept, and Smith ridiculed it. "I disagree completely with the apparent conclusion that we should target a relatively small number of mass population centers instead of a much larger number of military facilities. I think that if this were done and the Soviets were so advised (as has been suggested), it would not only weaken the deterrent but sharply reduce US standing in world public opinion. Even if the idea seemed to offer practical advantages, I believe it would be completely immoral," Smith told Dulles in a memo on April 9, 1958.[28]

Was it morally wrong to target nuclear weapons at cities rather than military forces? The devastation caused by the nuclear bombs dropped on Hiroshima and Nagasaki had been staggering, and many people around the world saw their toll on civilians as a moral indictment against the United States. However, intelligence estimates concluded that the massive nuclear strike force that the United States had already built by 1958 was so powerful that, once launched, its explosions and far-reaching fallout would indiscriminately kill both soldiers and civilians. In fact, existing SAC targeting plans already specified military targets in major cities. With each blast hundreds of times more powerful than Hiroshima or Nagasaki, their effect would devastate entire populations. Bobby's push for targeting population centers recognized that reality — and called for constructing and deploying far fewer nuclear weapons.

On May 1, General Twining, the chairman of the Joint Chiefs of Staff, and the chiefs of all the military services entered the Cabinet Room for an NSC meeting to take up the revision of the Basic National Security Policy. After CIA director Allen Dulles gave his customary review of security developments across the world, Bobby briefed the NSC on the proposed revision of the policy and moved promptly to discussion of his own proposed alternative, which was a "split," one of the disputed policies that the NSC took up for consideration. Bobby outlined eleven factors that he and other members of the Planning Board had considered in preparing the alternative. Distributed under Bobby's initials prior to the meeting, Bobby's "alternative version" called for the United States military to "develop further and maintain a capability to oppose limited military aggression wherever US security interests are involved."[29] With the military leaders in the room, Bobby made his case in dispassionate, succinct language, arguing that he was seeking chiefly to preserve a commander's flexibility. Until now, he had suggested that money spent on a soaring nuclear weapons arsenal could be better spent on strengthening conventional forces to protect the United States and its allies in Europe and elsewhere from an attack not involving nuclear weapons —

so-called limited aggression. Yet, perhaps hoping to avoid the appearance that he was overtly calling for a cut in spending on nuclear forces, Bobby made no specific mention of such a fiscal rationale. Instead, Bobby said simply that this revision was necessary so that the United States "could determine the application of force best serving US interests under the circumstances existing in each case of limited military aggression."[30]

Bobby, conducting the meeting as usual, then asked the participants to comment, beginning with Defense Secretary McElroy. McElroy said that the issue of limited war was "of very great gravity." He noted that he and General Twining had just returned from a meeting of NATO defense ministers at which the Turkish defense minister had pressed him as to whether the United States truly viewed an attack on one country as "an attack on all." If yes, McElroy suggested, the existing Basic National Security Policy dictated that a Soviet attack against Turkey would require the United States to launch a massive nuclear attack on the Soviet Union. The defense secretary said Bobby's proposal was "of the very greatest importance," but more time was needed to review it. Finally, the fiscal impacts of Bobby's proposal were not lost on McElroy. The defense secretary said, "The changes proposed by General Cutler as to increased capabilities for limited war could cost a great deal more money if they were not balanced by reductions in our expenditures to maintain our nuclear deterrent capability for massive retaliation."

Bobby then called on Quarles, the deputy defense secretary, who warned that a strategy of "limited war" had its own risks. "It would be extremely dangerous, for example, to allow a concept to get out that if we were attacked in Berlin we would not apply all the necessary military force required to repel the attack," Quarles said. This would have the effect of "inviting a Soviet attack," he warned.

Next, General Maxwell Taylor, the army chief of staff, voiced strong support for Bobby's proposal. Taylor had earned President Eisenhower's respect years before. As commander of the 101st Airborne, he had parachuted with his troops into Normandy on D-Day in June 1944. After the war, he served as superintendent at West Point before commanding the Eighth Army in Korea and then taking over as army chief of staff in 1955. In 1957, Ike had ordered Taylor to send a thousand soldiers from the 101st Airborne to enforce a federal court ruling desegregating Central High School in Little Rock, Arkansas. Now, addressing the president and other NSC members in the Cabinet Room, Taylor called for the "immediate adoption" of Bobby's policy alternative. He urged "greater flexibility in our military capabilities so that we were not faced with the alternatives of reacting to Soviet aggression by a massive nuclear strike or simply retreating in the face of the aggression." Taylor, who had repeatedly resisted air force efforts to expand reliance upon nuclear weapons, said he was not calling for reducing the nuclear deterrent capability but rather for "more adequate capabilities to resist limited aggression."

General Thomas White, the air force secretary, then spoke, urging rejection of the policy alternative on "limited war." He argued that the new draft policy, without Bobby's proposed alternative, already envisioned that the United States would provide "main but not sole reliance on nuclear weapons." In addition, White said, the new draft policy already provided for the US military to maintain adequate forces to "keep hostilities from broadening into general war."

General Twining then voiced his own opposition to the proposed policy change, arguing that it would weaken America's relationship with its allies, embolden the Soviets to start wars, and undermine our own troops' confidence. He said, "A deterrent would cease to be a deterrent if the enemy came to believe we had lost our will to use it." Indeed, he suggested that Bobby's proposal amounted to a failure of will to use nuclear weapons: "He felt that no fire power of any kind is of any use if there is no will to use it." Beyond these psychological reasons, Twining said he believed that the United States already had "strong capabilities for fighting limited war," but in places like China, Korea, and Indonesia decisions had been made for political reasons not to use those capabilities. Finally, Twining opposed any change in strategy that might lead to reduced expenditures on nuclear weapons, saying, "We must accept the fact that any expansion of tactical type forces at the expense of the strategic deterrent is unacceptable at this time."

Foster Dulles now took his turn. He underscored the loss of confidence in Europe that the United States would launch its nuclear weapons to defend them from a Soviet attack. He said the United States needed to develop "clean" nuclear weapons as part of "a new strategic concept" to maintain alliances in Western Europe. Dulles was not sure whether the current strategic policy would permit development of forces for "limited war," as General Twining had asserted. The secretary of state expressed the hope that the basic security policy "won't compel us to allocate so much of our resources to maintenance of the nuclear deterrent that we will weaken our capability for limited war." In the end, however, Dulles stopped short of endorsing adoption of Bobby's proposal and instead called for more time to study the issue.

Bobby then asked if others had comments, and President Eisenhower, having listened to all the others, finally spoke up. Ike cast doubt on the notion that wars could be limited, particularly in NATO countries. "Each small war makes global war the more likely," he said. The president dismissed the notion that if the Soviets attacked Austria, for example, it would be "a nice, sweet, World War II type of war." He said the issue needed to be studied further. Second, he felt that the proposal to increase limited war defenses posed a choice regarding military costs: How would the nation pay for such an increase? He said, "Either we do so by decreasing the strength of our nuclear deterrent force, or else we will have to accept a massive increase in the resources to be devoted to our military defenses." Then he issued a searing warning about the cost of pursuing both strategic objectives: "These methods would almost certainly involve what is called a controlled economy, but which in effect would amount to a garrison state." From the start of his New Look military policy years earlier, Ike had made it a core principle to reduce taxes and military spending costs to boost the national economy. Ike's comments made it clear that he did not intend to support both the current nuclear deterrent strategy and an increase in the nation's capacity to fight limited wars with conventional arms. He ended by indicating that he was prepared to launch a nuclear attack against the Soviets, saying that "he would not want to be the one to withhold resort to the use of nuclear weapons if the Soviets attacked in the NATO area."

The president's remarks appeared to end the debate, but the Dulles brothers had more to say in support of increasing the nation's capacity to fight limited wars. The secretary of state believed that the allies needed "at least the illusion that they have some kind of defensive capability against the Soviets other than the United States using a pushbutton to start a global nuclear war." In response to this, Eisenhower expressed bewilderment. "What possibility was there, he asked, that facing 175 Soviet divisions, well-armed both with conventional and nuclear weapons, that our six divisions together with the NATO divisions could oppose such a vast force in a limited war in Europe with the Soviets?"

Allen Dulles then argued that it was in the developing countries, not NATO, that the United States was suffering the hardest blows. "We were quite thin in our resources to meet situations such as that in Indonesia at the present time and situations like it which might develop very soon in Laos." He thought the government needed another fifty million dollars to respond to such events. Secretary of State Dulles returned to the issue of defending Western Europe. He "hoped that the President would order a nuclear war if the Soviets attacked Berlin, but he doubted very much whether the President's successor would issue such an order." When the president observed that the US and NATO conventional forces were certainly incapable of defending Berlin from a Soviet attack, Foster Dulles said that our current policy was to launch a nuclear war if there was a Soviet attack on Berlin. The Soviets believed this was our policy, and it "was extremely important that they continue so to believe," Allen Dulles added. With that, the discussion of Bobby's limited war proposal ended. Ultimately, the NSC adopted the new Basic National Security Policy, dismissing Bobby's alternative proposal to shift strategy away from its focus on building a massive nuclear strike force.

The meeting ended in a defeat for Bobby's proposed policy, yet in a letter to Skip two days later, on May 3, he called the NSC meeting "terrific." He said the Joint Chiefs "erupted over my personally drafted alternative on limited aggression," while the president and Foster Dulles were on opposing sides. "Many thought it the best meeting ever," he added. "I felt that I had made a major contribution: the P said in debate it was the most interesting paper he'd looked at in 6 months." Bobby sent the letter via regular mail to Skip in care of the American embassy, in a plain white envelope emblazoned THE WHITE HOUSE with ROBERT CUTLER typed above it, and marked, in Bobby's handwriting, PERSONAL in the lower left corner.[31] There is no sign Bobby's letters to Skip, containing accounts of secret NSC activities, ever fell into the wrong hands.

Bobby's letter also mentioned his being overworked. The cure, he said, was spending time with Skip on their vacation together, planned for the following week. "And the best way to begin is to begin: and that is to be with Dr. Koons, his advice, his kindness, his wisdom, and I believe indeed his love." Reviewing the plans for their time in Paris, he asked,

"Should we take in the Opera Comique one night? Don't feel you have to come to Orly [airport], it's so early."

On Thursday, May 8, J. Edgar Hoover sent Bobby a letter describing an FBI program aimed at interrupting the operations of the Communist Party in the United States. The letter revealed that the agency had launched the program in 1956, using informants to engage in controversial discussions and send anonymous mailings to foment suspicions within the party. The program had succeeded in causing "disillusionment" and "defection." Two decades later, a congressional committee headed by Senator Frank Church would say this letter to Bobby was the earliest acknowledgment by the FBI of COINTELPRO, a counterintelligence program that eventually expanded far beyond the Communist Party, targeting civil rights and anti-war groups and violating their members' constitutional rights to freedom of speech.[32] There was no record of Bobby responding to Hoover's letter, the committee said. At this point, he was consumed by his escape with Skip.

21

VENICE, MIDNIGHT

On May 10, Bobby flew to Paris to be with Skip, to stroll in the streets and visit museums and sit in cafés. On Sunday, they went to church with US ambassador to France Amory Houghton and his wife and had the Houghtons over to dinner at Skip's apartment.[1] On Tuesday, Bobby sent Steve a postcard showing the spire of Notre Dame Cathedral. "Skip is marvelous — Never saw him look better or more attractive," Bobby wrote, noting that the Paris weather was cloudy and cold. "Venice tomorrow to get warm. B."

The same day, perhaps huddled in a café while Skip was at work at the embassy, Bobby took pen in hand to write on two small pieces of paper, pondering what love, and in particular love between men, meant to him as a Christian:

> Love is the bread of life, as love in Jesus produced a radiance that has illuminated 2000 years, so in each one of us it turns mortality into the divine . . . Deep love is sturdy and harmonious. It survives death and human faults. It overleaps distance. It is as sweet tomorrow as a year ago. Being divine, it never grows old . . .
>
> I believe the most perfect arrangement is happy marriage — the needed complementing of the two sexes, elevated and made enduring by love. But there is, also, no impediment to the marriage of true minds. Such friendships have gone ringing down through history, from David and Jonathan to Damon and Pythias to the rich friendships of our own youth cruelly cut short by World War I . . .[2]

As a Christian, Bobby would have known the Old Testament's Book of Samuel II and its story of the friendship of David and Jonathan, and David's statement that to him the love of Jonathan "was more wonderful than the love of women."

Bobby and Skip flew from Paris to Venice on May 14. They checked into a hotel; the sleeping arrangements — whether they shared a room — are unknown. They walked through the city's narrow ancient streets, enjoying churches, palaces, and canals. They saw a performance of Verdi's opera *Il Trovatore* and dined in elegant restaurants. Here Bobby began keeping a diary of his relationship with Skip. At first, he wrote on small sheets of paper, which he later taped into a bound notebook.[3] The first entry begins:

> Venice, Midnight, May 16/58. This day will be richly remembered in the years that lie ahead. We talked — at the Colombe, on some narrow calle, for three hours over a delicious lunch and brandy; at the Edwardian elegance of the Grand for two hours at a fine dinner: — of things close to us both: our lives and the living of them — my limitations, and the issues of youth and age and the shaping of himself. How many people would have — could have — spent so many hours in conversation over the gossamer web of friendship? And how many come out from this anvil, well rewarded by sense and noble purpose? To understand each other, to appreciate, to deal with facts, to hold nothing back — and now we are both assured that these days have a gold harvest . . . and thinks of the other's regard as a treasure beyond price in his life — and would answer the call of his friend in the same quality and spirit in which the call was given.
>
> We have opened the windows in each other's houses and looked in: we have seen all that there is to see: however different the content from the other's way, each has understood and, valuing and appreciating, said: here is a life in which — so long as we live — I wish to share.

The next day, May 17, Bobby wrote that he had shown his diary entry to Skip. "He read this at lunch and said it was a perfect expression of our understanding." In a later entry, Bobby seemed less sure that Skip would approve of the diary:

> I fear this book will appall him at first, when and if he reads it. Who but RC could have produced such self-laceration and unnecessary suffering and the creation of

a vast romantic world about one wonderful young man? Only my friend, unhappy in his youth, suffering in his heart in his young manhood, wise, understanding, intellectual, lover of beauty, balanced — can understand if he reads it all. For an older man to care so for a younger could be deemed by the "general" to be unwholesome, abnormal — like Thomas Mann's Aschenbach's feeling for Tadzio?

Here Bobby is referring to Thomas Mann's novel *Death in Venice*, which tells the story of a German writer, Gustav von Aschenbach. Aschenbach goes on vacation to Venice, where he begins to have desires for Tadzio, a handsome Polish youth vacationing with his family. Aschenbach's passion for him is tormented, and Aschenbach doesn't dare to approach him. Finally, just as Aschenbach seems on the verge of reaching out to the boy, Aschenbach dies of a plague striking the city. Bobby saw the similarities between Aschenbach's love for Tadzio and his own love for Skip. Yet Bobby noted a significant difference: Tadzio remains at a distance and knows almost nothing of Aschenbach's passion for him.

But my friend knows all about me, my character, the twist that fate gave when Nell brushed me aside 30 years ago, then this long slavery of work of all kinds in an enforced continence: why should not the sudden breaking of this divine beauty in my dark world almost turn me inside out? After so many, many lonely years, to have found a rose among thistles. And when he reads it all he will see what is so critically fine between us: that our mutual esteem and devotion transcends flesh and partakes of the spirit, is for me a primitive move into a better, nobler, purer sphere than I have known before. He will understand.[4]

Now that he was confessing his passion for Skip in a written diary, it was deeply personal and also could be dangerous evidence of a forbidden love, and Bobby took steps to keep it secret. He wrote on its cover in cursive, in blue ink:

PERSONAL VOL I
Robert Cutler
41 Beacon St
Boston
Note to a finder on my death
If I die, give this without
Reading to Tilghman B Koons,
American Embassy, Paris France
For him to keep and read,
Robert Cutler

The two men took photos from their visit to Venice — Bobby in St. Mark's Square, Skip smiling broadly in a restaurant, Bobby looking down a quiet canal with a gondola in it — more than a dozen of which Bobby soon pasted in his diary. They visited Villa d'Este, the Renaissance villa and museum near Rome, before flying back to Paris.[5] On Sunday, May 18, as he was departing Orly airport for home, Bobby wrote:

We have just said happy good-byes after these eight incredible happiest days of my life. His last expression was a hopeful expectation to see me in August. Two people of such disparate ages could hardly have a more lovely communion. It dwells in the realm of spirit and mind, of a translucent purity; without the affection of flesh. We have arrived in these days at many understandings: that he is a man, with manly emotions; that in his private life he may elect courses — and will — wholly different from my narrow, cruelly blighted channel; that he may have mistresses for relief of his strong life stream; that while he has drawn close to marriage sometimes, he never quite wanted to cross the line and may not, that he has other friends . . . there may be others, very dear to him . . . that older men have expressed love for him before, but none before has ever really won his love as I have . . .

22

"I LOVE HIM . . ."

When Bobby returned to Washington, he plunged into a national security debate on how to break Eastern European nations free from Soviet control. In the NSC meeting on Thursday, May 22, Bobby said that there was a split in policy between the Joint Chiefs of Staff and the NSC Planning Board over how to achieve this goal. The Planning Board had unanimously agreed that "the dominated peoples should seek their goals of greater independence from Moscow gradually and generally without resort to violence."[1] The Joint Chiefs, on the other hand, believed that Soviet Bloc nations would only achieve independence with some fighting and that the United States should discreetly encourage violent uprisings and guerrilla operations "on a calculated basis when we are ready to cope with the Russian reaction."

General Nathan Twining, chairman of the Joint Chiefs, said the military leadership felt the Planning Board's position was "much too weak." Secretary of State Dulles, who had previously advocated an aggressive approach to confronting Communism, now endorsed gradualism. "Broadly speaking . . . we in the State Department believe that the best hope of bringing about an acceptable evolution toward greater freedom for the satellites is the exertion by the satellites of constant pressure on the Soviet Union and on their own regimes, in the hope of effecting a change in the thinking of the Soviet rulers." To bolster his case, he cited Hungary, where "the elements that we most depended upon had been liquidated by the resort to violence." The NSC adopted the gradualist version, and President Eisenhower approved it.

On the other side of the world, the CIA's covert action against Sukarno's government in Indonesia had faltered. On May 18, the same day Bobby was flying back from Paris, Indonesian anti-aircraft fire had shot down a B-26 bomber on a raid in support of the rebels. Its pilot ejected safely and was quickly captured. Documents he was carrying revealed him to be Allen L. Pope, a decorated Korean War veteran until recently stationed at Clark Air Base in the Philippines. In fact, less than a month prior to the fateful mission, Pope had been released from the US Air Force on temporary assignment to Civil Air Transport, a CIA front company used to supply the rebels.[2] Pope's documents also revealed a string of other bombing missions he had performed for the rebels in the preceding days, striking military bases, ships, warehouses, and even a church.[3] News of the crash reached Allen Dulles within hours, and he quickly called his brother. "We're pulling the plug," Allen said.[4] The CIA's attempted coup in Indonesia, never disclosed to the public, thus received a quiet burial. Pope later was tried and sentenced to death but would ultimately be released by the Indonesian government in 1961.

As Bobby worked in the NSC fighting the Cold War, he again turned to his diary to sort through his feelings for Skip, which he considered in harmony with his Christian faith:

> If I desire to live the normal life of a Christian gentleman —
> and not some narrow imperfection born of my reactions,
> my youth and young manhood — then HERE, NOW,
> glorious and radiant, is a sound purpose for living out a life.
> *I* have a *friend* in the highest, noblest and purest sense. We
> understand all about each other's private lives; we accept
> the differences in them as men respect in Christian way the
> integrity of other men; we take happiness in being together,
> especially because we dwell in a rare affinity which finds in
> the beauty of nature, of places, of ancient structures, of art,
> of literature, of music the true measure of friendship. The
> normal life — the only happy life — there can be no more
> to ask; and it is given freely, gravely, serenely by my friend
> to me. It is as *Thou* wilt, Heavenly Father, not as I wish.
> And, in this love, Thy will is directly manifest to me and I
> shall serve it all my days.[5]

Bobby revealed in his diary that he understood his old age made him unappealing to Skip, but he resisted concluding that his passion for Skip was unrequited. Bobby noted that he had eight pictures of Skip in his bedroom as well as another eight in a "pocket book" he carried with him, while Skip had just one photo of Bobby and Ike in his office. "What means so much to me, so incredibly much, means nothing to him," he recorded on May 27. "But what is important is this: there is no conclusion to be drawn from this difference, that I love him but he does not love me. People are not the same. And I have drawn endless anguish upon myself by concluding that his failure to act as I would means that he does not care as I do. This kind of thinking is arrant nonsense."

He continued:

> It is now 9 days since I saw him last. The impact of his personality, upon me, like a mighty press, has begun for the first day to lift. I am no longer cast down, living in yesterday, bleeding afresh as each anniversary hour tolls, stricken in heart by the long separation which lies ahead. I am getting back into balance.
>
> So great an upset in my life — so deep, so continuous, so overwhelming — has not occurred before. The impact of his character, intellect, breeding, and quality completely routed my ability to live as myself. What a testimony to the quality of this extraordinary man. In every area, he swept me down like a great wind, irresistible, overpowering, filling every nook and cranny. It was unconditional surrender to one who never sought, or dreamed of, such a thing.

In his letters to Skip, Bobby held back his aching lamentations and instead focused more on their mutual enjoyment. Two days earlier, May 25, Bobby had written to Skip, "You were responsible for giving me eight sovereign days of unequaled and unforgettable deep satisfaction. Perhaps never in my life have I had such a happy time, felt so continuously partner in a rare affinity of mind and spirit and appreciation of so many beautiful places and arts and music, and in just doing things together."[6] Still, he acknowledged feeling anguish as he returned from this "lofty plain of sharing with someone who means so much" to his position at the White House. "The sadness came from the realization I have so little time, and of those months how very little can be spent with you."

Seeking to escape from Washington pressures, Bobby retreated to Boston. One evening, he had dinner with Chan and Peggy Bigelow at

Cabot Lodge's home in Beverly Farms, an evening that included Cabot's son Harry "(one of my pets)" and "his little wife," as Bobby recounted in a letter to Skip. "Cabot was in high spirits. In a way, it was just like the old days 20–30 years ago when Chan, Cabot and I were always together." He also spent time at Fair Harvard.[7]

On June 3, Bobby described in his diary receiving a letter from Skip that "plunged me in bitter, hard to control disappointment and shock." Even so, he struggled to tame his emotional response, admitting to himself that Skip had other love interests in his life. "He is young, and I am old and ugly with age. He has people his own age whom he loves a good deal — his German girl, Alexander, possibly Steve [Benedict]," he wrote. "Why then should he make violent protestations to an aging *intruder* in his life?"

In a letter to Skip days later, Bobby chided him. "When people love you and you love them, please don't take them for granted. This is profligate."[8] But he also pulled back from his emotional response, saying that he had learned from Skip that the difference between the two men might lie not in their feelings for each other but in how they express those feelings. "You know, however, it would not be R. C. unless I should always hope for a little honey on my bread." He said he would look at any time for "some clear, winning word of love." He added, "Any time you can spare one, there is an old dog under the table." Then, in a postscript, Bobby noted that he would soon be sending plans for an August vacation in Europe. "Don't be alarmed. I understand. I shall not ask anything you don't want to give."

Bobby soon received a letter from Skip dated June 6 that "raised me into the empyrean," he effused in his diary. Skip spoke with "tender delicacy" of Bobby's birthday — he turned sixty-three on June 12 — and Skip said he would send a gold cross to Bobby when he could afford to buy it. "My heart filled up with confidence in our tie together, as swiftly as the tide comes racing in from Mt. St. Michel — dwarfing and drowning all doubts and fears," Bobby wrote in his diary. In a reply letter, he informed Skip that he had made arrangements to resume his position as chairman of the Old Colony Trust Company with a salary that would enable him to "be of practical help to you."[9] He had recently had lunch with Viscountess Betty Harcourt at the Metropolitan Club, and she had invited him to visit her estate in England. "Betty thinks, after hearing me describe you, you are IT. (You are, too.)"

On June 23, Bobby delivered his letter of resignation to the president. In a separate personal note to Ike, he outlined preparations for Gordon Gray to take over his post effective July 21. Bobby also set the stage for a possible return to service, saying that in a year or so he might take "some Commissionership or Embassy which you would then be wishing to fill." He also praised the president for his remarkable ability to get men to perform their best. "I continue every day to think you are a wonderful man. The current slings and arrows of outrageous fortune will not be seen when history judges your sound beliefs and fortitude and ceaseless labor for honorable peace. God will keep watch over so faithful a servant. Your affectionate friend, Bobby." The next day, the White House issued Bobby's formal letter of resignation, which said only that he was departing for "wholly personal reasons."[10] The White House also released a letter from Ike to Bobby, saying in part:

> I must, of course, abide by your decision and accept your resignation as you requested, but I do so with a personal feeling of loss most difficult to express.
>
> The dedication with which you have carried out your responsibilities during the past year and one-half is matched only by that which marked your earliest service beginning in 1953. It has been very fortunate for the Nation — and for me — that you have been willing repeatedly to lay aside your personal concerns and give wholeheartedly of your many talents to the study of these complex problems that must be deliberated and solved for the security of the Nation. All of us responsible in these matters recognize that, thanks to your painstaking efforts, our work has been made easier. I am sure I can speak for all of us in saying, "Thank you from the bottom of our hearts for all that you have done. We shall miss you." . . .
>
> With warm personal regard,
As ever,
Dwight D. Eisenhower

Bobby continued his work in the NSC, acquainting Gray with the operations of the council, the Planning Board, and the Operations Coordinating

Board. Meanwhile, the drumbeat of nuclear warfare developments continued. For months, the news about the missile program had been mostly bad. In April 1958, the Defense Department submitted a report to the president stating that there had been a string of failed tests in three key rocket programs — Atlas, Thor, and Jupiter. On June 30, however, Defense Secretary Neil McElroy reported to President Eisenhower that a Jupiter rocket test flight had been successful, as the nose cone reached an altitude of 335 miles and reentered the atmosphere with minimum damage.[11] "The flight provided the first concrete proof of the survival of a full-scale IRBM nose cone through reentry to impact," McElroy wrote.

Bobby, who still resided at The Family at 1718 H Street, took long bike rides to help regain his spirits and his emotional balance. He had cocktails with Lady Harcourt and went to see the movie *Gigi* with Gordon and Nancy Gray. He wrote a poem for Ike and Mamie's sixty-second wedding anniversary on July 1, and that same day he delivered to the president a twenty-eight-page memorandum on the national security mechanism he had created for Ike five years earlier and its subsequent changes.[12] He also traveled alone with the president to Quantico, Virginia, for a meeting. By the time he wrote Skip later that day, he had stepped back from the brink of despair. He noted that Steve was traveling to Geneva. "He hopes so much to be with you, whom he regards as a star apart."[13] Bobby added that he gave Steve a hundred dollars for the trip. "I seem to be the family banker."

Bobby's mood soared anew when Skip sent him his birthday gift, which Bobby consecrated with a prayer, as he described in his diary. "This is a solemn night. I have read from the Book of Common Prayer the Evening Prayers and the blessed prayer for the Absent, and then have placed about my neck the fine gold chain and dull gold cross which he has given to me for my birthday. What moment in time has meant more to me than this: as if some mystical, beautiful chain were cast about us both."[14]

Days later, Bobby's spirits plummeted again when Skip sent him a letter saying he would only have a short period with Bobby during his trip to Europe in September, and no time in August. He scrawled in the diary:

> I am falling apart. My nerves are uncontrollably on edge.
> I cannot sleep . . . Dexamil every day to keep going. Two

drinks at night for relief. And then dreary hours of night watch.

Now my spirit is so dark that I can only think of his letter saying he could not see me in September — that was set apart for self and others to whom committed. Not committed to me. No commitment to my love. No, shove that into another month where it won't intrude or interfere. What a desolate heath this gesture leaves me upon, bare and dusty and gray . . .

It is dreg-moments like this when life seems such a pitiful little flame that to snuff it out would make no one's world darker.

Then, yet again, his spirits rebounded days later when he received letters from Skip. "What medicine for this sullen, dark, despairing mood. He has agreed to two of our August visits together and offered to add a day to one of them; also, he is sure he can see me before I fly home in late September. Certainly, this was the letter of a true and closest friend. It is I who am deficient, wickedly self-centered, unthinking of his comfort and rest and happiness."[15]

In the Middle East, the Cold War's alliances, enmities, and proxy wars once again surged to the fore. A coup attempt led by Kermit Roosevelt against the government of Syria had failed the year before, but it fueled fears in Syria of an invasion by the United States. Seeking a bulwark against Western powers, Syria's Ba'ath Party Socialists forged an alliance with Gamal Abdel Nasser, the Arab nationalist leader and firebrand from Egypt. The CIA and British Secret Intelligence Service (SIS) had developed a plan in 1957 to carry out covert actions that made Syria appear to sponsor armed attacks against Jordan and other countries, creating a pretext for an invasion that would oust the pro-Soviet government in Syria. Following the mold set with the Iran coup, Roosevelt led the effort for the CIA. The coup plan included provisions for use of tribal forces, radio broadcasts, and the "elimination" of key figures.[16] Yet the plan failed to materialize, and in February 1958 Syrian president Shukri al-Quwatli signed a pact with Nasser creating a pan-Arabist state, the United Arab Republic, which combined Syria and Egypt as one nation spanning the Mediterranean Sea. In June 1958, the leaders of Lebanon, allied with the

US and other Western countries, claimed Syria was sending armed troops onto their territory in an attempt to overturn the Lebanese government.[17] In Iraq, Ba'ath Party members conducted a coup on Monday, July 14, murdering King Faisal II and imposing a Ba'athist regime. Amid extreme international tension, Lebanon's president, Camille Chamoun, a Christian, called for Western nations to support his government militarily.

In Washington, on that same Monday morning, July 14, one week before Bobby's resignation was to take effect, Eisenhower called the Dulles brothers, Joint Chiefs chairman Twining, Vice President Nixon, Army Secretary Anderson, Deputy Defense Secretary Quarles, Bobby, Gordon Gray, and others into the Oval Office to discuss the Lebanese situation.[18] As the meeting drew to a close, the president said it was clear what needed to be done: "To lose this area by inaction would be far worse than the loss in China, because of the strategic position and resources of the Middle East." Eisenhower gave his orders, refining them in meetings throughout the day, and the next day US Marines landed in Beirut and joined with the Lebanese army protecting the government.

The next day, Bobby's emotional distance from his White House position appeared to grow, even in conversations with his boss:

> This morning with the Commander-in-Chief for ten minutes, on a particular thing. He couldn't have been more like old times (in the midst of the Lebanon affair) — talked at some length about Jim Forrestal, as if he thought I was going to end that way and needed to get out. It was a marvelous close and friendly time . . . a long day of work, capped by the PB [Planning Board] farewell party; friendly eulogia, pleasant from dearly liked associates: but there is not now for me a measurement except it has my friend in account. So the reckoning, though pleasant, is a dead reckoning.[19]

That night, Bobby hosted a cocktail party for friends at his quarters at The Family. Secretary of State Dulles, consumed with Lebanon and unable to attend Monday's NSC meeting, sent Bobby a farewell letter Wednesday that was warm but also acknowledged their policy disagreements:

CHAPTER TWENTY-TWO

Dear Bobby,

Perhaps it is just as well that I was not at the Security Council meeting to hear your "swan song." I would have been too depressed. The drive, energy and clarity of thinking and expression which you have put into the work of the Security Council has been of immense value to me and, what is far more important, to the nation . . .

Among other things, I shall certainly miss the personal relationship and the wit and good spirit which permeated even our most difficult deliberations and made them more bearable.

With every good wish, I am,

Faithfully yours,

John Foster Dulles

On Wednesday, Bobby participated in a meeting of the 5412/2 Designated Representatives who met secretly to approve covert action programs. The group, including Bobby's friend Undersecretary of State Christian Herter, approved one program, though its exact nature remains classified.[20]

On Monday, July 21, officially Bobby's last day in the office, Ike gave him a medallion set in antique wood from the White House, engraved, TO ROBERT CUTLER, SPECIAL ASSISTANT, FROM HIS DEVOTED FRIEND, DWIGHT D. EISENHOWER, 1953–1958. Ike wrote on the card, "Dear Bobby, This is a poor thing as a memento of your long and brilliant service in your vitally important post in the administration. But at least you will not forget the face of your devoted, and most appreciative friend. Always, DDE."[21] That evening, Gordon Gray hosted a dinner of thirty-five guests, including Eisenhower, Nixon, Sinclair Weeks, Allen Dulles, and Jack McCloy. Gray's eloquent toast that evening praised Bobby's work in the Pentagon, the Psychological Strategy Board, and finally the NSC. He noted that it was Bobby's work at the PSB, with Gray, that prompted him to recognize the problems with national security policy and set out to cure the flaws he saw. He gently ribbed the honoree, saying he "guided, or was it directed," 179 meetings of the NSC and 504 meetings of the Planning Board. "Well here Bobby Cutler is. He has been variously described in the public press: The President's Right Hand for National Security; Washington's Mystery

Man; Keeper of the High Secrets; Suppressor of Information; Concealer of Bad News from the President; Bouncy Boston Banker; Advertising Solicitor for *Aviation Week*." By this time, the audience was likely roaring with laughter. Gray pressed on:

> Let me give you my version: Profane, yet a devoted churchman; testy, but basically tolerant; often hypochondriacal, yet the most strenuous worker among us; flexible to a point, and then Hell couldn't shake him loose; devoted to his party, yet non-partisan in national security; quondam novelist; excellent bicyclist; scholar, yet a practical man; bachelor, yet wedded to his country's security with consuming passion; bluntly concise, and concisely blunt, yet maintaining a great reservoir of charm and tact; formidable raconteur; flinty-eyed banker, yet an incurable romantic; possessing the characteristics of aristocracy but yielding to a tremendous sense of community, and therefore a laborer in the community vineyard; self-reliant, yet a tremendous family man loving those who meet his standards no more perhaps than those who do not; a gentleman and a friend; indeed rara avis.

Gray presented Bobby with his "Council Chair" from the Cabinet Room. It was a heartwarming evening, yet when Bobby got home he turned to his diary and revealed, on a night of crowning recognition for his years of service to his country, just how much Skip dominated his emotions and how much he longed for his affection. "It was a non-forgettable night. Certainly, poorly as I felt, I enjoyed and savored it. Good things of course were said of me: how else? But I do not lay such flattering unction to my soul. If *he* is my friend, and thinks well of me and my doings, *that* is better than this kind of thing, delight and fun as it was."22

The next day, Bobby stopped in at the White House to pack, dictate a few letters, and say a few final farewells, spending half an hour with Mamie and giving her a kiss on parting, with the same for Ann Whitman. Then he got a jarring phone call from Mrs. Lutz, Skip's mother. She had just returned from visiting her son in Paris and said the State Department was eavesdropping on him. Bobby sent Skip his notes of the call, reporting: "Mrs. L believes that TBK's telephone in the apartment is tapped, that 'they' spy on State Dept personnel."[23] After sending this correspondence, Bobby apparently dropped the matter. He was busy moving out of Washington, returning to Boston and Fair Harvard, and preparing for his trip to Europe where he'd again spend time with Skip.

At Fair Harvard, he took long bike rides and spent time with Bill and Ruth Sullivan, cut wood, and sought to avoid the sleeping pills he had been using. "Trying to sleep — not wholly satisfactory, but I'm trying not to take dope. I seem to be in a different world: no cares, no worries, just health to gain," he wrote in his diary on July 26.[24] Liberated from his White House obligations, Bobby gave free rein to his feelings about Skip. "In two weeks, I shall be with my friend. I think constantly of this meeting, and of him, and of what he has added to my last years: giving them a purpose — to help him and to pay back his friendship, with the best in me."

Bobby boarded the *Queen Elizabeth* at New York on July 30 for the transatlantic voyage. After the relaxing trip across the ocean and docking at Southampton, he still felt uneasy. "Curious that with the cage door open, I am still a prisoner. His love — perhaps only — can make me free," he wrote in his diary.[25] Arriving at his favored hotel, the Cavendish near Piccadilly Circus in London, he bought himself a new Raleigh bicycle, then had dinner with Ambassador Jock Whitney and others at the US embassy in Regent's Park. The next day, Bobby left Windsor Castle on a thirty-six-mile bike ride through Buckinghamshire. "Most of the time through farmland, gorgeous deciduous trees — the Chiltern Hills are famous for their beech trees, with scarlet poppies dappling the golden grain fields." After the day of biking, he had a double sherry and a bath, feeling rejuvenated and pleasantly exhausted, and took a walk around the ancient town of Aylesbury and a church there. "The organist was practicing, and I sat listening in this ancient structure, relating my present to their 1300 years of settlement on this hilltop." The next day, he was up and off again, biking another thirty miles or more through the countryside from Aylesbury to Stanton Harcourt, the village where Viscountess Betty Harcourt welcomed him at the historic manor house.

Bobby returned to London on August 8, then met Skip at the airport upon his arrival from Paris. "We had some drinks, dressed, to the Ritz for more cocktails, champagne, brandy — to bed at 12 in great content,"

Bobby recorded in his diary, apparently writing late at night. The diary is silent on sleeping arrangements at the Cavendish, though it is most likely they slept in separate rooms as planned. Their conversation ranged over friends and what Bobby called "a congregation of two," as well as Skip's health, his mother's visit, and his tangled finances:

> I am gradually understanding him better and loving him more as I learn more from him. Ignorance is not bliss, nor is it folly to be wise. The more I know of him the better I can help and care. I see more that in his way, at his age, I am as precious and necessary to him as he, in my way at my age, is to me. Let it be so recorded forever in my heart. We never had a less troubled more lovely time together.[26]

The time with Skip now transported Bobby into a passion, as they enjoyed a musical and dining out: "champagne cocktails, dressing, to MY FAIR LADY in the front row, so exquisite and lovely you wanted to cry, then to supper at the Caprice until 12:30 AM with lovely, close, fine talk."[27] The next day was Sunday, and Skip and Bobby went to communion at St. James's Church near the Cavendish, and then Skip drove Bobby out for another visit to Harcourt House.

Even during this blissful interlude with Skip, Bobby experienced dark moments, mostly because he had a seemingly untamable hunger for expressions of affection from Skip. When they went shopping the next day, Skip bought an item for a former girlfriend, Anna Marie Duisenberger, whom he called Mouchy.[28] Skip spoke at length about other young friends, including Steve and Ronnie Milford. "There is no honey on my bread. He hides his inner self from me, and treats my love as spendthrift. On this 3 days together, his letters went to Mouchy and Ronnie; where did his thoughts go?" Bobby wrote in his diary on August 11.

Yet Bobby's emotions rebounded again the next day, when he took Skip to the airport to return to Paris. He jotted in his diary: "He said that this had been one of the pleasantest weekends of his life, spoke with his charming gravity, full of meaning. Be still Bobby and comfort yourself in a truer, deeper friendship than you deserve or ever had. Now — off for 8 days of health cycling."[29] From Stanton Harcourt, he traveled fifty miles by bike through the village of Woodstock to Warwick, delighting in that town's vast ancient castle. Then, after taking a bath and having a hot whiskey at an inn, he returned to his diary and summed up his time with Skip:

> Looking back at those 3 days and 4 nights, in sober reflection: I find nothing but purest gold. Despite every effort on my part to drive him away, to profane his manly reserve, to try to make him into another — he remains as devoted and close and fine a friend as I have ever had or will have. There is no other road. He is the last place on the line. God make me learn to cherish this love he has for me, not divert it.

Whether the relationship Bobby was pushing Skip into included physical expression is unclear. Bobby added more hints as he continued his solo bicycle trip through the English countryside, notching fifty-seven miles the next day from Warwick via Stratford on Avon to Tewkesbury.[30] At Bath, he reported that he was struck by insomnia that was "broken at last by seconal," visited the home of the vice chairman of Imperial Tobacco, and went to communion in a village church.[31] He wrote poems to Skip in the diary, agonizing about his need for Skip's love and Skip's ambiguous distance and affection and the ever-present question of their age difference. Bobby continued on his bike trip, charting what he later calculated in a letter to Ann Whitman as 413 miles over ten days in all.

A few days later, Bobby flew from London to Paris to rejoin Skip, staying in his apartment at 134 rue de la Pompe. It was a joyous reunion, as Bobby recounted the next morning:

> This is written in Skip's big bed, into which he insisted I move, he vacating to the study.
>
> Last night he met me at Le Bourget — we drove through the Bois [de Boulogne] — had dinner at Armenouvelle — long talks there — then a further long talk in the car in the Bois . . . Never was there so happy a time, so complete a rapport, so much his giving up his apartness and explaining himself in the kindest and most intimate way. There are no more surprises. Steve, Ronny, and I —

and the Count — and lesser than these Mouchy. But I am as certain of his love as I can be of anything. And if every night were like last night, I would be the happiest fellow in the world. The poems were received and understood. We are a congregation of two.[32]

That day, Bobby went with Skip to buy a new car, advancing Skip a thousand dollars to put down on a new Mercedes to replace his three-year-old Thunderbird, and to look at a new apartment Skip was considering renting. The following day, Steve arrived in Paris and spent the day with Bobby and Skip, causing a moment of jealousy for Bobby as he was packing to drive with Skip alone to Deauville. "Only when I was packing in another room I could hear the murmur of his and Steve's voices talking in French, I felt a sudden cold apartness from these younger men," Bobby wrote.[33] Yet the moment passed, and Bobby and Skip went out for dinner at a restaurant overlooking the Seine and from there on to Deauville, on the Normandy coast.

They visited the site of Allied troop landings on D-Day in 1944 and saw the dramatic cemetery and memorial in honor of the American soldiers who gave their lives in that historic battle. The memorial is centered on a striking bronze statue of a nude man raising his arms.[34] Bobby sent a postcard of the statue, called *The Spirit of American Youth Rising from the Waves*, to President Eisenhower at the White House:

> Dear Mr. President,
> Skip and I drove over in his car to see these areas of your great landing and to pay our respects. It is very impressive, and interesting that the large crowds of visitors on Saturday were mostly French.
>
> > Yours,
> > Bobby

Back at Skip's apartment, Steve was there, and Steve and Skip shared the bed in the library, while Bobby slept alone in Skip's big bed. Bobby recounted, "When he said goodnight, in his room, before I undressed for bed, he stood close by me and put his arms around me: and my arms about him."

Bobby arose early on the morning of August 25 to prepare to depart to Denmark and Sweden, where he visited friends. In Sweden, he wrote a diary entry clearly expressing that his passion for Skip was deeply sensual:

> I have been thinking of Michaelangelo's depictions of Sacred and Profane Love. Sacred Love has the Divine qualities of the spirit and mind; it elevates and ennobles; it is above earth and flesh; its passion is pure and unselfish and related to service of an almost sacred flame. Profane love dwells in and is of the body; the fleshly trappings of the human being transcend the soul within; the sensual desire to touch, to embrace, to mingle seems the highest gratification and objective. Yet these emotions cannot truly be separated.
>
> Nothing I have ever experienced is more superior and fine than my love for my friend. It is far more a part of the Divinity in man than man itself. Yet, as I have said to him truly, it is not disembodied, living only in the mind, a sterile hymn. Not at all. I think him as beautiful as any human I have ever known, his smile, his lips, his teeth, his large hands, his thoughtful gravity, his exquisite tact and expressions of thoughtfulness. The temple of his soul delights me as does his soul within.[35]

From Sweden, Bobby traveled to Belgrade, Yugoslavia, where his beloved niece Mary Cutler O'Shaughnessy, daughter of his late brother George and his wife, Margaret, had just given birth to a baby, Elise. Bobby sent a picture of himself holding the baby in a letter to Ike. Bobby also noted in his diary that he had been reading Thomas Mann's *Tonio Kruger*, whose title character has both homosexual and heterosexual relationships, just like Skip. "I have finished 'Death in Venice' and begun 'Tonio Kruger' — these stories Skip loves so much. 'He who loves the more is inferior and must suffer,' — Tonio Kruger. There is much in Tonio's love for Hans, so different from him, that is redolent of my friend. As I read more, perhaps I shall learn to know him better."[36]

After traveling to Switzerland, Bobby flew back to London, where he biked around the city and on a Sunday morning attended matins at

St. Paul's Cathedral.[37] The next day, after more biking and dinner with an old Harvard friend, Bobby reflected on the battle between good and evil in John Milton's *Paradise Lost*, in which the angel Abdiel smites Satan and other angels who revolt against God. In his diary, Bobby compared Skip to Abdiel, adding revealing comments on sex. "My friend is my personal Abdiel. His intellect and thinking and character are pure and clean as morning," Bobby wrote. "It may be at the same time that his sex life differs from that which I have been accustomed to in the few other men who have meant much to me; but this neither troubles me, alters what I have written, or is other than a manly and sensible release. It is he that is right, I that have been wrong."[38]

Bobby then traveled to the Netherlands for meetings with friends, bankers, and US embassy personnel. He biked almost three hundred miles through the Dutch countryside, from Haarlem to the Zuiderzee and on to Edam, over several days. He then returned to England and resumed his bike trip once more. Doubts about his relationship with Skip began to creep in; he wondered why he had not received a letter from Skip since he was in Venice on September 6:

> This book, this record of an old man's rebirth from clean,
> pure love for a young man, this renaissance, this drink
> from the well where water has been troubled by the angel,
> these hardly credible pages are a many-splendored thing:
> like a faery castle it shimmers and hangs glistening radiant
> in the sky, made of gossamer and silken filament. It is the
> very light of a new dawn. What will bring it down, blow
> it away, melt its fantasy? One thing only — the finding
> that these airy towers and battlements and casements were
> builded with the hands and the heart and the love of only
> one partner; they are his concept; not a mutual, shared-in
> loveliness. Then like the sun burns off the spidering skeins
> in the dew wet grass at dawn, the airy splendor will vanish
> and be gone and only dust remain.[39]

These painful thoughts had time to pervade his mind as he was again biking in England. His mind also turned, as it so often did, to the president. On September 26, he wrote Ike a letter, noting that he had biked more than a thousand miles since July 26 and lamenting the news that Sherman Adams had resigned amid a scandal over gifts he'd accepted from a businessman. "I cannot understand the blind spot that brought in this whirlwind, nor do I care. Sherm is a good man, if ever one lived," he wrote.[40]

Bobby planned to take up the post of Old Colony Trust chairman when he returned to Boston, but first he had another rendezvous with Skip in Paris. He flew to Le Bourget airport on September 29, met Skip at the Versailles Palace, then spent the next twenty-six hours — by his calculation — with Skip in unadulterated joy. The next day, "I woke him at 8 AM after the best and most wonderful sleep, he said, in years. To see him bronzed and handsome against the pillow with his affectionate welcoming smile," Bobby wrote.[41] "This is no ordinary thing between us. We are not ordinary men — our mutual love has been brushed by an angel's wing. To its beauty and nobility, may now be added the certainty, that this love is mutual, exists, thrives, is understood by each." Before he left, Bobby gave the diary to Skip. It included eighty-four entries, from the Venice trip in May until this moment in Paris — more than twenty-six thousand words, with twenty-two photos taped in — spread over 112 pages of the single composition notebook with marbled green covers. Bobby had ended the volume with a brief entry saying, "I am leaving this book with my friend, with all my love. These two days have been marvelously beautiful, rich, and full days, promising a future which we both will love."

23

INVESTIGATIONS — AND AGONY

The three young men — friends and former lovers — who once lived in the Dr. Dick House had dispersed across the planet by early 1958, all of them working for the US Information Agency (USIA). Skip Koons was in his post at the US embassy in Paris, working for the US Information Service, part of the USIA. Steve Benedict had left his position at the White House in 1955 to take a job at USIA headquarters in Washington. And Gayl Hoftiezer, who had gone to work for the USIA in Pakistan in 1955, remained and found he enjoyed the life he had made for himself there in the city of Chittagong.

In early 1958, Gayl grew suspicious after being denied an expected promotion. He wrote Steve an anguished letter from Chittagong on February 3: "Could you find out, as discreetly as possible, why I didn't receive a promotion? Something is definitely wrong, I feel. I'm not as upset about not getting a promotion as I am the reason. Everything seemed to be in order at the time. My efficiency report was a five with a very good recommendation attached . . . I hope and pray there is nothing bad in my personnel file or 'some other file.'"[1] Steve was not in a position to find any information, and the worry was put aside — until it was recalled with regret months later.[2]

When Steve arrived at his office at USIA on September 16, 1958, he found two investigators from the agency's Office of Security wanting to question him. They asked whether he was a homosexual, and Steve flatly denied the suggestion, Steve recalled. He also lied to his boss, USIA deputy director Abbott Washburn, the former national director of Citizens for Eisenhower who knew both Steve and Bobby well from the 1952 campaign.[3] After being questioned, Steve wrote a letter to Washburn on September 30, 1958, denying that he was gay: "I have never engaged in sexual relations with persons of my own sex. Any allegation, implication or suspicion that I have engaged at any time in homosexual relations is false and without basis in fact."[4]

For gay people in this era, being able to mask and evade was a matter of professional survival, and Steve had honed the skill of hiding his sexual orientation to a fine art. "Like almost everyone, I have most likely known homosexuals," he continued in his letter to Washburn. "As one long interested in music, literature and the arts, fields in which the incidence of sexual abnormality is high, I have probably had more occasion than many people to know such persons. I do not consider the fact of any such associations to be in any way inconsistent or incompatible with my moral or professional obligations." Steve laid it on so thick that his protestations would almost seem a satire, were the potential consequences not so great. He closed on a note of indignation: "I believe the foregoing statements accurately reflect the substance of the testimony that I have given orally. I trust the matter may be terminated at this point."

But the investigation was just getting started. The USIA Security Office had launched an inquiry that spread overseas and threatened to touch the White House itself. After all, Steve was the former White House security officer. After McCarthy's censure and fall from power in 1954, he was reported to drink heavily and died in 1957. His fevered hunt for homosexuals and Communists in government had been discredited. Still, Ike's Executive Order 10450 remained in force, and exposure of Steve's homosexuality could be a serious development.

Steve alerted Skip to the investigation, using the veiled language that the two men had mastered over the years. Skip wrote back on October 11 assuring him that he was receiving the important communications: "I have received all your letters. Your promptness in writing them, your details are greatly appreciated. I have studied them thoroughly." He told Steve to send "innocuous" letters to his apartment, but to take secretive measures for letters with "something out of the ordinary" by sending them to his friend Patrice Astier. "Do not put any return address on outside envelope — which should be addressed to Patrice, inside envelope marked — for Skip." He also warned that sending letters to him at the American embassy was not "reliable." Then the patriotic former intelligence officer and NSC staffer unburdened himself of the agony the investigation was causing him:

> Some days are gloomier than others, of course. I am revolted and disgusted in general — and violently outraged most of

the time. Waiting is very hard, I know for you, though the worst you may already have gone through. What a crazy world — that all that is great and good in America and the cause we serve could have this hideous, wrong side to it. Incredible.

I find the waiting myself a great strain because nothing has happened yet . . .

I am very sick at heart, for you, for G. [referring surely to Gayl], for Bobby, for . . . etc. etc. trying to avoid indulging in self-pity, or being demented by fear.

This is such injustice and must be so in the eyes of God, should he exist . . . but the injustices of this world are myriad and men are so weak in their efforts to create truth and beauty . . .

Fight, have courage.

S

By this time, Gayl had left his position with the US Information Agency in Pakistan. Decades later, a lover of Skip's, Jean-Jacques Cortambert, said Gayl was discovered to have had a homosexual relationship with a member of the staff at the US embassy in Pakistan.[5] According to Cortambert, Skip believed the exposure of Gayl's affair in Pakistan started the investigation of Skip and Steve. Gayl's exact reasons for quitting his job have not been documented, but it fit a pattern seen repeatedly in the Lavender Scare: Once accused of homosexuality, a federal employee would make the choice to resign abruptly rather than fight the charge and undergo an investigation that could impugn friends and associates.

Bobby, meanwhile, had returned to his job as chairman of Old Colony Trust after two months in Europe. A letter from Ike, dated October 1, was waiting for him. "Dear Bobby: Today is the date you are due back at the Old Colony, so in a sense this note is both a welcome to your desk and an acknowledgment of your letters and cards from Europe," the president wrote. Ike said that he agreed with Bobby's defense of Sherman Adams and mentioned some other White House personnel changes. The president closed the letter saying, "I hope that one of these days you will come wandering into the White House; it will be good to see you. With warm personal regard, As ever, D. E."

As the 10450 investigation advanced, Skip turned to Bobby for help in finding a new job. Bobby was happy to do this and quickly spoke with and sent letters to business leaders he knew, such as General Motors vice president Roger Kyes, who previously was assistant secretary of defense in the Eisenhower administration, and an executive vice president at Standard Oil.[6] Bobby also recommended Skip for a position at First National Bank of Boston, Old Colony Trust's parent company. Bobby sent a memo to his friend Latimer Gray, First National's senior vice president for international banking, lauding Skip's background and achievements: "I have found 'Skip' to be able, hardworking, penetrating in analysis, sound in his observations and reporting, firm in his views developed after study and consideration, unusually mature for his age; readily accepting and discharging responsibilities far beyond his years."[7]

Skip was on duty at the embassy on a quiet Saturday, October 11, when he finally found time to read the diary volume Bobby had given him. Setting aside worries about the investigation, Skip responded with a letter. "My dear Bobby, I am so deeply touched by your love, so raised on high by the happiness I sometimes can give you, so saddened when I cause you pain and suffering . . . regretful I am inadequate too often to, in my own way, make your life more serene and happy, fearful that I know not how best to build and guide our 'congregation' from my troubled mind, yet hopeful that it will bring good more on balance than evil, and strong in my ultimate faith in the rightness of my attachment to you, and yours to me . . ."[8] He said he felt "warm, devoted, hopeful despite some of the frightening next to last pages," referring to Bobby's despair in September.

In Boston, Bobby continued urging bank officials to consider hiring Skip. First National soon invited him to Boston for interviews and to take a series of tests in New York. Skip arrived in Boston on October 31, spending the day at the bank. Bobby had arranged for dinner with Sherman and Rachel Adams and Chan and Peggy Bigelow. Skip spent the night in Bobby's apartment at the Somerset Club annex at 41 Beacon Street. The next day, Saturday, Bobby took Skip to Fair Harvard, in the scenic countryside west of Boston, where they took a walk with Bill Sullivan to a lake. Now "they know and like each other," Bobby wrote contentedly in his new second volume of the diary, which he emblazoned, as with the first volume, with a request that it be given to Skip "for his reading only."

On Sunday, Bobby and Skip flew to New York, having lunch with the Vanderbilts on Long Island before returning to Manhattan. That evening, Bobby took Skip to the Harvard Club, on West 44th Street, for dinner. In the intimacy of the club's Slocum Room, a former card room with high ceilings and dark wood paneling on the club's third floor, Skip signaled to Bobby that there could be trouble ahead. Bobby recounted Skip's words in the diary the next day: "Some colleague had read a letter I wrote him and he had left on his desk addressed 'mon petit frère' — there must be care in what I wrote though he was guilty to leave such a letter about. But he had 'taken care' of the matter. He said he had saved everything I ever wrote him — locked up in a box not at the office or his flat."[9]

It is unknown whether in fact an employee at the American embassy in Paris had read one of Bobby's letters on Skip's desk — or whether this was merely a ruse by Skip to invent a cause for the investigation other than suspicion falling on the three gay men who had lived together in the Dr. Dick House. It is possible that Skip was trying to prepare Bobby psychologically for the blow that would come if an investigator were to contact him. Yet this was likely not the hardest message for Bobby to hear that night. He wrote in his diary:

> He [Skip] said, with palpable difficulty, it was very hard for him to have me display tactile affection — it reacted against his love for me — please to try not to — to let the expression come from him as it would more readily if not alarmed away and his back "put up" by my actions.
>
> He spoke of Ronnie and his fondness for this handsome, younger, dependent, rather effeminate looking man — whom he could help and who looked up to him and would do things gladly for him (wash dishes for example). I made clear what is so: why shouldn't he like Ronnie or another, as I do Bill? It is a different thing in the expansible heart of man. On this, I gave him good assurance.

The next day in New York, Skip took the First National Bank of Boston tests and then caught a flight back to Paris. Reflecting on the conversation they had at the Harvard Club, Bobby's diary entry returned to the emotional dilemma that had vexed his relationship with Skip since its first bloom in the summer of 1957:

> I want to have his love. I believe him the most superior young man I know. I believe he loves me as an older man, more than he had ever loved an older man before . . .
>
> He does not love me as he loves a young man his age. I love with a burning heat: he loves with a calm balance. I cannot take Ronnie's part — how could that be possible? But he wants me to love him and be his friend. This is the great Arcanum. This is the Ark of the Covenant.[10]

Within two weeks, the positive results of Skip's tests were reported to the bank, and Latimer Gray offered him a position beginning with a two-year training period. Skip accepted the offer and began to make preparations to terminate his position at the embassy. "O Skip, I am so proud of you," Bobby wrote to him.[11]

The USIA investigation, meanwhile, ground forward. The "security people are furious at me for my 'attitude,'" Skip reported in a letter to Steve on November 26. "Undoubtedly I shall have the pleasure of more charming go arounds with them." Skip said he intended to "pull all stops and get satisfactory assistance both in and out of government in order to show them how to behave decently."[12] After reviewing the latest operas he'd seen, he returned to the subject of the investigation, denouncing senior officials as spineless and condemning the tactics of the investigators. "My temper is so boiling at these slobs . . . I think a nice public exposé of the Cohn and Schine pair USIA seems to have as their authorities would be a good thing."

It is not clear whom Skip might have thought he would turn to for assistance, but most likely this was Bobby, who had remarkable access to a man who had the power to end the investigation — President Eisenhower. There is neither evidence that Bobby knew of the active investigation of his friends nor that Bobby himself had been targeted by the investigators. On December 16, Bobby went to the White House for an evening of drinks with Ike and Mamie. Bobby's account of the evening, in a letter to Skip, makes no suggestion that Bobby made any special plea of any sort: "Such a nice visit with the P and Mamie on

Tuesday upstairs in the Mansion from 6–7:30 PM. He was wonderfully relaxed and in fine fettle. Took 2 Scotches, while I had 3 Old Fashioneds. It was just like old days. Both he and Mamie seemed so glad to see me again. He insisted on going down in the elevator, getting me a car, and showing me to the front door in person."[13]

Bobby had long known there were other young people enjoying Skip's affections or friendship — Ronnie, Steve, and "the Count," Alessandro Albrizzi. In mid-December, Bobby had a dream about Skip that expressed the desperation he felt in competing with young people for his favor, and he described it in his diary:

> This dream was of him and me beside a clear, fast river of small size (like Bonaventure). We were swimming, or going in or coming out from swimming. There was some-one with him whom he liked and was his companion: man or woman, I do not recall. There were two others also in the dream, another young man and his companion, man or woman — all in the character other than my friend were vague and shadowy — unmemorable and forgotten. But he was clear and beautiful: shining in the morning sun like a color movie: in bathing trunks, with brown legs and arms and chest — probably a flashback to the color photo-graphs of him at Dumbarton which are on my bureau and I look at every night. For an instant while, it was a happy dream: he and I there on the stream's sunny bank, his dark gold hair, his full mouth and white teeth, his large hands, his smile. Then he and his comrade disappeared into the water, as did the other two: and I was alone. In the next scene, I was in some kind of simple house or bath house, and my friend had come back from swimming, and some-how I was in utter despair. He had gone off without me, into the water with someone else. He did not care for me, then. He had left me alone. I was in a heavy tragic mood. And then I awoke.[14]

Bobby was concerned about alienating Skip further with his desperate mood swings and demands for attention. Thus, when he recounted the dark dream in a letter to him later that day, he depicted it in bright tones and omitted the part where Skip left him alone and he felt despair. He wrote: "The scene was very clear, though the setting unknown, and you were entirely clear. Very pleasant — I wish I could have such visions more often."[15]

An investigator for the US Information Service (USIS) — the USIA division in which Skip worked — soon interviewed two of Skip's former colleagues. Both of the men were now working for a securities firm, Shields & Company, on Wall Street. One was Ed Willett, who had worked with Skip under Navy Secretary James Forrestal in 1946. The other was Will Cates, who had worked with Skip at AMCOMLIB, the CIA-backed anti-Soviet radio operation in Munich. Cates's wife, Inge, had recently given birth to a baby girl, Barbara, and the couple had asked Skip to be her godfather.[16] News of the USIS investigator's visit came in a jarring way when the Cates family sent Skip a Christmas card with a photo of Barbara in a high chair on its front. Inside, below the printed Christmas wishes, Will jotted a chilling holiday note:

> Dear Skip,
> I hope you recognize your goddaughter in her first campaign picture.
> The other day a fellow from USIS came to ask about your associations. I slurred over the ones I've always considered questionable and then let Ed Willett snow him with reminiscences about Forrestal in 1946. You should have seen the poor fellow bleating: "and Mr. Willett, did you know of Mr. Koons' social acquaintances at the time?"
> Hope you get a nice plush job.
> And we hope this will all bring you to New York, when we'll let you feed Barbara.
>
> Merry Christmas
> Barbara, Inge & Will

At the time, Will and Inge Cates were well aware that Skip was gay, their daughter said later.[17] When the USIS investigator started with his questions, Will had evidently covered for Skip, and he suggested that Ed Willett had done the same. Will's expression of hope that Skip would "get a nice plush job" suggests that the investigator may have told Cates and Willett his inquiry was related to Skip's pursuit of a new position — not a sexual perversion investigation under Executive Order 10450.

After Skip announced his intention to leave his federal position, Steve received word that his own investigation had been resolved. On January 28, 1959, Paul McNichol, the director of USIA's Office of Security, sent Steve a letter informing him that "your case has been considered by the Office of Security and a decision made that your security clearance under Executive Order 10450 will remain in effect."[18] Steve had beaten the investigation, yet the ordeal also prodded him to seek a position outside of government. He had taken an interest in the Rockefeller Brothers Fund, the prominent philanthropy, and Bobby wrote a letter to his acquaintance David Rockefeller, then vice chairman of the Chase Manhattan Bank of New York, recommending Steve in superlative terms. After a meeting with the fund's director, Steve was offered a position. He left the USIA in July and began work at the Rockefeller Brothers Fund in September.[19]

Bobby spent the first weeks of 1959 preparing for Skip's arrival in Boston. He spoke with his old friend Chan Bigelow, the Tavern Club's treasurer, and arranged for Skip to get a "visitor's card" and stay in rooms on the club's third floor, near the theater where Bobby had put on so many plays decades earlier.[20]

With Skip coming to work at the bank in Boston, Bobby's emotional swings became even more pitched. Skip agreed to meet Bobby at the Harvard Club in New York on the night his ship arrived, January 30. After a long evening of dinner and drinks, Bobby wrote in his diary in a slanting, slightly off-kilter hand:

> I feel in my heart and soul and body a need for him. He does not have any such feeling for me . . .
>
> When I took his hand and held it a moment in mine, when we said goodnight, and kissed the warm strength, he permitted it. There was no counter gesture. Why should there be? Where there is no feeling, there is no overt evidence.
>
> I am really a great fool, a laughing-stock, a silly old broken monument.[21]

Bobby appeared at times to accept the bitter truth that Skip did not want a close physical relationship with him. It was an emotionally difficult time, and complicated. Skip was fond of Bobby and grateful to him for all of his assistance — and they continued to spend much time together. In February, Skip traveled with Bobby for four days to visit Harold Vanderbilt at the Vanderbilts' estate in Lantana, Florida. There, Bobby pined for Skip's affection, picturing him as he wrote in the diary after returning from the trip:

> How radiantly beautiful he was by the pool, slender, brown, powerfully limbed, thoughtful, grave, richly smiling. It is hardly conceivable that so beautiful a physical embodiment shall not pass into another's love . . .
>
> Look at him, cycling beside me, in shorts, his shirt off and tucked at his belt, the wind ruffling his hair. A Donatello marble in male beauty.[22]

Living at the Tavern and working at First National Bank, Skip seemed unable, or unwilling, to pull away from Bobby. There were visits to the farm and dinners with the Lodges, the Weekses, and friends from the bank.[23] Skip was becoming part of Bobby's regular Boston life.

In late March, Bobby's spirits plunged downward again. At the end of a long diary entry expressing agony over not receiving greater expressions of Skip's love, he wrote, "I will continue on in my impossible way until death comes to end the torment of unrequitedness."[24] After dinner at the Tavern that night, Skip walked Bobby home in a light rain across Boston Common, and they stopped for a tender moment of reconciliation at the Fox Hill Revolutionary War memorial in the park. The next day, Bobby wrote a letter expressing gratitude to Skip for his efforts to console him. Skip replied a few days later on Tavern Club stationery: "Thank you for your letter. As you know, it has been my continual wish that you can find a way to greater emotional and mental happiness. It should be a lasting, not transitory thing, when you achieve it."[25]

Bobby chronicled it all in his diary, and in April he completed the second volume, comprising ninety-nine entries spread over 124 pages, a total of more than twenty-seven thousand words. Many entries complain of Skip's emotional distance, while in others Bobby lashes himself for his selfishness and emotional neediness. There is no indication that Bobby gave Skip Volume II to read at this time. By May 1959, Bobby was well into the third volume, and his spirits were high. He did not complain in the diary after Skip told him that he had asked Ronnie to help move his belongings from the Tavern Club to an apartment he rented on Chestnut Street, two blocks from Bobby's home at the Somerset.

Bobby also sought to rebuild his relationship with Skip by helping him buy a sailboat. Bobby arranged with Chan to obtain a loan on good terms from South Boston Savings Bank, where Chan worked, in the name of a partnership that would be created to borrow the money and own the boat.²⁶ Bobby assured Skip that the effort would cause "no embarrassment." "My name will not appear in this or elsewhere as you are the Managing Partner," Bobby wrote in a letter May 2.²⁷ Three days later they formed the partnership Koons & Cutler. Near the end of the month, on May 27, Bobby wrote in his diary: "He does not love me as I do him. No one ever could or will. But he loves me more than anyone else has since Nell. And we are a unit now that only my faultiness will dissever. So strive mightily to be good enough. Look at the sun: the shadows will fall behind."²⁸

Yet Skip continued to feel stifled by Bobby — his stream of letters, his constant expressions of anguish over what he saw as Skip's failure to show sufficient love, his need to spend time with Skip. The tension came to a head when Bobby invited Skip, along with more than thirty other guests, to his sixty-fourth birthday party at the Somerset Club on June 12. Skip arrived an hour late, and they went into a small room to talk. Bobby recorded in his diary later that day that Skip blurted out: "I have seen you 4 out of the last 6 days. I have to have some time for others, to do my work, to be by myself . . . If you have these periods of doubt and depression, I can't help you . . . That is for you to do." Finally, he added: "You should go to your guests who expect you in the next room."²⁹ Bobby was devastated. He wrote in his diary:

> His glacial exterior in that little room was evidence he did not feel what I felt, did not want to talk about it, wished he were elsewhere with other than me.
>
> It was incredible. Just incredible.
>
> I found myself off the two-year platform of my life, without the love I thought I had: exactly like that night

I bade farewell to Nell in 1928 in the B&M Station. I was rejected, thrown out, cancelled — not for another, but because I was not good enough for the grade. He just did not want so much of me . . .

This means that my life here in Boston is coming to an end. I must find another life, another way, without love, or any kindness that makes life lovely. I must be a hermit, a monk, an absentee. Perhaps back to Washington and a life alone there, of work and forgetting.

This love was the last great spasm of my life. It has failed. Be fair, he likes my friendship, wants my help, has some admiration for me . . . but not love not love — that is for Ronnie and Steve and Alex and many others. I am too old to be loved, too selfish to be loved, too demanding.

Two days later, when Bobby returned from Fair Harvard to the Somerset annex at 41 Beacon Street, Skip was waiting for him. Skip believed Bobby had driven past him and Steve in the Mercedes on the highway, intending to avoid them, a claim Bobby denied:

When I arrived at #41, he was at the door to greet me. "Well you have been avoiding me for 10 miles, may I come in for a drink?"

So we went upstairs to my apartment, and had a drink each.

I tried to greet him as a friend, with a handclasp and a fraternal kiss — which was not received. [30]

Bobby said Skip laid out his charges, including: "He violently objects to my appearing to be saying that we are 'great friends' — this kind of thing he believes will hurt us both . . ." Skip also said, "He dislikes my passionate ardor to talk about our friendship," and "he is appalled, made frigid, and repulsed by this kind of event between us: it freezes him up and destroys what I seek." The argument once again left Bobby in despair:

Well, I have been taken apart and dissected and weighed and found wanting. After this, I don't see how any world can ever be the same again. For the thing that made it light was my belief I had forced someone to love me as I love him. But no,

O dark dark dark irrecoverably dark
Amid the blaze of moon.

And yet Bobby proceeded with the plan to buy Skip his sailboat. On June 24, Bobby put up two hundred shares of General Electric stock as collateral for a ten-thousand-dollar loan to make the purchase.[31] Skip promptly renamed the boat *Chaika*, the Russian word for "seagull" — and the name of a play by Chekhov.[32] Bobby got a friend to help Skip join the Eastern Point Yacht Club, where he moored the boat.[33] A few weeks later, Bobby went out for a Sunday sail with Skip and was overjoyed with the experience. "To have so wonderful a man be willing to spend so much time with me is a wealth far beyond my deserts," Bobby wrote in his diary.[34]

Yet another sailing outing, this time with Skip and Ronnie, caused Bobby's emotions to plummet amid jealousy. "I was an outsider, an extra, everything was between them. Little things, Ronnie's pills, cooking for Ronnie, helping Ronnie with the sails, a supervening kindness which, beside his politeness to me, told so much," Bobby wrote. "How can you make a person love you? You can't. It's there or not. With him, it isn't. I thought it was. It isn't. Today proved it."[35]

When Bobby and Skip met for drinks at the Parker House Hotel a few nights later, Bobby tried to apologize, but Skip said no apology was necessary and that it would be better if the cause for the apologies had never arisen. "I fall deeper in the quagmire, with every thought, day, hour. There is no apparent way out. For every time we are together, his indifference to my love is like a *poignard* turning in my heart. How disgusting he must think it that so old and formerly respected an old man is such a poor stick of a man. He is really ashamed that I love him, wishes it were not so. The manifestations are offensive to him, and they will hurt his position."[36] Two days later, after Bobby picked up Skip and a friend at the yacht club, Skip declined Bobby's invitation for a bike ride the following weekend. As they parted, Bobby asked Skip if he cared what was in his heart, and added, "I very much doubt if he did or gave a damn."[37] By the end of the night, he had taken Skip's pictures down in his apartment and put them in a drawer.

Skip, who often restricted his letters to quotidian facts and planning, with limited expressions of emotion, was angry and exasperated. "I am not going to repeat any further assurances of my affection and devotion tonight. Those are constants which you can count on always," he wrote on July 20, 1959.[38] "I fully recognize that a close, satisfactory relationship between men — as well as between men and women — can become very difficult when charged with uncontrolled emotion . . . When paranoia enters the picture — then it is time to rest on the oars — and see if time will help in straightening things out." Then he wrote:

> I am neither your wife, your mistress, nor your son, nor daughter. I am however, deeply attached to you, and fond of you for those things in you I appreciate, admire and respect.
>
> I am your friend, your closest, if you wish.
>
> However, Bobby, "if that flower with base infection meet, the basest weed outbraves his dignity."

Here he quoted Shakespeare's Sonnet 94, an enigmatic poem often considered a meditation upon the virtues of modesty and constancy.

> There is no sense my being with you if it involves, inevitably, slammed doors, cutting remarks, dour silences to friendly advances, and miserable looks.
>
> This is upsetting to me, and not good. Neither is it good for you . . .
>
> I am sorry, Bobby, but as this is going it makes no sense. Nor can I stand it. I cannot feel obligated to undergo inquisitions, needless and unjustified emotional pouts, nor a possessiveness which would shake any family to its foundations.

He went on to say that he had started discussions that day to sell the *Chaika* — which had been bought only the month before. He said Bobby had violated their agreement, which was that the partnership was "for our personal knowledge and tax purposes, but that the boat was mine." Now the boat "must go," he said. "The results of your comments on 'my' and 'our' boat have been quite enough."

Despite the turmoil, Skip invited Bobby to Nantucket to join him for a weekend of sailing along with Steve and Nick, a twenty-one-year-old friend from England. As Bobby began once again to feel rejected by Skip, he tried to maintain his reserve. "Why, O Father, does this have to be the end of what promised to be the most beautiful thing in the world?" he wrote in his diary.[39] Ultimately, Bobby had to leave the island early to attend the funeral of his friend T. Jefferson Coolidge and then go on to meetings in Washington, and he felt maltreated when Skip failed to say good-bye to him as he boarded the ferry, only waving from the dock. Skip, realizing that he had made a misstep, sent Bobby a telegram in Boston from Nantucket: "Sorry to miss you on bow while we waved thermos to stern, on balance hope you enjoyed last days as I did. Best of luck in Washington and a fervent hope for increasing calmness of spirit and less tension. Skip."[40]

Since leaving his White House post, Bobby had maintained regular contact with the president. On July 1, 1959, he had gone to the White House to celebrate Ike and Mamie's anniversary, writing another of his witty poems for the occasion. That night, Bobby had dinner with Allen Dulles and Lewis Strauss and their wives, and a few days later he was issued a pass card as a White House consultant.[41] Ike had urged Congress to create the Inter-American Development Bank, which would finance development projects in Latin America, and on August 7 he had signed legislation approving the bank.[42] Days later, after leaving Skip in Nantucket, Bobby met with the president, Treasury Secretary Robert Anderson, Federal Reserve Chairman William Martin, and others regarding the new bank. Ike wanted Bobby to direct it. Bobby saw the position as a way to serve Ike once again but also as an escape from the emotional gloom that had begun with his birthday party at the Somerset Club back in June and had hung over Bobby and Skip through the Nantucket trip and beyond.

"My life is now a flight from reality," Bobby wrote in a diary entry on August 12. "Reality could be luring with Skip, the greatest love I have ever felt in my life — sharing, helping, mutually enjoying. Why can't it be so? Why must I flee away to loneliness or Washington and try to drown this pain in work, instead of love?"[43]

As the summer of emotional agony wore on, Skip revealed to Bobby a new worry — his mother, Peggy, was concerned about how much time the two men spent together. Bobby wrote, "He said his mother had wondered about our relationship . . . I hope I never have to deal with her again!"[44]

On October 16, Bobby reflected in his diary on the events of the past summer, insisting that he had truly come to terms with what had happened:

> The concept of a companion-for-life — we two as closest friends in a congregation of ourselves, however lofty and pure — was ridiculous. Our ages — look at the picture of me, an old man. His young need for contemporary friends to lead contemporary life with. The malicious tongues of gossip seeking only to injure a young lovely life and an old vanishing one. But especially, his ineffable sense of "the fitness of things." It just couldn't be . . . with him.
>
> So I am punished real hard. And it took a frightful emotional struggle to accept and understand what had happened. I understand now. I accept.

The next day, Bobby added:

> For a while I thought he loved me as I love him, needed me as I need him. I was quite wrong as I have learned. It darn near killed me to learn it, and in the course I caused him much pain. But know it now. It is only a little life . . .
>
> But that's what the shouting is all about . . . So let us cross the River, then, and lie down and rest awhile on the other side.

By the time he wrote these lines, Bobby had already made firm plans to return to government service under the man he revered, Eisenhower, and to try to forget the young man he loved.

24

IKE'S MAN IN LATIN AMERICA

Concerned that poverty in Latin America was fueling the spread of Communism, President Eisenhower hoped the creation of the Inter-American Development Bank would finance development projects and strengthen economies so as to improve people's lives. Ike's brother Milton Eisenhower, who was president of Johns Hopkins University, had traveled to Latin America at Ike's request. Milton urged investment, aid, and reforms in Latin America, and he supported the IADB, as the bank was called. On October 14, 1959, Ike announced his appointment of Bobby as the first US member of the IADB board of executive directors. "My appointment of Mr. Cutler to this position evidences my deep personal interest in the successful carrying out by the Inter-American Bank of its important mission," the president said.[1]

With The Family no longer operating as a boardinghouse, Bobby rented a room in the adjacent Metropolitan Club, one of his favorite Washington haunts. He had stationery printed showing the club as his residence. The day before Ike announced his appointment, Bobby flew with him on the presidential jet to Ike's hometown of Abilene, Kansas, for the groundbreaking ceremony of his presidential library. During the trip, they discussed the mission of the new bank. "This will be the most challenging task I have ever undertaken," Bobby said in a letter to Skip's mother, Peggy Lutz. "It will call for tact, diplomacy, and clear thinking, dealing with a different people with whom I have had little contact."[2]

Social and economic upheaval continued to roil Latin America. In Cuba, revolutionary leader Fidel Castro had taken control of the capital, Havana, driving out dictator Fulgencio Batista, who flew to exile in Miami on January 1, 1959. Castro professed to embrace democratic values, and in early 1959 Allen Dulles viewed him as likely not a Communist. But by the time Castro planned a visit to the United States in April 1959, the CIA director was far less sanguine about the nature of his revolution. Days before Castro was to arrive, Dulles sent Vice President Nixon a memo reporting that Castro "has permitted Communists almost free rein in their infiltration of armed services, secondary labor ranks and educational and cultural institutions." On his trip to the US, Castro visited a school, rode a miniature train at the Bronx Zoo, ate a hot dog, held babies — and insisted publicly that he opposed Communism. He had seen what happened five years earlier when US officials began to perceive Guatemalan president Jacobo Arbenz as influenced by Communists. After he met with Nixon, the vice president said publicly that he did not believe Castro was a Communist but was likely "incredibly naïve" about Communism. Evidently seeking to win Castro's favor, Nixon also announced publicly that he supported a policy of non-intervention in Latin American countries.

But after Ernesto "Che" Guevara, an Argentina-born revolutionary, was named head of Cuba's National Bank, Allen Dulles told the National Security Council on December 1, 1959, that it was a blow to those who thought the Cuban government would not move toward the left. He said Guevara's assumption of his new position was the first step toward a nationalization of Cuba's banks.

These events underscored why Bobby was a logical choice to be the US executive director of the Inter-American Development Bank. As the president's former special assistant for national security, Bobby could be relied upon to make decisions that supported President Eisenhower's interests in both economic development and national security. What's more, he had a unique understanding of the financial issues at stake in Cuba. Old Colony Trust's client United Fruit produced all of its raw sugar on plantations it owned in Cuba. In 1958, it produced 157,000 tons of raw sugar on the island. By the end of 1959, the Cuban government had seized a small portion of United Fruit's land, twenty-two thousand acres.[3] Old Colony's parent, First National Bank of Boston, also had branches and considerable business spread across Cuba. First National reported a decline in its net income when, in 1959, the Cuban government barred the bank from sending profits from its Cuban branches to the United States.[4] Ultimately, under Guevara's leadership, Cuba refused to join the IADB and seized the assets of First National Bank of Boston and other US corporations, leading the United States to sever relations between the two nations.

Meanwhile, the American people had become entranced by a story of political intrigue, Allen Drury's blockbuster novel *Advise and Consent*.

Published in August 1959, the novel tells the story of a president so eager to appoint a left-leaning secretary of state that he uses political blackmail — threatening to reveal the homosexual past of a senator opposing the nomination, Senator Brigham Anderson of Utah. After the nominee's most unscrupulous backer in the Senate threatens to give a speech revealing damning information about Anderson, the senator commits suicide in a nearly empty Senate office building. The novel mirrored the tragic story of Lester Hunt, the Democratic senator from Wyoming who committed suicide after other senators threatened to reveal his son's arrest on a morals charge in Lafayette Square. Drury's tale transposed the events surrounding Hunt's suicide through a political prism, but the crux of the story was the use of homosexuality for political extortion.

Advise and Consent soared to the top of bestseller lists and stayed there for two years. Published more than a decade after Kinsey's *Sexual Behavior in the Human Male*, the novel depicts Anderson sympathetically as a family man who loves his wife and children but who had a homosexual experience after unexpectedly meeting a man on the beach while on leave in Honolulu during World War II:

> Suddenly the whole surging loneliness of the war, his own tiredness and questioning of himself, the burden of so much agony everywhere in the world, the need for a little rest and a little peace without fighting anymore with himself or anybody, had seemed unbearable, and like two children in a trance they had returned to the hotel together and from then on for nearly a month they were never apart for long. Any other time, any other place, he knew it never would have happened; but many things like that happened in war, he had observed, and no one noticed and no one cared.[5]

The novel seemed a clarion call to readers to recognize that, as Kinsey's research had indicated, sexual attraction exists along a continuum, and a large share of men could have homosexual experiences, even if ultimately choosing, as the fictional Senator Anderson did, to pursue traditional heterosexual relationships.

Just as *Advise and Consent* was published, Bobby's nomination was delayed. Democrats in control of the Senate were holding up a number of nominations, and there is no evidence that opponents sought to use a homosexual smear against him. Once again, there is no record of a background check being performed for his nomination. Had one been performed, it might have exposed the Bullitt accusations, the charge by the accused homosexual employee of the White House that Bobby was gay, or the USIA investigation of Skip and Steve. The pending confirmation hearing and its risks were not lost on Skip's mother, Peggy Lutz, who sent Bobby a letter congratulating him on his nomination, in which she wrote: "Advise & Consent was a fascinating book, one couldn't put it down. Am so glad you found time to read it. My copy is going the rounds, everyone wants to read it."[6]

Days after Ike announced Bobby's appointment, Bobby wrote his final diary entry in Volume III, recounting an evening that he and Skip spent drinking wine, having dinner, and walking through old Boston streets in the moonlight. Starting the fourth volume of his diaries, Bobby vowed it would be a new departure. "This Book, my fourth record of my great friendship for Skip, is to be the Happy Book," he wrote in the volume's first entry, on October 27, 1959. "There will be no more mullings and drama and damaged souls, no more *casser la tête*, no more imagining the worst, — only a pervading gladness that God has given to me, all undeservedly, this true and noble friend to love."[7]

Yet a month later, already settling back into Washington life, Bobby was again acknowledging in the diary that he was desperate for Skip's love:

> Here is a frantic obsession. It has pursued me now for 2-1/2 years. Long enough to know where I stand and he stands. I do know.
>
> I love him with all my heart, more than ever I cared for any human being. He is my No. 1 occupation in life. Nothing else is of equal importance. That is what love is. He knows love, he has been scourged and uplifted and crushed by love. But between us — me 64-1/2, he 32-3/4 — the thought of love to his normal, serene soul is out-of-course. The full revelations of it would make him consider,

be fearful, wish it would go away. Normal people are not this way. Yet that my love is more beautiful, more lofty, better than anything I have ever known may save a little. For he will see, as his high bright intelligence can penetrate, that there is no baseness here, no thing for him to disdain and fling from him.[8]

Bobby managed to irritate Skip less with his possessiveness, though that may have been because Bobby was now spending more time in Washington and was not able to hover so closely. Meanwhile, First National Bank had appointed Skip to a post in Paris, and he would start a European training program in January.

On December 4, Bobby went to Skip's apartment on Chestnut Street in Boston for drinks. "He was charming, interested, friendly, a perfect time till 8:20 then to the Polynesian Room at the Somerset Club — a dinner of exotic foods, with drinks — a walk home, — after — one more at the Harvard Club, — down the Esplanade under a baby moon." Perhaps knowing he was soon to return to Paris, Skip let himself express affection for Bobby. "He said: you should know that there has not been another person in my life for whom I have had such affection and love as for you," Bobby noted.[9] Three days later, he again rebuilt his vision of his love for Skip in the diary: "For now, I have a cause to live for: now I do not wish to end, but to live; now, I have heard from his own lips quietly, almost whisperingly in the dark of the Esplanade, that he has had more affection and love for me than anyone he ever knew."[10] At Christmastime, Steve and Gayl visited Skip at the Lutzes' home in Haverford, and Skip sent Bobby a card with a picture of a sailboat festooned with Christmas lights.

In January 1960, Senator Leverett Saltonstall, a Massachusetts Republican and an old friend of Bobby's, wrote a letter to Senator J. W. Fulbright, the Arkansas Democrat who chaired the Foreign Relations Committee, urging Bobby's confirmation. A week later, the committee approved Bobby, and he passed the full Senate shortly thereafter. On February 2, Bobby went to the White House, where Ike swore him in during a ceremony in his office, and on the same day he traveled to El Salvador to attend IADB organizational meetings. The bank's original capitalization was $400 million, of which the United States contributed $150 million.[11]

While Bobby helped establish the bank's offices in Washington, he would be required to travel extensively in Latin America.

Later in February, Bobby traveled with Ike and other administration officials to Brazil, Argentina, Chile, and Uruguay, countries seeking to improve their citizens' well-being but also harboring significant distrust of the US. Bobby struck up friendships with the IADB's directors from other countries. One of them, Guillermo Walter Klein — Argentina's treasury secretary — wrote him in April 1960, "I well remember the impression you left among our fellow delegates at El Salvador by visiting, on one of your first promenades through the city, the quarters of the poor." Yet Klein also noted: "American military interventions in the Caribbean and Middle American area, and a certain high-handed way it is said Americans had with nationals of those countries, had of course profound repercussion all over the Continent among people so jealous of their dignity and so touchy in much less important matters."[12]

In March, Bobby met Skip in New York, a whirlwind visit that began with lunch and drinks at the Princeton Club, visits to the Metropolitan and Guggenheim museums, drinks with Steve at his apartment, then to see *The Flying Dutchman* at the Metropolitan Opera, where Bobby and Skip sat in opera director Rudolf Bing's box. Finally, Steve and Gayl joined Skip and Bobby for dinner at the Algonquin Hotel. Months of separation had not muted Bobby's intense feelings for Skip. "He does not *love*, as I do. It is an 'arrangement,'" Bobby wrote later in his diary. "With him it will not be love, or passion as he calls it, which fades. It will be a sensible arrangement for living by two people who find sympathies together. This, then, accounts for so much. Why he never feels or expresses feeling for me . . . In this arrangement, I am as close to him as it is possible for one to be — closer, I think and believe, than Steve," he wrote. "I am no longer torn by vulture's talons."[13]

The following month, when Bobby and Skip were invited by former commerce secretary Sinclair Weeks and his wife to spend time at Catbow, their home in New Hampshire, Bobby wrote in the diary:

> If we could be natural, if I would not insist on talking and making him talk, if I would only by deed and fact show my love, then he would not wince internally and fear and feel he must go away from me. There is a deep love there,

a true love. Why can't I recognize and be with him — as I said I wanted to be, as with Chan and Bill, not filled with emotional instant need but taking the long road to home and happy harbor.[14]

But of course, Bobby's torments were not done, and each time he saw Skip, his passion for the younger man would spring up anew, as would his frustration over not receiving love in return. At Catbow, Skip gave Bobby a photo of an etching of himself made by a Russian painter, a gift that Bobby saw as a sign of love. "There is a story here. A story of how great love waxed like a mighty river rolling down from little brooks and then how it lost itself in a vast sea of incapability to understand," Bobby wrote in his diary. "Oh my God, what a terrible tragedy."[15]

As the presidential race of 1960 began to heat up, one prospective candidate, Senator Stuart Symington, the Missouri Democrat who had long demanded increasing expenditures on nuclear weapons and bombers, attacked the Eisenhower administration over the "missile gap," the allegation that the United States was lagging behind the Soviet Union in nuclear missile capabilities. This contentious claim, which first began when portions of the Gaither Panel report were leaked, now had new currency. Symington asserted not only that there was a gap but also that the administration had misled the American people. "I charge this administration with using intelligence information in such a manner that the American people have been given an inaccurate picture of what is necessary for our national defense," he said.[16] Shortly after Symington repeated his assertions, Eisenhower fired back, "If anybody — anybody — believes I have misled the American people, I'd like to tell him to his face what I think about him. This is a charge that I think is despicable . . ."[17]

Senator John Kennedy of Massachusetts, a leading Democratic candidate, also asserted there was a missile gap. Though Kennedy stopped short of charging that the administration had intentionally deceived the public, he accused Eisenhower and his top assistants of constantly trying to reduce costs, leaving the nation lagging behind the Soviets. "An 'Operation Candor' was considered, to lay bare to the public the facts of Soviet missile development — but it was rejected when 'wiser counsels' prevailed, to use Robert Cutler's term, fearing that it might spur demands for military spending that would unbalance the budget," Kennedy said in a speech on the Senate floor on February 29, 1960.[18]

In fact, the administration had pressed ahead in its aggressive buildup of nuclear weapons systems, even developing plans to place IRBMs in Turkey targeting the Soviets. Yet these aspects of the US military measures remained largely secret. In contrast, one highly classified defense program, reconnaissance missions by the U-2 spy plane, was dramatically exposed when, on May 1, the Soviets shot down a U-2 that was on a mission from Pakistan to Norway over their territory. The administration initially denied authorization of the flight, but nearly a week after Soviet premier Nikita Khrushchev appeared before the United Nations and announced the capture of the plane's pilot, Francis Gary Powers, Secretary of State Chris Herter acknowledged that the mission had President Eisenhower's approval.[19] Herter had been named secretary of state by Ike after Foster Dulles died of cancer in April 1959. The Soviets soon announced they would refuse to participate in a summit meeting that had been planned to take place in Paris to consider nuclear disarmament and a proposed nuclear test ban. Critics around the world vigorously faulted the Eisenhower administration for the violation of Soviet airspace and the ensuing collapse of the nuclear negotiations.

The attacks by Democratic candidates and the collapse of nuclear negotiations intensified one last public policy battle Bobby would wage — over his and Ike's management of the NSC. Democrats were eager to attack the Eisenhower administration's management of nuclear policy, a tactic that could also wound the likely Republican nominee, Vice President Nixon. Senator Henry Jackson, a Washington Democrat who called for more spending on nuclear missiles, announced he would hold a series of hearings on the machinery for deciding national security programs.[20] While Jackson initially positioned the hearings as a nonpartisan examination of policy making, it quickly became clear that the subcommittee's work would be highly politicized.

Kennedy, who had taken the lead in the race for the Democratic Party nomination, went to the floor of the Senate on June 14 and gave a speech calling for an overhaul of US foreign policy, an event reported on the front page of *The New York Times*, along with a full transcript of his remarks. Kennedy described Jackson's investigation as a "brilliant legislative inquiry" and said the government had failed to reappraise the

National Security Council and other tools of foreign policy. "We are forced to rely upon piecemeal programs, obsolete policies and meaningless slogans. We have no fresh ideas to break the stalemate in Germany, the stalemate over arms control — we have as our grand strategy only the arms race and the Cold War." He continued, "Coordinated efforts — with all agencies and all allies — have faltered without strong direction from the top; and strong direction from the top has faltered because the President was not kept fully informed."[21] Kennedy's broadside against the administration also tarred Nixon, and within a month the two men were squaring off as the presidential nominees of their respective parties. Just as Eisenhower and Bobby had done by attacking Truman over the NSC eight years earlier, Kennedy had turned the NSC into a campaign issue.

Bobby testified before Jackson's subcommittee in a closed session on May 24, 1960, dismissing any suggestion that the president was not fully informed. He described Ike as readily participating in discussion in the NSC meetings and deciding issues rapidly, if necessary. He said the president "almost always entered into debates and asked questions, ferreting out answers and listening with greatest interest, turning his head from one side to the other as they debated around him."[22]

Bobby threw himself into work at the IADB, and on June 5 he began the fifth volume of his diaries, again writing on its cover that if he died it should be delivered "without reading" to Skip, who by this time was working for the First National Bank in Paris. The new volume began with an entry about a car ride Bobby took with Peggy Lutz in which she recounted a list of women whom she said Skip had had relationships with dating back to his boyhood. It's possible that Peggy was trying to convince Bobby that Skip was heterosexual so that he would pull back from his obsession with him. Or perhaps she was seeking to elicit information from Bobby about her son's homosexuality.

Bobby also wrote often in his diary of his long, tempestuous relationship with Bill Sullivan and of his fondness for Bill's wife, Ruth, and their children. The couple named one of their sons, born in June 1951, Robert Cutler Sullivan.[23] In his diary, Bobby described his difficulties trying to help Bill in his struggles with alcohol and his estrangement from Ruth. Bobby had let the family reside in Fair Harvard, his house west of Boston. In August, Bobby gave the house outright to Ruth, and a year later she decided to sell it.[24]

Bobby's diary entries became increasingly bleak with a strong strain of self-loathing. "These diaries are a shocking revelation of my paranoia (as Skip called it once, in unforgotten anger). I am a see-saw, a burst passion, a mind filled with false, ignoble suspicions. I have no trust, faith, confidence," Bobby wrote on June 27, 1960. He went further: "How can I let Skip read this record? It will make him wish never to have seen or known so base a creature. For I have insulted, suspected, been faithless to the finest love of the finest man I have ever known. Again and again, I wish I were dead and no longer in this life to do him harm. Here is one condemned to Hell: his name is Robert Cutler: his name is written in water."[25] On July 7, Bobby wrote: "Indeed I am alone and spent and wish for death — now, quickly, in a flash."

Bobby kept up old friendships in the administration, including with Ann Whitman, Eisenhower's secretary. She, like Steve Benedict, had known Bobby since the days of the 1952 campaign. Bobby invited Steve and Ann to supper and then to see a new English movie, *The Trials of Oscar Wilde*, starring Peter Finch. "I have loved very much people younger than I — but *not* certainly like Oscar," Bobby wrote to Skip.[26]

In August, he wrote in his diary:

> You never understood (quite) the great passion I have for you. And, as you understand it, you did not like and were repelled by it. You thought it unnatural, unmanly, perhaps a little wrong — though your respect for my life service troubled you on the other side. You wished it would go away. You never realized that it was a great love, something you had a share in and that can't be turned aside without immeasurable harm. You kept away from realization. So it has been thrown aside. And the bloody damage has been done . . .[27]

As his agony continued, Bobby seemed to try to talk himself out of his misery and focus instead on excellence in his work. He noted that he had dinner with Allen Dulles and met with Gordon Gray to discuss Panama. "Well, I want to succeed in what I do," he wrote. "Why? If I am in the business I want to do it well."[28] Yet in the same entry he sounded pitifully lonesome for Skip: "What is he thinking right now? Of me? Of some young woman? Of his work? Of his health? *Quien sabe?* And I sit in my little room here at the M.C. [Metropolitan Club], ringed with his photographs, still thinking of him."

In the fall, Skip wrote Bobby a series of letters that once again resurrected Bobby's hopes for love. In a diary entry October 3, he underscored his view that, at the very least, his "Christian" love for Skip was undeniable: "But no fate can take from me the bare fact that I loved deeply and truly and nobly the best man I have yet to come across. Just loving someone like this, appreciating him, is a triumph in Christian loving."[29]

Trying to remain healthy, Bobby had continued riding his bicycle regularly, often riding out from the Metropolitan Club into the Virginia countryside to destinations such as Great Falls on the Potomac River. On Saturday morning, November 5, the day after the president gave a speech in Pittsburgh attacking Kennedy and praising Nixon and his running mate, Henry Cabot Lodge Jr., Bobby met with Ike at the White House. "He seems in excellent morale and health, friendly, pleased I came to speak, modest as ever of his accomplishments. Four hours later stopping on my bicycle ride for a beer in a poor slattern bistro I sat with riff-raff, all pro-Kennedy," Bobby noted in his diary.[30] Three days later, Kennedy and his vice-presidential running mate, Senator Lyndon Johnson of Texas, won the election.

Kennedy's victory raised expectations that the new president would reform how the White House devised national security policy, and Senator Henry Jackson's subcommittee soon prepared its crowning indictment of the Eisenhower administration's national security apparatus. On December 19, the subcommittee released a critical report suggesting that much of the NSC's work was inconsequential and a waste of time. "NSC papers are policy only if they result in action. They are policy only if they cause the Government to adopt one course or another. It appears that many of the papers now emerging from the council do not meet the test of policy in this sense." The report denounced the NSC for its "highly institutionalized procedures." It also called for the abolition of the Operations Coordinating Board. In a front-page *New York Times* story about the report, Jackson said President-Elect Kennedy "should undertake a major overhaul of the National Security Council."[31]

With the impending change of guard in Washington, Bobby decided to throw a dinner party on January 6 at the Metropolitan Club for many of his friends from the Eisenhower administration. The guest list of forty people included UN ambassador Cabot Lodge, Secretary of State Herter, CIA director Allen Dulles, Admiral Strauss, Charles Bohlen, and national security advisor Gordon Gray. Many came with their spouses, and Bobby included the widows of T. Jefferson Coolidge and Foster Dulles. Bobby introduced the guests with "little stories or comments," he wrote Skip. "It was great fun and I've had letters from 10 wives."[32]

Eisenhower, meanwhile, had prepared a vital yet stern message for the nation, which he delivered in a nationally broadcast farewell address on January 17. After pointing to the insidious threat posed by the hostile, atheistic ideology of Communism, he warned that the United States had built a vast armaments industry and that its influence was being felt in government, the economy, and even the spiritual and cultural spheres of life. "In the councils of government, we must guard against the acquisition of unwarranted influence, whether sought or unsought, by the military-industrial complex. The potential for the disastrous rise of misplaced power exists and will persist." He also said the arms race had been accompanied by a "technological revolution," in which government contracts and "the power of money" were playing a vast role in the nation's universities. He added that "in holding scientific research and discovery in respect, as we should, we must also be alert to the equal and opposite danger that public policy could itself become the captive of a scientific-technological elite."

Before President Kennedy took office on January 20, 1961, he named McGeorge Bundy, Harvard's dean of the Faculty of Arts and Sciences, to serve as special assistant to the president for national security. Bobby knew Bundy quite well. He was friendly with his father, Harvey Bundy, the prominent Boston Republican under whom he worked when he first joined the War Department staff in 1942. McGeorge had later co-written the memoirs of Henry Stimson, who praised Bobby. Bobby also had helped shield McGeorge's brother William Bundy when Joe McCarthy turned his furor on him. And Bobby served on the board of overseers at Harvard, where McGeorge had been a rising star ever since being appointed dean at the age of thirty-four in 1953.

Despite this familiarity, Bundy was not interested in preserving Bobby's NSC system. He and the new president swiftly and sharply downgraded the importance of the NSC, preferring instead to set national security policy through private meetings the president held with Bundy and a small number of other administration officials, including Secretary of State Dean Rusk and Secretary of Defense Robert McNamara. Kennedy abandoned the Eisenhower NSC's rigorous schedule of weekly meetings; there were only three NSC meetings in the president's first three months in office.[33] He also abolished the Planning Board, the core senior staff of the NSC that Bobby had directed to develop policy recommendations. James Lay, who had served as the NSC's executive secretary since the Truman administration and through the Eisenhower years, resigned. In February, the new president issued an executive order abolishing the Operations Coordinating Board; the White House would now be responsible for coordinating execution of policy by the various government agencies. Kennedy gave the Department of State a lead role in formulating national security policy, though he soon expressed frustrations with the department's inefficiencies and relied increasingly on Bundy. "Damn it, Bundy and I get more done in one day at the White House than they do in six months in the State Department," presidential adviser Arthur Schlesinger Jr. later quoted the president as saying.[34]

Kennedy and Bundy did preserve one key aspect of Bobby's 1953 NSC reorganization plan: the position of special assistant for national security affairs. They abandoned Bobby's model for it, however, as an honest broker who enabled a robust discussion of conflicting views of national security matters by multiple agencies for the president's consideration. Instead, Kennedy and Bundy redefined the position as an adviser, a confidant who reviewed policy options and then advocated for the policy he or she felt was best. While the position retained its formal title, it increasingly became known by a less formal name that reflected the advocacy aspect of the role — national security advisor. Bundy also moved the special assistant's office from the Old Executive Office Building adjacent to the White House to the White House's West Wing, near the Oval Office.

"I feel a little depressed that all that I created for Ike is now swept away," Bobby confided to Skip in a letter March 5.[35] "But of course JFK should have it as he wants it. This is the great virtue of the National Security Act, as I told Mac Bundy. But they will find, as we did, that you can't do all this on a personal, ad hoc basis, and in a year or so they will build it all back somewhat as we had it."

Kennedy's approach to national security policy was soon put to the test, as he approved a CIA-led invasion to overturn the regime of Fidel

Castro. The media had been reporting the massing of invasion forces in Guatemala for months, but it wasn't until April that Kennedy approved the mission. CIA deputy director Richard Bissell, involved in planning the 1954 Guatemala invasion, also devised the invasion of Cuba, including a planned assassination of Castro. In what would later be recognized as a bizarre — and, to many, morally corrupt — series of choices, the CIA worked secretly with the Mafia to execute the plan, including the passing of poison pills to an intended assassin in Havana. The plan failed.[36] Bissell and Allen Dulles met personally with the president to win approval of the invasion plan, and Kennedy revised it before giving the green light. About fourteen hundred CIA-backed troops landed at the Bay of Pigs on April 17, and the Cuban army thoroughly routed them within seventy-two hours of their landing. More than a hundred anti-Castro fighters were killed, and others were captured.[37] The defeat was a major failure for Kennedy less than one hundred days into his new administration. The debacle undermined the outpouring of goodwill that people around the world had displayed for Kennedy following his election.

Kennedy was eager to show a united front — and build bipartisan support — in the wake of the Bay of Pigs failure, and so he met with Eisenhower at Camp David on April 22. That same day, Kennedy and Bundy held their fourth NSC meeting, with US policy toward Cuba at the top of the agenda. Eisenhower and Bobby remained silent on the issue publicly, but Bobby poured his thoughts out in a letter to Skip days after the invasion collapsed. "It looks like Uncle Allen [Dulles] might have missed a little," he wrote sarcastically. "Some of the mish-mash might have come from the too rapid liquidation of NSC and Cabinet procedures — only 4 NSC meetings in 90 days. All the staff is gone, including Lay; the OCB is demolished."[38] Bobby added that Walt Rostow, McGeorge Bundy's deputy, "told me on the street one day 'maybe we have been a little too quick, but we thought it better to destroy and then rebuild anew.' Rather a poor way to handle machinery as complicated as the US."

Bundy acknowledged problems with national security management years later:

> Oh sure, there are things I would do differently. I would certainly not allow the processes of judgment and decision to be as disconnected as they were in the first few

months . . . Were we unwise to dismantle the machinery,
let's say, of the Planning Board, of the OCB? I think I
would say that it had to be dismantled because of the fact
that was the only way of turning loose forces that otherwise couldn't have been turned loose. But I think I would
have tried to keep a sound instrumentation in being and
tried to have developed early in that time a sense of staff
work . . . interdepartmental staff work for the President,
because I have concluded that you can't get along without
something of that sort . . .[39]

In fact, while Bundy and Kennedy held only three NSC meetings in
the three months prior to the Bay of Pigs, they held seven in the first
month after the invasion collapsed. Yet the meeting frequency tapered
off sharply after that, and Kennedy's personal management style resumed
and was eventually adopted by President Lyndon Johnson.[40]

Kennedy's management style was diametrically opposed to that of
Eisenhower, who preferred to have open discussions in front of a full
council, enabling a vigorous debate by many participants, often relying
on an orderly preparation of policy papers weeks or, if possible, months
in advance so that all parties could prepare and state their views. In
some regards, the NSC system was the optimal blend of the views of
Eisenhower, a general who knew he needed a frank discussion of all the
facts to win on the battlefield, and Bobby, a lawyer who believed that
proper procedure enabled contrary views to be considered so the best
decision could result. Of course, Eisenhower still made numerous decisions on the basis of private meetings with one or more advisers — key
decisions on the coups in Guatemala and Iran did not play out before
the full NSC. Yet for Eisenhower, the NSC policy process provided a
foundation for analysis of intelligence, national defense assets, and
policy. Kennedy, in contrast, was not accustomed to planning an agenda
for future meetings to facilitate policy development, Bundy said. "You
couldn't make Jack Kennedy say that he would agree two weeks from
now to receive an interdepartmental report."[41] In addition, Kennedy, not
eager for debates in the council setting, developed "a reticence in the
presence of a number of people which is too bad," Bundy said.

Bobby was now the Kennedy administration's man at the IADB, once again crossing party lines and serving under a Democrat. Kennedy called for $394 million in new funding for the bank to spur development and fend off Communism in Latin America. In March 1961, news reports said leading Democrats, such as Senator Hubert Humphrey, questioned whether Bobby was too conservative to continue serving as the US executive director for the IADB under the new Democratic president.[42] But on March 25, Bobby was comforted after he and the bank's president, Felipe Herrera of Chile, met with Kennedy at the White House. Kennedy "was warm, intimate, interested, affirmative about the [IADB] and my part in it. This was enormously reassuring to me. He said he would make a statement. Let us hope so, for it will help the Bank," Bobby wrote in his diary.[43] Eventually, President Kennedy supported Bobby, and he remained in the position.

Bobby threw himself anew into his work with the IADB while still holding close to his friendship with Eisenhower. In May, he visited Ike and Mamie at their farm in Gettysburg. "A really charming time, as old friends and trusted ones. A real enjoyment," Bobby wrote in his diary.[44] Even though he had not seen Skip in more than a year, Bobby continued to be emotionally focused on him, and once again was deeply hurt when he received a letter from Skip in June that suggested an emotional distance: "It is amazing that after one year and over of absence, my love for him is as strong, as fundamental in my loving, as ever it was. My reaction was almost as paroxysmic as after that awful Nantucket departure in August/59."[45] He then ended Volume V with the plaintive wish, "There will be another better, wiser, surer time when we can be together in harmony and love."

Bobby soon developed a fondness for Skip's former boyfriend Gaylord Hoftiezer, who had returned from Pakistan and was working for the chemical company Ciba and living in Mount Tabor, New Jersey. Gayl visited Bobby over the July 4, 1961, weekend; they bicycled along a canal on Saturday, and then went to church at the Washington Cathedral on Sunday morning. "Gayl's visit was a wonderful time. Such a fine, clean, manly, intelligent, feeling man, quiet and orderly, but responsive to affection," Bobby related in what was now his diary's Volume VI. Bobby and Gayl then drove to Gettysburg to "have drinks with Ike and Mamie on their porch — had a long talk with Ike about political turnings and the world — Mamie charming to Gayl, who was intoxicated with the whole thing."[46]

Two weekends later, Bobby and Gayl had dinner Friday evening at the Harvard Club in New York, then, back at Gayl's bungalow in Mount Tabor, stayed up "tippling and talking deeply and of ourselves and of the possibilities of friendship." The next day, they traveled to Skytop Lodge in the Pocono Mountains in Pennsylvania and hiked in the woods to a waterfall. "We shared a room together, and he said I only snored once," Bobby wrote in a diary entry.[47] He poured forth his thoughts and feelings about Gayl:

> He is the kind of man you trust and respect: sincere, sober, earnest, with intellectual and artistic reachings and individuality in taste and effort quite extraordinary in a boy reared in a South Dakota town of 480. I don't think I ever met a more manly wholesome decent fellow: big, strong, (his hands like Ike's) are twice as big as mine and he has the body of a football fullback, simple handsome as big strong men are, gentle, friendly. I respect him. He is the kind of a person I like to be with for I am bitten by his moving honesty and clearness of spirit . . .
>
> So now I shall have Gayl here and Skip there to fill my life and make it worth living and give me two objectives to live for — He will be 31 next month — height 6 foot 1 inches, weight 180 lbs — it is like a dream that there is in me something that can attract the love of this fine fellow and make me pray every night I can be good enough to deserve his love.[48]

Bobby's feelings for Gayl grew stronger, as became clear after Bobby went to Paris in August 1961 for a troubled visit with Skip. Filled with musical performances and visits to art museums, Bobby's time with Skip in Paris was emotionally tormented, chiefly because he perceived Skip's behavior as dismissive and uncaring. "He does not want my love and is not constituted to return it," Bobby wrote in his diary.[49] "Gayl is different. He is responsive. He gives me comfort and joy. But Skip can't and won't. And I must make the best of two possible worlds." Still, at the end of the trip, after leaving Skip at Orly airport, Bobby reflected on his love of Skip and their conflict over expression of emotion. "We are disparate in many ways, but in many ways alike. That is the way, I think, a great enduring love has to be. Ours is such a love and will endure forever."[50]

After returning home, Bobby spent more weekends with Gayl, including one in New Hope, Pennsylvania, with Steve Benedict and a friend. On another occasion, Bobby took Gayl with him to visit philanthropist and socialite Brooke Astor, whom Bobby was asking to contribute to Harvard's Peter Bent Brigham Hospital. They met at the Astor estate in Rhinebeck, New York, with Brooke and other Astor family members. "They all took to Gaylord which pleased me highly," Bobby wrote in his diary.[51]

Yet Bobby had his frustrations with Gayl, too. In December, he arranged a vacation for himself and Gayl in Nassau, the Bahamas, including a visit with Harold and Gertrude Vanderbilt in Lantana, Florida. Bobby confided in his diary:

> Gaylord at Nassau when someone asked him what he did: "Oh, I am a gigolo." What an odd cruel thing to have said. Perhaps because the night before I had said something about what people might think of an old man being there with a young one, and helping to pay for the vacation. To say that, though, of a lofty lovely relation — he said as a joke, with a laugh, but why was it in his mind. It is another little cross for me to carry . . .[52]

Ultimately, though, Bobby's diary entries revealed that while he was deeply fond of Gayl and grateful for his affection, he still loved Skip profoundly and thought of him constantly, pining over Skip's failure to return his love.

Bobby remained focused on his work at the IADB, and he was pleased with the bank's effectiveness in making loans for development projects. In a letter to Skip, he described his work hours at the bank as hellish, "really worse than my NSC schedule." Mentioning that he and the other directors had recently voted through approvals on four loans for a total of $20 million, he said the bank expected to reach $275 million in loans in total in 1961, its first year of lending. "Naturally, I take pride in this great accomplishment — my last 'performance' so to speak . . ."[53]

In the spring of 1962, Bobby attended meetings of the bank's leadership in Brazil and then in Buenos Aires, shortly after a coup d'état overthrew the Argentine government. "Wonderful, in my late sixties, to learn and enjoy a new and fascinating enterprise and to be accepted as a trusted, loved friend by people from Latin America and find among them trusted, loved friends. I had moved a long way from the little boy in Brookline of the prior century and from the Yankee banker of later years," he wrote.[54] Yet the fierce intensity of sixty-hour work weeks exhausted him. On April 9, Bobby wrote President Kennedy resigning effective July 15, 1962. He sent Skip a copy of the letter, noting, "Well, you see I have crossed the Rubicon. A big leap forward. Very tired. Love B."[55]

25

"THAT WHICH I AM, I AM"

In the fall of 1962, Skip Koons became embroiled in a dispute at the First National Bank of Boston and impetuously sent bank chairman Lloyd Brace a letter resigning from his post at the bank's Paris office effective October 1. Skip privately told his French lover that someone at the bank had discovered his homosexuality and was using it to force him out.[1] After Skip telephoned Bobby from Paris, Bobby called Brace on June 20 and asked him to disregard the resignation letter. A few days later, though, Brace wrote Bobby saying there was an "atmosphere" at the bank that would not "be fair to Skip or constructive to the Bank," and he accepted the resignation.[2] Within two weeks, Bobby had written letters to friends, each the chairman of his respective company — Standard Oil of New Jersey, Corning Glass, General Motors, and Chase Manhattan National Bank — recommending Skip with highly laudatory remarks and details of his achievements.

Chase Manhattan chairman David Rockefeller, brother of New York governor and onetime Eisenhower administration official Nelson Rockefeller, recalled meeting Skip a few years earlier and having been impressed by him. "It might be that we will have a place for him in our International Department, and I would very much like to see him," David Rockefeller replied to Bobby.[3] Bobby told Rockefeller in a phone call that Skip would come to the US in October after finishing his duties in Paris. Within a matter of months, Chase Manhattan hired Skip, launching an international banking career that would last more than two decades and bring him into a close working relationship with David Rockefeller.

Gayl Hoftiezer was observing all the gyrations from afar in Bombay. "Bobby is again content with you because he feels you need his help," he wrote in a letter to Skip. "The only thing I have to offer is a little money and a hell of a lot of love."[4] He continued: "What is it, Skip, that we are trying for? Is it love or wealth or recognition? . . . I've known the Eisenhowers, the Vanderbilts, and the Astors — now what, and what for you."

Bobby, meanwhile, had set a grand tour to mark his retirement: four months of travels to varied places such as Aspen, Colorado; Tahiti; New Zealand; India; and France, finally returning to his home at the Somerset in late January. The longest stay in any one place was to be a three-week visit with Gayl in Bombay, where Gayl was working for the Swiss pharmaceutical company Ciba. Bobby continued to hold close his friends from the Eisenhower administration, and he met with some of them to say farewell before departing on his travels. After having a lunch with Ann Whitman, she wrote him a note lamenting "that one more friend's path is diverging," adding, "Do give Gayl and Skip my love."[5]

When Bobby arrived in Bombay on December 4, 1962, Gayl gently mocked him in a letter to Steve Benedict for his complaints about politics and his health: "Met B this morning. He looked fine — tan and healthy. Knee still bothering him a bit. Before we reached the house from the airport he had given me his narrow opinion on the India Sino conflict, damned Kennedy for not taking action seven months ago on Cuba, damned Nehru, Ayub [Pakistan's leader, General Ayub Khan], and generally complained how ill he was, is, and is going to be."[6]

Bobby enjoyed his visit with Gayl but remained passionate about Skip. On February 20, 1963, he returned home after spending three weeks with Gayl in Bombay and twelve days with Skip in Vienna and London. He wrote in his diary that he was planning to see Skip, now working at Chase Manhattan, in his New York office and apartment that night, though he had not heard from him recently. "This depressed me deeply, as his failure to communicate always does . . . It's the difference in age, outlook, psyche, chemistry. We're different. I suppose that's why I still love him best."[7]

Bobby also suggested his infatuation with Skip actually began more than ten years earlier, which would have placed the first spark of passion around the first time they met in May 1953, not when their hands interlaced after a night at the movies in 1957. This confession comes in a diary entry of May 26,1963, that begins with Bobby responding to an apparent chide of Skip's at Bobby's emotionalism:

> Yes, I am emotionally immature, as you say. And I thank
> God for it. For the alive freshness of early and penetrating
> feelings, rushing through me like a wild west wind, has

done most to carry me forward in whatever levels my little life has attained . . .

Emotional immaturity continued into older age distresses and repels some men. Perhaps they have known it; perhaps having in youth experienced its melodramatic pang, they as grown men strangled and buried it beneath the glacial slabs of conformity to social rules.

I realize I am an "accident," a "sport." But it is too late now to change, even if in my case it made sense.

But, of course, one can't have the exquisite happiness of mutual love (see Balzac) without a sharing partner. So then, in the eleventh year, my imagined dream of mutual love shatters on a cold half-contemptuous note: yet my dream differed from that of other men in its divinity and gentleness and perfectionate reach for happiness. But its melody will linger on, like music that has ceased. And when I die a vagrant breeze will sometime blow around my dearest friend. And he will, wondering, ask "Why, what was that?" And never guess that it was an old love transfigured into a gentle breath of wind.[8]

Freed at last from his work regimen, Bobby remained active serving the institutions in Boston that he loved — Harvard, Peter Bent Brigham Hospital, and others — and periodically gave speeches in support of Republican causes, usually punctuated by rigorous support for former president Eisenhower and his policies. Yet now he also found time to spend with friends and family, including the widows of his deceased brothers, his nieces and nephews, and even his great-nieces and -nephews. Among these was Winthrop Aldrich, grandson of Bobby's eldest brother John, a Porcellian member who would graduate from Harvard in 1965. Aldrich, who eventually enlisted in the army and volunteered for duty in Vietnam, remembers "Uncle Bobby" telling stories before a large group at Porcellian Club dinners.[9] "He was very entertaining, particularly when he was on. He loved an audience," he said, recalling that in male company, Bobby's jokes usually turned quite bawdy.

A roommate of Aldrich's at Harvard, Owen Walker, said Bobby's humorous stories typically drew people in from other rooms to listen.[10]

One of these jokes, which he remembered Bobby telling at a Porcellian event, went like this:

> On the 50th anniversary of the Boston department store Jordan Marsh, a throng of people arrives to take advantage of complimentary items to be given away in celebration of the anniversary. A lady from Maine is among the first to get into the store. She approaches a salesman in the linen and towel department, and she asks for a free set of hand towels with initials on them.
>
> "Very good, madam, what is the first initial?" the salesman asks.
>
> "F"
>
> "And the second letter?"
>
> "U"
>
> "And the third letter?"
>
> "C"
>
> By this time, the salesman is getting very nervous. "Are there more initials, madam?"
>
> "Oh yes," the lady replied. "Three more," the lady replied. "K"
>
> "And the next letter?"
>
> "M"
>
> The salesman by now is clearly agitated and he is almost afraid to ask. "And the last letter?"
>
> "E"
>
> In shock, the salesman says: "Madam, I do not believe this is an appropriate legend to put on a towel on the occasion of Jordan Marsh's 50th anniversary!"
>
> "Why not?" she replies. "It's for the First Union Church of Kittery, Maine."

The story drew roaring laughter, Walker said.

Many people who knew Bobby assumed he was gay, according to Bronson Chanler, a Porcellian Club president and member of the Harvard class of 1947. "I think everybody assumed that without caring much about it," he said.[11] Many members of the Cutler family also felt confident Bobby was gay. Among these was Bobby's niece Patricia Cutler Warner, daughter of his eldest brother, John, who was close to her uncle. She had six children and lived in the Boston area, and Bobby inserted a picture of the children in the last volume of his diary. Warner, a veteran of the OSS and a participant in 1960s civil rights protests, said Bobby's sexual orientation became more obvious in later years as he spent more time with young men.

As the years passed, Bobby remained close friends with Ike. The former president flew to Boston to celebrate Bobby's seventieth birthday on June 12, 1965. Bobby arranged lunch at the Somerset Club, a round of golf at the North Shore Country Club, and dinner at the Tavern Club with Cabot Lodge, Sinclair Weeks, George Humphrey, and about twenty-five other former Eisenhower administration members, including Skip.[12] *The Boston Globe* reported in a story about the festivities that before Ike arrived at the Tavern, Bobby ignored his birthday and said simply, "This dinner is in honor of President Eisenhower."

Despite Ike's visit on Bobby's birthday, and their correspondence in later years, Bobby received relatively little mention from Ike in his writings. By and large, Bobby's strategy of keeping a low profile, compounded by the fact that he considered his primary role that of advocating for the president and not of pushing his own views, contributed to his receiving limited mention from historians and in memoirs. On the few occasions when Bobby did argue for a policy — for candor with the American public on nuclear weapons or for abandonment of the "massive retaliation" nuclear weapons strategy — it was in the secrecy of meetings with Ike or the NSC. The rise of conservatives Barry Goldwater in 1964 and Richard Nixon in 1968 coincided with Bobby's disappearance from Republican Party politics. His legacy as a progressive Republican, a behind-the-scenes opponent of McCarthyism, and the nation's first national security advisor is virtually unknown today.

Bobby threw himself into writing his autobiography, *No Time for Rest*, which was published in 1966 to little acclaim. It told of Bobby's adoration for his family and his experiences in the military, writing his novels, in the practice of law, in banking, and as national security advisor to President Eisenhower. It displayed Bobby's wit and intelligence and his reverence for men like Theodore Roosevelt, Stimson, Marshall, and Eisenhower and his friendships with Henry Cabot Lodge Jr. and others. Bobby also used the book as a platform to proclaim his vision of how best to manage national security and of the roles to be played by the NSC and the national security advisor. By the time his memoir was published, McGeorge Bundy had resigned as national security advisor, replaced by his assistant, Walt Rostow, who continued performing the same sort of personal advisory role that Bundy had for both President Kennedy and President Johnson. The concept of providing a true council, in which all agencies could be heard and their ideas vetted so that the president could make his own choice, had been eclipsed. In *No Time for Rest*, Bobby defended his vision for the national security advisor post, the NSC, and its staff: "I was convinced that the procedures we had developed were the Chief Executive's best protection against pressure for ex parte decisions, special pleading, imprecise guidance, and suppression of conflicting views. These dangerous impurities were washed out in the acid bath of the Planning Board, which brought every side of every question out into the clear light of day."[13]

In subsequent years, Bobby's management of the NSC came to be described by scholars as serving as an "honest broker."[14] Bobby acknowledged in *No Time for Rest* that he occasionally advocated for some actions — urging Ike to meet with the prime ministers of France and England, a change in nuclear weapons strategy, creation of a Latin American bank — but he returned to his neutral role. "A special assistant who takes such individual action has to be very sure of himself and his employer, for he is bound to step on the toes of interested department chiefs. Such forays would sometimes bring down on my head an adverse storm. But if debate was intensified on a germane issue, it was worth a knock on the head," he wrote.[15]

Because Bobby acted so thoroughly as an honest broker, some observers might suggest that it is wrong to call Bobby the first "national security advisor," and that position only began when McGeorge Bundy took over. (Gordon Gray, who succeeded Bobby in 1958, generally maintained Bobby's approach to the job.) President Nixon restored some aspects of the Eisenhower-Cutler model for the NSC following his election in 1968, though many national security advisors have adopted Bundy's advocacy model. Henry Kissinger served as both national security advisor and secretary of state for a two-year period during the Nixon years. During the Reagan administration, Admiral John Poindexter's service as national security advisor included arranging illegal covert weapons shipments to

Nicaraguan rebels, which he claimed he intentionally never informed President Reagan of so that the president could have "deniability." While NSC records from George W. Bush's administration remain largely classified, national security advisor Condoleezza Rice was a prominent advocate for launching the Iraq War, which ultimately led to the deaths of more than three thousand American soldiers and radically destabilized the Middle East. However, Brent Scowcroft, the national security advisor to Presidents Ford and George H. W. Bush — and the only person other than Bobby to hold the post twice — acknowledged the importance of serving as an honest broker: "If you are not an honest broker the system doesn't work well. The first thing you have to do is establish in the minds of all of the members of the NSC that their views will be presented honestly and straightforwardly to the president . . . Once they are comfortable with that, they certainly expect that you will present your own views but that you will do it in a way that doesn't disadvantage theirs."[16]

Throughout his years with Ike, Bobby often appeared to cross a political line separating him from his Republican colleagues in order to do what he deemed right. By defending Robert Oppenheimer's recommendation of being candid with the American public about nuclear weapons, Bobby helped Ike himself embrace such a policy, for example. By forcing Allen and Foster Dulles to subject their policy proposals to the NSC review process, Bobby helped Ike maintain control over his foreign and national security policy at a time when the Dulles brothers often sought to pursue extreme anti-Communist actions. His proposal in 1958 to curtail the nuclear weapons buildup put him in opposition to many administration officials and military leaders. On the other hand, it was Bobby who advocated for adoption of the security rules that subjected "sexual perversion" to scrutiny and in effect banned gays from federal employment. And when it came to fighting the perceived spread of Communism in Iran and Guatemala, Bobby raised questions about US strategy but ultimately voiced support for the CIA-led coups in those countries. The 1953 coup in Iran engendered hatred of the United States throughout the Middle East. Eventually, the shah's brutal regime fell in 1979 to the coup led by Ayatollah Ruhollah Khomeini, fanning the flames of religious extremism and intolerance across the Middle East. In Guatemala, where the CIA's 1954 coup crushed that nation's young tradition of electing its presidents, the country plunged into a civil war that lasted more than three decades, costing the lives of an estimated two hundred thousand Guatemalans. Remarkably, because these coups were so successful from a short-term military and intelligence standpoint, they served as models that enticed subsequent administrations into foreign interventions hoping for rapid success — the Bay of Pigs under President Kennedy in 1961, the military coup advocated by Henry Kissinger and backed by the CIA in Chile in 1973, and President Reagan's support of the war against the Sandinista government in Nicaragua, to name only a few.

The nuclear policies that Bobby helped launch would echo loudly in the following decades. The International Atomic Energy Agency, spawned in part by Bobby's support for Oppenheimer's policy of candor, has played a central role in international efforts to control proliferation of nuclear weapons. During Bobby's tenure, the NSC discussed placing nuclear weapons in Turkey as early as 1957, and when the Soviet Union responded by placing its own nuclear missiles in Cuba, the result was the Cuban Missile Crisis of October 1962. The crisis was resolved partly by President Kennedy's decision to remove the US missiles from Turkey.

Remarkably, the "missile gap," which Paul Nitze and other members of the Gaither Panel had trumpeted and which President Kennedy had warned about in his 1960 election campaign, was found by US intelligence to be nonexistent by the end of 1961.[17] And General Maxwell Taylor — who had sided with Bobby in his 1958 push for abandonment of the "massive retaliation" strategy — led a negotiating team that secured a breakthrough agreement, the nuclear test ban treaty that President Kennedy signed with the Soviets in 1963. Yet the two superpowers continued building their massive nuclear arsenals for decades, acquiring tens of thousands of nuclear warheads, a staggering global threat that remained keyed to the same strategy of massive retaliation that Bobby tried to overturn. Ironically, it was Nitze, the hard-liner whom Bobby rejected for an NSC post, who led the way in negotiating the agreement slowing production of nuclear weapons, the Intermediate Nuclear Forces Treaty. Nitze was eighty when President Ronald Reagan and Soviet leader Mikhail Gorbachev signed the treaty in 1987.[18]

No Time for Rest revealed Bobby's emotionalism, his failed romance with a woman (though she was not named), and his fondness for male friends, including Chan Bigelow. He described numerous instances of dressing up as a woman, and he provided a slightly mysterious description of the summer of 1922, when he began work on his second novel. "With a younger friend, in love and beginning his *first* novel, I lived on a farm in New Hampshire. We worked with the pen in the morning and evening. Under the hot August sun of afternoon, we helped to get in the hay, wearing a minimum of clothing."[19] Who was this younger friend, and with whom was he in love? All unsaid. Bobby seemed heedful of public perception of his fondness for young men, of which he revealed only a glimpse. Skip received a brief mention — the one in which, during the NATO conference in December 1957, Bobby said he dined with Skip and Lewis Strauss in Paris. "That night, I was Madame George Sand and Admiral Strauss was Victor Hugo."[20] A footnote offered a complimentary summary of Skip's career, ending with the note: "We have been close friends for many years." In the book's photo section, under the title "More Friends," Bobby included three individual pictures of younger men: the Reverend Richard Knight of St. Paul's, Skip Koons, and Gaylord Hoftiezer. Gaylord is shown in a white tuxedo with a black tie, smiling broadly. Perhaps sensing that a more liberal view of gay rights was coming, Bobby revealed in *No Time for Rest* that in 1945 he had had resolved the congressional investigation of five soldiers mistakenly accused of Communism because they merely were cases of "suspected sexual perversion." In retrospect, these snippets from his autobiography look like a trail of clues Bobby left about his sexual orientation.

In May 1966, Bobby visited Skip at a house he had purchased in East Hampton on Long Island. Gayl and his new lover, Ruedi Brack, a Swiss sculptor and athlete, were there, too. Bobby left feeling snubbed by Skip. "He was close to Ruedi and Gayl but polite to me," Bobby complained in his diary.[21] He also compared his relationship with Skip, marked by their dramatic difference in ages, to that between himself and Owen Wister, whom he called Uncle Dan, nearly half a century earlier. "The whole thing was a mystery. Our relations are very altered. I do not discount his kindness, his politeness, his care of an older man. But any showing of love — certainly not. Why should a fellow 40 show love to one 71? Did I to Uncle Dan Wister?"

Shortly before Christmas 1966, Bobby traveled to New York for an evening of dinner and drinks with Skip at the Harvard Club and then a visit to "our well-loved Maxfield Parrish Room at the St. Regis," the storied King Cole Bar graced by a mural by the painter Parrish. "All the problems talked out, against the background of his grave, profound wisdom of intellectual and loving kindness," Bobby wrote. "He is to have the diaries and the journals. He wanted them he said, not from idle curiosity, but so as to know me better and continue our friendship all *his* life."

On February 17, 1967, Bobby and Skip went to the Metropolitan Opera in New York and then out to dinner to celebrate Skip's forty-first birthday. At dinner, Bobby presented the diary to Skip in a fitted leather carrying case, along with a letter. "This letter comes with the six volumes of Diary which concern my life and yours. I give them to you now as a birthday present in their specially made carrier because you have said you wanted them to continue our friendship in later years and because they will be more discreetly kept in your care from misunderstanding readers and destroyed when you die."[22] He continued: "Had I your good sense and depth of understanding I might have been a better friend, one more comfortable and comforting to you. But to paraphrase 'Ulysses' — 'that which I am, I am.' While I cannot change my essential emotional high voltage nature any more than you can make yourself anew (which God knows I would not wish), I can — in whatever future relations we may have — learn to rejoice in what you give me."

He said he was uncertain about what to do with another set of eight diary volumes, which he had written from 1911 to 1928. "I am not so concerned at the sorry picture they make of me, lack of constancy in friendship, false values, priggish, harsh in judgment (except perhaps on myself), at the end a wicked violation of my principles with my neighbor's wife, for all of which I have been punished in life and will be in death," he wrote, in an apparent reference to Nell Sears. "Why should you want them? To make a Freudian study?"

Skip was now five years into his career at Chase and a vice president. The following month, when he and Bobby visited the Vanderbilts at Eastover in Florida, Skip had read the diaries and wrote Bobby a note about them: "Today, all these years later, they can in no way subtract from that core of affection which, however inadequate, was always there, as I used to tell you, and remains today. They do help me to understand much. Thank you, dear Bobby."[23]

While Bobby maintained his unrequited love of Skip, and continued to see him and correspond with him for the remainder of his life, he also pursued romantic interests with other young men. One of these was Anthony Favello, whom Bobby met while on a trip to Puerto Rico in 1968 with Gayl. Favello grew up in Boston, where his father was a maintenance man at Suffolk Downs horse racing track. "I was staying in a hotel with some other friends of mine, and we got invited over for a cocktail party," recalled Favello, who went by "Tony."[24] Having served in the air force, then failing to build an acting career in New York, Tony was working as a landscape architect. Suddenly he was swept up in Bobby's world — the Somerset Club and wealthy and famous people. "I was just a working man," he said. "I was quite blown away by the whole thing. I didn't fit into all of his friends. I was into yoga and meditation. I was not in the circle he traveled in."

Bobby and Tony soon spent lots of time together, including going to church. They took a trip to Europe later in 1968, visiting England, Switzerland, Greece, Italy, even having lunch with Henry Cabot Lodge Jr. at the embassy in Rome. At the time of their European tour, Bobby was seventy-three and Tony was thirty. "Bobby and I never had a physical relationship, but he liked to hold hands," he said. "I was not willing to let it go beyond that . . ." He noted that Bobby "told me once that he had had sex with one man in his life, but he had to keep it all hidden in those days." When Bobby privately published a collection of favorite poems and other writings as *The Bedside Companion* in 1969, he dedicated it "For Anthony" with a quote from Henry David Thoreau: "Thou meanderest forever at the bottom of my dream."

In April 1969, Bobby prepared a codicil to his will setting out how, upon his death, his personal possessions at 41 Beacon Street were to be distributed to a long list of people dear to him. In terse legal language, Bobby wrote that a steel cabinet in his study held "letters to me from Anthony Favello and certain private papers of mine relating to Favello: these should be turned over to Favello without being read; or, if he is deceased, should be destroyed without reading." The codicil set aside for Skip all of the letters Skip had written him and other personal papers, memorabilia, and photographs. Bobby also noted he had given Skip his six-volume diary and revealed his decision to destroy the eight volumes of diaries from his youth — "I have destroyed by burning my early diaries." The codicil then enumerated the books, antiques, and other cherished items to be given to each of fifty people, with each item seemingly selected with meaning in mind for the recipient. Chan was at the top, followed by Skip, Tony, Gayl, and Ruedi Brack. The Sullivans were to get an armchair and five Eisenhower medallions. Bobby's beloved niece Mary Cutler O'Shaughnessy was to receive, among other things, his mother's wedding ring, which Bobby had worn on his pinkie since her death. "NOTE: THIS RING MUST BE CUT OFF MY FINGER BEFORE CREMATION," he wrote. Then there were friends from his political and business life — Henry Cabot Lodge Jr. was to receive two elephants carved from "pale rose-colored stone," a signed edition of Stimson's *On Active Service in Peace and War*, and a 1914 leather-bound edition of Owen Wister's book about Harvard, *Philosophy Four*.

Bobby was healthy but, foreseeing his own end, he began saying farewell to the people he loved. When his seventy-fifth birthday party came in June 1970, he invited a group of younger friends, all gay men, to a birthday party at Skip's new town house in New York's Chelsea neighborhood. Bobby's invitation paraphrased English writer Samuel Johnson: "Friendship is the cordial drop which makes the nauseous draught of life go down." To this, Bobby added his own plea: "Shall we not try that draught once again together before time runs out?"

Skip, meanwhile, had developed relationships with a number of other men, including Jean-Jacques Cortambert, whom he had met on a trip to Paris in 1966. Jean-Jacques and Skip traveled together throughout Europe, often meeting in places where Skip had banking business to do, and they remained close for decades.[25] Another of Skip's enduring partners was Edgar Glazbrook, a native of Alice, Texas, who had moved to New York in 1969. They picked each other up one night walking near Glazbrook's apartment on Christopher Street in Greenwich Village.[26] "We passed each other on the street . . . We started talking, and he asked me if I wanted to come home with him," Glazbrook said. "He was so masculine that I wasn't sure that he was gay. I had just moved to New York, and I was afraid of being mugged or being arrested by plainclothes cops."

Skip was not interested in a committed relationship. "We began seeing each other after that, and for me it was love at first sight. I felt like he was the person I was looking for all my life," Glazbrook said. "But he was already involved with one or two other people, and that was frustrating for me." In June 1969, the Stonewall Riots erupted when members of the New York Police Department Vice Squad Morals Division raided the

Stonewall Inn, a gay bar located a few blocks from Glazbrook's apartment. On the night the first riot broke out, Ed and Skip had taken a trip out of town and were at an inn on the Hudson River. They soon heard about the riots. "We did feel this liberation," Ed said.

Skip's banking career flourished at Chase. He was named a vice president of international banking in 1965, with responsibilities for special projects that included acquiring banks in many other countries. In 1969, for instance, he traveled to London for discussions Chase held with two British banks about forming a new international bank.[27]

As Skip continued to advance in his banking career, Bobby became increasingly weak and senile. Patricia Warner often took the lead in caring for him, and she arranged for him to move to a nursing home in Concord. As Bobby's dementia worsened in 1974, Dr. Henry Vaillant, an internist who served the facility, sought to work with the old soldier's fading memory. He had Bobby's room decorated to look like a World War I military tent, complete with a field telephone, and hired a recently released psychiatric patient named Arthur to role-play with "General Cutler." Bobby was only a military policeman in World War I, but his fading mind evidently overlooked such details, and he soon fell into an imaginary world. "He often believed that Arthur was his aide de camp, and he gave him orders and directions of one kind or another, which Arthur would carry out with unvarying kindness," Vaillant said. Bobby died quietly on May 8, 1974, at the age of seventy-eight.

The Cutler family arranged a memorial service at the Cathedral Church of St. Paul, the historic Episcopalian cathedral Bobby loved, situated a few blocks from the Tavern Club and just across Boston Common from the Somerset Club. The memorial would, perhaps for the first and last time, bring together the disparate worlds of Bobby's life. Those attending, along with members of the Cutler family, included friends and colleagues of Bobby's own generation, such as Henry Cabot Lodge Jr. and Chan Bigelow, and many of the younger men with whom Bobby had continued to travel and socialize long after his time in government service ended, such as Skip, Steve, Gayl, and Gayl's latest boyfriend, Barry Wayne. "There were no innuendos. Everybody knew what was going on, but nothing was discussed," Wayne said.[28]

Tony Favello missed the funeral. He and a boyfriend had moved to Cape Cod to run a catering business in Provincetown. Tony later moved to New Mexico, obtained a nursing degree, and began a new career in his chosen profession. Tony said years later that Bobby's circle of close gay friends revealed a truth about Bobby's life. "He didn't drop people. He never dropped me," he said. "He had room for us all."

Obituaries in *The Boston Globe* and *New York Times* profiled Bobby as the mysterious keeper of national security secrets of the Eisenhower administration, the manager of the NSC, a raconteur, a man devoted to Harvard and Boston, and a bachelor. Chan's eulogy the following week at the Tavern was a tribute that made no mention of their close bond but instead sketched Bobby's professional career and noted his dedication to hard work.

Bobby's steadfast refusal to leak secrets to the press led to a posthumous attack from Joe Alsop. After the Eisenhower administration, Alsop continued his prominent career as a columnist through the Kennedy, Johnson, and Nixon administrations, although his fierce support of the Vietnam War would tatter his reputation in later years. In his memoir, *"I've Seen the Best of It,"* published in 1992, three years after his death, Alsop recounted the story about Avis Bohlen knocking over the tea table to avert conflict between her husband and Bobby, including the barb that Bobby "brought with him from Boston a well-established reputation for what the eminent English historian Edward Gibbon called 'incorrect tastes in love.'"[29] He continued, "There may have been something to this, for when he died Bobby left a large part of his fortune to his ever-loyal personal masseur." This appeared to be a reference to Bill Sullivan, with the false claim that Bobby left him "a large part of his fortune." He had in fact given the house to Ruth, and had done so more than a decade before his death. Beyond such quibbles, the charge of "incorrect tastes in love" was Alsop's final attack on Bobby. Alsop himself had married a Washington socialite in 1961 and divorced her in 1975; his stepson said Alsop admitted he was gay to his wife, was insecure about homosexuality, and "would make caustic jokes about gay men."[30] Tellingly, in his nearly five-hundred-page memoir, Alsop made no mention of his own homosexuality or the Soviet intelligence sting that targeted him in Moscow. In fact, Alsop's memoir exposed just one person as gay — Bobby. Bobby's life choices, which differed sharply from Alsop's, may have inspired the journalist's enmity. Bobby had rejected the path of a marriage of convenience, and instead chose to live life as a bachelor — as difficult as that might be — seeking love as he must.

After the gay liberation movement grew in the 1970s, the AIDS epidemic took its toll in the 1980s and '90s. "The unprotected sex we were having backfired on us. Skip and I lost so many friends, countless friends, to AIDS," Ed Glazbrook said.[31] One of those was Xavier Fourcade, Skip's friend from Paris, who had moved to New York after receiving visa help from Bobby and opened an art gallery that became prominent. Fourcade died in 1987. Another was Gayl, who died of complications from AIDS in 1994. Gayl had founded a marketing company and two small hotels, one near New York's Meatpacking District and another in Key West, Florida. In later years of his life, he reconnected with the tiny hometown he had left in the 1950s, Castlewood, South Dakota, and upon his death he bequeathed $1.8 million to its historical society.

Skip continued working in Chase Manhattan's international division on projects around the globe. He retired from the bank at sixty-two in 1988. A few years later, when David Rockefeller was preparing his memiors, he asked Skip to share his recollections about the bank's international expansion. Rockefeller later wrote Skip a thank-you letter, saying, "It was great fun spending time with you and reminiscing about the many experiences we shared over our years together at the Chase."[32] Skip, who smoked for decades, suffered a pulmonary embolism in 1999 and later was diagnosed with emphysema. With his health declining, he sold a house he owned on the Greek island of Samos. He and Ed Glazbrook moved in together in Skip's house in East Hampton, partly so Ed could care for him. "It was wonderful living together finally, under one roof, full-time," Ed said. After a protracted struggle with emphysema, Skip died on July 7, 2005.

Skip's death left Steve Benedict as the last man standing among the original close group of Bobby's friends in the Eisenhower years. Steve spent fifteen years with the Rockefeller Brothers Fund, where his work as program officer for the arts included supporting a wide range of organizations and projects, especially in minority communities. In 1963, he helped found the Theatre Development Fund, a New York nonprofit that supports the performing arts through a discount ticket program, and he served as the fund's president twice in his forty-three years of involvement with the organization. After working for the National Endowment for the Arts, in 1979 Steve founded the Master's Program in Arts Administration at Columbia University, which he went on to direct for ten years. He also helped create — and served for many years as president of — the Center for International Theatre Research, which supported the experimental theater of the British director Peter Brook. Steve worked closely with Brook on his group's trips to Iran, West Africa, and the United States. Steve also maintained connections with Eisenhower administration colleagues, and in October 2017, at the age of ninety, he was a featured speaker at the Eisenhower Foundation's gala honoring the 1952 election campaign.

After Skip's death in 2005, Steve, whom Skip had named executor of his estate, began the painstaking task of sorting through his voluminous personal records, which included many of Bobby's documents. Steve sent about twenty thousand pages of documents, photographs, and other items to the Robert Cutler Papers at the Eisenhower Library in Abilene, Kansas. In the office of Skip's townhouse, Steve discovered Bobby's six-volume diary — more than 163,000 words on 725 pages — safely stowed in the leather carrying case Bobby had made for it. He also found more than six hundred letters, telegrams, and postcards — nearly two thousand pages of correspondence in all — between Bobby and Skip.

Among them was a letter Skip handed Bobby in 1967, in Florida, after he had read the diaries. In it, he said:

> . . . I can only feel the greatest humility, and sense of marvel, before your love and affection. Indeed, it was marvelous, a beautiful thing.
>
> And yet . . . a passionate type of love, which, indeed I could never satisfy in your terms.[33]

Bobby experienced deep anguish because of his unrequited love for Skip, yet there is no sign that emotional turmoil ever impeded his performance of the patriotic duties that he embraced throughout his life, from his youth through both world wars and beyond. Bobby persevered in his service to the country at a time when anti-gay investigators were in the ascendant, the love of his life spurned him, and Bobby's own questions about his sexual orientation were profound. Serving Ike, the president whom he exalted, Bobby reformed the NSC, set a high standard for performance in the national security advisor post he created, and helped guide the country through the challenges of the Cold War.

ACKNOWLEDGMENTS

I wish to thank many people for their assistance with this book. First among them is Stephen Benedict, a close friend of Robert Cutler, who made this book possible through his tireless support of my research efforts, his remarkably accurate memory and his willingness to share papers from his personal archive of materials relating to his own work in the Eisenhower Administration, Bobby's and that of Steve's former lover, Skip Koons. After Skip's death in 2005, Steve preserved a treasure trove of documents and photos from Skip's estate. When we first met in July 2008, Steve gave me Bobby's diary and a box of letters between Bobby and Skip. In the following years, as I pieced the story together, Steve supported me constantly and generously, helping me interpret the diaries, providing insights and sending me a stream of letters, documents, photographs and audiotapes. Ultimately, he gave me more than 3,000 pages of documents.

My mother, Judith Cutler Shinkle, and her sister Patricia Cutler Warner were among many Cutler family members who supported and, in some cases, provided interviews for this project, as did Laura Cutler, John Cutler, and Mary Cutler Buell. Similarly several of my first cousins provided reminiscences and pertinent information – Robert Fowler, brothers Richard and J. Winthrop Aldrich, and brothers Christopher, Nicholas, and Joshua Warner. My cousins J. Winthrop Aldrich and Robert Fowler read and provided helpful comments on the manuscript. Special thanks go to my cousin Rosalind Aldrich Michahelles, who provided family history information, helpful connections, and food and housing when I visited Boston for research purposes.

I also was aided by Alistair Horne, who became a beloved member of our family when my mother's family took him in as a bundle from Britain during World War Two. Uncle Alistair, as my generation called him, mentioned Bobby as a member of Ike's inner circle in his second book, *The Land is Bright*, published in 1958. After going on to write highly lauded histories of wars and biographies of men like Napoleon and English Prime Minister Harold Macmillan, he was knighted by the Queen in 2003. Years before his death in 2017, Uncle Alistair encouraged my research and sent me a letter of Bobby's. He also helpfully pushed me to address one question: did Bobby's being gay really matter? Did it cause a war, avert a war or determine a national policy? Ultimately, I concluded the question cannot be answered with certainty. Some observers might argue Bobby's homosexuality shaped how he handled the NSC or that it led him to resign in 1955. I wondered whether Bobby might have objected to the effective ban on "sexual perversion" in Ike's Executive Order 10450 if he were not trailed by rumors of his own homosexuality. Ultimately, however, there is no clear evidence that his being gay affected Bobby's performance of his governmental duties.

Harry Lodge, the son of Henry Cabot Lodge Jr., provided valuable insights into Bobby's character and also introduced me to the world of Boston's Tavern Club. Harry and two other members, Christopher Smallhorn and Carol Bundy, daughter of William Bundy, helped me understand the club's unique history and culture at a lunch they graciously hosted for me in the fall of 2015. The club generously dredged from its aged file cabinets copies of Bobby's plays, which he performed in the 1930s on the club's stage.

Avis Bohlen kindly commented on the chapter concerning her father's appointment as US ambassador to Moscow.

Two women, Barbara Cates and Lynne Willett Knox, searched through their family documents to help me piece together the story of how their fathers, Will Cates and Ed Willett, both friends of Skip's, threw a USIS investigator off Skip's trail during the anti-homosexual investigation under Executive Order 10450 that targeted Skip and Steve in 1958.

Ed Glazbrook, Skip Koons' lover in later years, provided me with documents and photos. Ed's support has been a testament of his enduring love for Skip.

A number of historians have provided helpful reviews of the manuscript and other aid. Jeffrey Frank shared with me copies of correspondence between Joseph Alsop and Bobby. Gregg Herken provided helpful comments as well as insights on an FBI memo relating to Oppenheimer and Bobby. Michael Birkner, former member of the Eisenhower Institute at Gettysburg College, provided extraordinary assistance by commenting at length on the manuscript. David Nichols and Kai Bird also provided insightful comments. R. Eugene Parta, my former boss at Radio Free Europe/Radio Liberty who has written about the history of American broadcasting to the USSR, kindly read the chapters concerning Skip's work at AMCOMLIB. To receive such kind assistance from so many historians has been an honor. Any errors remaining in the book are entirely my own, of course.

This project benefited from the excellent work of the staff of the Eisenhower Presidential Library, including deputy director Timothy Rives and archivists Michelle Kopfer, Jim Leyerzapf and David Haight. Time and again over the past seven years, Michelle Kopfer provided prompt and detailed answers to my questions, and courteously handled my numerous requests for declassification of documents. I was also impressed by the professionalism and assistance of archivists at the Columbia University Libraries, Harry Truman Presidential Library, Harvard University Archives, Herbert Hoover Presidential Library, John F. Kennedy Presidential Library, Library of Congress, Massachusetts Historical Society and Yale University Library. The staff at the National Archives and Records Administration in College Park, Maryland, and in particular supervisory archivist Onaona Guay, provided remarkable assistance.

My agent Jacques de Spoelberch offered sound advice on the shape of this story and, even after many publishers declined the project, remained a strong advocate.

Chip Fleischer, publisher of Steerforth Press, and Tom Powers, an excellent historian and co-founder of Steerforth, embraced this project and provided commentary with depth. Chip's incisive editing improved this book tremendously.

My lifelong friend Clark Russell, a gifted artist with a passion for history, gladly dove into helpful discussions of the Eisenhower era.

Finally, I am endlessly grateful to my wife Meg, son Amos and daughter Rosalind, who abided and encouraged my borrowing of family time to work on this book over the past decade. Meg also read the manuscript and made very helpful comments. Truly, their love and support made this book possible.

NOTES

ABBREVIATIONS USED IN THE NOTES

CCOH   Columbia Center for Oral History, Columbia University, New York City

CIAFRR   Central Intelligence Agency FOIA Reading Room, the online location for documents the CIA has released in response to requests under the Freedom of Information Act, located at https://www.cia.gov/library/readingroom.

DNSA   Digital National Security Archive, a private not-for-profit research institute and library, Washington, DC.

EL   Dwight D. Eisenhower Presidential Library, Abilene, Kansas.

EPP   Eisenhower's Papers as President at the Dwight D. Eisenhower Presidential Library, Abilene, Kansas

FBIFRR   Federal Bureau of Investigation FOIA Reading Room, https://vault.fbi.gov.

FOIA   Freedom of Information Act.

FRUS   *Foreign Relations of the United States*, a publication series of records of the US Department of State.

MFC   Dwight D. Eisenhower, *Mandate for Change, 1953–1956: The White House Years* (Doubleday, 1963).

MHS   Massachusetts Historical Society, Boston, Massachusetts.

NARA   National Archives and Records Administration, College Park, Maryland.

NSC   National Security Council.

NTFR   Robert Cutler, *No Time for Rest* (Little, Brown, 1967).

NYT   *New York Times.*

OSANSA Office of the Special Assistant for National Security Affairs.

RCD   Robert Cutler Diaries, 6 vols., provided by Stephen G. Benedict to the author.

SGBD   Documents, letters, sound recordings, photographs, and other items provided by Stephen G. Benedict to the author.

PREFACE

1 See Fred I. Greenstein, *The Hidden-Hand Presidency: Eisenhower as Leader* (Basic Books, 1982), 124–38.

1. BOSTONIAN REPUBLICANS

1 Robert Cutler, *Whereof We Are Made* (Stinehour Press, 1965), 22–26.

2 NTFR, 25–27.

3 Ibid., 30–33.

4 Ibid., 117.

5 Ibid., 69.

6 Ibid., 69–70. Pavlova gave a series of performances at the Boston Grand Opera from 1914 to 1917.

7 Ibid., 31.

8 The Fish family traced its lineage to Peter Stuyvesant, the last Dutch governor of New York.

9 NTFR, 54.

10 The closeness of Wister's friendship with Roosevelt was revealed in the author's handling of his story "Balaam and Pedro," which had drawn objections from Roosevelt shortly after its publication in

1894. The story, which makes reference to the biblical tale of Balaam's ass, describes the cruel treatment that a cowboy named Balaam inflicts upon his horse, Pedro. Balaam uses his hand to gouge out the horse's eye, then shoots it in the leg carelessly, then shoots it in the head to kill it. Wister often visited the White House at length during Roosevelt's presidency, and the men exchanged views on all manner of subjects. Wister visited the White House at the time he was drawing together "Balaam and Pedro" and other stories, blending them with new writing to create *The Virginian*. When President Roosevelt told him that he still objected to the story, Wister redacted it to remove Balaam's plucking out of Pedro's eye. He dedicated the novel to Roosevelt, noting: "Some of these pages you have seen, some you have praised, one stands new-written because you blamed it; and all, my dear critic, beg leave to remind you of their author's changeless admiration."

11 NTFR, 59.

12 Robert Cutler, *Commencement in 1916*, (Stinehour Press, 1966), 7

13 Douglass Shand-Tucci, *The Crimson Letter: Harvard, Homosexuality, and the Shaping of American Culture* (St. Martin's Press, 2003), 109–10.

14 Susan Cheever, *E. E. Cummings: A Life* (Pantheon, 2014), describes the poet's homosexual feelings toward his Harvard friends on page 34 and elsewhere, and recounts the poet's speech citing Amy Lowell on pages 38–39.

15 NTFR, 31–32.

16 Robert Cutler, "And the Flood Was Forty Days Upon the Earth," *The Nation*, February 1, 1917.

17 This letter and others by Cutler to Wister are in the Owen Wister Papers, Box 17, Library of Congress Manuscript Division. By May 1918, Bobby was assigned to the 302nd Infantry and still stationed at Fort Devens. His brothers John and Elliott were both in Europe in the army, with Roger set to go by June 1 and George set to depart a month later. Bobby, meanwhile, had spent time as an aide-de-camp to a brigadier general. "But I soon found the job with no action attached as pleasant and 'clubby' as one might wish for but not the kind of job that a young man who wants the Kaiser dead, Germany kerwalloped, and the war over is looking for. 'Cushy' it would have been on the other side, too, and that would have been unconscionable there with the blood of so many dear, brave young friends being poured out daily in the trenches behind which at a safe distance with your general you sipped vin de pays. No, I couldn't bear it. So I asked him to let me go back into the line and he, a perfect old trump! — said he understood, and gave permission and now I am in the thick of company duties again."

18 NTFR, 54.

2. BACHELOR

1 Geoffrey Palmer and Noel Lloyd, *E. F. Benson: As He Was* (G2 Entertainment, 2013), 32.

2 Neil McKenna, *The Secret Life of Oscar Wilde: An Intimate Biography* (Basic Books, 2005), 276–77.

3 Palmer and Lloyd, *E. F. Benson*, 63.

4 E. F. Benson, *Queen Lucia* (Watchmaker Publishing, 2010), 31.

5 Cutler letter to his father, July 12, 1921, Box 1, Series I: Early Life, Robert Cutler Papers, EL.

6 Cutler letter to his father, August 11, 1921, Box 1, Series I: Early Life, Robert Cutler Papers, EL.

7 Michael Rocke, *Forbidden Friendships: Homosexuality and Male Culture in Renaissance Florence* (Oxford University Press, 1996), 94–111.

8 In the fall of 2015, the Tavern Club, under leadership of its secretary at the time, Christopher Smallhorn, invited the author to visit the clubhouse, offered insights into the club's history, and provided access to some of Bobby Cutler's plays. Many of the club's records, including Cutler's member file, are preserved at the MHS.

9 NTFR, 72.

10 Owen Wister, *Watch Your Thirst: A Dry Opera in Three Acts* (Macmillan, 1923).

11 *Beyond the Behind*, a play by Robert Cutler, Tavern Club archives.

12 NTFR, 106.

13 *England Expects Every Man to Do His Duty*, a play by Robert Cutler, Tavern Club archives.

14 Douglass Shand-Tucci, *The Crimson Letter: Harvard, Homosexuality, and the Shaping of American Culture* (St. Martin's Press, 2003), 281.

15 Richard Norton Smith, *The Harvard Century: The Making of a University to a Nation* (Simon & Schuster, 1986), 85.

16 Amit R. Paley, "The Secret Court of 1920," *Harvard Crimson*, November 21, 2002; see also William Wright, *Harvard's Secret Court: The Savage 1920 Purge of Campus Homosexuals* (St. Martin's Press, 2005), passim. As it happened, the professor who recommended Bobby Cutler for a post in the army, Chester N. Greenough, was an acting dean in 1920 and served as a chief investigator and prosecutor in the court's pursuit of the homosexuals at Harvard.

17 The photo is reproduced in William J. Miller, *Henry Cabot Lodge: A Biography* (Heineman, 1967).

18 Shand-Tucci, *Crimson Letter*, 149–55.

19 The anonymous valentine is from Robert Cutler member folder, Tavern Club Records, MHS.

20 Ellen P. Cabot, *Changing Times*, a privately published memoir, 10.

21 The photo album is among Cutler family documents released to the author by EL.

22 Cabot, *Changing Times*, 10.

23 NTFR, 121. While NTFR does not mention Nell by name, Bobby mentions her by name repeatedly in his later diary and letters with Skip Koons.

24 NTFR, 120.

25 Miller, *Henry Cabot Lodge*, 119–21.

26 Ibid., 126.

27 See Jack Beatty, *The Rascal King: The Life and Times of James Michael Curley (1874–1958)* (Da Capo Press, 1992), passim.

28 Cutler letter to Lodge, December 3, 1935, Henry Cabot Lodge Papers, MHS.

29 Undated letter of Cutler to Lodge, Henry Cabot Lodge Papers, MHS.

30 NTFR, 134.

31 Lodge letter to Cutler, February 16, 1939, Henry Cabot Lodge Papers, MHS.

32 NTFR, 133–35.

33 Famous Cutler Brothers Relax in Mountains, Boston Sunday Globe, October 27, 1940.

34 NTFR, 140–144.

3. WARTIME

1 In NTFR, Bobby obscured who called him to urge him to work for the War Department, saying only on page 147 that he responded to the caller by saying, "All right, Charlie." This was apparently a ploy by Bobby to mask the name of the caller, likely Harvey Bundy, a Boston Republican who was a friend of Bobby's and who became his immediate supervisor in the War Department. "During my law and banking years in Boston, Harvey Bundy (a senior partner in Choate, Hall & Stewart) was a personal friend of mine; in Washington, he took a kind interest in my work and first introduced me among 'the whales,'" Bobby wrote on page 150. At the time Cutler's autobiography was published, in 1965, Bundy's son, McGeorge Bundy, was the special assistant for national security to President Johnson. McGeorge Bundy also had helped Stimson write his postwar memoirs, and had served as a dean at Harvard. In writing his autobiography, Bobby might have obscured Harvey Bundy's role in hiring Bobby in 1942 out of concern that it would create an impression that there was a Boston cabal, with a Harvard pedigree, controlling national security policy for most of the period from 1953 to 1966.

2 NTFR, 150.

3 Davis letter to Cutler, August 21, 1942, Box 3, War and Defense Departments, Robert Cutler Papers, EL.

4 NTFR, 153.

5 Ibid., 155.

6 Soldier Vote Seen Aiding Democrats, NYT, June 30, 1943, 22.

7 NTFR, 164–66.

8 Ibid, 167.

9 Ibid, 169.

10 *Congressional Record—House*, November 29, 1943, 10091.

11 *Congressional Record—Senate*, December 3, 1943, 10281.

12 Ibid, 10289.

13 Ibid., 10290.

14 Senators Clash on Soldier Vote, NYT, December 8, 1943, 1.

15 *Congressional Record—House*, February 2, 1944, 1087.

16 Ibid., January 10, 1944, 14.

17 Text of the President's Message on Servicemen's Voting, NYT, January 27, 1944, 13.

18 Republicans Back Vote Bill Changes Amid Warm Debate, NYT, January 28, 1944, 1.

19 NTFR, 170.

20 *Congressional Record—House*, January 28, 1944, 895.

21 Soldier Vote Message and Digest of Law, NYT, April 1, 1943, 9.

22 NTFR, 172–174.

23 Ibid., 180–81.

24 Adieu to the Taft Amendment (opinion), NYT, August 16, 1944, 18.

25 NTFR, 181–82.

26 Henry L. Stimson and McGeorge Bundy, *On Active Service in Peace and War* (Harper & Brothers, 1948), 340.

27 NTFR, 213–16.

28 In *No Time for Rest*, Bobby identifies the trainee by the pseudonym Jim. However, the committee's attorney, Ralph Burton, presented a report to the committee in July 1945 listing Lash among the suspected subversive soldiers, and the profile of "Jim" as a friend of the First Lady is the only one that matches Lash's. See *Hearings Before the Special Committee on Subversive Influences in the Army of the Committee on Military Affairs, House of Representatives*, 79th Cong., 1st sess., July 18, 1945 (Government Printing Office, 1945). Lash had testified to Congress in 1942 that he had been a Socialist prior to the war. In that year, he also became a friend of the First Lady. After the war, he cofounded the organization Americans for Democratic Action with Mrs. Roosevelt and went on to a career as a journalist at the *New York Post* before writing *Eleanor and Franklin*, a widely read biography of the First Lady and President Roosevelt.

29 NTFR, 230–31.

30 Ibid., 241.

31 Ibid., 222.

4. FROM OLD COLONY TO PSYCHOLOGICAL WARFARE

1 T. Jefferson Coolidge Jr. was an early investor in telegraph and telephone businesses, including American Telephone & Telegraph. Calvin Coolidge, who served twice as governor of Massachusetts before becoming US president in 1923, was not a family relation.

2 Ben Ames Williams Jr., *Bank of Boston 200: A History of New England's Leading Bank 1784–1984* (Houghton Mifflin, 1984), 261.

3 Ibid., 380.

4 Author interview of Patricia Cutler Warner, daughter of Bobby's brother John Cutler and his wife, Rosalind Fish Cutler, March 11, 2012. Patricia Cutler Warner is the author's aunt. She said that she learned of the phrase used to describe Bobby's office from her husband, Charles Warner, who worked at the bank during Bobby's tenure.

5 Letter from Henry Cabot Lodge Jr. to Robert Cutler, October 10, 1946, MHS.

6 Republicans Poll Big Bay State Vote, NYT, November 7, 1946, 6.

7 Cutler letter to Lodge, March 17, 1947, Lodge Papers, MHS.

8 Judith Cutler married Jackson J. Shinkle in October 1947. They are the author's parents. She died in 2011, five years after the author began working on this biography of Robert Cutler. (Author's note: My mother on one occasion late in her life expressed disdain for Bobby because of his sexual orientation. After my mother's death, I discovered this June 1947 letter from Uncle Bobby to her among documents in her office. Its presence there posed a riddle: Did she truly disdain him as she claimed, or did she in fact admire him but struggle with how to cope with his sexual orientation? Why exactly did she keep the letter for more than six decades? These questions appear unanswerable.)

9 The name Galatea, for the sculpture-turned-woman, did not appear in Ovid's recounting; it arose only in versions of the story that became popular in Europe after the Renaissance. The story of Pygmalion and his sculpture was widely reinterpreted in art and literature, perhaps most famously in George Bernard Shaw's 1912 play *Pygmalion*, which itself was reinterpreted in the musical *My Fair Lady*.

10 Lodge interview with author, December 8, 2007.

11 RCD, vol. 3, entry of May 3, 1959.

12 Author interview of Maura Sullivan Dudley, October 10, 2009.

13 Author interview of Robert C. Sullivan, November 8, 2009.

14 Dr. Cutler Is Dead; Boston Surgeon, 59, NYT, August 17, 1947, 52.

15 Robert M. Zollinger, MD, *Elliott Carr Cutler and the Cloning of Surgeons* (Futura Pub, 1988), 176–77.

16 NTFR, 122.

17 Gore Vidal, *The City and the Pillar* (E. P. Dutton, 1948), 246. Novels featuring lesbian characters also appeared, including Patricia Highsmith's *The Price of Salt*, published in 1952.

18 Alfred C. Kinsey, Wardell B. Pomeroy, and Clyde E. Martin, *Sexual Behavior in the Human Male* (W. B. Saunders, 1948), 639.

19 NTFR, 243.

20 Ibid., 243.

21 Ibid., 247.

22 Steven Leonard Newman, "The Oppenheimer Case: A Reconsideration of the Role of the Defense Department and National Security" (PhD diss., Department of History, New York University, 1977), 31–34.

23 NTFR, 253.

24 Ibid., 256.

25 Ibid., 258.

26 Douglas T. Stuart, *Creating the National Security State: A History of the Law That Transformed America* (Princeton University Press, 2008), 188–202.

27 Townsend Hoopes and Douglas Brinkley, *Driven Patriot: The Life and Times of James Forrestal* (Knopf, 1992), 446–68.

28 William J. Miller, *Henry Cabot Lodge: A Biography* (Heineman, 1967), 198.

29 The agenda of the Platform Committee on June 18, 1948, Cutler Papers, Box 7, 1948 Convention, EL.

30 David M. Oshinsky, *A Conspiracy So Immense: The World of Joe McCarthy* (Free Press, 1983), 108–9.

31 David K. Johnson, *The Lavender Scare: The Cold War Persecution of Gays and Lesbians in the Federal Government* (University of Chicago Press, 2004), 16–17.

32 Westbrook Pegler, "Homosexuals in the State Department" (column), *Cincinnati Enquirer*, March 27, 1950.

33 Johnson, *Lavender Scare*, 105.

34 Ibid., 108.

35 Ibid., 109.

36 *Employment of Homosexuals and Other Sex Perverts in Government: Interim Report Submitted to the Committee on Expenditures in the Executive Departments*, 81st Cong., 2nd sess. (Government Printing Office, 1950), 4, 5, 24, 25.

37 Ibid., 5–6.

38 Hoover memo, "Re: Sex Deviates in Government Service," June 20, 1951, FBIFRR.

39 Hoover memo, "Re: Sex Deviates in United States Government Service," September 7, 1951, FBIFRR.

40 Richard Gid Powers, *Secrecy and Power: The Life of J. Edgar Hoover* (Free Press, 1987), 172.

41 Anthony Summers, *Official and Confidential: The Secret Life of J. Edgar Hoover* (Putnam, 1993), 93–94.

42 President Truman letter to James Lay, July 14, 1951, appendix of NSC 113/1, Truman Library.

43 Cutler letter to Eisenhower, October 11, 1950; Cutler list of guests at dinner November 22, 1950; Eisenhower letter to Cutler, November 29, 1950, Dwight D. Eisenhower: Papers, Pre-Presidential, 1916–52, Principal File, Box 29, EL.

44 Jerry W. Sanders, *Peddlers of Crisis: The Committee on the Present Danger and the Politics of Containment* (South End Press, 1999), 71.

45 Kai Bird and Martin J. Sherwin, *American Prometheus: The Triumph and Tragedy of J. Robert Oppenheimer* (Knopf, 2005), 418–19.

46 Cutler background report by the FBI, January 22, 1953, forwarded by Hoover to Adams at the White House, Henry R. McPhee Records, Box 17, file of Cutler, Robert, EL. The portion of the report disclosing Cutler's consulting relationship with the CIA was declassified in May 2016 after a mandatory review appeal by the author.

47 Report to the President by Gordon Gray, February 22, 1952, President Truman File, Box 3, PSB Series, 1952 (1), Gordon Gray Papers, EL.

48 One Year History of the PSB, NSC Staff Papers, PSB Central Files Series, Box 23, Background Materials for PSB (1), EL, 28.

49 John Prados, *Presidents' Secret Wars* (William Morrow, 1986), 87.

50 Sarah-Jane Corke, *US Covert Operations and Cold War Strategy: Truman, Secret Warfare and the CIA, 1945–53* (Routledge, 2008), 124–25.

51 Gregory Mitrovich, *Undermining the Kremlin: America's Strategy to Subvert the Soviet Bloc, 1947–1956* (Cornell University Press, 2000), 70.

52 Ibid.

53 Ibid., 71.

54 NTFR, 266.

5. WITH IKE TO VICTORY

1 Abilene Welcomes Eisenhower Home in Biggest Celebration in Its History, *St. Louis Post-Dispatch*, June 22, 1945, 1.

2 MFC, 7.

3 Ibid., 9.

4 Text of Eisenhower's speech, Columbia University Archives, Central Files, 1895–1971, Office of the President, Box 411.

5 Medicine: For a Sick World, *Time*, May 17, 1948.

6 Correspondence between Ginzberg and Eisenhower, Columbia University Archives, Central Files, 1895–1971, Office of the President, Box 406; Eli Ginzberg, *The Eye of Illusion* (Routledge, 1993), 49–56.

7 MFC, 16–18.

8 Ibid., 16.

9 Eisenhower Sweep Foreseen by Lodge, NYT, December 10, 1951, 24.

10 Eisenhower Says He's Deeply Moved, NYT, March 13, 1952, 1.

11 MFC, 23.

12 *Harvard Crimson*, March 22, 1952.

13 Cutler letter to Eisenhower, March 24, 1952, Dwight D. Eisenhower: Papers, Pre-Presidential, 1916–52, Box 29, Robert Cutler file, EL.

14 NTFR, 268–9.

15 Ibid, 270.

16 Ibid.

17 MFC, 45.

18 Memos by Cutler, July 1952, Lodge–Cutler Correspondence, MHS.

19 Dirksen Blasts Gov. Stevenson Over Scandals, *Chicago Tribune*, August 5, 1952, 3.

20 Adams letter to Cutler, September 8, 1952, Lodge–Cutler Correspondence, MHS.

21 NTFR, 273.

22 Top GOP Group Drops 10 Members, NYT, September 14, 1952.

23 Eisenhower Picks a 'Cold War' Chief, NYT, February 17, 1953, 16.

24 NTFR, 283–84.

25 Benedict oral history interview, September 13, 1968, 29, SGBD.

26 Benedict notes on campaign train, September 21, 1952, SGBD.

27 MFC, 60.

28 NTFR, 278.

29 Ibid., 277.

30 Benedict identified the fifth and sixth cars forward as housing the campaign staff and press corps.

31 NTFR, 275.

32 Katherine Howard oral history interview, 1971, CCOH, 419–20.

33 NTFR, 284.

34 Stephen Benedict Papers, 1952–1960, 9-19-52 Remarks on Nixon Fund, Box 1/1, Preservation, EL.

35 Ike Has Confidence in Nixon, *Kansas City Times*, September 20, 1952, 1.

36 Benedict notes on campaign train, September 25, 1952, SGBD.

37 Robert R. Bowie and Richard Immerman, *Waging Peace: How Eisenhower Shaped an Enduring Cold War Strategy* (Oxford University Press, 1998), 76.

38 Fred I. Greenstein, *The Hidden-Hand Presidency: Eisenhower as Leader* (Basic Books, 1982), 125.

39 Eisenhower speech in San Francisco, October 8, 1952, Eisenhower's Papers as President, Speech Series, Box 2, September 26 1952 to October 13 1952 (3), EL.

40 Senator Joe McCarthy, *The Story of General George Marshall* (self-published, 1952), 169.

41 Dwight D. Eisenhower, *Crusade in Europe* (Doubleday, 1948), 14–16, 50.

42 David A. Nichols, *Ike and McCarthy: Dwight Eisenhower's Secret Campaign Against Joseph McCarthy* (Simon & Schuster, 2017), 3.

43 Cutler letter to Lodge, September 17, 1952, Lodge–Cutler Correspondence, MHS.

44 Eisenhower, *Crusade in Europe*, 457–78.

45 Emmet John Hughes, *The Ordeal of Power: A Political Memoir of the Eisenhower Years* (Atheneum, 1963), 41.

46 Benedict notes from campaign train, dated October 29, but Benedict stated were properly dated September 29, SGBD.

47 Hughes, *The Ordeal of Power*, 41–42.

48 Kohler oral history interview, December 1970, CCOH, 19.

49 Eisenhower Wants Korea to Bear Brunt of Fighting, NYT, October 3, 1952, 1.

50 Sherman Adams, *First-Hand Report: The Story of the Eisenhower Administration* (Harper, 1961), 30–31.

51 Eisenhower Scores President on Reds; Supports McCarthy, NYT, October 4, 1952, 1.

52 Adams, *First-Hand Report*, 31.

53 Eisenhower Scores President on Reds, NYT, October 4, 1952, 1.

54 Kohler oral history interview, 28.

55 Adams, *First-Hand Report*, 32.
56 Stephen Benedict Papers, Box 4, 10-3-52 Milwaukee WI (1), EL.
57 Hauge oral history interview, March 1967, CCOH, 16–17.
58 Benedict notes on campaign train, October 16, 1952, SGBD.
59 Adams, *First-Hand Report*, 140.
60 NTFR, 288.
61 Eisenhower Scores President on Reds.
62 NYT, October 6, 1952.
63 Truman Declares General Betrays Moral Principles, NYT, October 8, 1952, 1.
64 Cutler letter to Lodge, October 8, 1952, Lodge-Cutler Correspondence, Lodge Papers, MHS.
65 MFC, 71–72.
66 Text of Eisenhower's Address at the Boston Common, NYT, October 22, 1952, 16.
67 Cutler letter to Eisenhower, dated November 5, 1952, 5:00 PM, and Eisenhower response, November 12, 1952, EPP, Robert Cutler 1952–1955 (5), EL.
68 MFC, 271.

6. TRANSITION

1 Jean Edward Smith, How to End a War (opinion), NYT, April 11, 2009.
2 Cutler letter to Eisenhower, EPP, Robert Cutler 1952–1955 (5), EL.
3 A group of bachelors who were early members of The Family pooled their money and bought the house from its original owner in 1914. One of The Family's early members was Willard Straight, who served as a diplomat in China and later founded *The New Republic* magazine. Others who resided at the house as bachelors included Boston mayor Andrew Peters, New York Federal Reserve Bank governor Benjamin Strong, and ambassador and undersecretary of state David Bruce. The house, a small brick building that could not accommodate more than about eight bachelors at a time, was a social hub in the earlier decades of the twentieth century, according to documents preserved by the Historical Society of Washington. The guest book shows that Nicholas and Alice Roosevelt Longworth, daughter of President Teddy Roosevelt, were guests.
4 City directories show the Lafayette Chicken Hut at 1720 H Street. For more information on the bar, which became known as simply the Chicken Hut, see David K. Johnson, *The Lavender Scare: The Cold War Persecution of Gays and Lesbians in the Federal Government* (University of Chicago Press, 2004), 163–65.
5 See Stephen Kinzer, *The Brothers: John Foster Dulles, Allen Dulles, and Their Secret World War* (Times Books, 2013), 9–22 and passim.
6 Ibid., 24–25.
7 Ibid., 49–51.
8 Ibid., 50.
9 Ibid., 51.
10 Leonard Mosley, *Dulles: A Biography of Eleanor, Allen, and John Foster Dulles and Their Family Network* (Doubleday, 1978), 96.
11 Dwight D. Eisenhower, *Crusade in Europe* (Doubleday, 1948), 36–39.
12 Transcript of Cabinet Meeting, Eisenhower's Papers as President, Cabinet Series, Box 1, Cabinet Meeting of January 12–13, 1953, 4.
13 Ibid., 23–36.
14 FBI assistant director Nichols memo to Tolson, December 9, 1952, filed in the US Supreme Court as an exhibit in the amicus curiae brief of the Mattachine Society of Washington, DC, in the case of *Obergefell v. Hodges*.
15 For Hill's background, see Douglas M. Charles, *Hoover's War on Gays: Exposing the FBI's "Sex Deviates" Program* (University Press of Kansas, 2015), 133.
16 Hoover memo to Tolson, Nichols, and Ladd, January 5, 1953, filed in the US Supreme Court as an exhibit in the amicus curiae brief of the Mattachine Society of Washington, DC, in the case of *Obergefell v. Hodges*.

17 Vandenberg memo to Adams, background file of Vandenberg, Box 71, Files of Henry R. McPhee, EL.

18 Hoover letter to Adams, January 8, 1953, Vandenberg file, Box 71, Files of Henry R. McPhee, EL. The file was declassified in 2008.

19 Grant Vandenberg Leave of Absence Because of Health, Associated Press, *Jacksonville (Illinois) Daily Journal*, January 14, 1953, 1.

20 Eisenhower letter to Vandenberg, January 17, 1953, filed in the US Supreme Court in an amicus curae brief by the Mattachine Society of Washington, DC, in the case of *Obergefell v. Hodges*.

21 Randy Shilts, *Conduct Unbecoming: Gays and Lesbians in the US Military* (St. Martin's, 1993), 107–8.

22 Allan Bérubé, *Coming Out Under Fire: The History of Gay Men and Women in World War II* (Free Press, 1990), 128–48.

23 Eli Ginzberg, *The Lost Divisions* (Columbia University Press, 1959), xvii–xviii.

24 Snyder letter to Ginzberg, December 21, 1951, Ginzberg Papers, EL.

25 Ginzberg described his friendship and collaboration with Eisenhower in his autobiography, Eli Ginzberg, *The Eye of Illusion* (Routledge, 1993), 181–95.

26 Cutler FBI background report, January 22, 1953, and Hoover letter to Adams, January 22, 1953, Henry R. McPhee Records, EL.

27 While Benedict and the other world federalist activist provided an account of their homosexual affair in an interview in 2015, they requested that the second party not be named.

7. THE GAY SPY

1 Koons biographical statement, SGBD.

2 Author interview of Benedict, October 2012. Koons letter to his mother, June 8, 1945, SGBD.

3 Koons biographical statement, SGBD.

4 Townsend Hoopes and Douglas Brinkley, *Driven Patriot: The Life and Times of James Forrestal* (Knopf, 1992), 266–68.

5 Ibid., 267.

6 Officer's Qualification Record of Koons, completed by Captain C. F. Espe, Operational Branch, Office of Naval Investigations, August 14, 1946, SGBD.

7 Souers's appointment calendars reflecting the meeting in May 1946 were released pursuant to a FOIA request by the author.

8 Koons reported to his station as "Assistant Intelligence Officer; Russian specialist," reporting to the "Commander Naval Western Forces Pacific," according to US Navy orders, SGBD.

9 Koons biographical statement, SGBD.

10 Underscoring Russia's intent to settle old accounts, the secret accord at Yalta noted that it was intended to restore the former rights of Russia "violated by the treacherous attack of Japan in 1904," a reference to Japan's stealth attack in 1904 on the tsarist Russian navy in Port Arthur, which ignited the Russo-Japanese War. In a faint nod to Chinese sovereignty, the Yalta agreement said that Roosevelt "will take measures" to win Generalissimo Chiang Kai-shek's concurrence in the agreement "on advice from Marshal Stalin." At the time, Chiang was the leader of the nationalist government in China, having at times been allied with the Communists but also having been their bitter opponent. At the time the Yalta accord was signed, the war was raging on in the Pacific, and Germany had not been vanquished. Under those circumstances, it would be a strategic blunder to reveal that Stalin was planning to shift forces to the Pacific theater, and so the Yalta accord was kept secret.

11 David M. Glantz, *The Soviet Strategic Offensive in Manchuria, 1945: 'August Storm'* (Routledge, 2003), 182–90.

12 Kennan telegram to Secretary of State James Byrnes, March 25, 1946, *FRUS 1946*, vol. 10, *The Far East: China*, 1157–58.

13 Benninghoff cable telegram to Smith, August 2, 1946, *FRUS 1946*, vol. 10, *The Far East: China*, 1179–83.

14 Marshall telegram to Acheson, October 16, 1946, *FRUS 1946*, vol. 10, *The Far East: China*, 1186–87.

15 In March 1946, senior US diplomat George Kennan warned in a telegram from Moscow to the US secretary of state James Byrnes that the Soviet commissar for foreign affairs, Vyacheslav Molotov, had told US officials that Soviet state security officials would be exercising control in Dairen. Kennan also said that the Soviets could be expected to "cut off contact between members of our consular staff and local inhabitants" and take other measures to convince the United States to abandon the consulate in Dairen. See *FRUS 1946*, vol. 10, *The Far East: China*, 1157–58. A month earlier, in February 1946, Kennan wrote Byrnes a fifty-five-hundred-word essay called "Long Telegram," which warned that the Soviet Union was driven to expand its territory and called for a policy of containment. The telegram came to the attention of navy secretary James Forrestal, for whom Koons and Willett had produced a similar analysis. When Consul Benninghoff finally was able to set up offices, the Soviets permitted him to do so in the former Yamato Hotel, now known under Soviet control as the Red Star Hotel.

16 Davis telegram to Byrnes, December 23, 1946, *FRUS 1946*, vol. 10, *The Far East: China*, 1194–96.

17 Koons's orders, December 16, 1946, SGBD.

18 Deck Log of LCI-1090, November and December 1946, Task Force Group 78.4, NARA.

19 Davis telegram to Byrnes, December 23, 1946.

20 William H. Newton, Scripps Howard correspondent, "Soviet Ultimatum Forces US Vessel to Go from Dairen," NYT, December 24, 1946, 1.

21 The intelligence report, in SGBD, continues: "The attitude of the guard officers to the ship's company was cool, and they purposely refrained from contact with the latter. When drawn into conversation, however, they appeared friendly and eager to talk. Their morale is best described as 'fair' to 'poor'; all were tired of duty in Dairen and the Far East in general and desired demobilization or duty in European Russia."

22 Koons letter to Professor Walter P. Hall, dated December, 1946, SGBD.

23 Koons draft intelligence report, undated, 13 pages, SGBD.

24 Koons email to Bill Bowring, September 27, 2000, SGBD.

25 NYT, December 24, 1946. The time of the Russian major's boarding of the ship is drawn from the Deck Logs of the LCI (L) 1090, November and December 1946, Task Force Group 78.4, NARA.

26 Davis telegram to Byrnes, December 23, 1946.

27 Newton, Soviet Ultimatum Forces US Vessel to Go from Dairen.

28 Plainfielder Says Reds Issued Ultimatum Despite US Denial, *Courier News* (Bridgewater, New Jersey), December 27, 1946, 1.

29 Editorial, NYT, January 1, 1947.

30 Why 7 is Not 8, *Time*, January 6, 1947.

31 *Life* photographer Mark Kauffman's pictures in Dairen remained in the *Life* Photo Collection, and one is reproduced in this book.

32 McCarthy speech, June 14, 1951, as reprinted in Senator Joe McCarthy, *The Story of General George Marshall* (self-published, 1952), 51.

33 John Lewis Gaddis, *George F. Kennan: An American Life* (Penguin Press, 2011), 258.

34 Intelligence Report, Central Intelligence Group, "Subject: Political Information: Sino-Russian Newspaper; Russian Emigrants Association Relations with the Paper," released by the CIA to the author in September 2015 in response to a request under FOIA. It is possible that Koons wrote this report, but portions of it remain classified and its author is not identified.

35 Bologoff letter to Koons, July 6, 1948, SGBD.

36 US Pacific Fleet orders, SGBD.

37 In February 1952, Skip wrote in a letter to Steve discussing salary options for a new position, "But on salary will put down 8,000 minimum. Hels bells [sic] I was offered two 5,000 jobs by CIA when I left Navy, and that was before I had BA even, let alone PHD's books etc." SGBD.

38 Tilghman B. Koons, "United States Foreign Policy Towards China, 1941–1949" (senior thesis, Woodrow Wilson School of Public and International Affairs, Princeton University, May 1949).

Koons noted that Marshall later testified to a congressional committee in 1947 that he could see no "concrete" evidence that the Soviets were aiding the Chinese Communists, despite such recognized facts as the Soviet forces providing captured Japanese arms to the Chinese Communists. Yet Koons also sought to balance his thesis, including a footnote in which he faulted Republicans on congressional committees for "playing politics" in their attempts to discredit the Democrats.

39 Colligan, US Department of State, letter to Koons, September 19, 1949, SGBD.

40 Benedict statement to author, November 18, 2012.

41 Stephen Benedict, "A Visit to Santayana," *St. John's Review* 48, no. 2 (2005).

42 Author interview of Benedict, July 29, 2008.

43 Vidal was very open about his interest in anonymous sex with other men, but Benedict said that Vidal never made a pass and their relationship never became sexual. "I could certainly have been seduced by him sexually in a second, but that never happened," Benedict later said in a written account to the author in November 2012.

44 Ned Rorem, *Knowing When to Stop: A Memoir* (Simon & Schuster, 1994), 288–89.

45 Thomas Larson, *The Saddest Music Ever Written: The Story of Samuel Barber's Adagio for Strings* (Pegasus Books, 2010), 90. Barber and Menotti bought a home in Mount Kisco, New York, in 1943, which they named Capricorn and became a sort of cultural center and a gathering place for gay composers and artists, some of whom were lovers of Barber or Menotti. While Barber and Menotti both took other lovers, the two men remained close friends all their lives.

46 Barber and Turner remained lovers for years and were friends until Barber's death in 1981. Turner died in 2003. The relationship between Barber and Turner is illuminated in letters between the two men contained in the Turner papers at the New York Public Library for the Performing Arts. Among the European performances, Turner played Barber's music, including the Adagio for Strings, on February 15, 1951, in Frankfurt.

47 Leonie Rosenstiel, *Nadia Boulanger: A Life in Music* (W. W. Norton, 1982), 94, 117, 121, 134–35. Paronian also was very close to Nadia Boulanger's sister, Lili Boulanger, a gifted composer and musician who died at the age of twenty-four in 1918.

48 Benedict email to the author, July 31, 2015.

49 Koons naval records, SGBD.

50 Koons letter to Benedict, dated "October 1951," SGBD.

51 Koons letter to Benedict, dated "Friday afternoon," estimated early December 1951, SGBD.

52 Koons letter to Benedict, undated but estimated November 11, 1951, due to references in letter, SGBD. All of Steve's letters to Skip from this era have disappeared, though Steve kept Skip's and so they have survived.

53 Koons letter to Benedict, December 1951, SGBD.

54 Koons letter to Benedict, January 18, 1952, SGBD.

55 Benedict statement to author, November 18, 2012.

56 Koons letter to Benedict, undated, but references suggest March 17, 1952, SGBD.

57 Frank Wisner memo, "History of Project," August 21, 1951, to CIA deputy director Allen Dulles, Wilson Center Digital Archive.

58 A. Ross Johnson, *Radio Free Europe and Radio Liberty: The CIA Years and Beyond* (Stanford University Press, 2010), 28.

59 Koons letter to Benedict, dated only "Friday, October," but its references clearly suggest 1952, SGBD.

60 Johnson, *Radio Free Europe and Radio Liberty*, 31.

8. REFORMING AND RUNNING THE NSC

1 Dwight D. Eisenhower Inaugural Address, January 20, 1953, CSPAN Archives, https://www.c-span.org/organization/?4031/Archives.

2 Eisenhower Appointment Book, January 21, 1953, Eisenhower Foundation, http://www.dwightdeisenhower.com/209/Appointment-Books.

3 Cutler's term on the Harvard Board of Overseers was 1950–56, while Alsop's was 1951–57, according to the Harvard University Archives.

4 NTFR, 317–20.

5 Joseph W. Alsop with Adam Platt, *"I've Seen the Best of It": Memoirs* (W. W. Norton, 1992), 58, 60, 391, 392, 379, 380.

6 Alsop letters to Cutler, February 12, 1953, and Cutler letter to Alsop, February 16, 1953, Joseph Alsop Papers, Box 8, Library of Congress.

7 NTFR, 318–19.

8 Hoover letter to Cutler, January 28, 1953, and Cutler letter to Hoover, January 30, 1953, released by the FBI in response to an author FOIA request.

9 Minutes of the 129th Meeting of the NSC, January 29, 1953, microfilm, Minutes of the Meetings of the National Security Council, University Publications of America.

10 Peter Grose, *Gentleman Spy: The Life of Allen Dulles* (Houghton Mifflin, 1994), 335.

11 Stephen Kinzer, *The Brothers: John Foster Dulles, Allen Dulles, and Their Secret World War* (Times Books, 2013), 89.

12 See for instance, David Eisenhower, *Eisenhower at War 1943–1945* (Random House, 1986), 160–61.

13 Eisenhower letter to Cooke, February 18, 1953, in Louis Galambos (ed.), *The Papers of Dwight David Eisenhower*, vol. 14 (Johns Hopkins University Press, 1970), 54.

14 NTFR, 320–21.

15 Memorandum of Discussion, 135th Meeting of the NSC, March 4, 1953, Eisenhower's Papers as President, NSC Series, Box 6, EL.

16 NTFR, 320–22.

17 Cutler memo for the president, March 16, 1953, and Report of Recommendations Relative to the NSC, March 16, 1953, p. 7, Papers of the OSANSA, NSC Series, Administrative Subseries, Box 6, NSC — Organization Functions (7), EL.

18 S. Nelson Drew (ed.), *NSC-68: Forging the Strategy of Containment* (National Defense University, 1996), 22.

19 Ibid.

20 NTFR, 300.

21 Report of Recommendations Relative to the NSC, by Robert Cutler, March 16, 1953, p. 7, OSANSA Papers, NSC Series, Administrative Subseries, Box 6, NSC — Organization Functions (7), EL.

22 Eisenhower letter to Cutler, March 17, 1953, OSANSA Papers, NSC Series, Administrative Subseries, Box 6, NSC — Organization and Functions (7), EL.

23 *Time*, April 6, 1953.

24 Benedict memo to Cutler, April 2, 1953, SGBD.

25 Benedict letter to Koons, April 4, 1953, SGBD.

26 Benedict memo to Cutler, April 6, 1953, SGBD.

27 Cutler cabled Koons on May 1, 1953, saying that he "will expect you to report for work as near May Eleventh as possible have cleared with Stevens." SGBD.

28 The Eisenhower Presidential Library has no record of a background report for Koons. The library does have an NSC routing slip that mentions a Koons personnel file at CIA, but it makes no mention of a background report. Portions of the memo were classified for approximately sixty years. After an appeal by the author, the CIA agreed in December 2014 to declassify the portion of the memo that said, "One is in your personnel file at CIA, and . . ."

29 NTFR, 308.

30 Ibid., 308–9.

31 Ibid., 309.

32 Dwight D. Eisenhower and Robert H. Ferrell (ed.), *The Eisenhower Diaries* (W. W. Norton, 1976), 237.

33 Cutler memo, *FRUS 1952–1954*, vol. 2, 323.

34 James Doolittle sent Cutler a letter on June 1, 1953, commending Koons for his "outstanding cooperation" and his "courtesy, efficiency, and constant availability" in his work with Operation Solarium. By that time, Koons had been in his new post at the White House for less than a month.

35 Cutler undated notes on "Paul Nitze," and letter of Nitze to Wilson, June 20, 1953, NSC Series, Administrative Subseries, Box 7, Planning Board-Org. and Personnel, March 1953–December 1959, EL.

36 Top-secret memo by Cutler, July 16, 1953, *FRUS 1952–1954*, vol. 2, 397–98.

37 NSC 162/2, *FRUS 1952–1954*, vol. 2., *National Security Affairs*, 577–97.

38 Saki Dockrill, *Eisenhower's New-Look National Security Policy, 1953–61* (Macmillan, 1996), 19–42.

9. IKE'S PECULIAR BAN ON GAYS

1 Text of Eisenhower's State of the Union Message on New Domestic and Foreign Policies, NYT, February 3, 1953, 14.

2 Brownell letter to Eisenhower, January 20, 1953, draft executive order, undated; and draft news release, undated, US Department of Justice records, Records Group 60, Box 530, File 146-200-2-04 Section 2B, NARA.

3 NSC 113/1, May 2, 1952, RG 273, NSC Policy Papers, Box 15, NARA.

4 Cutler letter to Eisenhower, January 21, 1953, NSC Series, Administrative Subseries, Box 7, Personnel-Security Programs [March 1953–May 1956] (1), EL.

5 Eisenhower's memo of January 21, 1953, to Brownell, at the EL, bears Cutler's initials and includes, in Cutler's handwriting, the notation, "Given to Brownell at 8:30 PM Jan 21/53." The memo is found in NSC Series, Administrative Subseries, Box 7, Personnel-Security Programs [March 1953–May 1956] (1), EL.

6 David K. Johnson, *The Lavender Scare: The Cold War Persecution of Gays and Lesbians in the Federal Government* (University of Chicago Press, 2004), 125.

7 Ibid., 125.

8 Memo on Creation of a Combination Government Official Plus Private Citizen Advisory Committee, by Rockefeller Committee, January 10, 1953; memo by Milt Hill to General Persons, January 12, 1953, Eisenhower's Records as President, Official File, Box 414, Folder: OF-104-J Security and Loyalty Program of Government Employees 1952–53 (1), EL.

9 Hoover memos of January 23, February 4, February 11, February 26, March 18, April 6, and April 10, 1953, US Department of Justice records, Records Group 60, Box 530, File 146-200-2-04 Section 2B, NARA.

10 Eisenhower letter to Vandenberg, March 3, 1953, filed in the US Supreme Court as an exhibit in the amicus curiae brief of the Mattachine Society of Washington, DC, in the case of *Obergefell v. Hodges*.

11 MFC, 212.

12 Douglas M. Charles, *Hoover's War on Gays: Exposing the FBI's "Sex Deviates" Program* (University Press of Kansas, 2015), 121.

13 Ibid., 98–100.

14 FBI memo on Bohlen by Ladd to Rosen, March 16, 1953, J. Edgar Hoover's Official and Confidential file on Bohlen, NARA.

15 Robert D. Dean, *Imperial Brotherhood: Gender and the Making of Cold War Foreign Policy* (University of Massachusetts Press, 2001), 98.

16 Charles, *Hoover's War on Gays*, 123.

17 FBI report on Offie, February 11, 1953, White House Office, OSANSA, Records: 1952–61, FBI Series, Box 3, FBI O-R (1), EL, 3.

18 Memorandum of Conversation with the President, by John Foster Dulles, March 16, 1953, John Foster Dulles Papers, JFD Chronological Series, Box 1, Chronological — JFD March 1–17, 1953 (1), EL.

19 FBI to J. Edgar Hoover from L. B. Nichols, March 16, 1954, The J. Edgar Hoover Official and Confidential File, microfilm, Charles Bohlen, Reel 11, University Publications of America.

20 J. Edgar Hoover memo to Tolson, Ladd, and Nichols, March 18, 1953, The J. Edgar Hoover Official and Confidential File, microfilm, Joseph McCarthy, Reel 15, University Publications of America.

21 Charles E. Bohlen, *Witness to History: 1929–1969* (W. W. Norton, 1973), 324.

22 Dean, *Imperial Brotherhood*, 130.

23 Ibid., 131.

24 MFC, 213.

25 Dean, *Imperial Brotherhood*, 133.

26 Joseph W. Alsop with Adam Platt, *"I've Seen the Best of It": Memoirs* (W. W. Norton, 1992), 349–50.

27 Top-secret memo of Richard Helms to CIA director Allen Dulles regarding "Attached FBI Report," March 27, 1953, CIAFRR.

28 "Thayer Resigns Munich Post in Screening Protest," *Sandusky (Ohio) Register*, March 26, 1953.

29 John Foster Dulles Papers, Telephone Conversation Series, Box 10, White House Telephone Conversations January to April 1953, EL. This quote corrects an inversion of two words in the original phrase, which reads, ". . . until we all have of these clearances . . ."

30 MFC, 309.

31 Cutler memo of March 9, 1953, released by NARA in response to a FOIA request by the author.

32 New Security Plan Issued; Thousands Face Re-Inquiry, NYT, April 28, 1953, 1.

33 Memorandum of Discussion, 141st Meeting of the NSC on Tuesday, April 28, 1953, Eisenhower's Papers as President, NSC Series, Box 4, EL, 13–14.

34 David M. Oshinsky, *A Conspiracy So Immense: The World of Joe McCarthy* (Free Press, 1983), 117.

35 Discussion at the 141st Meeting of the NSC on Tuesday, April 28, 1953, Eisenhower's Papers as President, NSC Series, Box 4, EL, 14.

36 Ibid., attached Cutler memo re Senator McCarthy, April 30, 1953.

37 Letter of Deputy Attorney General William P. Rogers to National Gallery of Art acting president F. L. Belin, US Department of Justice records, Records Group 60, Box 530, File 146-200-2-04 Section 11, NARA.

38 Civil Service Commission chairman Philip Young report to the National Security Council, October 21, 1953, Record Group 59, Department of State, Bureau of Security and Consular Affairs, Lot Files 62-D-146, Decimal Files 1953-60, Box 13, File EO 10450, Employee Security Program, I-E/3.1, NARA.

39 Benedict statement to the author, September 8, 2016.

10. THE PASSION OF OPPENHEIMER

1 Kai Bird and Martin J. Sherwin, *American Prometheus: The Triumph and Tragedy of J. Robert Oppenheimer* (Knopf, 2005), 332.

2 The US Army's investigation and tolerance of Oppenheimer's Communist associations, and the FBI's surveillance and investigation of Oppenheimer, are discussed in detail in *American Prometheus*, passim.

3 McGeorge Bundy edited *The Pattern of Responsibility* (Houghton Mifflin, 1952), which placed statements by Secretary of State Dean Acheson in context of historical events.

4 Report by the Panel of Consultants of the Department of State to the Secretary of State, January 1953, FRUS, 1952–1954, Volume II, Part 2, National Security Affairs, document 67.

5 Transcript of Oppenheimer's talk "American Weapons and American Policy," February 17, 1953, McGeorge Bundy Personal Papers, Series 3.4, Box 28, John F. Kennedy Presidential Library.

6 Memorandum of Discussion, 134th Meeting of the NSC, February 25, 1953, Eisenhower's Papers as President, NSC Series, Box 4, EL.

7 Report to the National Security Council by the NSC Planning Board, May 8, 1953, FRUS, 1952–1954, Volume II, Part 2, National Security Affairs, document 88.

8 Nichols memo to Tolson, May 11, 1953, released by NARA in response to a FOIA request by the author.

9 Hoover memo to Tolson, Ladd, Belmont, and Nichols, May 19, 1953, released by NARA in response to a FOIA request by the author.

10 Priscilla J. McMillan, *The Ruin of J. Robert Oppenheimer: And the Birth of the Modern Arms Race* (Viking, 2005), 162–64.

11 Cutler letter to Eisenhower, May 24, 1953, Eisenhower's Records as President (White House Central Files), Official Files, Box 280, 72-F, NSC 1953, EL.

12 Cutler letter to Michelson, June 29, 1954, Eisenhower's Records as President (White House Central Files), Official Files, Box 280, 72-F, NSC 1954, EL.

13 Cutler confidential memo to staff, May 25, 1953, Eisenhower's Records as President (White House Central Files), Official Files, Box 280, 72-F, NSC 1953, EL.

14 Bobby almost certainly would not have brought Oppenheimer before the NSC without getting Ike's approval first, though the meeting minutes state, "At the invitation of Mr. Cutler, Dr. Oppenheimer made a brief statement to the Council as to how the original panel of consultants . . . had reached the conclusions which were now set forth in NSC 151." Memorandum of Discussion, 146th Meeting of the NSC, May 27, 1953, Eisenhower's Papers as President, NSC Series, Box 4, EL, 8.

15 Ibid., 9.

16 Ladd memo to Belmont, June 5, 1953, released by NARA in response to a FOIA request by the author.

17 Hoover memo to Tolson and Ladd, June 24, 1953, released by NARA in response to a FOIA request by the author.

18 The Texts of Eisenhower Speeches at Dartmouth and Oyster Bay, NYT, June 15, 1953, 10.

19 Kai Bird, *The Color of Truth: McGeorge Bundy and William Bundy: Brothers in Arms* (Simon & Schuster, 1998), 163.

20 Ibid., 163.

21 McCarthy Strikes at Allen Dulles, NYT, July 10, 1953, 1.

22 McCarthy and CIA Plan Inquiry Deal, NYT, July 15, 1953, 16.

23 Richard G. Hewlett and Jack M. Holl, *Atoms for Peace and War, 1953–1961: Eisenhower and the Atomic Energy Commission* (University of California Press, 1989), 55.

24 Strauss memo on Candor, Strauss Papers, Box 428, Folder 1, Herbert Hoover Presidential Library.

25 Hewlett and Holl, *Atoms for Peace and War*, 57–58.

26 Ibid., 63.

27 Desk Books of Oppenheimer, September 1, 1953, Papers of J. Robert Oppenheimer, Library of Congress.

28 Cutler memo to Strauss and Jackson, September 10, 1953, *FRUS 1952–1954*, vol. 2, part 2, *National Security Affairs*, document 104.

29 Ibid.

30 Lewis Strauss memo to the president, September 17, 1953, Eisenhower's Papers as President, Administration Series, Box 5, Atoms for Peace, EL.

31 Gregg Herken, *Brotherhood of the Bomb: The Tangled Lives and Loyalties of Robert Oppenheimer, Ernest Lawrence, and Edward Teller* (Henry Holt, 2002), 267–68.

32 Barton J. Bernstein, "The Oppenheimer Loyalty-Security Case Reconsidered," *Stanford Law Review*, July 1990, 1439.

33 FBI memo, Belmont to Ladd, November 19, 1953, cited in ibid.

34 Hoover memo to the attorney general, December 3, 1953, J. Robert Oppenheimer FBI Security File, Scholarly Resources Inc., microfilm, Reel 2.

35 Hoover memo to Tolson, Ladd, and Nichols, December 2, 1953, released to the author by NARA in response to a FOIA request by the author.

36 Bird and Sherwin, *American Prometheus*, 479.

37 Eisenhower and Ferrell, *The Eisenhower Diaries*, 259.
38 Coyne memo to Cutler, December 3, 1953, under Cutler reply to Coyne, and Coyne memo to Hoover, December 4, 1953, J. Robert Oppenheimer FBI Security File, microfilm, reel 2, section 5.
39 Hoover memo to Tolson, Ladd, Belmont, and Nichols, December 4, 1953, released by NARA in response to a FOIA request by the author.
40 Eisenhower and Ferrell, *Eisenhower Diaries*, 260.
41 Hoover memo to Tolson, Ladd, Belmont, and Nichols, December 4, 1953, released by NARA in response to a FOIA request by the author.
42 Text of Eisenhower's Address to the U.N. Assembly, NYT, December 9, 1953, 2.
43 Cutler memo on JRO, Lewis Strauss Papers, J. Robert Oppenheimer Correspondence and Memoranda, 1953, Box 497, Folder 1, Herbert Hoover Presidential Library.
44 Bird and Sherwin, *American Prometheus*, 481–84.
45 Ibid., 484.
46 In the matter of J. Robert Oppenheimer, hearing transcript, 3.
47 NTFR, 319.
48 Transcript of FBI wiretap recording, March 12, 1954, released by NARA under a FOIA request by the author.
49 FBI investigative report NK 100-31936, undated, released by NARA under a FOIA request by the author.
50 J. Robert Oppenheimer National Security File, microfilm, Sections 23 and 24, Hoover letters of March 25, 1954, to Strauss and Brownell.
51 Hoover letter to Cutler, March 25, 1954, released by NARA in response to a FOIA request by the author. Cutler response to Hoover, March 30, 1954, J. Robert Oppenheimer National Security File, microfilm, Sections 24.
52 FBI memo, Branigan to Belmont, March 31, 1954, J. Robert Oppenheimer National Security File, microfilm, Section 31.
53 Herken, *Brotherhood of the Bomb*, 290.
54 Oppenheimer Action Late, McCarthy Says, NYT, April 14, 1954.
55 Bird and Sherwin, *American Prometheus*, 524.
56 Strauss letter to Gray, April 14, 1954, and C. A. Rolander Jr. letter to Strauss, April 17, 1954, Lewis Strauss Papers, J. Robert Oppenheimer Correspondence and Memoranda, March 1954, Box 497 Folder 3, Herbert Hoover Presidential Library.
57 Bird and Sherwin, *American Prometheus*, 537.
58 In the matter of J. Robert Oppenheimer, hearing transcript, 171.
59 Ibid., 565.
60 Ibid., 726.
61 Bird and Sherwin, *American Prometheus*, 541.

11. THE IRAN COUP

1 Donald Wilber, *Overthrow of Premier Mossadeq of Iran, November 1952–August 1953* (National Security Archive).
2 Kermit Roosevelt, *Countercoup: The Struggle for the Control of Iran* (McGraw-Hill, 1979), 120.
3 Tim Weiner, *Legacy of Ashes: The History of the CIA* (Doubleday, 2007), 83.
4 Memorandum of Discussion, 132nd Meeting of the NSC, February 18, 1953, Eisenhower's Papers as President, NSC Series, Box 4, EL.
5 CIA memo for the president, Subject: The Iranian Situation, NSC Staff Papers, Box 65, Disaster File, Iran (3), EL.
6 Mohammad Reza Pahlavi, the Shah of Iran, *Answer to History* (Stein & Day, 1980), 45–48, 59–60.
7 Memorandum of Discussion, 135th Meeting of the NSC, March 4, 1953, Eisenhower's Papers as President, NSC Series, Box 4, EL, 6.

8 Ibid., 8.

9 Memorandum by the Secretary of State of a Meeting at the White House on the Evening of March 4, 1953, *FRUS 1952–1954*, vol. 6, 894, document 378.

10 United States Delegation Minutes of the Second Meeting of Secretary of State Dulles and Foreign Secretary Eden at the Department of State, March 6, 1953, 10:15 AM, *FRUS 1952–1954*, vol. 6, 917, document 381.

11 Memorandum by the Secretary of State of a Meeting at the White House on March 6, 1953, at Noon, *FRUS 1952–1954*, vol. 6, 919, document 382.

12 Memorandum of Discussion, 136th Meeting of the NSC, March 11, 1953, Eisenhower's Papers as President, NSC Series, Box 4, EL, 13–17.

13 Memo to James Lay, Executive Secretary of the NSC, First Progress Report on Paragraph 5-a of NSC 136/1, "US Policy Regarding the Present Situation in Iran," EL.

14 Wilber, *Overthrow of Premier Mossadeq of Iran*, 2–3.

15 Eden Bars US Right to Subpoena Oil Data, NYT, December 12, 1952.

16 NSC 138/1, January 6, 1953, *FRUS 1952–1954*, vol. 1, part 2, *General: Economic and Political Matters*, 1318–36.

17 Nancy Lisagor and Frank Lipsius, *A Law Unto Itself: The Untold Story of the Law Firm Sullivan & Cromwell* (William Morrow, 1988), 199–212.

18 Memorandum of Discussion, 139th Meeting of the NSC, April 8, 1953, Dwight D. Eisenhower Papers, NSC Series, Box 4, EL, 1–3.

19 Wilber, *Overthrow of Premier Mossadeq of Iran*, 5.

20 Ibid., 12.

21 Ibid., appendix B, 3–4.

22 Ibid., 7–12.

23 Ibid., 18–19.

24 Ibid., 11–12.

25 Ibid., 12.

26 Roosevelt, *Countercoup*, 1, 18.

27 Wilber, *Overthrow of Premier Mossadeq of Iran*, 18.

28 Memorandum of Discussion, 157th Meeting of the NSC, July 30, 1953, Eisenhower's Papers as President, NSC Series, Box 4, EL.

29 Roosevelt, *Countercoup*, 139–43.

30 Wilber, *Overthrow of Premier Mossadeq of Iran*, 24–25.

31 Ibid., 37–38.

32 Stephen Kinzer, *All the Shah's Men: An American Coup and the Roots of Middle East Terror* (Wiley, 2008), 15.

33 Wilber, , *Overthrow of Premier Mossadeq of Iran* 50–52.

34 Ibid., 52–53.

35 Ibid., 63.

36 Ibid., 64.

37 Ibid., 65.

38 Kinzer, *All the Shah's Men*, 189.

39 Christopher de Bellaigue, *Patriot of Persia: Muhammad Mossadegh and a Tragic Anglo-American Coup* (Harper, 2012), 256–61.

40 Burton I. Kaufman, *The Oil Cartel Case: A Documentary Study of Antitrust Activity in the Cold War Era* (Praeger, 1978), 58–59, 100–01.

41 Ibid., 101.

42 MFC, 163.

43 Dwight D. Eisenhower's Papers as President, DDE Diary Series, Box 4, "DDE Diary Oct.–Dec. 1953," EL.

44 NTFR, 370.

12. MYSTERY MAN

1 Samuel Lubell, "Mystery Man of the White House," *Saturday Evening Post*, February 6, 1954, 27 et seq.

2 White House Mystery Man is Is the Top Secret Keeper of Eisenhower Regime, *St. Louis Post-Dispatch*, March 7, 1954, p. 33.

3 Untouchable, Unreachable, Unquotable, NYT Magazine, January 30, 1955, 12.

4 Drew Pearson, The Washington Merry-Go-Round, *Journal-Standard* (Freeport, Illinois), January 6, 1954, 8.

5 NTFR, footnote 1, chapter 17, 402.

6 Goodpaster Memorandum of Conference with the President, November 24, 1954, Dwight D. Eisenhower's Papers as President, Ann Whitman Diary Series, Box 3, folder "ACW Diary November 1954 (1)," EL.

7 Evan Thomas, *Ike's Bluff: President Eisenhower's Secret Battle to Save the World* (Little, Brown, 2012), 149–50.

8 Top-secret letter from Hoover to Cutler, September 16, 1953, FBI Series, Box 2, D-G (1), OSANSA Affairs: Records, 1952–1961, EL.

9 Dwight D. Eisenhower and Robert H. Ferrell (ed.), *The Eisenhower Diaries* (W. W. Norton, 1976), 60–69, 103.

10 Brian Hoey, *Mountbatten: The Private Story* (Sidgwick & Jackson, 1994), 91.

11 Benedict statement to the author, July 14, 2013.

12 Letters and memoranda by J. Edgar Hoover to Robert Cutler and the Office of the Special Assistant for National Security Affairs, 1952–61, FBI Series, EL.

13 John Prados, *Keepers of the Keys, A History of the National Security Council from Truman to Bush* (William Morrow and Company, Inc., 1991).

14 Cutler letter to Allen Dulles, November 24, 1953, CIAFRR.

15 Cutler poem for Eisenhower anniversary, July 1, 1953, EPP, Robert Cutler 1952–1955 (5), EL.

16 Note dictated by Eisenhower for delivery to Cutler, November 26, 1953, EPP, Robert Cutler 1952–1955 (4), EL.

17 Cutler memo regarding "Gettysburg Address . . . It might have been," August 18, 1954, Office of the Special Assistant for National Security Affairs, Special Assistant Series, Presidential Subseries, Box 2, President's Papers 1954 (1).

18 Roscoe Drummond, "Rough Path Today for Gettysburg Address," *Kansas City Star*, September 22, 1954, 22.

19 *Report to the President*, June 30, 1953, Box 14, President's Committee on International Information Activities: Records, 1950–53, EL, 90.

20 Memorandum of Discussion, 160th Meeting of the NSC, August 28, 1953, Eisenhower's Papers as President, NSC Series, Box 4, EL.

21 Eisenhower Sets Up New Security Unit, NYT, September 4, 1953, 1.

22 Minutes of the First Meeting of the Operations Coordinating Board, September 17, 1953, *FRUS, The Intelligence Community 1950–1955*, document 160, 459–61.

23 Cutler letter to Eisenhower, March 20, 1954, EPP, 1952–1955, Robert Cutler (4), EL.

24 Eisenhower letter to Cutler, March 23, 1954, EPP, 1952–1955, Robert Cutler (4), EL.

25 Memorandum for the President by Cutler, July 20, 1954, Ann Whitman Administration Series, Robert Cutler 1952–1955(3), EL.

26 Glantzberg letter to Eisenhower, July 12, 1954, Ann Whitman Administration Series, Robert Cutler 1952–1955(3), EL.

13. THE GUATEMALA COUP

1 Memorandum of Discussion, 132nd Meeting of the NSC, Wednesday, February 18, 1953, Eisenhower's Papers as President, NSC Series, Box 4, EL.

2 Stephen Schlesinger and Stephen Kinzer, *Bitter Fruit: The Untold Story of the American Coup in Guatemala* (Doubleday, 1982), 103.

3 Ibid., 69.

4 Piero Gleijeses, *Shattered Hope: The Guatemalan Revolution and the United States, 1944–1954* (Princeton University Press, 1992), 149.

5 Ibid., 150.

6 Memorandum from the chief of the CIA's Western Hemisphere Division, J. Caldwell King, to the agency's deputy director for plans, Frank Wisner, *FRUS 1952–1954, Guatemala*, 2–4.

7 Ben Ames Williams Jr., *Bank of Boston 200: A History of New England's Leading Bank 1784–1984* (Houghton Mifflin, 1984), 236, 244, 261.

8 Holland memo of April 19, 1954, *FRUS 1952–1954*, vol. 4, *The American Republics*, 841–42.

9 Stephen Kinzer, *The Brothers: John Foster Dulles, Allen Dulles, and Their Secret World War* (Times Books, 2013), 148.

10 Schlesinger and Kinzer, *Bitter Fruit*, 106.

11 Ibid., 83.

12 Robert J. Donovan, *Confidential Secretary: Ann Whitman's 20 Years with Eisenhower and Rockefeller* (Dutton 1988), 2, 160.

13 Report by the NSC Planning Board, June 1, 1953, *FRUS 1952–1954*, vol. 4, *The American Republics*, 191–94.

14 Ibid., 193.

15 Memorandum of Discussion, 148th Meeting of the NSC, Thursday, June 4, 1953, Eisenhower's Papers as President, NSC Series, Box 4, EL, 7.

16 Ibid, 8.

17 Wisner memo to CIA director Dulles, *FRUS 1952–1954, Guatemala*, 86.

18 Memorandum of Discussion, 159th Meeting of the NSC, Thursday, August 13, 1953, Eisenhower's Papers as President, NSC Series, Box 4, EL.

19 Memo drafted for submission to the NSC by the Bureau of Inter-American Affairs, US Department of State, August 19, 1953, Office of the Historian online, https://history.state.gov.

20 Allen Dulles memo of December 9, 1953, *FRUS 1952–1954, Guatemala*, 155–56.

21 Memorandum of Conversation, Assistant Secretary of State for Inter-American Affairs (Cabot), *FRUS 1952–1954, Guatemala*, 1095–97.

22 CIA and Guatemala Assassination Proposals 1952–1954, CIA History Staff Analysis, Gerald K. Haines, June 1995, CIAFRR.

23 E. Howard Hunt, *Undercover: Memoirs of an American Secret Agent* (Berkley, 1974), 96–98.

24 Cutler top-secret letter to Allen Dulles, March 15, 1954, CIAFRR.

25 Allen Dulles top-secret letter to Cutler, March 16, 1954, CIAFRR.

26 Martin A. Lee and Bruce Shlain, *Acid Dream: The Complete Social History of LSD: The CIA, the Sixties, and Beyond* (Grove Press, 1994), 27–35; Carl Bernstein, "The CIA and the Media: How America's Most Powerful News Media Worked Hand in Glove with the Central Intelligence Agency and Why the Church Committee Covered It Up," *Rolling Stone*, October 20, 1977.

27 CIA memorandum to Koons, April 19, 1954, CIAFRR.

28 Memorandum by the Assistant Secretary of State for Inter-American Affairs (Holland) to the Acting Secretary of State, April 20, 1954, footnote 3, *FRUS 1952–1954*, vol. 4, *The American Republics*, 1100-1101.

29 Communist Arms Unloaded in Guatemala by Vessel from Polish Port, US Learns, NYT, May 18, 1954, 1.

30 A secret CIA cable of May 18, 1954, speculated that the arms included mortars. CIAFRR.

31 Guatemala Hints UN Case on Arms, NYT, May 23, 1954, 1.

32 John Foster Dulles Papers, Telephone Conversations Series, Box 10, Folder White House Telephone Memos Jan 1, 1954–June 30, 1954 (1), EL.

33 Dulles appointment calendar, May 26, 1954, John Foster Dulles Appointment Schedule Series, Box 2, May 1954, EL.

34 Hoover memo to Cutler, July 26, 1956, with attached copy of Labor Youth League pamphlet, OSANSA, Records: 1952–1961, FBI L-N (1), EL.

35 Memorandum of Discussion, 202nd Meeting of the NSC, June 17, 1954, Eisenhower's Papers as President, NSC Series, Box 5, EL.

36 Nick Cullather, *Secret History: The CIA's Classified Account of Its Operations in Guatemala, 1952–1954*, 2nd ed. (Stanford University Press, 2006), 88.

37 Ibid., 90–92.

38 Schlesinger and Kinzer, *Bitter Fruit*, 180–81.

39 MFC, 425–26.

40 Schlesinger and Kinzer, *Bitter Fruit*, 182.

41 Ibid., 199.

42 Ibid., 209, 210.

43 NYT, July 3, 1954.

44 The litigation history is provided in an appeals court ruling, 410 F.2d 553, *USA v. United Fruit Company*, No. 26801, United States Court of Appeals Fifth Circuit, April 25, 1969.

45 MFC, 425–27.

46 NTFR, 370.

14. THE DR. DICK HOUSE, JOE McCARTHY, AND "SEXUAL PERVERSION"

1 Dr. Dick assisted at Washington's deathbed and performed a Masonic service when Washington was buried at Mount Vernon on December 18, 1799, according to Mary Lindsey, *Historic Homes and Landmarks of Alexandria, Virginia* (Newell-Cole, 1962).

2 Author interviews of Benedict.

3 Cutler letter to Mrs. Lutz, January 26, 1954, SGBD.

4 Benedict email to the author, June 2, 2015.

5 Benedict statement to the author, December 10, 2017.

6 Adams memo to Benedict, May 24, 1954, Eisenhower's Records as President (White House Central Files), Official File Series, Box 273, folder OF 72-A-16, EL.

7 Benedict statement to the author, March 22, 2015.

8 Benedict FBI background report, July 14, 1953, with cover letter of Hoover to Adams, January 16, 1953, Henry R. McPhee Records, Box BE-BN, EL. Elisabeth Mann Borgese, the youngest daughter of German writer Thomas Mann, fled from Nazi Germany with her family. Her husband, Giuseppe Borgese, was an Italian journalist and author who fled Mussolini's fascism in Italy in 1931. The two met in Zurich and married in 1939, when Borgese was thirty-five years older than she was.

9 Benedict FBI background report, 10.

10 Benedict email to the author, October 21, 2009.

11 David K. Johnson, *The Lavender Scare: The Cold War Persecution of Gays and Lesbians in the Federal Government* (University of Chicago Press, 2004), 128.

12 Ibid., 128–29.

13 Ibid., 129, 158.

14 Hank Greenspun with Alex Pelle, *Where I Stand: The Record of a Reckless Man* (David McKay, 1966), 219–22. Greenspun, originally from Brooklyn, had been convicted in July 1950 of illegally smuggling weapons to an armed Jewish defense organization, the Haganah, which sought to protect Jews from armed Arab groups in the newly formed state of Israel. Greenspun also had worked briefly for the Flamingo, a Las Vegas hotel controlled by mobster Bugsy Siegel until Siegel's murder in 1947. Greenspun's critics used these activities to undermine his credibility, yet his claims in the *Las Vegas Sun* asserting that McCarthy was homosexual nonetheless reverberated across the country.

15 Robert D. Dean, *Imperial Brotherhood: Gender and the Making of Cold War Foreign Policy* (University of Massachusetts Press, 2001), 148–49.

16 Touring Senator Levels Wrath at Sun's Publisher, *Reno Gazette Journal*, October 14, 1952, 1.

17 Hoover memo to Tolson, Ladd, Belmont, and Nichols, May 19, 1953, released by the FBI to the author under a FOIA request.

18 Eisenhower State of the Union Address, January 7, 1954, EL online, https://www.eisenhower
.archives.gov/all_about_ike/speeches/1954_state_of_the_union.pdf.

19 Johnson, *Lavender Scare*, 134.

20 Joseph and Stewart Alsop, Did Ike Buy Lemon on Commie Issue, Detroit Free Press, January 20,
1954, 10.

21 The series subsequently won a Pulitzer Prize in journalism for the writer, Anthony Lewis.

22 David M. Oshinsky, *A Conspiracy So Immense: The World of Joe McCarthy* (Free Press, 1983),
372–77.

23 Drew Pearson, Washington Merry-Go-Round (column), *Daily Telegram* (Eau Claire, Wisconsin),
March 8, 1954.

24 David A. Nichols, *Ike and McCarthy: Dwight Eisenhower's Secret Campaign Against Joseph
McCarthy* (Simon & Schuster, 2017), 149.

25 Kai Bird, The Chairman, John J. McCloy, *The Making of the American Establishment* (Simon &
Schuster, 1992), 419

26 Nichols, *Ike and McCarthy*, 56–59, 162–65.

27 Michael J. Birkner, "Eisenhower and the Red Menace," *Prologue Magazine* 33, no. 3 (Fall 2001),
https://www.archives.gov/publications/prologue/2001/fall/eisenhower-and-red-menace-2
.html#nt20.

28 Text of Army Report Charging Threats by McCarthy and Cohn Interceding for Schine, NYT,
March 12, 1954, 9A.

29 Cohn Says Army Tried to Use Hold on Schine to Stop Inquiry, *St. Louis Post-Dispatch*, March 15,
1954, 15.

30 Nichols, *Ike and McCarthy*, 210–12.

31 Robert Shogan, *No Sense of Decency: The Army-McCarthy Hearings, A Demagogue Falls and
Television Takes Charge of American Politics* (Ivan R. Dee, 2009), 173.

32 Army-McCarthy hearings transcript, April 30, 1954, US Government Printing Office, Part 14,
543.

33 Shogan, *No Sense of Decency*, 178.

34 Testimony of John G. Adams, Army-McCarthy hearings transcript, May 14, 1954, US
Government Printing Office, Part 33, 1221–222.

35 Shogan, *No Sense of Decency*, 210.

36 Ibid., 213–14.

37 Army-McCarthy hearings transcript, June 9, 1954, US Government Printing Office, Part 59,
2417–419.

38 Ibid, 2427, 2429.

39 McCarthy Hearings End on 36th Day as Potter Suggests Perjury Action, Removal of Top Aides
on Both Sides, NYT, June 18, 1954, 1.

40 Shogan, *No Sense of Decency*, 235–39.

41 Drew Pearson, Threats Drive Senator to Suicide, *Daily Reporter* (Dover, Ohio), June 23, 1954, 6.

42 Ibid.

43 Nichols, *Ike and McCarthy*, 289, 293.

44 Letter of Theodore Streibert, director of the US Information Agency, to Cutler, August 20, 1954,
SGBD.

45 Document, declassified in 2015, attached to Benedict's FBI background report, Henry R. McPhee
Records, Box BE-BN, EL.

15. EXPLOITING SOVIET VULNERABILITIES

1 Koons letter to Allen Dulles, January 15, 1954, with enclosed top-secret memo, "US Policy on the
Exploitation of Soviet Vulnerabilities," CIAFRR.

2 Dulles memo to C. D. Jackson, November 16, 1953, CIAFRR.

3 Barnes memo to Dulles, November 18, 1954, CIAFRR.

4 Bissell memo to Dulles, February 9, 1954, CIAFRR.

5 Cutler letter to Allen Dulles, January 26, 1954, CIAFRR.

6 Allen Dulles letter to Cutler, February 10, 1954, CIAFRR.

7 James R. Killian, Jr., *Sputnik, Scientists and Eisenhower, A Memoir of the First Special Assistant to the President for Science and Technology* (The MIT Press, 1977), 68–85, 115–16.

8 Ted Morgan, *Valley of Death: The Tragedy at Dien Bien Phu That Led America into the Vietnam War* (Random House, 2010), 265–66.

9 Evan Thomas, *Ike's Bluff: President Eisenhower's Secret Battle to Save the World* (Little, Brown, 2012), 123.

10 Memorandum of Discussion, 191st Meeting of the NSC, April 1, 1954, Eisenhower's Papers as President, NSC Series, Box 4, EL.

11 Cutler memo to Smith, *FRUS 1952–1954*, vol. 8, *Indochina*, 1445–48.

12 Thomas, *Ike's Bluff*, 128–29.

13 Memorandum of Discussion, 195th Meeting of the NSC, May 6, 1954, Eisenhower's Papers as President, NSC Series, Box 5, EL, 3, 4.

14 Cutler memo to the secretary of defense and Joint Chiefs of Staff, May 7, 1954, in *The Pentagon Papers: The Defense Department History of United States Decision Making on Vietnam: The Senator Gravel Edition*, vol. 1 (Beacon Press, 1971), 501–03.

15 Morgan, *Valley of Death*, 556–59.

16 Memo to Cutler from Horace Craig, Paul Comstock, and T. B. Koons, June 8, 1956, with attached Report on US Policy for the Exploitation of Soviet Vulnerabilities, June 8, 1954, p. 3, OSANSA, NSC Series, Box 18, USSR — Report on US Policy for Exploitation of Soviet Vulnerabilities, EL.

17 Report on US Policy for the Exploitation of Soviet Vulnerabilities, 7–9, 13, 14.

18 Ibid., 10–12, 22.

19 Eisenhower letter to Allen Dulles, July 26, 1954, CIAFRR.

20 Stephen Kinzer, *The Brothers: John Foster Dulles, Allen Dulles, and Their Secret World War* (Times Books, 2013), 187.

21 Thomas, *Ike's Bluff*, 144.

22 Report on the Exploitation of Soviet Vulnerabilities, November 30, 1954, White House Office, NSC Staff Papers, 1953–61, Special Staff File Series, Soviet Vulnerabilities (2), EL, 27. For clarity, the author has added a comma to this quote from the report.

23 Ibid., 57.

24 Memorandum of Discussion, 236th Meeting of the NSC, January 27, 1955, Eisenhower's Papers as President, NSC Series, Box 5, EL, 6.

25 Ibid., 7.

26 James Lay note to the NSC, January 31, 1955, NSC 5505/1, OSANSA, NSC Series, Policy Papers Subseries, Box 14, folder NSC 5505/1 — Exploitation of Soviet and European Satellite Vulnerabilities (2).

27 Greg Barnhisel, *Cold War Modernists: Art, Literature, and American Cultural Diplomacy* (Columbia University Press, 2015), 4, 127–32.

28 Arch Puddington, *Broadcasting Freedom: The Cold War Triumph of Radio Free Europe and Radio Liberty* (University Press of Kentucky, 2000), 136.

29 Gregory Mitrovich, *Undermining the Kremlin: America's Strategy to Subvert the Soviet Bloc, 1947–1956* (Cornell University Press, 2000), 172.

16. "LOSING MY RIGHT ARM"

1 Memorandum of Discussion, 239th Meeting of the NSC, March 3, 1955, Eisenhower's Papers as President, NSC Series, Box 6, EL.

2 Cutler letter to Eisenhower, March 8, 1955, and Eisenhower's reply to Cutler of the same date, EPP, Robert Cutler 1952–1955 (2), EL.

3 Cutler letter to the president, dated August 18, 1954, EPP, Robert Cutler, 1952–1955 (3), EL.

4 Cutler to Quit as Assistant to President, *Washington Post*, March 7, 1955; "Security Council Sparkplug" (opinion), *Washington Post*, March 11, 1955.

5 Hoover letter to Cutler, March 9, 1955, released by the FBI to the author under a FOIA request.

6 NTFR, 329.

7 Cutler's thank-you note to Ike and Mamie, dated March 14, 1955, and President Eisenhower's reply of March 15, 1955, EPP, Robert Cutler, 1952–1955 (2), EL. Cutler explained in a note later, found in the same location at the Eisenhower Library, that his French phrase was a reference to the French national anthem, "La Marseillaise," whose second line is: "*Le jour de gloire est arrivé.*"

8 Cutler letter to John Foster Dulles, March 11, 1955, Koons Day File, Box 7, Robert Cutler Papers, EL.

9 Koons letter to Robert Cutler, March 30, 1955, SGBD.

10 NTFR, 330.

11 NTFR, 331.

12 Eisenhower Appointment Book, March 1955, Eisenhower Foundation, http://ks-eisenhower presidentiallibrary.civicplus.com/209/Appointment-Books

13 Report to the President, April 1, 1955, Box 8, Robert Cutler Papers, EL.

14 NSC 5412/1, March 12, 1955, US Department of State Office of the Historian online, https://history.state.gov.

15 Rockefeller memo to Cutler, April 2, 1955, Koons Day File, Box 7, Robert Cutler Papers, EL.

16 In response to a FOIA request by the author for documents about Bobby, the FBI said in 2007 that two files that were "potentially responsive" to the request were destroyed in 2003 and 2006 "pursuant to routine records retention schedules."

17 Cutler letter to Nixon, April 6, 1955, released to the author by the Richard Nixon Presidential Library and Museum.

18 Cutler letter to Eisenhower, April 7, 1955, EPP, Robert Cutler, 1952–1955 (2), EL.

19 Cutler letter to Whitman, April 21, 1955, EPP, Robert Cutler, 1952–1955 (2), EL.

20 Eisenhower letter to Cutler, dated May 31, 1955, EPP, Robert Cutler, 1952–1955 (2), EL.

21 Cutler letter to Eisenhower, dated November 17, 1955, with enclosed reprint of speech, EPP, Robert Cutler, 1952–1955 (1), EL.

22 Joseph and Stewart Alsop, "Security vs. Democracy," *Washington Post*, June 15, 1955.

23 Cutler letter to Nixon, September 7, 1955, Richard Nixon Presidential Library and Museum.

24 NTFR, 339–40.

25 Eisenhower letter to Cutler, November 21, 1955, EPP, Robert Cutler, 1952–1955 (1), EL.

26 $460,000 Is Raised by Bay State GOP, NYT, October 16, 1955.

27 Eisenhower letter to Cutler, December 20, 1955, DDE Diary Series, Box 11, December 1955 (2), EL.

28 Robert Cutler, The Development of the National Security Council, *Foreign Affairs*, April 1956.

29 NTFR, 343.

30 Cutler letter to Koons, postmarked June 28, 1956, SGBD.

31 Nichols memo to Tolson, June 19, 1956, obtained from the FBI by the author under a FOIA request. The author first received the document in highly redacted form and began a series of appeals. In 2016, ten years after the first request, through appeals the author received a version of the document revealing that it was Mitchell who reported Bullitt's homosexuality allegations to the FBI.

32 White Is Accused as Foe of System, NYT, April 7, 1954.

33 We Accuse . . . Sumner Welles, *Confidential*, May 1956.

34 Rushmore testimony August 27, 1940, to the US House of Representatives Subcommittee of the Special Committee to Investigate Un-American Activities, the so-called Dies Committee.

35 79 in Hollywood Found Subversive, Inquiry Head Says, NYT, October 23, 1947, 1.

36 David M. Oshinsky, *A Conspiracy So Immense: The World of Joe McCarthy* (Free Press, 1983), 252, 318.

37 Ladd memo to Belmont of the FBI, June 15, 1953, concerning Walter Winchell broadcast of June 14, 1953, Walter Winchell Records, Part 32 of 58, FBIFRR.

38 Henry E. Scott, *Shocking True Story: The Rise and Fall of Confidential, "America's Most Scandalous Scandal Magazine"* (Pantheon, 2010), 130.

39 Cutler Aids Campaign, NYT, September 19, 1956.

40 Turner letter to Benedict, November 19, 1955, SGBD.

41 Recording of conversation at the Dr. Dick House by Benedict, September 26, 1956, SGBD.

42 Dillon Anderson oral history interview, December 30, 1969, CCOH, 20, 106.

43 David A. Nichols, *Eisenhower 1956: The President's Year of Crisis — Suez and the Brink of War* (Simon & Schuster, 2011), 235–36 and passim.

44 Ibid., 124–25, 283.

45 Ibid., 162–63, 189.

46 Eisenhower letter to Cutler, November 24, 1956, EPP, Robert Cutler, 1956–1957 (3), EL.

47 Hoover letter to Cutler, November 28, 1956, and Cutler reply to Hoover on December 6, 1956, released by the FBI in response to a FOIA request by the author.

17. THE RETURN

1 Cutler letter and memo to Allen Dulles, January 7, 1957, CIAFRR.

2 Executive Order 10700, signed by President Eisenhower on February 25, 1957.

3 Cary Reich, *The Life of Nelson A. Rockefeller: Worlds to Conquer, 1908–1958* (Doubleday, 1996), 616–17.

4 NSC 5412/2, undated, though an accompanying NSC memo indicated that it was signed by Eisenhower December 28, 1955, FRUS, 1950-1955, The Intelligence Community, document 250.

5 See, for instance, Allen Dulles Memorandum for the Record, meeting of the Designated Representatives, 6 March 1957, NSC Series, Policy Papers Subseries, Box 10, NSC 5412/2 — Covert Operations, EL.

6 Memo of OCB meeting, January 9–10, 1957, CIAFRR.

7 Memorandum of Discussion, 309th Meeting of the NSC, January 11, 1957, Eisenhower's Papers as President, NSC Series, Box 8, EL, 1-5.

8 Ibid., 3–4.

9 Ibid., 7–11.

10 Alec Kirby, David G. Dalin, and John F. Rothmann, *Harold E. Stassen: The Life and Perennial Candidacy of the Progressive Republican* (McFarland, 2012), 166–70.

11 Ibid., 184.

12 Memorandum of Discussion, 315th Meeting of the NSC, March 6, 1957, Eisenhower's Papers as President, NSC Series, Box 8, EL, 15–17.

13 Memorandum of Discussion, 316th Meeting of the NSC, March 14, 1957, Eisenhower's Papers as President, NSC Series, Box 8, EL, 8.

14 Ibid., 5; US Policy on Indonesia, NSC 5518, May 3, 1955, *FRUS 1955–1957*, vol. 22, *Southeast Asia*, document 95.

15 Stephen Kinzer, *The Brothers: John Foster Dulles, Allen Dulles, and Their Secret World War* (Times Books, 2013), 217–18.

16 Memorandum of Discussion, 316th Meeting of the NSC, March 14, 1957, Eisenhower's Papers as President, NSC Series, Box 8, EL, 5-6.

17 Alsop memo, attached to letter by CIA director Dulles to Hoover, April 1, 1957, CIAFRR.

18 Edwin M. Yoder Jr., *Joe Alsop's Cold War: A Study of Journalistic Influence and Intrigue* (University of North Carolina Press, 1995), 154–55.

19 Alsop memo, April 1, 1957.

20 Ibid.

21 Hoover memo to Tolson, Boardman, and Belmont, April 17, 1957, FBI Official and Confidential Files, microfilm collection of the University Publications of America.

22 FBI report on Joseph W. Alsop Jr. and Stewart Alsop, March 29, 1957, FBI Official and Confidential Files, microfilm collection of the University Publications of America.

23 Secret Service investigative report, April 18, 1957, in Hoover's Official and Confidential file on "White House Employees — Homosexuals," NARA, released to the author under a FOIA request.

24 Ibid.

25 Hoover memo to Tolson, Boardman, Belmont, and Nichols, April 18, 1957, FBI Official and Confidential Files, microfilm collection of the University Publications of America.

26 Ibid.

27 Domestic Intelligence Division routing slip with notation by Hoover, April 19, 1957, part of Hoover's Official and Confidential file on "White House Employees — Homosexuals," NARA, released to the author under a FOIA request.

28 Hoover memo to Tolson, Boardman, Belmont, and Nichols, May 10, 1957, part of Hoover's Official and Confidential file on "White House Employees — Homosexuals," NARA, released to the author under a FOIA request.

29 Hoover confidential letter to Robert Cutler, with attached memorandum, "March on Washington, May, 1957," both dated April 26, 1957, OSANSA: Records, 1952–1961, FBI Series, L-N(2), EL.

30 Cutler letter to McPhee, May 1, 1957, OSANSA: Records, 1952–1961, FBI Series, L-N(2), EL.

31 FBI copy of the article "Puritan — Up to a Point," NYT, May 24, 1957, with routing information and stamped with the file number 62-98899, the same number as the file that held reports alleging Cutler was a homosexual, released by the FBI under a FOIA request by the author.

32 Memorandum of Discussion, 324th Meeting of the NSC, May 23, 1957, Eisenhower's Papers as President, NSC Series, Box 8, EL, 1–7.

33 Ibid., 7.

34 Kirby, Dalin, and Rothmann, *Harold E. Stassen*, 188.

35 Ibid., 190.

36 Ibid., 191.

37 Cutler letter to Eisenhower, June 8, 1957, EPP, Robert Cutler 1956–1957 (2).

38 Cutler letter to Eisenhower, June 12, 1957, with attached memorandum, "US Position on First Phase of Disarmament," dated June 11, 1957, EPP, Robert Cutler 1956–1957 (2).

39 Cutler memo to Allen Dulles, June 6, 1957, NSC Series, Policy Papers, NSC 5412/2 folder, EL.

40 Cutler memo to file, June 19, 1957, NSC Series, Policy Papers, NSC 5412/2 folder, EL.

41 Cutler letter to Larson, director, US Information Agency, June 19, 1957, SGBD.

18. "THE GREATEST ADVENTURE OF MY LIFE"

1 RCD, vol. 1, entry of July 14, 1958.

2 RCD, vol. I, entry of June 30, 1958.

3 RCD, vol. 1, entry of July 18, 1958. The author inserted the colon in "1:30" for clarity.

4 Cutler letter to Koons, July 21, 1957, SGBD.

5 In the myth, Damon and Pythias travel to Syracuse, where Pythias is arrested for plotting against the tyrant Dionysius the Elder. Dionysius condemns Pythias to death but agrees to let him visit his home one last time as long as Damon remains in his place. Dionysius announces that he will kill Damon if Pythias fails to return by the agreed date. In the end, Pythias returns just in time to save his friend from death and explains that he had been thrown overboard during a storm. Dionysius is so astounded at the true friendship of the two men that he agrees to free them both. This mythical tale has been retold throughout the centuries, including in an English play in the 1500s. In 1864, a friendship society, the Order of the Knights of Pythias, was founded in Washington, DC; it eventually was reported to have some eight hundred thousand members. In 1871, Louisa May Alcott retold the story in her novel *Little Women*. In 1915, the story was retold in a book, and a movie followed.

6 The visit by Bobby and Skip to Dumbarton Oaks is referenced in several places in their correspondence and in RCD, including Cutler letters to Koons of August 18, 1957, and September 28, 1957, SGBD.

7 Note written by Cutler on the back of Koons's letter to Cutler of June 17, 1957, SGBD.

8 Cutler letter to Peggy Lutz, July 29, 1957, SGBD.

9 Cutler letter to Koons, August 5, 1957, SGBD.

10 Cutler letter to Koons, August 2, 1957, SGBD.

11 Cutler letter to Koons, August 1, 1957, SGBD.

12 Koons letter to Cutler, August 6, 1957, SGBD.

13 Cutler letter to Koons, August 5, 1957, SGBD.

14 Koons letter to Cutler, August 11, 1957, SGBD.

15 Cutler letter to Koons, August 12, 1957, SGBD.

16 Koons letter to Cutler, August 27, 1957, SGBD.

17 Koons letter to Cutler, September 11, 1957, SGBD.

18 Cutler letter to Koons, September 22, 1957, SGBD.

19 The poem was written by Félix Arvers.

19. SPUTNIK, TURMOIL, AND LOVE

1 Memorandum of Discussion, 333rd Meeting of the NSC, August 1, 1957, Eisenhower's Papers as President, NSC Series, Box 9, EL.

2 Hoover letter to Cutler, July 31, 1957, OSANSA, FBI Series, Box 1, Folder FBI A-B(1), EL.

3 Cutler memo to Eisenhower, August 7, 1957, with attached memos by General Thomas Farrell and Captain Jack Morse, DDEL, EPP, Robert Cutler, 1956–1957 (1).

4 Memorandum of Discussion, 336th Meeting of the NSC, September 12, 1957, Eisenhower's Papers as President, NSC Series, Box 9, EL.

5 Ad Hoc Interdepartmental Committee on Indonesia, September 3, 1957, *FRUS 1955–1957*, vol. 22, *Southeast Asia*, document 262.

6 Memorandum of Discussion, 337th Meeting of the NSC, September 23, 1957, Eisenhower's Papers as President, NSC Series, Box 9, EL, 1–5.

7 Paul F. Gardner, *Shared Hopes, Separate Fears: Fifty Years of U.S.-Indonesian Relations* (Routledge, 1997), 145–46.

8 Soviet Fires Earth Satellite into Space, NYT, October 5, 1957, 5.

9 Memorandum of Discussion, 339th Meeting of the NSC, October 10, 1957, Eisenhower's Papers as President, NSC Series, Box 9, EL.

10 Cutler letter to Koons, October 10, 1957, SGBD.

11 Intelligence and "Moon," NYT, October 7, 1957, 16.

12 Eisenhower Plans Talks to Nation on Urgent Issues, NYT, October 23, 1957, 1.

13 Cutler letter to Koons, October 23, 1957, SGBD.

14 Cutler letter to Koons, October 23, 1957, SGBD.

15 Moss and Snyder Clash on Secrecy, NYT, November 21, 1957, 18.

16 Cutler letters to Koons, November 25, 1957, and December 4, 1957, SGBD.

17 Cutler and Candor, *Medford (Oregon) Mail Tribune*, November 25, 1957.

18 *Washington Post*, October 31, 1957.

19 Eisenhower letter to Allen Dulles, November 5, 1957, CIAFRR.

20 NTFR, 356–57.

21 Security Resources Panel of the Science Advisory Committee (informally known as the Gaither Panel), *Deterrence and Survival in the Nuclear Age*, November 7, 1957, OSANSA, NSC Series, Policy Papers Subseries, Box 22, EL, 14.

22 Memorandum of Discussion, 343rd Meeting of the NSC, November 7, 1957, Eisenhower's Papers as President, NSC Series, Box 9, EL.

23 Memorandum of a Conversation Between the President and the Secretary of State, *FRUS 1955–1957*, vol. 19, *National Security Policy*, document 157.

24 Special National Intelligence Estimate Number 11-10-57, The Soviet ICBM Program, CIAFRR.

25 NYT, November 23, 1957, 1.

26 CIA Director Dulles Memorandum for the Record, November 23, 1957, NSC Series, Policy Papers Subseries, Box 10, NSC 5412/2 — Covert Operations, EL.

27 Audrey R. Kahin and George McT. Kahin, *Subversion as Foreign Policy: The Secret Eisenhower and Dulles Debacle in Indonesia* (University of Washington Press, 1997), 181.

28 Cutler letter to Koons, November 10, 1957, SGBD.

29 Eisenhower Note to Nehru Sees Peril in Atom Test Ban, NYT, December 16, 1957, 1.

30 NTFR, 359.

31 Cutler letter to Koons, December 28, 1957, SGBD.

32 Secret Report Sees US in Grave Peril, *Washington Post*, December 20, 1958, 1.

33 Gregg Herken, *The Georgetown Set: Friends and Rivals in Cold War Washington* (Knopf, 2014), 234–35.

34 Stewart Alsop, Gaither's Grim Report, *San Bernardino County Sun*, December 29, 1957.

35 Cutler letter to Koons, January 2, 1958, SGBD.

36 Cutler letter to Koons, January 7, 1958, SGBD.

37 Cutler letter to Koons, February 2, 1958, SGBD.

20. CHALLENGING US NUCLEAR STRATEGY

1 Memorandum of Discussion, 350th Meeting of the NSC, January 6, 1958, Eisenhower's Papers as President, 1953–1961, EL.

2 Cutler letter to Koons, January 7, 1958, SGBD.

3 Koons letter to Cutler, January 16, 1958, SGBD.

4 Cutler letter to Koons, January 24, 1958, SGBD.

5 Audrey R. Kahin and George McT. Kahin, *Subversion as Foreign Policy: The Secret Eisenhower and Dulles Debacle in Indonesia* (University of Washington Press, 1997), 133.

6 Admiral Charles Triebel memo to Cutler, February 10, 1958, FRUS 1958–1960, vol. 17, *Indonesia*, document 15.

7 Copy of Cutler letter to Eisenhower, January 31, 1958, enclosed with Cutler letter to Koons, February 2, 1958, SGBD.

8 Eisenhower letter to Cutler, February 5, 1958, EPP, Box 11, Robert Cutler, 1958 (3).

9 Cutler letter to Koons, incorrectly dated January 9, 1958, apparently February 9, 1958, with attached copy of Eisenhower's letter to Cutler, February 5, 1958, SGBD.

10 Statement of Policy of the NSC, Top Secret, US Objectives in the Event of General War with the Soviet Bloc, with cover memorandum regarding Statement of Policy Adopted by the NSC, NSC 5410/1, by James S. Lay, March 29, 1954, *FRUS 1952–1954*, vol. 2, part 1, *National Security Affairs*, document 114.

11 Cutler letter to Koons, March 10, 1958, SGBD.

12 Massive Exchange of Nuclear Weapons, memo by Cutler, March 16, 1958, *FRUS 1958–1960*, vol. 3, *National Security Policy, Arms Control and Disarmament*, document 11.

13 "Clean" Nuclear Weapons, memorandum by Robert Cutler, March 16, 1958, Nuclear Non-Proliferation, NP00399, DNSA.

14 Cutler letter to Koons, March 10, 1958, SGBD.

15 Cutler letter to Koons, March 17, 1958, SGBD.

16 Introduction: The Role of an NSC Consultant, memo by Robert Cutler, March 25, 1959, correspondence files of Robert Cutler, SGBD.

17 Cutler memo to Eisenhower, March 18, 1958, Subject: November, 1958, Net Evaluation, US Nuclear History, NH00370, DNSA.

18 Memorandum of Discussion, 359th Meeting of the NSC, Thursday, March 20, 1958, Eisenhower's Papers as President, NSC Series, Box 9, EL.

19 Cutler memo, March 21, 1958, Nuclear Policy folder, OSANSA, NSC Series, Briefing Notes Subseries, Box 14, EL.

20 Cutler memo to General Twining, March 24, 1958, Nuclear Policy folder, OSANSA, NSC Series, Briefing Notes Subseries, Box 14, EL.

21 Copy of Cutler letter to Bridges enclosed in a letter to Koons, March 30, 1958, SGBD. "I enclose a copy of a letter I wrote to that ———— Styles Bridges whose Meet the Press comments infuriated me. No answer, of course," Bobby wrote.

22 Memorandum of Discussion, 361st Meeting of the NSC, Thursday, April 3, 1958, Eisenhower's Papers as President, NSC Series, Box 10, EL, 7.

23 General Power would later become known for his gruffness and bluster in nuclear weapons strategy. After hearing a briefing on the need for restraint in nuclear targeting and strategy in 1960, he said, "Restraint! Why are you so concerned with saving *their* lives? The whole idea is to *kill* the bastards! . . . Look. At the end of the war, if there are two Americans and one Russian, we win!" according to Fred Kaplan, *The Wizards of Armageddon* (Simon & Schuster, 1983).

24 Cutler memo to Quarles, April 3, 1958, OSANSA, Special Assistant Series, Chronological Subseries, Box 6, folder April 1958 (1), EL.

25 Peter J. Roman, *Eisenhower and the Missile Gap* (Cornell University Press, 1996), 71.

26 Top-secret memo by Robert Cutler, April 7, 1958, John Foster Dulles Papers, White House Memoranda Series, Box 6, White House General Correspondence, 1958 (4), EL.

27 Operations Coordinating Board Report, January 29, 1958, *FRUS 1958–1960*, vol. 10, part 2, *Eastern Europe; Finland; Greece; Turkey*, document 305.

28 Smith memo to John Foster Dulles, April 9, 1958, Comments on Attached Memos by General Cutler, US Nuclear History, NH00100, DNSA.

29 R.C. Alternative Version of Paragraph 14, May 1, 1958, Records of the OSANSA, NSC Series, Policy Papers Subseries, Box 25, NSC 5810/1 Basic National Security, EL.

30 Memorandum of Discussion, 364th Meeting of the NSC, Thursday, May 1, 1958, Eisenhower's Papers as President, NSC Series, Box 10, EL, 3.

31 Cutler letter to Koons, May 3, 1958, SGBD.

32 Final Report of the Select Committee to Study Governmental Operations with Respect to Intelligence Activities, book 3, April 23, 1976, 65.

21. VENICE, MIDNIGHT

1 Cutler postcard to Benedict, May 13, 1958, SGBD.

2 Cutler writing, May 13, 1957, SGBD.

3 RCD, vol. 1, entry of May 16, 1958; Cutler letter to Peggy Lutz, May 18, 1958, SGBD.

4 RCD, vol. 1, entry of September 10, 1958.

5 RCD, vol. 1, entry of June 3, 1958.

22. "I LOVE HIM . . ."

1 Memorandum of Discussion, 366th Meeting of the NSC, May 22, 1958, document 5, Eisenhower's Papers as President, NSC Series, Box 10, EL.

2 Audrey R. Kahin and George McT. Kahin, *Subversion as Foreign Policy: The Secret Eisenhower and Dulles Debacle in Indonesia* (University of Washington Press, 1997), 181.

3 Stephen Kinzer, *The Brothers: John Foster Dulles, Allen Dulles, and Their Secret World War* (Times Books, 2013), 240.

4 Ibid., 241.

5 RCD, vol. 1, entry of May 19, 1958.

6 Cutler letter to Koons, May 25, 1958, SGBD.

7 Cutler letter to Koons, June 2, 1958, SGBD.

8 Cutler letter to Koons, June 9, 1958, SGBD.

9 Cutler letter to Koons, June 21, 1958, SGBD.

10 Cutler official resignation letter to Eisenhower, June 23, 1958; Cutler personal letter to Eisenhower, June 23, 1958; and Eisenhower official reply to Cutler, June 24, 1958, all SGBD.

11 Defense Secretary Neil McElroy letter to Eisenhower, June 30, 1958, DNSA.

12 Robert Cutler, "The Structure and Functions of the National Security Council," report with cover memo to Eisenhower, EPP, Robert Cutler 1958 (2), EL.

13 Cutler letter to Koons, July 1, 1958, SGBD.

14 RCD, vol. 1, entry of July 1, 1958.

15 RCD, vol. 1, entry of July 10, 1958.

16 Matthew Jones, "The 'Preferred Plan': The Anglo-American Working Group Report on Covert Action in Syria, 1957," *Intelligence and National Security* 19, no. 8 (Autumn 2004): 405–507.

17 Lebanese Charge Influx Increases, NYT, June 28, 1958, 4.

18 Jerry Persons memo of a conference with the president, White House, July 14, 1958, *FRUS 1958–1960*, vol. 11, *Lebanon and Jordan*, document 124, US Department of State, Office of the Historian.

19 RCD, vol. 1, entry of July 15, 1958.

20 CIA Memorandum for the Record, July 16, 1958, by Thomas Parrott, regarding a meeting of the 5412 Group, Documents of the 5412 Group, NSC Series, Policy Papers Subseries, EL.

21 Copy of Eisenhower's note and transcript of the engraved medallion, EPP, Robert Cutler 1958 (1), EL.

22 RCD, vol. 1, entry of July 21, 1958.

23 Cutler letter to Koons, July 22, 1958, SGBD.

24 RCD, vol. 1, entry of July 26, 1958.

25 RCD, vol. 1, entries of August 4, 6, and 7, 1958.

26 RCD, vol. 1, entry of August 8, 1958.

27 RCD, vol. 1, entries of August 9 and 10, 1958.

28 RCD, vol. 1, entry of August 11, 1958.

29 RCD, vol. 1, entry of August 12, 1958.

30 RCD, vol. 1, entry of August 13, 1958.

31 RCD, vol. 1, entries of August 15 and 17, 1958; Cutler letter to Ann Whitman, Whitman Administration Series, Robert Cutler 1958 (1), EL.

32 RCD, vol. 1, entry of August 21, 1958.

33 RCD, vol. 1, entry of August 22, 1958.

34 Cutler postcard to President Eisenhower, August 23, 1958, Whitman Administration Series, Robert Cutler 1958 (1), EL.

35 RCD, vol. 1, entry of August 28, 1958.

36 RCD, vol. 1, entries of August 31 and September 4, 1958.

37 RCD, vol. 1, entry of September 14, 1958.

38 RCD, vol. 1, entry of September 15, 1958.

39 RCD, vol. 1, entry of September 24, 1958.

40 Cutler letter to Eisenhower, September 26, 1958, Whitman Administration Series, Robert Cutler 1958 (1), EL.

41 RCD, vol. 2, entry of September 30, 1958.

23. INVESTIGATIONS — AND AGONY

1 Hoftiezer letter to Benedict, February 3, 1958, SGBD.

2 Benedict comments to the author, February 2016.

3 Benedict written comments to the author, April 2016.

4 Benedict letter to Washburn, September 30, 1958, SGBD.

5 Author interview of Jean-Jacques Cortambert, May 5, 2010.

6 Cutler correspondence with business leaders he contacted on Skip's behalf, including a letter dated November 25, 1958, from Emile Soubry, Standard Oil executive vice president, SGBD.

7 Cutler memo to Gray, October 10, 1958, enclosed in a letter that Cutler sent to Koons October 17, 1958, SGBD.

8 Koons letter to Cutler, October 11, 1958, SGBD.

9 RCD, vol. 2, entry of November 3, 1958.

10 Ibid.

11 RCD, vol. 2, entry of November 13, 1958.

12 Koons letter to Benedict, November 26, 1958, SGBD.

13 Cutler letter to Koons, December 19, 1958, SGBD.

14 RCD, vol. 2, entry of December 19, 1958.

15 Cutler letter to Koons, December 19, 1958.

16 Cates family Christmas card to Koons, postmarked December 14, 1958, SGBD.

17 Author interview of Barbara Cates, April 9, 2016.

18 McNichol letter to Benedict, January 28, 1959, SGBD.

19 Benedict email to the author, March 21, 2016.

20 Cutler letter to Koons, December 15, 1958, SGBD.

21 RCD, vol. 2, entry of January 30, 1959.

22 RCD, vol. 2, entry of February 24, 1959.

23 RCD, vol. 2, entry of March 8, 1959.

24 RCD, vol. 2, entry of March 30, 1959.

25 Koons letter to Cutler, April 4, 1959, SGBD.

26 Chandler Bigelow letter to Cutler, April 30, 1959, SGBD.

27 Cutler letter to Koons, May 2, 1959; partnership document, dated May 5, 1959, SGBD.

28 RCD, vol. 3, entry of May 17, 1959.

29 RCD, vol. 3, entry of June 12, 1959.

30 RCD, vol. 3, entry of June 14, 1959.

31 RCD, vol. 3, entry of June 24, 1959.

32 Benedict said in an email to the author on May 8, 2016, that Koons named the boat after the Russian word for "seagull" and the Chekhov play.

33 Cutler letter to Koons, May 11, 1959, SGBD.

34 RCD, vol. 3, entry of July 9, 1959.

35 RCD, vol. 3, entry of July 12, 1959.

36 RCD, vol. 3, entry of July 15, 1959.

37 RCD, vol. 3, entry of July 18, 1959.

38 Koons letter to Cutler, July 20, 1959, SGBD.

39 RCD, vol. 3, entry of August 5, 1959.

40 Koons telegram to Cutler, August 7, 1959, SGBD. Punctuation added for clarity.

41 Cutler letter to Koons, Tilghman Koons and Cutler Correspondence, 1959, 1961, Box 14, Robert Cutler Papers, EL.

42 *Baltimore Sun*, August 8, 1959.

43 RCD, vol. 3, entry of August 12, 1959.

44 RCD, vol. 3, entry of August 18, 1959.

24. IKE'S MAN IN LATIN AMERICA

1 "Statement by the President (Eisenhower) Regarding Appointment of Robert Cutler as US Executive Director of the Inter-American Development Bank," October 14, 1959, The American Presidency Project, http://www.presidency.ucsb.edu/ws/?pid=11558.

2 Cutler letter to Lutz, October 17, 1959, SGBD.

3 Annual Report of the United Fruit Co. for the year 1959.

4 Annual Report of the First National Bank of Boston for the year 1959.

5 Allen Drury, *Advise and Consent* (Pocket Books, 1961), 347 and, further, 547.

6 Lutz letter to Cutler, undated, SGBD.

7 RCD, vol. 4, entry of October 27, 1959. *Casser la tête* is a French expression that translates roughly as "causing headaches."

8 RCD, vol. 4, entry of November 23, 1959.

9 RCD, vol. 4, entry of December 4, 1960.

10 RCD, vol. 4, entry of December 7, 1960.

11 News release issued by Old Colony Trust, February 1, 1960, Papers of Robert Cutler, Box 9, Inter-American Development Bank, EL.

12 Klein letter to Cutler, April 27, 1960, Papers of Robert Cutler, Box 9, Inter-American Development Bank, EL.

13 RCD, vol. 4, entry of March 21, 1960.

14 RCD, vol. 4, entry of April 11, 1960.

15 RCD, vol. 4, entry of April 13, 1960.

16 Juggling of Missile Data is Charged by Symington, NYT, January 28, 1960, 1.

17 Angry President Denies he Misled U.S. on Defenses, NYT, February 21, 1960, 1.

18 Transcript of Kennedy speech, February 29, 1960, John F. Kennedy Library historic speeches online, https://www.jfklibrary.org/JFK/Historic-Speeches.aspx.

19 Herter Indicates Flights Will Go On, NYT, May 10, 1960, 1.

20 Senate Unit to Scan Adequacy of Policy on Science Issues, NYT, March 6, 1960, 19.

21 Text of Kennedy's Speech to Senate Advocating New Approach on Foreign Policy, NYT, June 15, 1960, 32.

22 President Pictured as of Decisive Mind, NYT, July 18, 1960, 46.

23 Author interview of Robert Cutler Sullivan, November 8, 2009.

24 RCD, vol. 5, entry of July 30, 1960; Cutler deed to Ruth Sullivan, August 2, 1960, found in Massachusetts Land Records online at http://www.masslandrecords.com.

25 RCD, vol. 5, entry of June 27, 1960.

26 Cutler letter to Koons, July 3, 1960, SGBD.

27 RCD, vol. 5, entry of July 29, 1960.

28 RCD, vol. 5, entry of August 12, 1960.

29 RCD, vol. 5, entry of October 3, 1960.

30 RCD, vol. 5, entry of November 5, 1960.

31 NYT, December 20, 1960.

32 Cutler letter to Koons, January 14, 1961, SGBD.

33 Karl F. Inderfurth and Loch K. Johnson, *Fateful Decisions: Inside the National Security Council* (Oxford University Press, 2004), 63; Index to National Security Meetings, Finding Aid, National Security Files, John F. Kennedy Presidential Library, Boston, Massachusetts.

34 Ibid, 65.

35 Cutler letter to Koons, March 5, 1961, SGBD.

36 Peter Kornbluh (ed.), *Bay of Pigs Declassified: The Secret CIA Report on the Invasion of Cuba* (New Press, 1998), 294.

37 Ibid., 1–3.

38 Cutler letter to Koons, April 20, 1961, SGBD.

39 McGeorge Bundy oral history interview — JFK#1, March and May of 1964, conducted by Richard Neustadt, John F. Kennedy Presidential Library, 185.

40 Index to National Security Meetings, John F. Kennedy Presidential Library.

41 McGeorge Bundy oral history interview — JFK#1, March and May of 1964, conducted by Richard Neustadt, John F. Kennedy Presidential Library, 186.

42 See, for instance, "Use of Bank for Latin Aid Assailed, Cutler Criticized as Conservative," *New York Herald Tribune*, March 18, 1961, 1.

43 RCD, vol. 5, entry of March 25, 1961.

44 RCD, vol. 5, entry of May 20, 1961.

45 RCD, vol. 5, entry of June 5, 1961.

46 RCD, vol. 6, entry of July 4, 1961.

47 RCD, vol. 6, entry of July 17, 1961.

48 Ibid.

49 RCD, vol. 6, entry of August 28, 1961.
50 RCD, vol. 6, entry of September 5, 1961.
51 RCD, vol. 6, entry of September 18, 1961.
52 RCD, vol. 6, entry of January 15, 1962.
53 Cutler letter to Koons, December 7, 1961, SGBD.
54 NTFR, 387.
55 Cutler letter to President Kennedy, April 9, 1962, copy sent to Skip Koons, SGBD.

25. "THAT WHICH I AM, I AM"

1 Author interview of Jean-Jacques Cortambert, May 5, 2010.
2 Brace letter to Cutler, June 26, 1962, SGBD.
3 David Rockefeller letter to Cutler, July 20, 1962, SGBD.
4 Undated letter from Hoftiezer to Koons, approximate date can be calculated because he says that he will be thirty-two years old in two weeks, which would date the letter in early August 1962, SGBD.
5 Undated letter of Whitman to Cutler, SGBD.
6 Hoftiezer letter to Benedict, December 4, 1962, SGBD.
7 RCD, vol. 6, entry of February 20, 1963.
8 RCD, vol. 6, entry of May 26, 1963.
9 Author interview of Winthrop Aldrich, February 27, 2008. Winthrop Aldrich is the author's cousin.
10 Author interview of Owen Walker, August 30, 2015.
11 Author interview of Bronson Chanler, January 29, 2008.
12 Ike Honors Old Teammate, *Boston Globe*, June 12, 1965.
13 NTFR, 300.
14 See, for instance, John P. Burke, *Honest Broker? The National Security Advisor and Presidential Decision Making* (Texas A&M University Press, 2009).
15 NTFR, 316–17.
16 Burke, *Honest Broker?* 7.
17 New Figures Close "Missile Gap," NYT, November 26, 1961.
18 Strobe Talbott, *The Master of the Game: Paul Nitze and the Nuclear Peace* (Knopf, 1988), 166–80, 337–39, 363.
19 NTFR, 65.
20 NTFR, 359.
21 RCD, vol. 6, entry of May 30–31, 1966.
22 Cutler letter to Koons, February 17, 1967, SGBD.
23 Koons note to Cutler, March 11, 1967, SGBD.
24 Author interview of Anthony Favello, August 16, 2008.
25 Author interview of Jean-Jacques Cortambert, May 5, 2010.
26 Author interview of Edgar Glazbrook, November 21, 2008.
27 International Banking, minutes of a meeting held at National Westminster House, July 16–18, 1969, SGBD.
28 Author interview of Barry Wayne, April 26, 2009.
29 Joseph W. Alsop with Adam Platt, *"I've Seen the Best of It": Memoirs* (W. W. Norton, 1992), 349.
30 William S. Patten, *My Three Fathers: And the Elegant Deceptions of My Mother, Susan Mary Alsop* (PublicAffairs, 2008), 202.
31 Author interview of Edgar Glazbrook, April 19, 2016.
32 David Rockefeller letter to Koons, January 21, 1993, SGBD.
33 Koons letter to Cutler, March 8, 1967, SGBD.

BIBLIOGRAPHY

Acheson, Dean. *The Pattern of Responsibility.* Edited by McGeorge Bundy. Boston: Houghton
Mifflin, 1952.

Adams, Sherman. *First-Hand Report: The Story of the Eisenhower Administration.* New York: Harper
& Brothers, 1961.

Alsop, Joseph W. *"I've Seen the Best of It": Memoirs.* With Adam Platt. New York: W. W. Norton,
1992.

Barnhisel, Greg. *Cold War Modernists: Art, Literature, and American Cultural Diplomacy.* New York:
Columbia University Press, 2015.

Beatty, Jack. *The Rascal King: The Life and Times of James Michael Curley (1874–1958).* Boston: Da
Capo Press, 1992.

Bellaigue, Christopher de. *Patriot of Persia: Muhammad Mossadegh and a Tragic Anglo-American
Coup.* New York: Harper Perennial, 2012.

Benson, E. F. *Queen Lucia.* Ocean Shores, WA: Watchmaker Publishing, 2010.

Bernstein, Barton J. "The Oppenheimer Loyalty-Security Case Reconsidered." *Stanford Law
Review,* July 1990.

Bérubé, Allan. *Coming Out Under Fire: The History of Gay Men and Women in World War Two.* New
York: Penguin Group, 1991.

Bird, Kai. *The Chairman, John J. McCloy, the Making of the American Establishment.* New York:
Simon & Schuster, 1992.

Bird, Kai. *The Color of Truth: McGeorge Bundy and William Bundy: Brothers in Arms.* New York:
Simon & Schuster, 1998.

Bird, Kai, and Martin J. Sherwin. *American Prometheus: The Triumph and Tragedy of J. Robert
Oppenheimer.* New York: Vintage Books, 2005.

Bohlen, Charles E. *Witness to History: 1929–1969.* New York: W. W. Norton, 1973.

Bowie, Robert R. and Richard Immerman. *Waging Peace: How Eisenhower Shaped an Enduring
Cold War Strategy.* New York: Oxford University Press, 1998.

Brinkley, Douglas, and Townsend Hoopes. *Driven Patriot: The Life and Times of James Forrestal.*
Annapolis: Naval Institute Press, 2000.

Burke, John P. *Honest Broker? The National Security Advisor and Presidential Decision Making.*
College Station: Texas A&M University Press, 2009.

Charles, Douglas M. *Hoover's War on Gays: Exposing the FBI's "Sex Deviates" Program.* Lawrence:
University Press of Kansas, 2015.

Cheever, Susan. *E. E. Cummings: A Life.* New York: Vintage Books, 2015.

Corke, Sarah-Jane. *US Covert Operations and Cold War Strategy: Truman, Secret Warfare and the
CIA, 1945–53.* Studies in Intelligence Series. London: Routledge, 2008.

Cullather, Nick. *Secret History: The CIA's Classified Account of Its Operations in Guatemala, 1952–
1954.* 2nd ed. Stanford, CA: Stanford University Press, 2006.

Cutler, Robert. *The Bedside Companion.* Lunenburg, VT: Stinehour Press, 1969.

———. *Commencement in 1916: A Backward Glance.* Lunenburg, VT: Stinehour Press, 1966.

———. *Louisburg Square.* New York: Macmillan, 1917.

———. *No Time for Rest.* Boston: Little, Brown, 1967.

———. *The Speckled Bird.* New York: Macmillan, 1923.

———. *Whereof We Are Made.* Lunenburg, VT: Stinehour Press, 1965.

Dean, Robert D. *Imperial Brotherhood: Gender and the Making of Cold War Foreign Policy.* Amherst: University of Massachusetts Press, 2001.

Dockrill, Saki. *Eisenhower's New-Look National Security Policy, 1953–61.* New York: St. Martin's Press, 1996.

Donovan, Robert J. *Confidential Secretary: Ann Whitman's 20 Years with Eisenhower and Rockefeller.* New York: E. P. Dutton, 1988.

Drew, S. Nelson, ed. *NSC-68: Forging the Strategy of Containment.* Washington, DC: National Defense University, 1994.

Eisenhower, David. *Eisenhower at War 1943–1945.* New York: Random House, 1986.

Eisenhower, Dwight D. *Crusade in Europe.* Baltimore: Johns Hopkins University Press, 1997.

———. *The Eisenhower Diaries.* Edited by Robert H. Ferrell. New York: W. W. Norton, 1981.

———. *Mandate for Change: The White House Years, 1953–1956.* New York: Doubleday, 1963.

Gaddis, John Lewis. *George F. Kennan: An American Life.* New York: Penguin Press, 2011.

Gardner, Paul F. *Shared Hopes, Separate Fears: Fifty Years of U.S.-Indonesian Relations.* Boulder, CO: Westview Press, 1997.

Ginzberg, Eli. *The Eye of Illusion.* New Brunswick, NJ: Transaction Publishers, 1993.

———. *The Lost Divisions.* New York: Columbia University Press, 1959.

Glantz, David M. *The Soviet Strategic Offensive in Manchuria, 1945: 'August Storm.'* London: Frank Cass, 2003.

Gleijeses, Piero. *Shattered Hope: The Guatemalan Revolution and the United States, 1944–1954.* Princeton, NJ: Princeton University Press, 1991.

Greenspun, Hank. *Where I Stand: The Record of a Reckless Man.* With Alex Pelle. New York: David McKay, 1966.

Greenstein, Fred I. *The Hidden-Hand Presidency: Eisenhower as Leader.* Baltimore: Johns Hopkins University Press, 1994.

Grose, Peter. *Gentleman Spy: The Life of Allen Dulles.* Boston: Houghton Mifflin, 1994.

Herken, Gregg. *Brotherhood of the Bomb: The Tangled Lives and Loyalties of Robert Oppenheimer, Ernest Lawrence, and Edward Teller.* New York: Henry Holt, 2002.

———. *The Georgetown Set: Friends and Rivals in Cold War Washington.* New York: Knopf, 2014.

Hewlett, Richard G., and Jack M. Holl. *Atoms for Peace and War, 1953–1961: Eisenhower and the Atomic Energy Commission.* Berkeley: University of California Press, 1989.

Horne, Alistair. *The Land Is Bright.* London: Max Parrish, 1958.

Hoey, Brian. *Mountbatten: The Private Story.* London: Sidgwick & Jackson, 1994.

Hughes, John Emmet. *The Ordeal of Power: A Political Memoir of the Eisenhower Years.* New York: Atheneum, 1963.

Hunt, E. Howard. *Undercover: Memoirs of an American Secret Agent.* N.p.: Berkley Publishing, 1974.

Inderfurth, Karl F., and Loch K. Johnson. *Fateful Decisions: Inside the National Security Council.* New York: Oxford University Press, 2004.

Johnson, A. Ross. *Radio Free Europe and Radio Liberty: The CIA Years and Beyond.* Washington, DC: Woodrow Wilson Center Press; Stanford, CA: Stanford University Press, 2010.

Johnson, David K. *The Lavender Scare: The Cold War Persecution of Gays and Lesbians in the Federal Government.* Chicago: University of Chicago Press, 2004.

Jones, Matthew. "The 'Preferred Plan': The Anglo-American Working Group Report on Covert Action in Syria, 1957." *Intelligence and National Security* 19, no. 8 (Autumn 2004).

Kahin, Audrey R., and George McT. Kahin. *Subversion as Foreign Policy: The Secret Eisenhower and Dulles Debacle in Indonesia.* Seattle: University of Washington Press, 1995.

Kaplan, Fred. *The Wizards of Armageddon.* Stanford, CA: Stanford University Press, 1983.

Kaufman, Burton I. *The Oil Cartel Case: A Documentary Study of Antitrust Activity in the Cold War Era.* Westport, CT: Greenwood Press, 1978.

Killian, James R. Jr., *Sputnik, Scientists and Eisenhower, A Memoir of the First Special Assistant to the President for Science and Technology.* Cambridge, MA: The MIT Press, 1977,

Kinsey, Alfred C., Wardell B. Pomeroy, and Clyde E. Martin. *Sexual Behavior in the Human Male.* Bronx: Ishi Press International, 2010.

Kinzer, Stephen. *All the Shah's Men: An American Coup and the Roots of Middle East Terror.* Hoboken: John Wiley, 2003.

——. *The Brothers: John Foster Dulles, Allen Dulles, and Their Secret World War.* New York: Times Books, 2013.

Kirby, Alec, David G. Dalin, and John F. Rothmann. *Harold E. Stassen: The Life and Perennial Candidacy of the Progressive Republican.* Jefferson, NC: McFarland, 2013.

Kornbluh, Peter, ed. *Bay of Pigs Declassified: The Secret CIA Report on the Invasion of Cuba.* New York: New Press, 1998.

Larson, Thomas. *The Saddest Music Ever Written: The Story of Samuel Barber's Adagio for Strings.* New York: Pegasus Books, 2010.

Lee, Martin A., and Bruce Shlain. *Acid Dreams: The Complete Social History of LSD: The CIA, the Sixties, and Beyond.* New York: Grove Press, 1985.

Lindsey, Mary. *Historic Homes and Houses of Alexandria.* Alexandria, VA: Newell-Cole, 1947.

Lisagor, Nancy, and Frank Lipsius. *A Law Unto Itself: The Untold Story of the Law Firm Sullivan & Cromwell.* New York: Paragon House, 1989.

McCarthy, Joe. *The Story of General George Marshall.* Self-published, 1952.

McKenna, Neil. *The Secret Life of Oscar Wilde: An Intimate Biography.* New York: Basic Books, 2005.

McMillan, Priscilla J. *The Ruin of J. Robert Oppenheimer: And the Birth of the Modern Arms Race.* New York: Viking, 2005.

Miller, William J. *Henry Cabot Lodge: A Biography.* New York: James Heineman, 1967.

Mitrovich, Gregory. *Undermining the Kremlin: America's Strategy to Subvert the Soviet Bloc, 1947–1956.* Ithaca, NY: Cornell University Press, 2000.

Morgan, Ted. *Valley of Death: The Tragedy at Dien Bien Phu That Led America into the Vietnam War.* New York: Random House, 2010.

Mosley, Leonard. *Dulles: A Biography of Eleanor, Allen, and John Foster Dulles.* New York: Dial Press, 1978.

Newman, Steven Leonard. *The Oppenheimer Case: A Reconsideration of the Role of the Defense Department and National Security.* PhD diss., Department of History, New York University, 1977.

Nichols, David A. *Eisenhower 1956: The President's Year of Crisis — Suez and the Brink of War.* New York: Simon & Schuster Paperbacks, 2011.

——. *Ike and McCarthy: Dwight Eisenhower's Secret Campaign Against Joseph McCarthy.* New York: Simon & Schuster, 2017.

Oshinsky, David M. *A Conspiracy So Immense: The World of Joe McCarthy.* New York: Oxford University Press, 2005.

Pahlavi, Mohammad Reza. *Answer to History.* New York: Stein & Day, 1980.

Palmer, Geoffrey, and Noel Lloyd. *E. F. Benson: As He Was.* Luton, UK: Lennard Publishing, 1988.

Patten, William S. *My Three Fathers: And the Elegant Deceptions of My Mother Susan Mary Alsop.* New York: Public Affairs, 2008.

Powers, Richard Gid. *Secrecy and Power: The Life of J. Edgar Hoover.* New York: Free Press, 1987.

Prados, John. *Presidents' Secret Wars: CIA and Pentagon Covert Operations from World War II Through the Persian Gulf,* rev. ed. Chicago: Elephant Paperbacks, 1996.

———. *Keepers of the Keys, A History of the National Security Council from Truman to Bush.* New York: William Morrow and Company, Inc., 1991.

Puddington, Arch. *Broadcasting Freedom: The Cold War Triumph of Radio Free Europe and Radio Liberty.* Lexington: University of Press of Kentucky, 2000.

Reich, Cary. *The Life of Nelson A. Rockefeller: Worlds to Conquer, 1908–1958.* New York: Doubleday, 1996.

Rocke, Michael. *Forbidden Friendships: Homosexuality and Male Culture in Renaissance Florence.* New York: Oxford University Press, 1996.

Roman, Peter J. *Eisenhower and the Missile Gap.* Ithaca, NY: Cornell University Press, 1995.

Roosevelt, Kermit. *Countercoup: The Struggle for the Control of Iran.* New York: McGraw-Hill, 1979.

Rorem, Ned. *Knowing When to Stop: A Memoir.* New York: Simon & Schuster, 1994.

Rosenstiel, Leonie. *Nadia Boulanger: A Life in Music.* New York: W. W. Norton, 1982.

Sanders, Jerry W. *Peddlers of Crisis: The Committee on the Present Danger and the Politics of Containment.* Boston: South End Press, 1983.

Schlesinger, Stephen, and Stephen Kinzer. *Bitter Fruit: The Untold Story of the American Coup in Guatemala.* New York: Doubleday, 1982.

Scott, Henry E. *Shocking True Story: The Rise and Fall of Confidential, "America's Most Scandalous Scandal Magazine."* New York: Pantheon Books, 2010.

Shand-Tucci, Douglass. *The Crimson Letter: Harvard, Homosexuality, and the Shaping of American Culture.* New York: St. Martin's Griffin, 2004.

Shilts, Randy. *Conduct Unbecoming: Gays and Lesbians in the US Military.* New York: St. Martin's Press, 1993.

Shogan, Robert. *No Sense of Decency: The Army-McCarthy Hearings, A Demagogue Falls and Television Takes Charge of American Politics.* Chicago: Ivan R. Dee, 2009.

Smith, Richard Norton. *The Harvard Century: The Making of a University to a Nation.* New York: Simon & Schuster, 1986.

Stimson, Henry L., and McGeorge Bundy. *On Active Service in Peace and War.* New York: Harper & Brothers, 1947.

Stuart, Douglas T. *Creating the National Security State: A History of the Law That Transformed America.* Princeton, NJ: Princeton University Press, 2008.

Summers, Anthony. *Official and Confidential: The Secret Life of J. Edgar Hoover.* New York: Pocket Star Books, 1993.

Talbot, Strobe. *The Master of the Game: Paul Nitze and the Nuclear Peace.* New York: Knopf, 1988.

Thomas, Evan. *Ike's Bluff: President Eisenhower's Secret Battle to Save the World.* New York: Little, Brown, 2012.

US Atomic Energy Commission. *In the Matter of J. Robert Oppenheimer: Transcript of Hearing Before Personnel Security Board, Washington, DC, April 12, 1954, through May 6, 1954.* Washington, DC: US Government Printing Office, 1954.

US Department of State. *Foreign Relations of the United States (FRUS) 1946,* vol. 10, *The Far East: China.* Washington, DC: US Government Printing Office.

————. *FRUS, The Intelligence Community 1950–1955.*

————. *FRUS 1952–1954, Guatemala.*

————. *FRUS 1952–1954,* vol. 1, part 1, *National Security Affairs.*

————. *FRUS 1952–1954,* vol. 1, part 2, *General: Economic and Political Matters.*

————. *FRUS, 1952–1954,* vol. 2, part 2, *National Security Affairs.*

————. *FRUS 1952–1954,* vol. 4, *The American Republics.*

————. *FRUS 1952–1954,* vol. 6, part 1, *Western Europe and Canada.*

————. *FRUS 1952–1954,* vol. 13, part 1, *Indochina.*

————. *FRUS 1955–1957,* vol. 19, *National Security Policy.*

————. *FRUS 1955–1957,* vol. 22, *Southeast Asia.*

————. *FRUS 1958–1960,* vol. 3, *National Security Policy, Arms Control and Disarmament.*

————. *FRUS 1958–1960,* vol. 10, part 2, *Eastern Europe; Finland; Greece; Turkey.*

————. *FRUS 1958–1960,* vol. 11, *Lebanon and Jordan.*

————. *FRUS 1958–1960,* vol. 17, *Indonesia.*

Vidal, Gore. *The City and the Pillar.* New York: E. P. Dutton, 1948.

Weiner, Tim. *Legacy of Ashes: The History of the CIA.* New York: Doubleday, 2007.

Wilber, Donald. *Overthrow of Premier Mossadeq of Iran, November 1952–August 1953.* CIA Clandestine Service History, written in March 1954. Accessed on the site of the National Security Archive, Washington, https://nsarchive2.gwu.edu/NSAEBB/NSAEBB28. This historical account of the coup was revealed in a report in the NYT on April 16, 2000. The document, with some portions of the text deleted, was later published on the website of the National Security Archive, a nonprofit organization dedicated to preserving declassified documents and supporting investigative journalism. The CIA has not declassified the document.

Williams, Ben Ames Jr. *Bank of Boston 200: A History of New England's Leading Bank, 1784–1984.* Boston: Houghton Mifflin, 1984.

Wister, Owen. *The Virginian.* New York: Pocket Books, 2002.

————. *Watch Your Thirst: A Dry Opera in Three Acts.* New York: Macmillan, 1923.

Wright, William. *Harvard's Secret Court: The Savage 1920 Purge of Campus Homosexuals.* New York: St. Martin's Press, 2005.

Yoder, Edwin M. *Joe Alsop's Cold War: A Study of Journalistic Influence and Intrigue.* Chapel Hill: University of North Carolina Press, 1995.

Zollinger, Robert M., MD. *Elliott Carr Cutler and the Cloning of Surgeons.* Mount Kisco, NY: Futura Publishing, 1988.

INDEX